'This is a "must have" for any therapist with an interest in ongoing improvement of practice. The book is a rich treasure of theories and illustrative case studies. It revisits Freud's original use of case study research and adds fresh new perspectives on both our general "being" and on therapeutic practice. It leaves you feeling enriched, rejuvenated and slightly changed – as only a really good book can.'

Dr Sofie Bager-Charleson, Director of PhD Programme, Metanoia Institute

'Although existential therapists have written widely on the philosophical perspective behind existential therapy, there has been too little in the way of case studies to illustrate how therapy works in practice. This book fills that gap and more. It is a splendid book about both theory and practice. The chapters feature therapists who have offered substantial contributions to contemporary existential therapy – individual, couple and group. Hooray for this book! I can now offer my students something concrete that will give them a wider view of how existential therapy works in practice, how theory informs practice – and the other way around.'

Betty Cannon PhD, Founder and President of the Boulder Psychotherapy Institute

'This book collects together an exceptional range of authors who have taken on the challenge of discussing the key themes of existential therapy from the standpoint of their encounters with their clients. In highlighting the relationally attuned engagement between therapist and client, the authors succeed in emphasising existential therapy's key principle of relatedness as it is lived. By doing so, they challenge readers to review the specific dilemmas under discussion more as "problems in living", rather than as some manualised (and dehumanised) psychological disturbance. More than this, in adopting a predominantly narrational focus, the authors revitalise the case study tradition such that each presentation serves to inform and inspire fellow practitioners. I was stimulated and provoked; whether strongly agreeing or disagreeing with the authors' views, I was always left with a desire to read more of what they had to say.'

Professor Ernesto Spinelli, author of *Tales of Un-Knowing: therapeutic encounters from an existential perspective* (PCCS Books)

Acknowledgements

With heartfelt thanks to all our clients and supervisees, past and present, without whose inspiration this book could not have been created.

CASE STUDIES IN EXISTENTIAL THERAPY

TRANSLATING THEORY INTO PRACTICE

Edited by
Simon du Plock

First published 2018

PCCS Books Ltd
Wyastone Business Park
Wyastone Leys
Monmouth
NP25 3SR
United Kingdom
contact@pccs-books.co.uk
www.pccs-books.co.uk

This collection © Simon du Plock, 2018
The individual chapters © the contributors, 2018

All rights reserved.
No part of this publication may be reproduced, stored in a retrieval system, transmitted or utilised in any form by any means, electronic, mechanical, photocopying or recording or otherwise, without permission in writing from the publishers.

The authors have asserted their right to be identified as the authors
of this work in accordance with the Copyright, Designs and Patents Act 1988.

Case Studies in Existential Therapy: translating theory into practice

British Library Cataloguing in Publication data: a catalogue record for this book is available from the British Library.

ISBN 978 1 910919 28 6

Cover design by Jason Anscomb
Typeset in-house by PCCS Books using Minion Pro and Myriad Pro
Printed in the UK by CMP, Dorset

Product code – 01202575

This product has been assessed as low risk and can be used safely without safety information.
The manufacturer's authorised representative in the EU for product safety is:
Easy Access System Europe – Mustamäe tee 50, 10621 Tallinn, Estonia
gpsr.requests@easproject.com

Contents

	Foreword Emmy van Deurzen	v
	Introduction Simon du Plock	1
1	Creative existential therapy with children: Tom in his therapy world Verity J Gavin	10
2	Why me, why now? On discovering that time is passing Martin Adams	29
3	Gay sexuality:' 'I am what I am; I am my own special creation' Helen Acton	44
4	Existential dream analysis Darren Langdridge	56
5	The unfinished self: inclusivity in experiential-existential therapy Greg Madison	71
6	'Three's company, two's a crowd': working existentially with couples presenting with issues of addiction Simon du Plock	84
7	Stoking the flames: coaching towards authentic and impassioned change Sasha van Deurzen-Smith	102
8	Existential group therapy Rimantas Kočiūnas	117
9	Trans and non-binary genders Christina Richards	137
10	Living ME: a case study of the experience of being diagnosed with a chronic 'psychosomatic' illness Simon du Plock	154
11	Finding meaning: cross-cultural existential therapy with a young refugee Zack Eleftheriadou	168

12	Spirite equus: what we can learn from equine-facilitated therapy *Julie Scheiner*	*182*
13	Out of it: addiction and recovery as lived phenomena *Ryan Kemp*	*200*
14	Ontological insecurity: the case of Henry James *Simon du Plock*	*213*
15	Time-limited existential therapy and counselling *Alison Strasser*	*233*
16	The face of abuse: the responsibility of the psychotherapist as witness *Georgia Feliou*	*249*
17	Lost for words: using existential experimentation in a GP practice *Mark Rayner and Randolph Quinault*	*265*
18	An existential view on traumatic grief: the four-worlds model *Chloe Paidoussis-Mitchell*	*282*
19	Two hats: the case study as viewed by the therapist-researcher *Prunella Gee*	*299*
20	Living towards death in a technologically mediated existence *Elaine Kasket*	*320*
	Afterword *Simon du Plock*	*333*
	Contributors	*334*
	Name index	*339*
	Subject index	*342*

Foreword

Emmy van Deurzen

Existential therapy is a dynamic, dialogic and collaborative form of therapy where therapist and client jointly trace the meanings of the client's experience and find new and more creative ways of tackling the challenges clients are facing. They work as a team and stand together in the waves of the client's difficulties in living to find a way to stem the tide of their dilemmas and crises. They work out the manifold and complex connections and interactions between the seemingly endless stream of events, things, feelings, thoughts, memories, hopes, values, projects and relationships that initially flood the therapist's consciousness when tuning into the client's world. The therapeutic task is to create order out of chaos and replace confusion with a new, deeper understanding of the human condition as experienced by this one individual. In the process of plumbing the depth of existence, both therapist and client learn a great deal in their encounter with a wide range of obstacles that they need to surmount and take into their stride.

The beauty of existential therapy is that its process is utterly free and eminently flexible. Its theory is based in philosophy and its methods in phenomenology and hermeneutics, with the sole objective of grasping human reality better. It does not impose a rigid theoretical framework or technique to curtail that freedom. Each existential therapist works in different ways and varies their attention and presence in relation to each client. In fact, at each session, in each moment, existential therapists attune themselves to the client's mood, their outlook, their struggle, the way they are engaged in the world. The work involves a great deal of resonance, while clarifying and elucidating the things that we often take for granted or that puzzle or paralyse our clients. There is an upsurge of meaning and purpose in the process as old values and a new life direction emerge from the darkness. Existential therapy is a therapy of freedom and paradox. This makes it hard to describe and teach in a generic or abstract manner. It is always direct and specific and relates to the situation of a particular client's predicaments. There is no better way to understand existential therapy than to experience it. The next best way of coming to grips with it is through reading and debating case illustrations.

This book is a goldmine of careful and clear accounts of existential therapy. It presents a wide range of different existential ways of working, from focusing to coaching. It illustrates existential practice in many different settings, from working with children to working with the dying. It details the great variety of methods, insights, dialogues, creative interventions and very personal interactions that different existential therapists bring to bear on their work.

I was proud to be the midwife to Simon du Plock's earlier volume of existential psychotherapy case studies (du Plock, 1997), which was unique in bringing these illustrations of existential work to the public at this early stage. In this new volume, Simon has surpassed himself as editor by selecting and showcasing a vibrant, lively and vital collection of new case illustrations. Not only is the range of these stories enormous; their quality is outstanding. From chapter to chapter, the focus of the accounts shifts from a very closely observed specific interaction to a masterful summing up to provide a broader perspective. All of it has been put together with much care, panache and passion. It will be a pleasure to read, teach and learn from and a resource to treasure. It takes in the whole landscape of existential practices, including different settings and modalities.

Each case study is like a short story that tells us something about human existence, something about one person's struggles and difficulties. But it also illustrates the therapeutic skill of illuminating the essence of that struggle, both at its zenith and its apogee. We follow the dynamic movement in time and we savour its resolution.

You will relish this offering and you will learn not just about existential therapy but also about human existence and its many troubling difficulties. You will find yourself thinking and feeling deeply about each situation depicted and will find yourself hooked, as if you were reading a mystery novel.

Reference

du Plock S (ed) (1997). *Case Studies in Existential Psychotherapy and Counselling*. Chichester: John Wiley & Sons.

Introduction

Simon du Plock

The case study tradition is well established as a teaching device. Freud's use of the case study was instrumental in communicating the concepts of early psychoanalysis, and the examination and writing of case studies continue to be central to the curriculum in all contemporary schools of therapy. Their status and value – as exemplars of good practice, vehicles for the dissemination of knowledge or as an arena for the problematisation of received wisdom – went unchallenged until the development of psychological testing and experimentation in the 1920s and 1930s provided alternative ways of examining theory and practice. While presentation and discussion of case studies has played a major role in the development and dissimulation of psychotherapy, their limitations, especially with regard to accuracy and reliability, have been much debated. The relevance of the case study is particularly called into question in a climate strongly influenced by demands for evidence-based practice, but whether we regard them as factual records or as useful fictions, their continuing popularity is evidenced by their ubiquity. A sub-genre of semi-fictional case studies has emerged in recent years – typically, short, literary psychoanalytic case reflections – and has found a large audience among a psychologically-minded general public.

The great majority of texts specifically designed to provide mental health practitioners with examples of how to work with clients focus primarily on the problem that the client presents, since they take the case study as a mnemonic device to illustrate abstract theoretical and research issues. As such, the case study serves a threefold purpose: 1) to describe a specific clinical problem; 2) to show how such a problem is viewed by experts in the field and how they treat it, and 3) to provide a place to discuss the epidemiology and aetiology of the problem.

While such an approach may initially appear valid, its usefulness is circumscribed by the way in which the individual client largely disappears, to be replaced by a presenting problem. At its most clumsy, this medical/scientific approach may fall into the error of positioning clients themselves as the problem and as nothing other than the problem, so that, for example, the rich and complex experience of the person presenting with particular anxieties becomes secondary to a diagnosis of generalised anxiety disorder. Similarly, someone exhibiting compulsive behaviours or reporting hallucinations comes to be viewed as obsessive compulsive or schizophrenic, and treated as such.

The development of systematic methods for undertaking case study research should be noted. Researchers have sought to introduce greater rigour by undertaking intensive 'single subject' analysis of individual clients, using multiple sources of information, constructing extensive databases to focus on evidence obtained across a large number of related case studies, and employing teams of researchers to independently analyse case studies. While each of these developments makes an important contribution to enhancing the reliability of the case study method, the underlying model endures. It may be suggested that it does so because, when done proficiently, it offers the reader a convincing story about a particular engagement with a specific client and their problem of living. The validity of this account rests, in large part, on the extent to which the author is transparent about their own personal and professional knowledge and motivation and the degree to which they present a coherent narrative. The 'narrative' knowledge offered by such accounts provides a vital counterbalance to 'paradigmatic' knowledge, which is presented in the form of abstract or general laws. As McLeod states:

> One of the central arguments for an important role for case study research in counselling and psychotherapy… is that it provides a source of narrative knowing that is needed to complement the findings of studies that generate abstract or paradigmatic knowledge. It is not that one form of knowing is better than the other, but that human sense-making (in any field of endeavour) requires both these modalities to exist in creative interplay. (2010: 8)

The contributors to this book all identify as existential phenomenological therapists and, as such, offer narrative descriptions of their encounters with their clients that focus on their way of being in the world – their existential position. Staying true to their espousal of phenomenology, they attempt to describe rather than interpret the client's way of being in the world, and are careful to stay close to and privilege the client's subjective experience, rather than impose objective, theory-based explanations. Furthermore, they argue for a perspective which is grounded in the primacy of the relationship between the therapist and client and, more precisely, in an appreciation of the importance of genuine encounter in which client and therapist meet in a democratic and transparent manner to consider what it means to be human and create a life in the face of the challenges and absurdities of the human condition. The individual clients who feature (albeit anonymised) in each chapter are just that – individuals rather than 'cases'.

The focus of the therapeutic alliance moves away from the individual client and their presenting problem and towards an understanding of the client as 'situated': that is to say, as always and inevitably existing and creating meaning in relationship. This notion of the client as 'situated' serves to remind us that psychological 'dis-ease' can best be understood not as intra-psychic phenomena (distress situated in the psyche or mind) but as the interaction of the individual with often complex and sometimes hidden social and material influences. The client, then, is understood as presenting with a 'problem of living', rather than an individual psychological illness.

While each contributor to this text sets out a distinct way of working, it is possible to outline certain assumptions that most existential therapists are likely to see as the foundation of their therapeutic practice. We may express them as follows.

1. Human beings are 'thrown' into the world in the sense that they find themselves in a situation that is given rather than chosen. A baby cannot choose to be born into one family with a particular set of circumstances and not another, or to be born with particular physical attributes and genetic make-up. Similarly, as we are all born, so too will we all die. While we cannot choose these existential givens, we can choose how we respond to them and it is in doing so that we create our own values and our own lives. As Sartre expresses it, men are condemned to be free (1958: 439, 485). While this may seem perfectly obvious, many clients (indeed all of us at certain times) resist such an active view of their place in the world, preferring to attribute the shape of their life to fate, chance, economics, upbringing or a hundred other 'external' factors that can be pressed into service.

2. Since human beings are thrown into the world, it makes no sense to attempt to understand them without also coming to grips with their context. This is necessarily true of human beings in the therapeutic relationship: neither

client nor therapist is in the room as *just* the client or therapist. As Cohn (1997) reminds us, when we see a client, their family, partner, social nexus etc are also present in the room. For the existential therapist, there is in fact no 'individual' therapy. This must also be the case for the therapist, though their context should not be permitted to impinge inappropriately on the client's work. In existential therapy, unlike psychoanalytic or psychodynamic therapy, it is understood that the therapist should not, indeed cannot, be a blank screen.

3. Since it is the 'phenomena' – those things that appear – that are of concern in existential therapy, the therapist should take care to be open to this and to engage with it as fully as possible. The therapist generally stays in the here-and-now of the client's experience and takes care not to introduce normative theories or gather evidence from previous sessions to support the hypotheses that such theories entail.

4. Just as clients invariably bring their context into therapy, so they bring their past and their hopes and fears for the future, as well as their experience of the present moment. Existential therapy is often misunderstood as discounting the past, but this is not so. However, it does reject the reductionistic notion so often encountered in therapy that the past 'causes' the present, since such a deterministic approach denies the ability of humans to be creative and to make choices about their lives. Many clients restrict themselves to living primarily in the past, or in the present or future, and in such cases much of the therapeutic work will be concerned with enabling them to experience themselves in relation to all three.

5. The existential approach is concerned with the whole being of the client and rejects dichotomies such as mind and body or psyche and soma. The way in which we relate to our body cannot be split off from any other of the dimensions in which we encounter the world.

6. If we can choose our response to those aspects of our lives that are given, it follows that we can also fail to choose or make choices that do not really reflect our needs. This necessitates the formulation of types of anxiety and guilt that are distinct from neurotic anxiety and guilt. The feelings we experience as a result of our attempts to evade authenticity are of a specifically existential nature and should be approached as such, if they are to be worked with effectively.

Each of the writers who have contributed to this book seek to offer the reader a sense of their therapeutic style when engaging with clients. They also aim to present an innovation in therapeutic theory and show how this informs their therapeutic practice. In the opening chapter, Dr Verity Gavin offers an approach to working with children that is grounded in an embodied phenomenological attitude. Originally trained as a social anthropologist, Gavin is particularly concerned to enter the client's world from their own experiencing and point of view. She describes how she uses participant observation to engage with her young client, Tom, in the co-creation of what she terms 'his therapy world'. Her creative existential therapy approach is rooted in what she calls 'three attitudes': applied phenomenology; being creative about opening up a relational space between therapist and client, and recognition of the client's 'cultural symbolic system'. Gavin shows us how her use of these three attitudes enables her to enter Tom's world and encourage his freedom of expression, both verbal and non-verbal. In the process of this, she helps him to express and confront his underlying existential themes and become increasingly confident.

Martin Adams, in Chapter 2, sets out into relatively uncharted territory to offer a model of human development consistent with the existential phenomenological view that human beings are the product of the choices and actions they make in the context of lived time. This model, as Adams explains, clearly contrasts starkly with the one widely adopted by psychotherapists that 'has tended to conceptualise human development in terms of stage theories that propose a fixed sequence of defined stages that we all go through, rather like going up a ladder'. This profound shift of perspective informs his case illustration, of work with a client whose presenting problems are to do with an awareness of passing time and ageing. Liberated from 'stage theory', Adams is able to focus on the client's original project and help her understand how this is related to her relationship with time.

Helen Acton's Chapter 3 is a contribution to recent debate in the existential therapy community between those who assert that our focus on an individual's ability to create themselves through the life choices they make logically extends to the conclusion that sexual orientation is a choice, and those who argue that this runs counter to clinical experience in which clients talk about their sexual orientation as a given – part of their facticity. Drawing on client work, she suggests that we need to be careful to ensure that our attention to the client's actual lived experience stays at the heart of existential practice.

In Chapter 4, Professor Darren Langdridge provides an overview of major approaches to dream analysis and critiques the theories propounded by

Medard Boss, the theorist most often associated with existential psychotherapy. Drawing on the writing of the French philosopher Paul Ricoeur, he goes on to present some of his own work in developing existential dream analysis, and illustrates this with a case study showing how he has expanded current existential ideas about working with dreams to include an appreciation of them as spaces for imagination and creativity.

Next, Dr Greg Madison (Chapter 5) introduces experiential-existential therapy, an approach that draws on existential therapy and focusing to move away from theoretical interpretation and cognitive analysis and arrive at a 'radically inter-subjective stance' that prioritises the bodily experience of both client and therapist. The emotional and therapeutic power of such a stance for both client and therapist is illustrated by his discussion of his encounters with a young man struggling with terminal illness.

In Chapter 6, I have attempted first to say something about the nature of addiction from an existential-phenomenological perspective, and second to present a model of working existentially with couples that I have developed (inspired by Spinelli's ground-breaking ideas on relational dimensions of therapeutic encounter) and used in my clinical practice for some years. While the two are explicitly linked by the fact that the particular couple I discuss present with issues about addiction, I go on to argue that it is clinically helpful to conceptualise 'addiction' as a form of 'self-medication' and a way for individuals to avoid responsibility for creating their own lives. I argue that, at its most radical, the identity of 'addict' can absolve the individual of any need to exercise personal agency.

Sasha van Deurzen-Smith presents her own contribution to the growing field of existential coaching in Chapter 7. She begins with an overview of the concept of coaching and what distinguishes it from psychotherapy and existential psychotherapy, and then illustrates her unique way of working in a case study of a young woman who presents with a number of goals that she wants to work towards. We see how the client is facilitated in a process that enables her to clarify her motivation for change and the ways in which she sabotages herself while also working on her goals. The key to holding the psycho-educational and psychotherapeutic focuses of this work seems to be the phenomenological attitude that the existential coach brings into play.

In Chapter 8, Professor Rimantas Kočiūnas presents a detailed model for an existential group therapy. We might expect to find a considerable literature on existential approaches to group therapy, not least because existential theorists have emphasised the *Mitwelt* or 'with-world' nature of human being, and the popularity of Irvin Yalom's classic text *The Theory and Practice of*

Existential Group Therapy (1970). Kočiūnas notes, though, that individual work with clients is far more popular than group work and speculates on the reasons why this might be so before arguing, with the help of examples from his practice, that groups have the advantage of enabling clients to gain direct and powerful insights into their ways of being-with-others.

Dr Christina Richards then introduces an increasingly important area of therapeutic work – how to engage with clients who are using therapy to help them decide which gender presentation and physicality are most congruent with their sense of internal gender identity. This process of choosing authentic identity is clearly at the core of existential philosophy and practice. Richards presents a case study that brings together aspects of her work as an NHS psychologist with a presentation of gender dysphoria to illustrate how an existential phenomenological approach can play a significant role in this emerging field.

In Chapter 10, I depart from the 'standard' model of the case study as a vehicle for the author to present some aspect of their work with a client, and instead ask the question whether it is possible for existential therapists to gain useful insights by focusing on *their own* experience of a 'problem of living'. While this might seem a radical reconceptualisation of the notion of the 'case study', I argue that it is a logical consequence of taking seriously the notion that the therapist's way of being determines the extent to which they are open to entering into a therapeutic relationship with a client. My exploration of the experience of being diagnosed with a chronic illness has, then, a number of implications for my way of engaging with clients both in general and those presenting with similar issues.

In Chapter 11, Dr Zack Eletheriadou presents a case study of a young person who became a refugee and presents with profound trauma in the context of multiple cross-cultural conflicts. Her work is particularly interesting for the way in which it draws on both existential phenomenological and psychodynamic theory to make sense of life-changing socio-psychological experience.

Dr Julie Scheiner then introduces her specifically existential approach to the field of equine-assisted therapy. She argues that the four dimensions of human existence model or framework, familiar to existential psychotherapists from the work of Binswanger and van Deurzen, offers a valuable way of developing practice to more fully consider the client's way of being in the world.

Next, in Chapter 13, Ryan Kemp sets out to describe the phenomenon of 'addiction' through the lens of existential phenomenology. Having done so, he goes on to argue that it provides an exciting new perspective with clinical relevance and he illustrates this through a case study of his work with a client in an NHS setting.

In Chapter 14, I seek to show how it is possible to explore a key existential concept, that of 'ontological insecurity', using an analysis of literature – in this instance, some examples of the fiction of Henry James. I argue that the particular way in which James sought to maintain a relationship with the world via a specific type of novel form provides us with helpful insights into our understanding of what may be called a 'schizoid process'.

In the next chapter, Dr Alison Strasser sets out her development of the well-known model of existential time-limited therapy, which she and her father, Dr Freddie Strasser, devised over two decades ago, and provides a case study showing how she uses the model to work with a client presenting with anxiety.

In Chapter 16, Georgia Feliou, an existential therapist based and practising in Athens, introduces the 'radical' phenomenology of the French theorist Jean-Luc Marion. Marion's work will not be familiar to the majority of UK existential therapists; Feliou's use of it, and in particular Marion's notion of 'saturated phenomena', in her work with a client presenting with issues of psychological abuse may inspire greater appreciation of its relevance for existential therapeutic practice.

In Chapter 17, Mark Rayner and Randolph Quinault describe how they have devised a model of existential therapy that can be applied in today's NHS primary care settings. Their case study shows how they use this method – which they call existential experimentation – with a client presenting with aphasia arising from a non-malignant brain tumour. This chapter is interesting both for its discussion of client work and also for the way in which it addresses some of the tensions inherent in working existentially in an increasingly evidence-based, goal-oriented NHS.

The four-worlds model comes to our attention again in Chapter 18, in Dr Chloe Paidoussis-Mitchell's discussion of working therapeutically with trauma and loss. She presents a four-worlds model of traumatic bereavement and loss and its application in her work with a client in her private practice.

Moving towards the end of the collection, and end-of-life issues, in Chapter 19 Dr Prunella Gee presents extracts from a longitudinal case study on the impact of retirement on men. Gee engages directly with the relationship between case study and research, exploring the extent to which psychological research methods and psychotherapy practice may each provide insights of value to the other. She also notes 'a remarkable symbiosis or "fit" between later-life issues' as they surface in her case study 'and the existential lens'.

The final chapter in this book is by Dr Elaine Kasket. Having started with childhood, it is fitting that we end with death. Kasket writes about the penetration of ubiquitous digital technology even into our relationship with death and the dead. With the help of a case study, she illustrates her way of working with a client caught up in 'technologically mediated mourning'.

Each chapter ends with a brief 'Discussion with the editor', which provides me with an opportunity to clarify further any concepts that the author has introduced or drill down further into aspects of their chapter that may be of particular relevance with regard to – remembering the subtitle of this book – 'translating theory into practice'. I want to extend my thanks to Dr Zack Eletheriadou for generously acting as interlocutor for my own contributions to the text. I hope that these dialogues will encourage readers to explore the work of individual contributors further and will inspire them to reflect on, and perhaps in turn write about, the way in which theory and practice come together to enrich their own clinical work.

References

Cohn H (1997). *Existential Thought and Therapeutic Practice: an introduction to existential psychotherapy*. London: Sage.

McLeod J (2010). *Case Study Research in Counselling and Psychotherapy*. London: Sage.

Sartre J-P (1943/1958). *Being and Nothingness* (H Barnes trans). London: Methuen.

Yalom I (1970). *The Theory and Practice of Existential Group Therapy*. New York, NY: Basic Books.

1

Creative existential therapy with children: Tom in his therapy world

Verity J Gavin

The French windows of my waiting room were open. I could see Tom, slightly behind his mother. She was holding his hand and seemed to be talking softly while pulling her son gently forward. Tom was not like most other children as he negotiated the stepping stones leading to the door. He held his head down. I stepped well back to help them make their joined-together entrance. For the first time, I saw this chubby child of six, leaning into his mother, thick brown fringe above dark eyes, dressed in a woollen chunky cardigan, coloured trainers and longish orange shorts.

As Tom turned into the room, our eyes met fleetingly. Behind his shyness I felt his curiosity. He looked around the room, then to the floor, then back to me, and offered a glimmer of a smile. I felt in no hurry to say hello. We were already there in this exquisite moment of the first contact. The response to my gentle smile was a smile through his eyes, then an inquisitive kind of frown as his eyes moved up towards his fringe.

I said: 'Hello Tom. You've arrived. I think you know my name.' I paused, hoping he might say my name, which he did not. 'It is Verity... Bonjour, Madame.' I shook hands with Tom's mother and returned directly to him. 'Would you like to see my workshop, with toys and other materials to play with? Your mum will stay here, in the waiting room.'

Tom walked hesitantly towards me and the open door as I gestured he could pass in front of me. Like all other clients of all ages, Tom went ahead of me into the practice workshop. He stood quietly, absorbing the unusual and attractive sight of a large space with different creative materials and unusual furniture.

'You can wander about to look more closely or touch whatever you like. It is you that chooses here… most of the time.'

Tom looked around, noticing the corner with comfy cushions and curtains, another one with a sand tray surrounded by shelves and drawers full of figurines and objects.

'We can sit and talk a bit too, whenever you wish to.'

Tom moved towards the table where he spotted a large box of soft pastels, charcoal, paints and a big, spiral-bound pad of drawing paper. I showed him a cardboard *pochette* and box for storing everything he drew or created. (Later, when I told him about the few workshop rules, I explained that nothing he drew or created left the workshop.)

Seeing his interest in the soft pastels, I said: 'You can sit here and use them or go to the wall panel and draw with them or use the paints and big brushes.'

When Tom sat down at the table, I sat to his side at right angles (never directly in front but to the side, with a good view of his face and upper body). After his initial diffident sketch of a tree and three blue flowers, I showed him several ways he could hold the pastels, moving my arms in slow and then wider and faster movements. For more than five minutes, Tom silently played with colours, creating new ones by superimposing one on the other. When I showed him that he could use his fingers to rub the colours together, he looked towards me in surprise for a split second, and then began a more body-engaging exploration with ample arm movement. However, there was still little variation in his facial expressions. Suddenly, realising his fingers of both hands were 'really dirty', he stopped and got down from his stool to wash them in the sink.

At this transitionary moment, while he took the towel, I told him it was good to see him exploring the workshop, which his parents had visited when they came to talk to me about his family and his life. But Tom was already looking at the clay tray, asking a question for the first time: 'How do you do with that?' Maybe because he had just carefully washed his hands, he decided to move on across the workshop towards the puppet corner. He took out and held a large griffon puppet and two panda and lamb puppets, and then just stood still, looking at a fish puppet on the top of the others in the big tub. He picked it up slowly: 'Mine was dead. It went dead when I was on holiday with Granny. I never saw how it is to be a dead fish. Mum and Dad showed me where they buried it. I go there sometimes and add a few little stones. I go in secret. Jack laughs at me.'

Tom's face was full of sadness, his body limp and his touch light, as if he were delicately holding a kind of 'deadness'.

'That was a very sad time for you, Tom, and you still seem to be sad when you remember your fish,' I said.

We were quiet together for a while. Then I added: 'You are standing near the quiet, sacred corner where you can think of someone, or some special time, and decorate that space.'

Tom did not take up either option. He played silently with the fish and several other puppets. As he left his first session, he placed the fish on a low surface next to the sacred corner and said, as we moved towards the door: 'I will look after you, fish. Stay here until next week, I'll take care of you.' Then Tom looked at me and said: 'Bubble was my fish's name.' Then fleetingly, I heard him say in a low voice: 'Jack said they didn't bury him, they threw him in the dustbin.'

For three quarters of an hour, Tom had explored the workshop world and several creative media. He had related to me tentatively, speaking a little more toward the end of the session. Clearly, he had the capacity to play alone in my presence (a crucial step in the development of a child (Winnicott, 2005)). His parents had already told me this. Indeed, he mostly played alone, and rarely with his elder brother Jack, who was four years older than him.

At the same time as Tom was developing a special, meaningful relationship with the fish puppet, he was initiating symbolic communications and showing his capacity to care. It seemed likely that the fish would become a transitional object in the developing of the therapeutic process. I could certainly begin to relate trialogically, speaking to this puppet, in the hope that he would converse indirectly back by animating the puppet or speaking directly to me.

Tom's therapist and three attitudes

I chose the introduction to this chapter to be six-year-old Tom's introduction to his therapy. I was first a social anthropologist, and then retrained in London in the early days of existential psychotherapy, and I always try to enter the client's world from their own experiencing and point of view. One of my main interests is the play between personal, interpersonal and cultural meanings. This is one of many links between these two disciplines. In both, the way of being, with a people or a person, is (in the former) and can be (in the latter) described as participant observation.

To participate with Tom in the co-creation of his therapy world, I maintained throughout a phenomenologically embodied observation of both Tom's and my own felt sense (Gendlin, 1978-79; Madison & Barnett, 2011) of being in each of the four dimensions of experiencing (Binswanger, 1963; van Deurzen, 2012). While fully engaged in an equality of being human with Tom, I participate professionally in an offering of my creative *Dasein*-opening to enrich this same process in him.

Figure 1.1 shows these dimensions of being, each one overlapping with each of the others, leaving a space in the centre for non-being. From this centre, the dimensions spread out to all three spheres and levels of *Dasein*-relating.

Figure 1.1: The three 'movings' of *Dasein* (3MD) and the four dimensions of felt sense experiencing (4D)

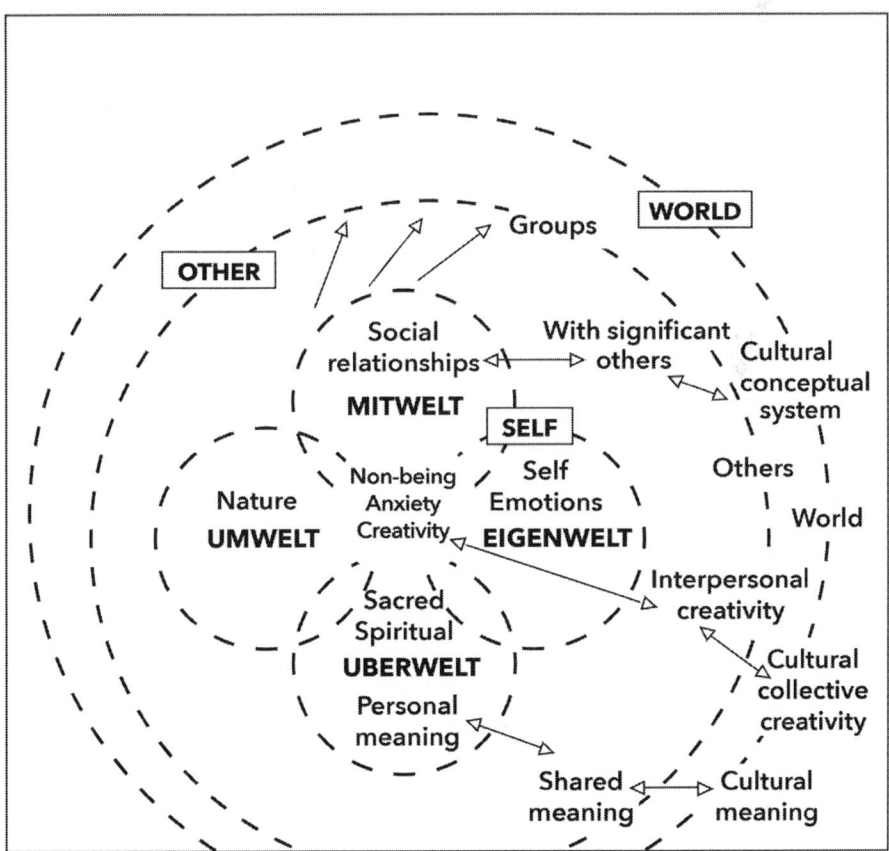

The phenomenological attitude, along with the two others I introduce to the creative existential therapists I train in France and Belgium, contributes fundamentally to my *Dasein*-opening, come what may, in – at times – challenging and intense interactions with clients. With quiet little Tom, my way of being encouraged him to explore, experience and express his potentiality of being. In so doing (or, rather, being), he gained the courage to confront the predominant existential themes underlying his distress.

At all times I kept in mind that Tom's therapy world was a privileged one within his wider world context of current significant relationships and his past relational history. He was, as we are always, at one and the same time relating to self, others and the world. These three levels, or what I call three movings of *Dasein*-relating, are indicated by the three spheres of Figure 1.1. In the world of my practice-workshop, Tom was encouraged to open creatively at each level, thus enriching his sense of being fully alive in all four dimensions of his being.

I have already presented the first of the three attitudes – the phenomenological one – that I progressively introduce to qualified psychotherapists in my two-year training in an, until recently, psychoanalytically dominated France and in Belgium, where a phenomenologically inspired creative therapy for children was also unheard of. Although I have always worked this way with adults, the dearth of appropriate therapy for child victims of negligence and abuse focused my practice for a while, and also the content of my two-year training for working with children and adolescents. When I added a post-post-training, this covered all age groups. I am hoping to introduce and encourage more creative existential work with adults and more theoretical existentially inspired work with children (Gavin, 2013).

Before I move on to the second attitude, I need to stress two points. If the therapist lives and attends to all three movings of *Dasein*, she is not in a mainly dialogical mode. The therapy world is open to all three. Tom was free to relate to the place, space and media as he chose, and to create his relating to me within. Creativity, then, in my approach, is of three kinds, based on the three movings of *Dasein*. Tom's innate 'personal' creative opening was encouraged in our interpersonal creative relating as we co-created our therapy world (see the lines connecting horizontally in Figure 1.1).

The second, trialogical, attitude of creative existential therapy is anchored in, and only possible because it is built on, the first, body-based phenomenological one. It is, simply put, the therapist's engagement in creative ways of opening up a relational space between herself and the client. She recognises the therapeutic importance of the client's opening at all three levels of relating or movings of *Dasein*: self, others and the world.

It could be argued that the trialogical attitude is natural for a healthy, happy child who is developing his capacity to play and symbolise. Relating with and animating objects using paint, modelling and other creative media are creative relational processes exploring different senses of self and forms of meaning. The respect for, and expansion of, the relation space encourages the client's freedom to be and to choose. At times I spoke with great respect directly to Tom's fish (who would then reply in a special fish-like voice); sometimes I animated a particular puppet to talk with Tom or his fish. When Tom himself initiated these trialogical exchanges, he was at the same times exploring and sharing emerging personal meanings.

The third attitude of symbolic meaning recognises the cultural symbolic system Tom has bathed in since birth and the enriching of his personal symbolism shared over time in the often non-verbal communication between us. Attending to these triple ways of relating and creating helped me acknowledge the three 'sources' of emerging meanings that any of us live in or, better still, are. Tom, as we will see, had struggled alone to make sense of his experiences and began exploring with me alternative ways of being with and seeing this world. My confirmation of all three dimensions of his being and his gained courage enabled him to creatively confront existential sources of his anxiety.

Unfolding early sessions in a practice workshop

Tom arrived for his second session behind his mother. He was negotiating the stepping stones with care and almost jumped into the room, smiled a little and walked past me with a slight hello. I said a quick 'Bonjour' to his mother as I was in a hurry to shut the waiting-room door and catch up with Tom

Tom went straight to his fish, which I had placed exactly where and how he had left it. 'Hello fish, you are still resting. Take these to get strong.'

He took two little coloured stones from a nearby basket in the sacred corner and placed them next to the fish's mouth. Then he said: 'Can I play in the water tray, Verity?'

He looked delighted as he put several stones into the water, clustering most of them into an alcove supported by a strong wall. After putting a few toy fish in the water, he hurriedly placed three frogs in the alcove, who called to the fish to come quickly as the nasty crocodile was coming. He grabbed a large crocodile with an open mouth and splashed it into the water, turning it from left to right as though searching for prey. A tiny frog jumped into the water and scurried off in a panicky movement to hide behind another stone. The frog called to the others to join him. 'There… look… he is dangerous… they are scared. Will they ever escape?' Tom told the frogs to stay quiet and wait. But the three together jumped away when the crocodile turned his head. The little one on its own stayed stuck in the corner.

'Oh, what can we do to save you? Think of a plan. Little frog, be brave. No one is there to help you. Find a bird for me; quick, Verity. He will fly past and pick the little one up'.

Luckily there was a puffin on the pile of figurines and Tom took it quickly from my hand, making it swoop down, and they both landed on a big stone next to the water tray. 'That's it! Saved!' said Tom, after this unusual spurt of co-ordinating thinking and moving, engaging me and emotions, and ending with relief.

Figure 1.2 illustrates Tom's other modes of being with self, myself and the material of the workshop. In these early sessions, Tom was opening out towards other corner spaces and creative materials in the practice workshop. He initiated a ritual of attending quietly and gently to his fish when he first arrived. He showed his capacity to symbolise in different kinds of play, communicating non-verbally, with some verbal comments or interactions. Each session, he returned to the water tray, where the little frog was still in danger of attack from the large crocodile. During scary, last-minute escapes, this little frog was often helped by a kind dolphin. However, his relating with me stayed relatively restricted and mostly indirect. I was not convinced there was a real poverty of Tom's intersubjective skills. There were sparks of spontaneity, openings of curiosity, and a developing kind of connivance, especially when his fish was close by or with us. It was evident that I would need to introduce new, creative ways of relating, communicating and expressing in order to facilitate his gradual opening of this particular moving of *Dasein*: relating with other(s) – the 'other' being in this case me, his therapist.

Figure 1.2 is just one kind of creative note-taking that I use to catch my global felt sense (4D) and creative resonance as soon as the client has left, as I do not take notes during sessions. This is to ensure my embodied presence to self, client and our potential space. Figure 1.2 also shows how it is possible to record the movements, expressions, themes and productions over space and in the time of a 45-minute session. Simple drawings record the child's creations and productions. Greater details of particularly significant moments can be captured in additional quick sketches, adding into it notes and phrases of verbatim exchanges. This way of describing a session as close in time as possible

Figure 1.2: Creative note-taking

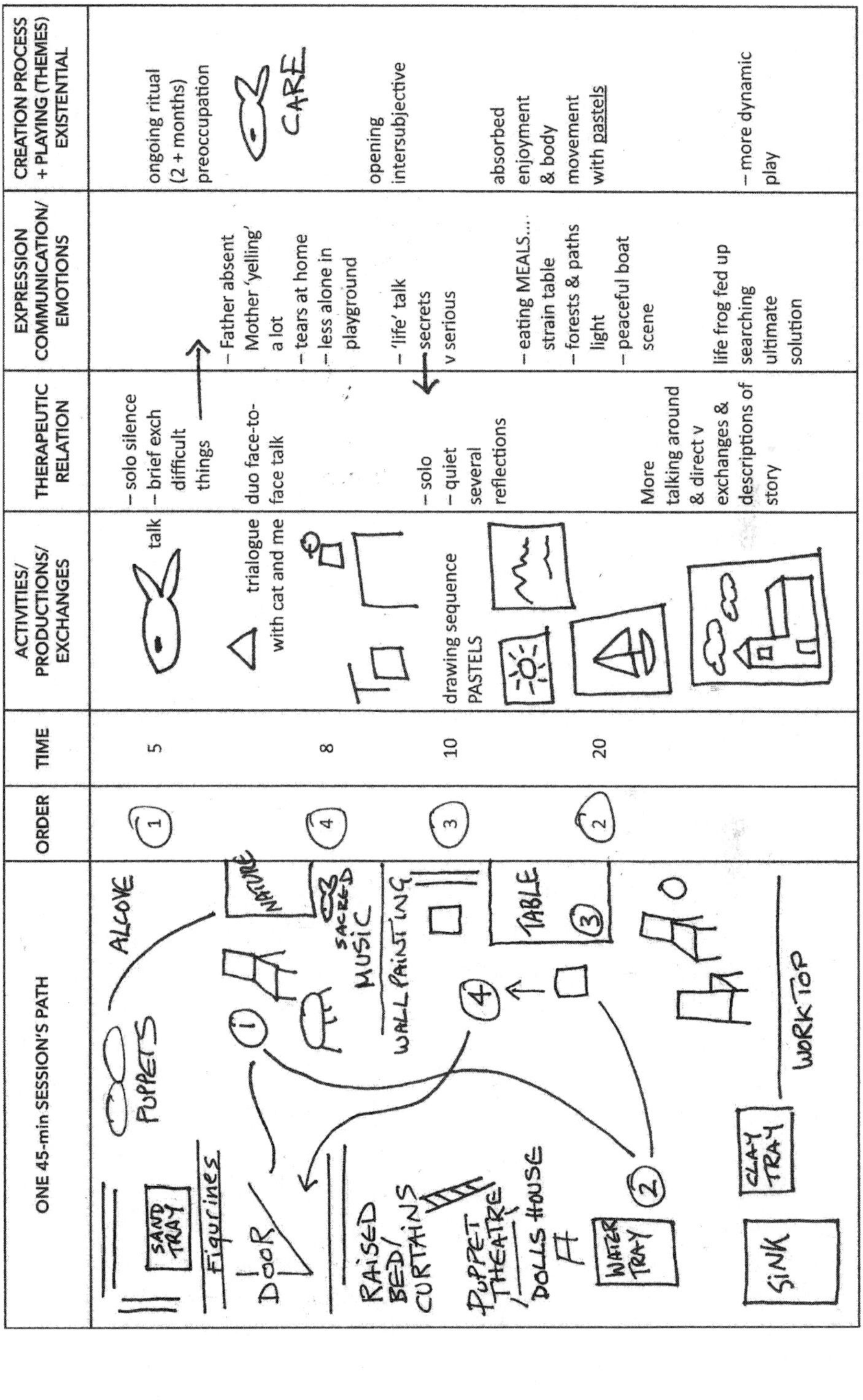

to its happening and to the immediate lived experience is my attempt to honour the three main principles of the phenomenological method (Spinelli: 2014), and to remember all four dimensions of felt experiencing (van Deurzen, 2012; Madison & Barnett, 2011).

Another form of 'bridging' theory and practice is my use of three interrelated projects: the Life Path, the Family Plan and the Scenery of Significant Others and Places. The therapist records information from parents in these three ways and keeps the whole in mind and alive throughout the therapeutic process. The child creatively engages in each project, sometimes briefly, sometimes extending over many sessions, using a wide variety of materials: paint, pastels, little stones, coloured wool. Members in the Family Plan may be made out of clay, corks, pipe cleaners etc.

Collaborating with parents

Collaborating with parents is part of the extended frame of child and adolescent psychotherapy. It too is subject, to my mind, to the healthy tension between a firm frame and a creative human way of being-with. A transparent collaboration, while respecting confidentiality, is not an easy task, for example with parents who may, like their children, have a heavy relational history. It is, I believe, the creative opening of the professional's way-of-being that offers parents a chance to generate new understandings of themselves and their child.

My meetings with the child's parents, either together or separately (whether separated, divorced or not) help me explore more deeply the three kinds of themes that are uppermost in creative existential therapy. These themes overlap, but for heuristic reasons they are considered separately, with bases in different disciplinary or theoretical traditions. The first are the existential themes, the second developmental themes, and the third the themes of playing and symbolising. They are interrelated and each one elaborated in different schemas that make up the conceptography of my approach for thinking about practice. Only the existential themes will be considered later in this chapter.

My preliminary meeting with Tom's parents was an initial move into Tom's relational world. While exploring their request for their son's therapy, their perception of him, the relational family context and Tom's relational history, I was developing a collaborative way of working with them and introducing a clear frame and my way of working therapeutically. Before accepting a child or an adolescent in therapy, I consider it essential that these are spelt out and the frame agreed upon. Many subsequent problems are linked with the fact that the therapist has not clarified the frame and has not reminded the parents of it in the course of the therapy. Three simple examples are the parents questioning their child about the content of the sessions, not discussing with the therapist an eventual ending before announcing it to their child, or not respecting the important ending phase by abruptly stopping the therapy.

Returning to the first meeting, this is likely to be particularly charged with (a) parent(s)' distress and great details of, for example, family events or secrets. I may propose a second meeting, in both cases without the presence of the child. The potential client, of whatever age, should not be introduced to the therapist in a climate that is predominantly negative, emotionally charged and problem orientated, where he is subject to adult forms of communicating. As I have already illustrated in the description of Tom's first session, children have a potential to adopt a new way of relating with their therapist.

I wanted to ask Tom's parents if Tom related anywhere in a more lively, direct, interactional inter-subjectivity. I was intrigued to know more about how Tom communicated with family and school friends, and how he expressed his feelings at home: had they noticed a heavy sadness at times or heard him ask thoughtful questions about life and death? I explored further their and Tom's sense of self-worth, and their and Tom's relationships with his brother Jack. I asked when and how they had dealt with the goldfish's death, and later on, in a meeting with Tom's mother only, I invited her to tell me more about her relationship with her own mother, and her reactions when she died, as well as those of Jack and Tom.

I then explored Tom's 'play' history in relation to each parent, which led the father to dwell on his own 'tough' upbringing and his great irritation with Tom's 'weaknesses' and 'fragility'. He had no choice, as a child, he said, but to 'get on', and had never found it easy to be physically cuddly or playful with either child or, indeed, with his wife. I spoke of privileged moments between one parent and one child and proposed several ideas to this father who was gradually opening to his own needs while exploring the needs of his son. We also explored why the two boys spent little time having fun together, which was not, I discovered, a recent situation linked with Jack's growing interests beyond the family. Here I heard comments about four-year-old Jack's difficulty in accepting the arrival of his baby brother, and also about Tom starting in primary school six months previously. Comments about 'boys being boys', Jack being a toughie and Tom too shy, left me more, rather than less, concerned about Tom. Now I knew that neither parent played much with their children and seemed to think it inevitable, because of their busy lives. Their children were similarly expected to 'get on' with their lives, mostly playing in their bedrooms.

The therapeutic process

In the following months, Tom chose a wider range of creative and play sequences, many of which belonged to the *Umwelt* body dimension. He spent quieter, more regressive moments in the cushioned alcove, enjoying the soft, tactile sensations, and behind the puppet theatre curtains, where he spoke with the puppets rather than getting them to perform in front of me. However, in both cosy settings, he showed great pleasure when I animated a toy or puppet with one of his in a trialogical talk. And it was in these often touching moments that I could communicate at a symbolic level, using his own, personal symbolism. Also, the puppet I animated would often think aloud, rather than ask questions, or take a different viewpoint to Tom's on what was going on.

'I wonder why we animals get so scared. How is it the monkey does not want to climb trees any longer? Oh, if the duck did that to me, I'd shout, "Stop! The pond is for everyone, not just for you, you big bully."'

My puppet would also initiate trialogical talk with Tom's fish, mostly about the mysteries and difficulties of living. Here, in quiet trialogical play, we began to open indirectly to experiencing a greater quality of intersubjective interaction. More active incarnating play involved Tom moving about with musical instruments or standing up to paint on the wall panel. He used, rather tentatively at first, the anger cushions and punching ball. This and other factors led Tom to begin to express, and then talk about, the hurt and anger he felt from his brother's treatment.

He used several kinds of what I call creative abreactions, tearing up drawings of 'worst' monsters, writing angry letters on 'nasty' writing paper and posting them in his shoebox letter box and throwing clay onto a particular spot on the tiled floor. During these moments, my felt resonating sense (at 4D – see Figure 1.1) was of his deep hurt and anger as he repeatedly hit the cushions or threw the clay. He would yell 'at' his 'brother', 'Beast, imbecile, I hate you,' and then flop down or lie on cushions and speak bit by bit about what had been happening in an escalating way over several years. Jack had hit, pinched and shaken his brother and had silenced him, it seemed, from his early years, with the threat of scary stories coming true. Suddenly scenes Tom had played out and passing remarks or questions he had made fitted into place. He was sharing the strain and distress of it through all four dimensions of his being: the release of built-up energy, the trialoguing with his brother, the expression of his feelings and the questioning why he 'deserved' this treatment and felt so different from others. Emerging personal symbolic meanings and shared implicit meanings I had felt, without fully understanding, were coming into a new light.

The gravity of Tom's experience and his loss of confidence in self and others were easier to understand when I heard Tom say, while talking to me or to his fish, the following sorts of comments: '… and they never buried you, just threw you in the bin… I couldn't say goodbye to Granny when she was dead. I was too much a baby. Now her body is eaten up like Mum's will be, and mine… Why didn't Mum or Dad stop Jack? I thought I was bad. It was my fault… Now I'm big I wonder why I couldn't tell them… The monsters had all that power… I was always scared.'

At home he began to speak his mind, share heavy feelings, but also enjoy moments of great fun and an awkward silliness that overflowed at times at school but was fortunately appreciated by his surprised teacher.

The ongoing background experiencing of what I call the 'transpotentiality' of creative relatedness in my therapeutic approach is more than, but greatly enriched by, those intense inter-subjective moments or sequences in which the client (or therapist in training) transcends her habitual mode of being. The latter may be moments of mutual engagement in active play, in which the child experiences mutual spontaneity and pleasurable exchanges, or times of quiet, predominantly non-verbal stillness together. The client may paint, sculpt, create a story or 'work' in the sand or water tray, or be in a quiet, half-dreaming kind of state.

Existential themes

The therapist's existential way of being is grounded in an embodied phenomenological attitude. As I hope to have shown, this attitude values and encourages the creative relational space and meaning composing between therapist and client. Referring again back to Figure 1.1, as I was entering Tom's world of being (3MD) my lived experience of creative resonating (4D) and relating was instantly and always effected by his progressive opening (3MD) and the enriching of the four dimensions of his experience (4D). Through my engagement, creative entry and confirming of Tom's whole being (4D), my quality of presence facilitated his creative opening and the emergence of universal ontological themes, which could then be addressed, both directly in words and indirectly through my non-verbal symbolic trialogical communications.

It is from the grounding of this way of being that the therapist will be more aware of, and sensitive to, the emerging existential themes that are central, I believe, to therapeutic work with all ages. When underlying existential anxiety is tamed in a confirming (4D), creative way (3MD), it is then possible

Creative existential therapy with children

to confront, often trialogically, specific existential themes. Parents, often unknowingly, offer a lot of information on their own underlying existential anxieties and how these are absorbed, shared and transmitted in family life.

Tom had expressed underlying existential themes, initially in non-verbal ways of relating (3MD) and in the content of his play (4D). As he initiated himself, and as he took up from me, certain creative propositions, he gradually empowered himself (4D) with the courage to create and confront these themes. His intense anxiety subsided and his sense of self-confidence grew.

In the content of his creating and playing, Tom had revealed, within the first few sessions, an anxiety and preoccupation with death, an unspoken fear linked with family life, and a lack of self-confidence (especially what I call 'embodied' or body-based confidence). As each of these themes were

Figure 1.3: Existential themes - Tom

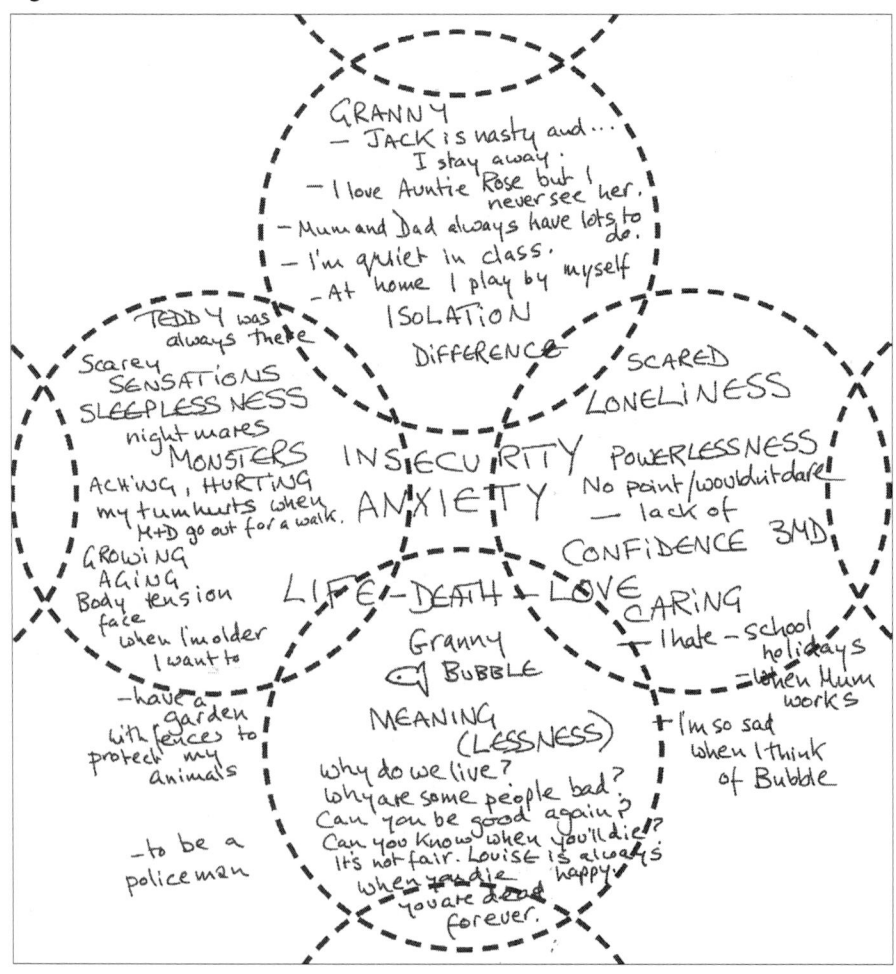

addressed creatively, either actively through different creative media or indirectly through 'drawing-exploring' or talking about life (and death), there was a positive change in Tom's body tonus and facial expressions, and a greater capacity to express himself, non-verbally and verbally. He was surprising himself with a new capacity to let go and have fun and engaging more and more with me in moments of heightened enjoyment.

Some of these themes are presented in Figure 1.3, which I offer as an example of a quick taking stock, in this case after six months of therapy.

Only when his parents witnessed this at times explosive and increasingly assertive Tom – most notably in his relating with his elder brother – did they begin to share and address their concern about not having protected Tom from Jack's scaring and bullying. They could not believe that Jack had managed to conceal this for several years. Why he had developed this power and been able to maltreat his little brother raised many crucial questions (*Mitwelt* related) about the family dynamics and the very different needs of the two children. The parents began a healthy self-questioning that challenged old assumptions and led to changes in some ingrained daily routines. They were also learning how to take care of their own needs. The mother began a personal therapy, as did Jack soon after.

Like so many children, Tom's fear of the monsters in his room and in his dreams reflected heightened existential anxiety. Falling asleep is not easy if you have a diffuse sense of insecurity about being alive and unshared questions about death. In the same way that Tom had been developing rituals to remember and care for his dead fish, he had also found a way of appeasing this anxiety. In the process, over several months of mourning Bubble and Granny, he was sharing with me, non-verbally at first, these unspeakable anxieties. Gradually he responded to some of my 'talkings about life' – which included not only talking but also exploring and drawing about death – with questions about what happens after death, who would look after him when his parents died, why people eat animals that could stay alive, and could his heart stop dead when he was very scared or hurting too much?

In the following six months of his therapy, there was a series of sessions where Tom enacted death-related themes in the sand tray: for example, a burial attended by his favourite animal and person figurines. He modelled clay into a tombstone and placed it in the sacred corner, on a round straw mat, which he decorated with little shiny pearls and shells, and 'drew' and signed a little card to Granny. In later sessions, he seemed to use this creative trialogical opening to start us talking about these and other existential issues:

for example, feeling different from others, not having friends, being isolated in general in his world. His sense of injustice and his preoccupation with protection and caring were closely related in the Überwelt dimension of fundamental values and the meaning(s) of existing.

In the following weeks Tom's mother rang to say that he was falling asleep more easily at night, eating well (yet still refusing any meat or fish) and yelled regularly at his brother. She said at first he would run immediately to one of his parents for safety but more recently he would stand firm, waiting for their support. At school he was making friends and seemed to be keeping them. He gradually participated more in class.

When the therapist has 'worked' creatively in her training and continues personal explorations of her own existential themes, she will identify more easily the way the client relates, communicates and expresses these themes, both verbally and non-verbally. She will also be more confident and creatively skilled in keeping open and exploring these themes. It is in her way of being, of talking about and creatively confronting issues relating to life and death, loneliness, freedom and responsibility that the client 'comes alive', liberating heavy emotions of the Überwelt dimension and progressively integrating traumatic experiences that affect all four dimensions of being.

Ending therapy and concluding this chapter

Tom's therapy was straightforward, in part because the parents collaborated and accepted support in questioning their assumptions about parenting. Also, I did not have to address through my creative relating serious attachment, incarnating, emotional and neural integration themes. Tom had already gained a reasonably secure attachment with both parents before Jack's behaviour began to undermine his security of being.

Tom's capacity for intersubjective relatedness needed to be enriched through my creative trialogical way of being, and the offering of some of the creative media and propositions I have developed over many years (Gavin, 2013). My mainly right-brain relating facilitated Tom's emotional integration and neural plasticity. Tom's potential fear provoked by Jack's negating of open, free and trustworthy relating had held him in a silent secrecy of submission. Jack had managed to maintain over time the heightened sense of insecurity he had produced in his brother. This was assisted by their parents' lack of awareness and availability when Tom needed extra support in dealing with the death of his Granny and then of his fish and his attempts to make sense of these experiences. Tom, very much alone, had linked both disasters with his lack of confidence in adults, or at least seen them as evidence that adults could not, in his understanding, be trusted to tell the truth.

In the last months of his therapy, Tom took increasing agency and responsibility for his freedom to be and to express these new ways of being in the therapy world. As the months passed, these changes became more and more embedded in his everyday life. Tom then gave me other causes to consider ending his therapy. One significant indicator was that he, for the first time, began to think about his future life. He also showed a new lightness of feeling, and at times even mischief. For the first time he wondered about other children who were in therapy with me or that he thought should come – notably, an 'enemy' at school, and his brother!

After careful collaboration with his parents, Tom and I spoke about the ending of his therapy five weeks before the last session, which he began to plan. Besides the favourite biscuits and fruit juice for himself, he found a way to prepare for saying goodbye to his fish: a stock of food (of painted pieces of dry clay) and a blue felt 'pond bag', 'for when he feels tired and needs to rest', Tom said. In the third to last session we talked about, and explored in sketches, how our heads become full of pollution when lies are spread in the air. During the second to last session, Tom talked at length about what he wanted to do in his life, why it was important to care for children and his sadness to leave me and the fish. The last session was mostly quiet. Tom looked through the drawings and paintings in his folder. We spoke of our journey and drew together, turn by turn, a pastel colouring, with many a 'teasing' kind of stroke. He walked around the workshop saying goodbye to favourite places and special toys. Then he handed over his fish into my care, explained what I must do, and gave him a big hug.

I told him I would remember him and wished him a life full of many explorations and fun. We said 'Au revoir' and he left the workshop, slipping past his mother to skip speedily from one stepping stone to the next.

Discussion with the editor

Simon: Can you expand a little on the context in which you were inspired to developed creative existential therapy and how it sits in relation to existential theory and practice in general?

Verity: The short answer is that I tend to give myself big challenges, and the longer answer is to do with why, which there isn't space to do here but I plan to do so elsewhere.

The personal context was my change of profession, from social anthropologist to psychotherapist. Having moved up in the academic world, I was further away from real people in grassroots research. But I also saw the negative impact of the arrival of the UK prime minister Margaret Thatcher on the concerns and issues that mattered to me. Family concerns also led me to consider this massive professional leap and later on my move to live in France.

I was developing my own creativity through personal work and art therapy training when I had unusual scope to develop and embody my ideas about psychotherapy while working in a therapeutic community based on Winnicottian thought. Throughout my training in existential therapy, in the days of Emmy van Deurzen, Ernesto Spinelli and Hans Cohn, I was considering how all that I was learning about therapy with adults was relevant and applicable to working with children and adolescents and wondering why there was so little creative work with adults in existential therapy.

When I moved to France in 1990, I developed two practice workshops, but I had no intention of starting a training course. The country-wide and local professional context was not encouraging. There was no official recognition of the profession of psychotherapist; there was a predominance of psychoanalysis, mostly Lacanian; 'existentiel' was reduced by many to the '68 movement', and there was no tradition of creative therapy – in my sense of the term – or experiential training for working with children and adolescents.

But enthusiastic pressures on me from therapists in Belgium and France led me to start a post-foundation training in 2005 for the three professions of clinical psychologists, child psychiatrists and psychotherapists specialising in therapy with children and adolescents. In 2012 I added a 'post-post-training', which includes working with adults.

Simon: And what do you regard as its distinguishing characteristics?

Verity: The most distinguishing characteristic of creative existential therapy is the creative opening that is offered to the client. The choices offered in a practice workshop and the creative quality of being of the therapist encourage the client's freedom of expression, verbal and non-verbal. The creative relatedness of this process is trialogical, not dialogical, which has only a talking and sedentary base. The opening and enriching of a potential space between therapist and client facilitate the emergence of, and creative confrontation with, existential themes.

The training introduces the creative media (for example, clay, paint, water, sand), and all kinds of creative propositions that I have devised to encourage clients to enter into the exploration of underlying themes. There are many other particularities I'd love to elaborate on but lack the space here.

Simon: You mention your current training activities. Can you say more about the ways in which you have been able to spread your approach more widely, and the success you have had and challenges you have encountered?

Verity: I am now completing my much overdue introductory book in French, which refers to practice with all ages. Then I will return to the draft of a book in English that goes into greater theoretical depth, again referring to all ages. It explores the centrality of creative relatedness to life, therapy and what I call our own, unique 'poemy' we compose in living creatively. What I argue for, and it is important to my mind to insist on it, is fundamental for existential therapy. The basic 'PhilosoVie' and principles are there for all ages, and highly flexible to adapt to the uniqueness of each person in therapy, whatever their age.

Simon: I was struck, reading your chapter, by what felt to me to be an interesting contract between the warmth and immediacy of your relationship with Tom and the complexity of your Creative Existential Therapy model – particularly with regard to the way the four dimensions of being and the triological attitudes are incorporated. How, in your work, do you balance, bridge, or perhaps 'embody' theory and practice?

Verity: The fact that the complexity of what you call my 'model' seems a great contrast throws up a permanent tension I felt while writing and cutting out or condensing sections to fit the length of the chapter. I hoped to give the feel of working with a child without abandoning the conceptual 'theoretical' integrative frame I have developed, which was supposed to point to various major contributions from contemporary existential work with adults.

This thinking-theory frame is embodied in my practice because the notions specific to creative existential therapy grew in the first place out of my experiencing the practice. My creative way of training has greatly strengthened this embodiment and my confidence and wish to transmit. It took two years for this frame to emerge experientially through my own practice. So my next plan is to disseminate the content and the creative 'existential' pedagogy to trainers of foundation and post-foundation courses.

References

Binswanger L (1963). *Being-in-the-World: selected papers of L Binswanger* (J Needleman ed). New York, NY: Basic Books.

Gavin VJ (2013). Creative existential therapy for children, adolescents and adults (with special reference to training. *Existential Analysis 24*(2): 318–341.

Gendlin ET (1978–79). Befindlinchkeit: Heidegger and the philosophy of psychology. *Review of Existential Psychology and Psychiatry 16*(1–3): 43–71.

Madison G, Barnett L (eds) (2011). *Existential Therapy: legacy, vibrancy and dialogue*. London: Routledge.

Spinelli E (2014). *Practising Existential Psychotherapy: the relational world*. London: Sage.

van Deurzen E (2012). *Existential Counselling and Psychotherapy in Practice*. London: Sage.

Winnicott DW (2005). *Play and Reality*. London: Routledge.

2

Why me, why now? On discovering that time is passing

Martin Adams

Human development has been largely overlooked by the existential-phenomenological therapeutic tradition until only very recently (Cohn, 1998; Adams, 2006, 2013a, 2014, 2018). This is curious because, with the exception of Heidegger, whose project was ontological and who had little personal or professional interest in biography, Kierkegaard, Nietzsche, Sartre, Beauvoir and Merleau-Ponty all wrote about it. Merleau-Ponty in particular regarded as a philosophical issue how things come to be the way they are, and Simone de Beauvoir considered both gender and old age from developmental and philosophical perspectives.

Psychotherapy in general has tended to conceptualise human development in terms of a fixed sequence of defined stages that we all go though, rather like going up a ladder. With the exceptions of Jung and Erikson, who look at the whole of life, psychotherapy theorists have also tended to focus on childhood and the early years of life. This way of thinking, derived from natural scientific principles of causation and essentialism, has come to dominate the profession.

Nevertheless, although some elements from such stage theories have some resonance with everyday experience, they are unable to account for the very qualities that are most distinctive about human existence: the ability to choose, to hope and to love, and our need for meaning and purpose in life.

An alternative approach has been taken by Baltes and colleagues (1987). Characterised by the propositions that development is both a lifelong process and an expression of biological, social, historical and cultural processes (Sugarman, 2001: 13), their life-span approach is more of an integrative umbrella under which different aspects of development can be explored and understood.

Although Baltes and colleagues do not explicitly refer to the ontological dimension, this orientation is closer to an existential perspective.

Thinking about human development existentially

As with many other subjects, we need to be careful about the terminology we use when referring to human development (Adams 2013b: 51). Words like 'instinct', 'maturing' and 'evolving' have biological resonances; words like 'transforming' or 'building' have technological implications. The current enthusiasm for neuroscience also distracts us from the project of trying to stay close to experience (Tallis, 2011; Crawford, 2010). Even the word 'development' itself is not immune from this distraction (eg. Burman, 2007). Borrowing from Heidegger's use of dis-closing or dis-covering, a word more consistent with the experience-near principles of phenomenology is 'opening', in the sense of a lifelong opening to the awareness of the givens of existence. Dreyfus (1991: 187) articulates this as the way, from birth, that the 'human organism starts *Daseining* gradually', and starts taking 'a stand on itself by pressing into human possibilities'.

This is echoed by Laing (1965), who writes:

> Biological birth is a definitive act whereby the infant organism is precipitated into the world... physical birth and biological aliveness are followed by the baby becoming existentially born as real and alive.' (1965: 41)

He is saying that physical birth is the starting point for a process of opening to the world. This is what he calls becoming existentially born.

Extending this, Merleau-Ponty (1964) suggests that as, from birth, we gradually open to existence, we are exposed to an endless succession of de-centring experiences in which our worldview is challenged. Some of these are easier to accommodate than others. Life is a constant process of de-centring and we are constantly reminded of our ungroundedness.

Existentially, we are both 'thrown' into our lives, in the sense that we do not choose to be born, and 'thrown' out of our lives, in the sense that we do not know when we will die. Our lives are influenced by the twin mysteries of natality – how we come out of nothing – and mortality – how we return into nothing. On our path through life from birth to death, we start with something we are given that is neither ours nor requested. Our life task is to make it into something that is personal and owned, but then we lose it when we die. The most basic challenge of life, of our development as human beings, is to find a way to live with this absurdity and to discover ways of being that give us what we decide we need, bearing in mind that what we need changes as we go through life. We have to learn to distinguish between 'thrownness' and 'fallenness', between those elements that we cannot change and those we can.

When Sartre (1946/1973: 29) wrote, 'Man is condemned to be free', he meant that we have responsibility for our lives whether we like it or not. We only see ourselves as fixed, or 'sedimented', because it evokes too much anxiety – existential anxiety – to acknowledge that we are the product of our choices and actions. We gain a resilient and coherent sense of self because of, not in spite of, our ability to be different in different circumstances. When we understand this, we can choose whether to be the active creator of our own life or a passive recipient of a life.

Sartre (1943/2003) suggests that, in our perpetual searching for reliable patterns, we gradually identify a fundamental (or 'original') project, on the basis of context-derived choices, which we subsequently apply to other contexts. In the desire to avoid the anxiety of freedom and responsibility and to make an autobiography that gives the impression of coherence and purpose, we view the original project as ineluctable, rather than chosen. We close down our possibilities, imagining that our life will become easier and simpler, and in a sense it does, except that it also becomes narrower and less flexible.

Although Sartre talks about the original project forming round a significant event, it is truer to say that we simplify our random and largely incoherent experiences into a small number of coherent and prototypical 'memories' that are actually constructions and that epitomise our relationship to others and to the world – to existence. The original project is more likely to be embodied rather than cognitive and is about our place in the world – our response to uncertainty.

The questions that arise from absurdity are unresolvable existential questions (Yalom, 1980). As such, they become the backdrop to the whole of our lives, and our awareness of time passing, our temporality, becomes an integral part of our thrownness. Time is like a thread that weaves through our lives. It is never not there. It is the water that we swim in, and we are always aware not only that our time on this earth is finite but also that it is up to us to make something of it, because it cannot be repeated.

These questions preoccupy us in different ways depending on our age, context and circumstances and are always in the form of paradoxes and dilemmas. They are ever present and never solved.

The paradox of physicality is that, although physical death will kill me and the denial of death will destroy the time I have left, the idea of death will save me in the sense that it will prompt me to live my life more resourcefully. The dilemma is that I know I am going to die but not when or what it will be like.

The paradox of relationality is that only awareness of my separateness can help me understand and respect the otherness of the other. The dilemma is that we have a need for individuality at the same time as a need to be part of a whole.

The paradox of individuality is that, by realising I am weak and vulnerable, I develop responsibility and personal power. As long as I pretend I am invulnerable, I cannot come to terms with my natural human vulnerability. The dilemma is that, even as we make our choices, we seek external validation.

The paradox of morality is that, when I discover there are no absolute rules to live by, I realise that my life will only become meaningful if I develop my own value system. The dilemma is that our need for ultimate meaning and purpose persists, even as we come to accept the relativity of our existence.

The summarising thread that runs through all these is: 'How can I live as if there is certainty while knowing that there is none?' We are subject to randomness and chance far more that we care to admit and there is an overarching paradox that absolutisms such as 'See you tomorrow' are delusions that are necessary for us to carry on everyday life (Stolorow, 2007). Meaning-making at every moment of our lives is born out of the perpetual tension evoked by these unsolvable dilemmas and paradoxes. We create meaning by struggling with courage through adversity and by gaining a successively richer understanding of the paradoxes of existence. This is what is meant by authenticity.

Existentially, then, the question with respect to human development is: 'How do we get from birth, when these paradoxes are not understood, to existential maturity and wisdom (which is by no means guaranteed anyway) when they are understood?'

Existential-phenomenological therapeutic practice

The developmental model most consistent with an existential-phenomenological view that a person is the product of their choices and actions taken in the context of lived time is a life-long process model concerned with the skills of living. In our desire to have 'continuity in time and a location in space' (Laing, 1965: 41), to be something rather than nothing, we actively construct a coherent sense of self out of the random events of our lives, in order to bring meaning and purpose. In this way, we daily encounter our thrownness and realise not only that our life is no one else's responsibility but our own but also that it is the product of chance and opportunity.

With respect to therapeutic practice the following conclusions can be made.

- Given the centrality of time and temporality, the questions 'Why now?' and 'Why me?' take on a greater importance and relevance. We need to consider what is going on for this particular client, at this particular time of life and in these particular circumstances, that has given them the gift of despair that brings them to therapy.

- Since life is process, our natural 'state' is one of change. In existential therapy, we do not work on 'change', we work on stopping stopping – on resistance to change. Clients come to us when they feel their autobiography is not making enough sense, when they are feeling existentially de-centred and are resisting re-centring. By reintroducing the client to change, we reintroduce them to personal responsibility and what I call the Law of Existential Consequence (Adams, 2013b), which states that, when I do something, something follows that I have to take responsibility for.

- Since the past is a matter of interpretation and presently being acted out, our task is to find out how past choices led to current actions and future intentions. Wellbeing does not depend on the successful search for a key memory and its correct interpretation; rather, it emerges from a fluid dialectic between story-making and story-breaking. It is about being able to update autobiography in line with current experience and realising that there is no guarantee that the current meaning will last beyond the present moment. When the client is able to identify the current meaning of their original project, they will be able to re-own it so that the choice can be revisited and remade. In the process, the existential realities of freedom, choice and responsibility come to replace the determinist fantasies of causation and passivity. When they understand this, the client can choose whether to be the active creator of their life or a passive recipient of a life.

When we care for someone what we care for is their autonomy, regardless of their chronological or existential age. As autonomy is so central to human meaning, the existential therapist will need to know how to adapt and monitor their practice so that an optimum amount of autonomy is present within the relationship (Karban, 2017).

Case illustration

The first contact Alex made with me was by email. She said that she had been to see an osteopath for recurrent back pain and he had suggested that she contact me about her anxiety, which he said was exacerbating her back pain. She also said that, although she had never seen a psychotherapist before, she felt the osteopath's suggestion was a good one because she knew she had a few things she needed to talk through.

She arrived on time for her first appointment, a few days later. I let her take a while to get accustomed to the room and then asked her to tell me a bit more about what brought her here today, what questions she needed to talk through. I wanted to start where she was and I needed to know 'Why now?'

Although she was new to therapy, she talked easily. She said she just wanted to know why she was feeling so anxious and depressed. She was 38 years old, but looked 10 years younger. She said there were three issues worrying her. One was her parents, who lived abroad. They were both in their early 70s but in the last year or so she had started to worry about them. She said: 'I don't know why, they are fine, they still do everything they used to… but now I worry that there's only me to look after them if anything happens.' An only child, she talked about her comfortable childhood and schooldays. She said it was 'pretty normal, nothing awful happened'. In her early school days, her parents moved frequently, often to different countries, because of work. Although she no longer knew anyone from her school days, she said it 'was good because I met lots of different sorts of people and I know so many different places. It was exciting'. The second issue, which she said was separate, was that she was finding it hard to get over a relationship that ended four years before. She said she found herself thinking of her ex-boyfriend, Jamie, more now than she ever did, even when they were together. The third issue was that she thought she was drinking too much.

I wasn't so sure that the three issues were unconnected but, as it was nearly the end of the first session, I left it and instead asked her, as I always do at the end of the first session, what it had been like talking to me for the last 45 minutes. She said, 'Odd but good. I don't know you, but I feel as if I do. I've said all sorts of things I've only ever thought about before... I'm surprised you could follow my rambling.'

In the next few sessions she talked more about her relationships with her parents and with Jamie, and about just feeling sad about 'everything'. But 'everything' was hard for her to put into words. She was looking at her life in a different way and what she was finding was confusing her. I decided to let it unfold in its own way.

She talked more about her childhood, about feeling that she didn't ever have a best friend, that she didn't belong anywhere, and of the relationship with Jamie, who pursued her and whom she met through work and who lived all the time in the US and was married anyway. She only saw him when he came to the UK. 'That's what I don't understand. It wasn't much of a relationship and I didn't expect much from it, so why do I think about it so much?' She talked about the dog her parents got when she was a teenager and back living in the UK. She said: 'I used to think of her as my dog, even though I moved away not long after we got her. It was great going back to see her.' Gradually, 'everything' became a shorthand for all the thoughts and feelings that came with her awareness of time, of age, of her own age. This came into sharp focus when she was reminded of her birthday. 'You know, I had genuinely forgotten it was my birthday and when I got a card from my parents, I thought, "It must be a mistake... I've only just had one."' But it wasn't a mistake; another year had gone past.

The surprise of another year going past opened up a more profound reflection about her relationship with time. She claimed she had 'never spent much time thinking about time or age', then corrected herself: 'No, that's not right, it's more that I spent a lot of time actively not thinking about it.' She didn't want to be reminded of her birthday, of getting older, of getting old, of her temporality.

She talked about working in a young person's industry, in different companies on short-term contracts, and of being surrounded by people nearly 10 years younger than her. She socialised with them too, which largely revolved around bars and clubs. She said, 'It was fun, I could do pretty much anything I wanted – go here, do that, like when I was a child. There's always tomorrow, something new, things will turn up... but...'

Things had indeed been good and fun but were rapidly becoming less so. She continued: '... it's like my second 40 years has collapsed in an instant and I'm suddenly old. Is this it? Is this as good as it gets? I haven't started. I feel 18. I thought I had all the time in the world. I feel older than my parents. I always thought old age happened to other people, but it's right here. I thought I was ageless – I mean, young.' She said she had never known death, no one close to her had ever died, and then corrected herself: '... except my dog… I really miss her, I think that's probably why I don't go back [to her family home] much.' She talked about how guilty she felt for not going to see her parents, especially as she was so worried about them. She realised that the excuse of her work was just that, an excuse.

She also returned periodically to the relationship with Jamie, 'if that's what it was', which was continuing to confuse her. She gradually realised that 'it was all a part of the same thing' – that there were two opposite things going on. One was that the relationship with Jamie was a distraction that didn't make any demands, an amusing but rather meaningless way to stop time passing. The other, which had only just occurred to her, was that, because the relationship was so on-off, she could allow herself to hope, to dream, without any danger of it being tested. The loss of the dream and its replacement with loneliness was why she had started to think about him more.

She talked about living in a shared house with other single people until three years ago: 'They all moved in with their boyfriends; they've all got children now.' I asked her what it was like living on her own now. 'Oh, it's OK I suppose… No, that's rubbish, it's not… I just stay in and drink on my own… I want what they've got… I never thought I'd say that.' She talked about having cultivated independence from a young age. What she meant by this was never needing anyone else. She said: 'It was a lie, wasn't it? I did need people but I never got them. Now I do, I don't know how to get them.'

She had two different dreams. One was her free and easy lifestyle, and the other, her relationship with Jamie. Except that they both had the same effect, to make her forget time passing… until now.

Even though we had been meeting for some months, I sometimes found it hard to remember what we had been talking about in the previous session, and I had rarely taken her to supervision. She was easy to be with and made few demands on me. It was easy, maybe too easy. I had only heard about the relationship with Jamie and I was curious about her other relationships. She never talked about any other relationships, or any other friendships, only work relationships. Were there any?

Something stopped me asking, and her saying. Also, although she was attractive and personable, there was something rather androgynous and asexual about her – something that kept her from making close relationships, perhaps. All these points came together for me when she missed a session 'because of work' and I found myself wondering whether I had said something wrong in the previous session. Or maybe I hadn't said something I should have. The next time she came, I asked her whether this was the case. She said, 'No I don't think so, it was just that I'm not sure what I'm doing in therapy any longer. It's OK but not that special any more. It's sort of stopped.' This was my experience too. Although important things were talked about, it was curiously repetitive. I asked her if all her relationships went like this, starting fine and then too quickly slowing down and stopping.

This led her to talking about how difficult it had always been to make close relationships: 'It has just never happened. I don't know how other people do it. I want to but don't know how.' She said that, although she did fancy people from time to time, they never seemed to fancy her or she didn't know what to do to make them interested in her. She continued: '... and the longer I go without, the more ashamed and embarrassed I get of never having had a boyfriend, unless you count Jamie... and I don't any more. I mean, what would people think of me if they knew? I've never had anyone and I don't belong anywhere.' For the first time, she cried about the place she found herself in.

Then, after a few minutes, she said: 'You know, I've wanted to do that ever since the first session but haven't dared because you would think I'm pathetic and weak.' 'What do I think?' I asked. She replied: 'You don't seem to, I suppose I knew you wouldn't. Anyway, it's nothing much to do with whether you think I'm pathetic, is it? It's about whether I do.' This led on to a deeper consideration of how she always felt herself to be flawed, an outsider, somehow more incapable than her peers; how she consequently needed to pretend to be more competent, more able, more independent and less needy than her peers, when she felt the opposite was true, and how she was getting more and more fed up with this double life. 'It just doesn't work, does it... and never did,' she said.

The more she came to accept her neediness, the more she was able to transcend it and take responsibility, rather than waiting for someone else to look after her. As she said: 'It never worked before, why should it work now?' As she became more able to be with herself, her solitary drinking faded away. Progress was slow and uneven but gradually she became more able to risk herself in relationships and allow carefully chosen others to know about her insecurities and her fallibility. She talked for the first time about finding men attractive and being attractive to them, and about being able to have closer relationships than she had had before.

Commentary

Life is not neat and tidy. There are many interlocking plots and narratives, only some of which we know. Life is the product of randomness, chance and opportunity, although we try to make it seem coherent and planned. When Sartre says (2003:115), 'At the moment of death the chips are down, there remains not a card to play,' he means that a life is only complete at death. There is no point saying anything until then, and probably not then either. Nevertheless, with this in mind, it is necessary to make some comments on the case illustration above.

When Alex came to therapy, her original project of independence from both time and intimate relationships was so well practised that she hardly knew it was there. She had certainly forgotten it was a way of being that she had chosen in childhood as a means to cope with her circumstances. It was embodied and had become a part of how she was physically, socially, personally and ethically. She had forgotten how to be an active agent in the world. It enabled her to forget birthdays.

As I said earlier, the original project is a context-derived choice that is then applied to later contexts. If it is not constantly updated, it is bound to cause problems, such as anxiety and depression. This was the case with Alex. She was trying to stop time and her original project was unable to accommodate the passing of time. She found herself in a vicious circle that could not be sustained. Feeling unsure of her place both in the world and in relationships led to her feeling ashamed, that it was her fault and she needed to hide this from others. This led her to avoid taking any risks with relationships, for fear the 'truth' was discovered: that she was a freak and that there was something irretrievably wrong with her.

She had got to the point where living a life of static inauthenticity was less tolerable than living a life of dynamic authenticity, and she made a choice to change her life.

Discussion with the editor

Simon: I wonder if you could say something about yourself and your professional and personal motivation for writing on this particular topic? I ask this as, while human development feels like a crucial factor in much therapeutic work, very few existential therapists have talked explicitly about it in a way that adds to existential-phenomenological theory and that may help other practitioners.

Martin: Professionally I came to existential work from psychology and psychoanalysis and, while both of these disciplines have a strong interest in developmental issues, I never found the way they talked about it, and about other issues too, very convincing because of their reliance on explanation and positivism. Life always seemed to me much richer than that. Something was missing from these perspectives – lived experience. Also, I had always found the richness of fiction closer to the way I live my life, closer to understanding where I am between birth and death and the dilemmas and paradoxes of what to do with the time in between. When I came to train existentially, I was surprised by the lack of importance given to developmental issues in general. This seemed to be driven by a need to create a distance from psychology and psychoanalysis and also by a rather one-dimensional understanding of the 'present'. It was an 'adult' rather than a whole-life perspective. Most importantly, though, it did not match with my experience, or with that of my clients or with what I found in the philosophy. The contributions of Sartre, de Beauvoir and Merleau-Ponty are enormous but were largely ignored. This led me to feel vindicated in my conviction and led me to work on an existential approach to human development. Also, as I have got older, it has seemed to me that life and what we call 'development' is far more subject to randomness, chance and opportunity than other theories acknowledge, that it is continuous and dynamic and that change only stops on death. I felt this needed to be reflected in the theory.

Simon: Personally, I have found enlightening Hazel Barnes' (1980) description of the way an individual's fundamental project emerges via unreflected actions in infancy. I resonated with it the first time I came across it, and I find it helpful to think about clients' fundamental (or original) project with her model in mind. I suppose it might be objected that it is of mainly theoretical interest and not necessarily applicable in the consulting room. Nevertheless, I wonder what your thoughts are on this, as it seems to take us back, quite literally, to the fundamentals of identity. And, thinking about it, it seems to underpin Betty Cannon's (1991) formulation of a Sartrean analysis.

Martin: This is an excellent point. I don't think it is simply of theoretical interest. Starting from a position of 'existence before essence' and our need to be something, anything, rather than nothing, it helps us to understand how it is that our beliefs of who we are, what we call our 'personality', and those times when we say things like, 'That's just who I am', or 'I'm like this because…' can feel so certain and our lives seem ruled by causation.

These ideas of how we are, in fact, are choices, but they are passive, reactive choices, in the sense that they are made without reflection. They have to be considered choices of a sort because, even though they are inevitably based on biological and social givens (ie. facticity), we are still making sense of these givens and they are therefore constitutive of identity in an existential sense. As Barnes (1980) puts it, they are individual but not yet personal. They have not been actively chosen and are therefore not fully owned; they have not been made personal. They are seen as things and given the status of facts. This fixity begins in childhood because the vulnerability and dependency of the early years means that the child is necessarily immersed in the world of others and this world is given to and largely accepted without reflection, without question, by the child.

The child quickly arrives at what is called, depending on the translation, their original or fundamental project. I prefer the term 'original' because it has implications of 'first', whereas 'fundamental' has implications of 'basic' in a quasi-genetic sense, which is not the case at all, although it may feel like that.

Original choices coalesce into the original project of how to be in the world, which is embodied rather than cognitive. Because of this, it is not easily available for reflection. It is me, it is the way I am, it just is. It is my worldview. Note the reifying third person pronoun, 'it'.

Reflecting on these choices is never easy, but it is made easier in therapy when the certainties of earlier times start to cause problems in current life, like they did with Alex. These certainties get past their sell-by date and questions – experiential, not intellectual questions – get asked about their alleged validity: 'It's what I'm familiar with but it just doesn't feel right'. These are what we know as 'symptoms'. In this way, the past is in the present, preventing free action into the future. Existential time has stopped but biological time has not. This is always an exciting and anxiety-producing time because the client comes to the realisation that something they always believed about themselves, that came to be a part of their identity, was not only not so then but is also not so now. The past can change; existential time can start again and the uncertain future can be revealed.

Therapy and existential change, then, is about going back to these unreflected choices and reconsidering them, or maybe even considering them for the first time ever and realising that they are not facts at all but choices. It is not necessary that they be changed; simply that they are owned after reflection and remade with a greater sense of deliberation and ownership than before, in a context-appropriate manner, bearing in mind that no choice can ever be for all time. This is the paradox: that we have to live with certainty, knowing there is none. That we are a nothing, trying to be a something.

Simon: I was intrigued by your notion of the Law of Existential Consequence – can you say a little more about it?

Martin: This follows on from the above. Sartre's notion of freedom evolved from the radical freedom of his early work to a situated freedom that incorporates randomness, facticity and the reality that not only are we defined by our actions but also it is not possible not to act. What Sartre means by freedom, then, is not that we are free to choose to be anything we like; this is a simplistic notion of freedom and possibility. He means we are always in a context and the world is one of 'scarcity'. Our freedom is always a situated freedom.

Existentially, freedom is not to do with selecting between options, anyway. It is to do with owning what is and making something of it. The only existential choice is 'to be or not to be', not 'shall I do this or that?' Commitment to a choice is being – that is, existential birth; denial of commitment to a choice is non-being – that is, existential death. This is the existential meaning of choice. Existentially, the only 'right' choice is the one that is taken and committed to. You can have hopes and expectations about a certain course of action, but you never know what will happen until you do it, and sometimes not until long after, if ever. The future is not only uncertain but also ambiguous.

Things rarely go according to plan and, even if they do, it is not for very long. The effects of chance, personal misjudgements and the effects of other people's actions all impinge on us and define our world far more than we like to admit. Since our power to influence the world is small, we have to take the opportunities it offers, which are mostly surprises and not predicted, and try to make them our own.

When we say things like, 'They made me do it' or, 'I couldn't help it' or, 'I didn't mean that to happen', these are all inauthentic acts of bad faith that we use to try to evade and deny our responsibility for our situation and the awareness that we are never anywhere else but where we are and no moment is any more real than the present moment.

We are bound by the existential reality that, when we do something, something usually unexpected follows that we have to take responsibility for, whether we like it or not. We may not necessarily have actively and deliberately brought it about, but it happened and needs to be lived with and actions taken that can be committed to. In this way, we live life actively, rather than being lived by life passively. We cannot pretend things are otherwise. It is the Law of Existential Consequence.

Simon: Insofar as you have suggested a specifically existential model of human development, can you say something about how you have promulgated it, its reception by existential therapists to date, and what you think may be its future impact?

Martin: This is interesting. The reception has rarely been one of indifference. Sometimes I've met with antipathy, suspicion and scepticism, but mostly with curiosity and interest. I have found that counselling psychologists have been the most receptive, probably because they have already had a developmental training, although an existential model is at odds with what they will have previously studied. I have designed and taught a doctoral-level module on an existential approach to human development for counselling psychologists at Regent's University, and for counselling psychologists and psychotherapists at the New School of Psychotherapy and Counselling, for some years. I have also presented the ideas at conferences and run CPD workshops on it, and the reception by participants at these live events has been overwhelmingly positive. I have also published papers in *Existential Analysis* and the *Counselling Psychology Review* and I am currently writing a book about it for Palgrave. Since I first started talking about it, interest has certainly grown, as evidenced by my inclusion in this book, and I would like to think that it will have an increasing impact in the wider psychotherapy world because of the irrelevance and inappropriateness of stage theories and the increasing interest in what existentialism and phenomenology can offer.

References

Adams M (2018). *An existential approach to human development: philosophical and therapeutic perspectives*. London: Palgrave.

Adams M (2014). Human development and existential counselling psychology. *Counselling Psychology Review 29*(2): 35–43.

Adams M (2013a). Human development from an existential-phenomenological perspective: some thoughts and considerations. *Existential Analysis 24*(1): 48–56.

Adams M (2013b). *A Concise Introduction to Existential Counselling*. London: Sage.

Adams M (2006). Towards an existential-phenomenological model of life span human development. *Existential Analysis 17*(2): 261–280.

Baltes PB (1987). Theoretical propositions of life span developmental psychology: on the dynamics between growth and decline. *Developmental Psychology 23*(5): 611–626.

Barnes HE (1980). Sartre's concept of the self. *Review of Existential Psychology and Psychiatry 17*: 41–65.

Burman E (2007). *Deconstructing Developmental Psychology*. London: Routledge.

Cannon B (1991). Sartre and Psychoanalysis: an existentialist challenge to clinical metatheory. Lawrence, KS: University Press of Kansas.

Cohn H (1998). John Bowlby's concern with the actual phenomenological aspects of attachment theory. *Existential Analysis 9*(1): 43–51.

Crawford MB (2010). The limits of neuro-talk. In: Giordano JJ, Gordijn B (eds). *Scientific and Philosophical Perspectives in Neuroethics*. Cambridge: Cambridge University Press: 355–369.

Dreyfus HL (1991). *Being-in-the-World: a commentary on Heidegger's being and time, division I*. Cambridge, MA: MIT Press.

Karban B (2017). Leaping-in and leaping-ahead: an exploration of Heidegger's notion of solicitude. *Existential Analysis 28*(2): 106–117.

Laing RD (1965). *The Divided Self*. Harmondsworth: Penguin.

Merleau-Ponty M (1964). The child's relations with others. In: *The Primacy of Perception* (W Cobb trans). Evanston, IL: North Western University Press (pp96–158).

Sartre J-P (1946/1973). *Existentialism and Humanism* (P Mairet trans). London: Methuen.

Sartre J-P (1943/2003). *Being and Nothingness: an essay in phenomenological ontology* (HE Barnes trans). London: Routledge.

Stolorow R (2007). *Trauma and Human Existence: autobiographical, psychoanalytic and philosophical reflections*. Hove: The Analytic Press.

Sugarman L (2001). *Life-Span Development: frameworks, accounts and strategies*. Hove: Psychology Press.

Tallis R (2011). *Aping Mankind: neuromania, Darwinitis and the misrepresentation of humanity*. London: Acumen.

Yalom I (1980). *Existential Psychotherapy*. New York, NY: Basic Books.

3

Gay sexuality: 'I am what I am; I am my own special creation'

Helen Acton

There is something of a debate currently raging within the world of existential therapy between those writers and practitioners who insist that, as existentialists, we must focus on a person's ability to choose and create themselves, even to the extent of choosing their sexual orientation, and those who recognise that such a position seems to run counter to clients' lived experience of their orientation as something they did not choose but that they must choose how to live with. As existentialists concerned with the primacy of choice and freedom, can we go too far? Is the notion of a fixed sexual orientation such a challenge to our belief in the elasticity of being that in this alone we choose to ignore the phenomenon? What is the impact when a trainee hears in supervision that 'existentially, sexuality is fluid and there is no such thing as gay' (Crabtree, 2009: 258)?

As a therapist, my client work is heavily influenced by the writings of Jean-Paul Sartre, and in particular his concepts of freedom, facticity and bad faith, which for me are the beating heart of an existential approach. In Sartrean philosophy, our freedom is limited only by a set of facts – those aspects of our situation over which we have no control and no choice – our 'facticity' (Sartre, 1943/1958). More often than not, since the human condition is fundamentally characterised by the tension between freedom (or 'transcendence') and facticity, therapy involves both confronting ways in which a client may be living in 'bad faith' by attempting to flee or deny either and exploring how the two work together. But in this chapter, I will argue that there has been, both in Sartre's earlier work and in ensuing interpretations, an over-emphasis on the form of bad faith defined as a denial of freedom and a tendency to pay less attention to the denial of facticity. Indeed, 'it is easy to ignore this [second] sort of bad faith because Sartre is so often fighting the battle against determinism. It is extremely important that we keep both forms of bad faith in mind' (Solomon 1972: 300).

In his later years, this is a phenomenon that Sartre himself recognised and regretted. In a journal interview he gave in 1969, republished in book form in 1974, he stated:

> ... life taught me *la force des choses* – the power of circumstances... Little by little, I found that the world was more complicated than this... I [had] concluded that in any circumstances, there is always a possible choice. Which is false. Indeed, it is so false that I later wanted precisely to refute myself... The conception of 'lived experience' marks my change since *L'Etre et Le Néant*. (Sartre, 1969)

While as a practitioner I endeavour to be mindful of this adjustment in Sartre's thinking and his acknowledgement of lived experience in all circumstances, nowhere is their pertinence more evident than in my extensive work with clients for whom sexual orientation is a concern. From a phenomenological standpoint, sexual orientation can most usefully, most realistically and most therapeutically be considered a component of an individual's facticity. If, as phenomenologists, we are concerned with lived experience, then we must heed the fact that, for many individuals, perhaps the majority, sexual orientation 'may not *feel* like a choice – may not be available to consideration by us in the way that we are used to choices being available' (du Plock, 1997: 67). To look at it in any other way would be to favour one particular interpretation of existential philosophy over lived experience – an insistence on theory and the imposition of that theory that should be anathema to an existential way of working.

As Medina so eloquently puts it, we must:

> guard against the adoption of a theoretical frame, however loose, that encourages us to interpret or intertwine the purity of the client's experience with the notion of the plasticity of sexuality for all, which is in reality the possibility of bisexuality or asexuality for some. (Medina, 2014: 122)

This is not to say that, for example, a gay man can in good faith state that he *knows* he will never be sexually attracted to a woman, for such occurrences are, of course, known. Indeed, people can experience major changes of sexual orientation in the course of a lifetime, and a phenomenological approach to lived experience would remain open to this. But I would suggest that what one cannot do is *choose* to experience a change in sexual impulse, and therefore in sexual orientation. Even bisexual individuals do not *choose* to be attracted to both genders. Many subscribe, as I do, to the idea that there is a wide spectrum of sexual orientation, with heterosexuality at one extreme end and homosexuality at the other, and many variations of bisexuality in between, but again I would posit that crucially one cannot *choose* one's position on that spectrum. To quote again from Medina: 'A spectrum of sexualities into which a population might fall does not equate to a spectrum of sexuality *within* us all' (2014: 127). For, bringing the discussion back to the phenomenology of *lived experience*, it is evident that 'few words grate on contemporary gay nerves like the word "choice". The idea of homosexuality as a deliberately chosen path runs counter to the personal experiences of gays and lesbians' (Moon, 2002).

In my experience, it is when a client has come to a point of either accepting or rejecting his or her 'given' sexual orientation that they find horizons opening up as to how they might choose to live that orientation. What seems to be most apparent is that true freedom 'is only initiated once boundaries have been explored' (van Deurzen 2002: 18), and this is a notion I shall explore through sharing my experience of working with one of my clients, Sam. There is much misunderstanding about what an existential therapy that recognises sexual orientation as facticity might look like. Rodrigues claims that 'to consider [sexuality] as facticity would be to give up on analysis' (2014: 49). I would argue that nothing could be further from the truth.

Case study

It was several months into our work together that Sam (as I shall call him) first began to allude to sexual orientation as an issue. He was a slim, plain-looking man in his mid-30s. He had suffered from depression and anxiety for many years but was unable thus far to make sense of why he felt so 'stuck'. He lived alone and, although successful in his career as a financial adviser, felt isolated and rejected. As he initially described it to me, his personal life was characterised by a never-ending succession of friendships gone sour, accompanied by a sense of mystification as to why he always ended up being scorned when he considered himself to be such a loyal and loving friend.

I had spent our early sessions working with Sam in as warm and engaged a manner as I could, endeavouring to hear and attend as fully and openly as possible to the material he shared. At times this was something of a struggle, as his resentful tone of victimhood made him difficult to like: the world had rejected him, done him wrong, and in this respect was a deeply bewildering and unjust place. He was 'done' with friendship, agonisingly stuck between his longing for connection and the belief that it only ever leads to pain. There were moments when the bitterness within him twisted and contorted his face as he spat out his words, and it didn't feel like a huge leap to imagine that this attitude might render friendships problematic.

In time it became clear that Sam felt accepted enough by me for me to begin gently to challenge some aspects of his stance, and to wonder aloud with him how he might have been experienced by some of these 'ex-friends'. As we worked through the tale of each of the relationships in question, a pattern began to emerge. Each time, the friend was a straight man to whom Sam had been drawn, with whom he had become close, then extremely close, and who had ultimately terminated the friendship and rejected Sam bluntly and categorically. Delving a little deeper and asking him to think about a time he remembered first feeling this particular kind of closeness followed by rebuff, he began to talk about his friendship with Thomas, a classmate he had been best friends with at age 11. As he did so, his bitterness began to melt into a much softer pain, and it was clear we had touched on a memory that stirred a part of him that was more vulnerable than angry. Thomas had meant the world to Sam and the two boys had been constant companions until the day that Thomas suddenly and cruelly told Sam to stay away from him. Other kids had begun to tease Thomas about the closeness of the relationship with his 'gay boyfriend', and Thomas responded by telling Sam to leave him alone, that Sam was 'gay' and 'disgusting' and that he wanted nothing more to do with him.

As Sam told me this story, he started to cry, and his pain and sense of loss were palpable in a way I had not seen before. As I tentatively asked him to stay with these feelings, we began to explore what this memory meant to him. Now, for the first time, the feelings he articulated seemed to be about himself, directed towards himself, rather than expressed as a venomous attack on the people around him. He seemed in that moment more broken than bitter and told me, through his tears, that Thomas had been right, that he was disgusting. Once again, I gently asked him to stay with what he was feeling. Treading carefully, I asked what was disgusting about him, and it was from there that Sam started to talk about his true feelings for Thomas – that the classmates had been right. He felt he had been drawn to Thomas in a way that was 'more than friendship', and before too long he was ashamedly revealing that he had been sexually attracted to men ever since, and that his few attempts to form sexual relationships with girls, which had all but ceased many years previously, had felt pointless and empty.

In the sessions that followed, we returned to Sam's experiences of the adult friendships that had caused him such pain. Now his attitude was less angry, less bitter and more reflective, although his feelings were no less painful. He began to open up about these friendships in a way that revealed the deep conflict there. He began to be more honest with himself about the true nature of his feelings. Where before he had been filled with a sense of bafflement and righteous indignation at the rejections he had experienced, he now started to see some of these experiences in a different light. Excruciating as it was for him to admit it, both to himself and to me, he very gradually came to an awareness that there was perhaps more of an explanation for what had happened than he had wanted to see. Rather than shining a harsh spotlight on the friends who had rejected him, he looked more closely at his own part in the breakdown of each of these relationships, and although he found it no less harrowing – rather, it was harrowing in a new way – he could at least begin to make some sense of what had happened. He had wanted more from these friends than they could give him.

But this was an extremely difficult process for Sam. At the age of 11 he had taken from his experience with Thomas the message that his sexuality, or the early stirrings of it, was a cause for rejection, a part of him so repellent that, upon its discovery, even his closest friend would want nothing more to do with him. And reflecting now on his adult friendships, he could begin to see that it was a message he had reinforced for himself time and time again. He had internalised what he perceived his 'being-gay-for-others' (Moon, 2002) meant – that his feelings for men rendered him rejectable and disgusting. Thus far, the only meaning he had ascribed to his 'being-gay-for-myself' was that being gay meant loss, and it angered him that he had lost so many friendships because of it. And so it had become, from the start, something to deny, push away and attempt to bury.

Had he made the choice to pursue relationships with men who were themselves attracted to men, who could potentially have reciprocated his feelings and welcomed his sexuality rather than rejecting it, Sam would have had to acknowledge to himself the truth of the nature of his longings. But by making straight men the objects of his affection, although he had in one sense kept himself 'safe' from that imperative, he had at the same time strengthened the message and ensuing belief that his sexual orientation alone rendered him rejectable. And this was the source of his 'stuckness' – the paralysing conflict between his longing for a deep, loving, sexual connection with a man and his belief that such feelings were 'wrong'. By consistently denying to himself his same-sex attraction, he was able to enter each new friendship with a straight man in the belief that this time it would be different – this time his increasingly desperate need for extreme closeness and possessive exclusivity would not be 'misinterpreted' and would not lead to rejection.

When Sam talked about his attraction to men, it was with a deep sense of shame. But as we considered together what had led to this shame – that it was the unkind reactions of straight men who could not reciprocate his attraction (and had chosen for their own reasons to react with blunt rejection) – it became possible to open up the conversation. Now that Sam's struggle with his sexual attraction to men had been brought into the light, it had for the first time become possible to look honestly at the ways in which he had been railing against it and ultimately denying it.

In adulthood he had occasionally revisited the hope that a romantic encounter with a woman might rescue him from his loneliness, but he was fundamentally repelled by any notion of sexual intimacy with a woman, and having accepted that he felt no sexual desire there, he had lost himself in a self-authored myth of asexuality intended to protect him from the rejection he perceived to be the only possible consequence of allowing himself a same-sex attraction. But by living in this form of bad faith – by refusing at a deep level to acknowledge the fact that he was sexually attracted exclusively to men – he had become stuck in a world where, once he began to really care for someone and express it with an intensity inappropriate for platonic friendship, his feelings inevitably led to rejection.

The paradox for Sam was that the self-denial that had led him to keep himself 'safe' by choosing straight men who could not return his feelings was precisely what was leading to the rejection becoming a self-fulfilling prophecy. However, as he slowly began to move away from languishing in bad faith with respect to his sexual orientation, I could see in Sam that 'existential choice regarding being sexual expresses the willingness, or lack thereof, to acknowledge "that which is there for me" as opposed to "what is imaginable but not present"' (Spinelli 2014: 37).

Now that he was able to acknowledge his homosexuality, over the weeks, the tone he used to talk about himself and the way in which he approached the topic gradually changed. As he began to understand something about the lens through which he had been viewing his sexuality and could see the meaning he had conferred upon it, he seemed to soften in his outlook on those around him and view himself with more compassion. It became possible for us to explore together the notion that it was not his homosexuality *per se* that was the cause of his pain, but rather the way he had interpreted it in his childhood and subsequently reinforced that interpretation. During this phase of the therapy, Sam's whole demeanour was shifting. Gone were the bitter facial contortions; gone was the confusion about how the world could treat him so unjustly, to be replaced by a gradual acceptance of himself as a gay man, and a glimpse of something approaching excitement about what this might now mean for him. And as his acknowledgement moved towards acceptance, increasingly evident in the therapy room was the principle that 'by coming to terms with a sense of fixedness or givenness in the arena of sexual attraction, the individual in turn paradoxically becomes unstuck and free to explore their sexual selves in more fruitful and meaningful ways' (Medina 2014: 123).

Sam began slowly to open up to the (now very real) possibility that he might at last find satisfying romantic and sexual connections in the world – ones that might for the first time lead to him being neither repulsed nor rejected. He was now able to start looking at his feelings and values around homosexuality squarely in the face, as he reflected on aspects of life as a gay man that he observed in the world around him. On some things he was clear: he had no interest in 'the gay scene', as he perceived it; he didn't identify with gay stereotypes of camp, and he wasn't keen on the promiscuity or non-monogamy that he associated with what is still commonly referred to as a 'gay lifestyle'. What he wanted, and began enthusiastically to imagine for himself, was to live a quiet life shared with a loving, male partner. Witnessing the enjoyment Sam was now able to feel as he pictured the life he wanted, and the kind of gentle, loyal, loving, sophisticated gay man he would be, I was reminded of the assertion that:

> much of the value of the concept of being gay is the way in which it provides a space which each individual can invest with a different meaning. One of the joys (and challenges) of being gay is the opportunity such an identification provides for inventing oneself. (du Plock 1997: 62)

In the closing weeks of our work together, Sam and I explored ways in which he might now choose to live his homosexuality in the world. Remaining congruent with the values he had clarified, he chose to eschew overtly gay-centric social environments and decided instead to seek ways to meet potential partners through an online dating site. It was with a sense of optimism that he began to engage with meeting and dating men who could potentially reciprocate his feelings, and it was with a nascent sense of peace that he now imagined making friendships that would no longer be sabotaged by the unwelcome, unwitting expression of suppressed and unexamined sexual feelings. Sam's 'being-gay-for-myself' now meant something very different from the inevitable loss he had previously attributed to it.

Afterword

This case study illustrates just how present Sartre's notions of *situated* freedom and *factical* possibility can be in the consulting room; how tangible facticity can be, as 'the contingent world which I did not create but which I must choose to live in some fashion or other' (Cannon, 1991: 46), with regard to sexuality. Rodrigues is critical of an existential approach that understands a person's sexual orientation to be an aspect of their facticity, asserting that 'from this perspective, all that is left for me to choose is how to respond to this particular given' (2014: 44). But dismissed in that little 'all' is an entire world of relations that opened up to Sam as he chose how to respond to the given of his homosexuality. Indeed, it is continuously evident to me that 'helping the client to explore the real freedom and "releasement" that can come from accepting a fixedness is ultimately the therapeutically beneficent and indeed existentially congruent way of working' (Medina, 2014: 135).

While he had been denying his homosexuality, or still entertaining the notion that he could choose to be attracted to women, there had been no possibility for Sam to live in true freedom. Mired in this bad faith, he was boxed in on all sides by denial (of himself), revulsion (in response to women) and rejection (by straight men). The disowning of his sexual orientation led only to a narrow, pinched experience of himself and the world. His 'being-gay-for-myself' was reduced to one interpretation – namely, that it meant rejection and loss – based as it was on a reinforced negative experience of his 'being-gay-for-others'. But once he had allowed his true sexual attractions to come to light within the safe space of therapy, and we had the opportunity to explore the significance he had placed on them, the work led Sam to an acceptance of his sexual orientation that ultimately illustrated just how 'fixing and anchoring in certain aspects of their being in fact opens the individual to the real freedom to… create their own path' (Medina, 2014: 135).

It is interesting to note how, even in the UK in 2017, it can be extremely difficult and shameful for a client to articulate his or her sexual orientation. I have had clients tell me they are gay by writing it on a slip of paper and handing it to me; by emailing me between sessions to tell me; by including the information in a Christmas card, and by asking if we could switch the lights off while they tell me something. For the vast majority of such clients, this moment comes as the culmination of many years of struggling with an aspect of themselves that they have tried hard to deny or reject. For a therapist to meet a client in that position with an insistence, or even a mere belief, that their sexual orientation is an existential choice would quite simply be 'allowing theory to overlay existence and experience' (Medina, 2014: 132) – the very antithesis of an existential approach to therapy.

Discussion with the editor

Simon: I think you have identified something rather important when you say that there is a debate raging within the world of existential psychotherapy between those who argue that we can choose our sexual orientation and those who argue that this runs counter to clients' lived experience. It seems to me, and you allude to this, that this debate is indicative of something beyond 'just' sexual orientation. I wonder if there is a wider debate here, and if so what that might mean for existential theory and practice generally?

Helen: I think that's a really important question – one I believe Sartre, in his 1969 interview, was addressing – and I wonder if what it in fact means is something of a parting of the ways between the theory and the practice. Is the question of sexual orientation revealing a key distinction between existential philosophy and existential psychotherapy in that one is something we do in a café, while the other, as deeply rooted in existential philosophy as it is, holds a value that lies in *actual* human experience? It seems to me that this distinction is what Sartre himself had begun to recognise.

In the context of my being an existential therapist, it's the client's lived experience that is fundamentally important to the practice. The theorists can carry on theorising about it – that's up to them, but what's really key is that, in our practice, we take as our primary concern the client's lived experience. Isn't that the point of therapy? Because what's the alternative? That we shoehorn clients into theory, while baulking against the shoehorning that many patients experience in psychoanalytic therapy? What *is* existentialism if it isn't rooted deep in the human experience of existence? You'll see that I'm raising more questions here than answers!

Simon: You quote me as saying that sexual orientation 'may not *feel* like a choice

– may not be available to consideration by us in the way that we are used to choices being available', and I think I agree with you when you state it's most useful to consider sexual orientation as part of a person's facticity. Indeed, your work with Sam illustrates this very powerfully. But for me the crucial word is *feel*: sexual orientation does not *feel* like a choice, but that doesn't mean it isn't a choice – it may be a very special kind of choice. I have made the case (2014, 1997) that sexual orientation can be understood as a *pre-reflective* choice. Hazel Barnes expresses this notion clearly in her exposition of Sartre's theory of a baby's self-development:

> My consciousness at first is purely non-reflective-consciousness: at this stage I am not aware of the world. I merely project myself out into the world, relating to it: I am pure intentionality. During this time my original project is shaped, the fundamental choice of my being is made: I choose myself through an attitude and action: I vote for my destiny with my feet and without making rational conscious choices. I become who I am by doing what I do. (Barnes, 1993: 42)

I think Cannon captures this well:

> These pre-reflexive choices, which include… *my way of relating to other people*, may never have been reflectively conceived… Yet… all of my concrete choices, all of my various ways of being, doing, and having are clues to my fundamental project of being – the meaning of my being in the world. (Cannon, 1991: 39, emphasis added)

So maybe Sam's pre-reflective choice can be taken as a clue to his, as Sartre terms it, 'original project'?

Helen: I'm afraid that I would need first of all to challenge the premise of your question, Simon. For me, the whole notion of pre-reflective choice can only ever be speculative and is therefore problematic. What in other modalities would be considered 'the unconscious', I see as speculation, and it's unclear to me why we existentialists would give so much weight or credence to this phenomenon that no one is or can be aware of, and which must therefore be considered a construct, at best. If we have no awareness of it, how useful is this construct of 'choice'? What meaning can it possibly hold? If such a thing exists, where does pre-reflective choice come from? To wonder about what might go on in a baby's head seems to me to be profoundly unphenomenological. What does the Barnes quote add to the project of therapy? What does it illuminate?

Even if we were to accept pre-reflective choice as more than just a hypothetical concept, I would argue strongly against the view that sexual orientation falls into such a category. I would invite the reader to revisit my case study and imagine approaching the therapy with Sam with the notion of 'sexual orientation as pre-reflective choice' in mind. Adopt the hat of a therapist taking that position. What follows? What does the therapy then offer? My sense is that such an attitude would leave the client feeling ultimately that he wasn't understood.

It's a familiar moment in existential therapy when we challenge a client on something they haven't experienced as a choice and which they initially believed not to have been a choice at all – a belief we might say is an expression of them living in 'bad faith' – and find that this challenge, when offered in a timely fashion, will in fact resonate with them at some level. They may well come to the recognition that they did make a choice, even if it didn't *feel* like a choice to them at the time, and that they did so for myriad reasons in response to myriad conditions. But sexual orientation is simply not one of those situations. Of course, we all choose what we *do* with our sexual orientation – *how* we live it, how we respond to it, how we act on it, what meanings we invest it with. But I challenge – and indeed, invite – anyone to show me an example of where a client has come to the recognition that they chose – *at any level* – their sexual orientation itself, be it homosexuality, bisexuality or heterosexuality. And if it doesn't resonate with them at any level and in any way, then what does it add? How is that phenomenological? How is it the human experience?

In earlier writing on this topic (Acton, 2010), I referred to an AE Housman poem, written at the time of Oscar Wilde's trial, which is based around a metaphor especially pertinent to the notion of sexual orientation as facticity: 'Oh they're taking him to prison for the colour of his hair' (Housman, 1939). If sexual orientation expresses an aspect of one's being, then for me it does so in the way that red hair does. What will the existential theorists arguing choice in this area have to say if (and when) sexual orientation is found to be genetic, biological or hormonal in some way?

Coming back to the question of a dissonance between existential theory and existential therapy practice, it seems that some theorists are stuck in their ivory towers talking about pre-reflective choice while, down on the ground, people are living their actual lived experience that simply does not reflect this theorising. This adherence to the concept of 'choice' at all costs seems to be leading some existential theorists very far away from lived experience – nowhere further than in the area of sexual orientation. As existential practitioners, we do not *have* to be led down that path. In all the years I've worked in this field, I can't think of a single example of a situation where the notion of sexual orientation as a choice of *any* kind – pre-reflective or otherwise – would have been either helpful to the client or in any way reflective of actual lived experience. Try this theory out with the young guy facing the death penalty in his own country for being gay and see how far you get.

References

Barnes H (1993). Sartre's concept of the self. In: Hoeller K (ed). *Studies in Existential Psychology and Psychiatry.* Atlantic Highlands, NJ: Humanities Press (pp41–66).

Cannon B (1991). *Sartre and Psychoanalysis: an existential challenge to clinical metatheory.* Lawrence, KS: University Press of Kansas.

Crabtree C (2009). Rethinking sexual identity. *Journal of the Society for Existential Analysis* 20(2): 248–261.

du Plock S (2014). Gay affirmative therapy: a critique and some reflections on the value of an existential-phenomenological theory of sexual identity. In Milton M (ed). *Sexuality: existential perspectives.* Monmouth: PCCS Books (pp141–159).

du Plock S (1997). Sexual misconceptions: a critique of gay affirmative therapy and some thoughts on an existential-phenomenological theory of sexual orientation. *Journal of the Society for Existential Analysis* 8(2): 56–71.

Medina M (2014). The freedom to be fixed: can I be a homosexual please? In: Milton M (Ed). *Sexuality: existential perspectives.* Monmouth: PCCS Books (pp119–138).

Moon P (2002). Sartre and sexual choice. *The Gay & Lesbian Review Worldwide* 9(5).

Rodrigues VA (2014). Are sexual preferences existential choices? *Journal of the Society for Existential Analysis* 25(1): 43–52.

Sartre J-P (1969). Itinerary of a thought. *New Left Review* 1(58): 43–66.

Sartre J-P (1943/1958). *Being and Nothingness* (H Barnes trans). London: Methuen.

Solomon RC (1972). *From Rationalism to Existentialism.* New York, NY: Harper & Row.

Spinelli E (2014). Being sexual: reconfiguring human sexuality. In: Milton M (ed). *Sexuality: existential perspectives.* Monmouth: PCCS Books (pp21–61).

van Deurzen E (2002). *Existential Counselling and Psychotherapy in Practice.* London: Sage.

4

Existential dream analysis

Darren Langdridge

Dreams have occupied an important place in many cultures throughout history, and also played a central role in the history of psychotherapy. For Freud (1900/1953), dreams were a means of working through unresolved anxiety by the production of transformed representations of (otherwise potentially disturbing) wishes. And, while dreams were a central feature of much early Freudian psychoanalytic practice, they have diminished in clinical importance in recent years, and are now understood primarily through the transference relationship (Loden, 2003).

The other key figure in the history of psychotherapeutic dream analysis is, of course, Jung (1963, 1974), and it is with the Jungian school of analytical psychology where we see dream work occupying a continuing, central, practical role (Vedfelt, 2002). Jung's theory of dreams is more general than Freud's, and has a number of central features. Dreams are primarily thought to be the products of the collective unconscious, the inherited record of human experience, that are expressed symbolically in the form of archetypes (universal patterns of experience). The purpose of most of these symbolic representations is compensation – the expression of aspects of the personality that are not adequately expressed in waking life.

There is little empirical evidence to support the theories of Freud or Jung. Most scientific analyses highlight significant flaws in these theories (see Domhoff, 2000). What these scientific analyses do reveal most strikingly, however, is the continuity between material in waking life and one's dreams (Hall & Nordby, 1972). It is here, with the consequent need to focus primarily on the manifest rather than latent nature of dreams, that the phenomenological method of existential dream analysis comes to the fore. Existential dream analysis is most often associated with the work of Boss (1957) and his attempt to move from a psychoanalytic focus on latent content towards a phenomenological focus on manifest meaning. Boss drew primarily on the philosophy of Heidegger (1962, 2001) to argue for a phenomenological stance in which material from the dream world is treated in the same manner as material produced in the waking world. That is, as existential therapists, we should avoid the imposition of predetermined frameworks of meaning on dream material and instead work collaboratively with our clients to discern the manifest meaning as presented in the here-and-now of the therapeutic encounter. Cohn describes this beautifully:

> Dreams are not something we 'have', they are an aspect of our being... They are not puzzles to be solved but openings to be attended to. (1997: 84)

Dreams are attended to for the insights they may offer into waking concerns that are currently inaccessible to the client. In other words, dreams, like our moods (Heidegger, 1962), show what matters to us at an ontological level by providing analytic access to current ontic concerns (Jaenicke, 1996). In tune with scientific understandings, Heidegger explains the relationship between dreams and waking life:

> The different way of being in dreaming and waking belongs to the continuity of the historicity of the particular human being... Waking and dreaming are not different objective realms, the difference between which could be recorded by the characteristics of their content... the dreamworlds belong to waking life. (2001: 229–230)

The central point here is how dreams are understood as an aspect of waking being-in-the-world that can only be understood in relation to the everyday concerns of waking life. The phenomenological approach to dream analysis founded on the work of Heidegger contrasts markedly with earlier causal psychoanalytic theories, in that it aims:

> not to give a causal explanation and derivation of the dreams, but to let the dreams themselves tell their own stories by what they say and

reveal in their orientation towards the world. Dreams are not symptoms and consequences of something lying hidden behind [them], but they themselves are in what they show and *only* this. Only with *this* does their emerging essence [*Wesen*] become worthy of questioning. (Heidegger, 2001: 245)

Boss (1957) explicated two principles for analysis that draw directly on Heideggerian concepts: bearing and possibility. The first concerns the bearing of the dreamer to other persons and the wider world in a dream, strongly emphasising the way in which a dreamer is embedded in a culturally and historically situated relational context. The second principle involves us asking whether there are possibilities in the dream that are ahead of the dreamer's waking experience, so looking at how the dream might offer access to insight that opens up a person's world.

All this notwithstanding, the innovative nature of the Bossian dream project has been somewhat overstated, given similar moves towards a more phenomenological stance among varieties of psychoanalytic theorists, past and present (from Fromm (1951) to Fosshage (2007)). Unfortunately, Boss also failed miserably to adopt a phenomenological method in his own analytic work with dreams, and wildly projected his own idiosyncratic interpretations onto his patients (Gendlin, 1977; Vedfelt, 2002). As Gendlin (1977) correctly points out, Boss might successfully have advocated for a move to a phenomenological theoretical position in the analysis of dreams but he failed to implement this methodologically in his own work. Regardless, it remains the fundamental foundation for dream work among most – if not all – existential therapists. Whether existential therapists work with dreams using this foundation is an interesting question and one worthy of empirical investigation. I suspect that some do, but I have a suspicion that many others either neglect the 'dreamworld' entirely or engage eclectically with a variety of theories.

Developing existential dream analysis

In my own work, I have sought to further develop existential dream analysis, building directly on the Heideggarian principles of Boss to produce a practical method of analysis that is strictly phenomenological (Langdridge, 2006, 2013). To this end, I have drawn on work in phenomenological and hermeneutic research methodology and method (Ashworth, 2003a, 2003b, 2016; Langdridge, 2007) that has not previously been applied to clinical practice to delineate a new way of working clinically with dream material in the therapeutic setting. There is a long tradition of psychologists developing rigorous phenomenological methods for the analysis of research data, starting with the work of Giorgi in the 1960s and 70s in the Anglophone tradition (see Giorgi, 2009 for an excellent account of his methodology). Following Giorgi have been many others who have further developed the family of phenomenological methodologies (Langdridge, 2007) that provide a rich array of practical methods for the analysis of research data that we can also use in our dream analytic work with clients.

Dreams retain an importance in my practice because I believe they offer client and therapist alike unique insight into current ontic concerns. That is, I see dreams as a fifth dimension of existence, akin to the three dimensions described by Binswanger (1958, 1963) of *Umwelt*, *Mitwelt* and *Eigenwelt*, and the later fourth addition of the *Überwelt* proposed by van Deurzen (2007; van Deurzen-Smith, 1988). The dimensions – which roughly translate respectively as the physical, social, psychological and spiritual – structure all aspects of existence, and are used as an analytic heuristic in much existential practice. Relatedly, I argue that dreams offer an imaginative space unfettered by the everyday demands/limits of conscious being-in-the-world, in which all four dimensions might be present without inhibition. In other words, we might understand dreams as an aspect of consciousness beyond the four dimensions of existence – a kind of meta-dimension, if you will (Langdridge, 2013). With the rules of everyday life subject to the possibility of temporary suspension, dreams offer us a creative play space for working through our ontic concerns that I believe has potential value for the therapeutic process. Boss argued that, while we may adopt a phenomenological mode of analysis, that does not mean dreams simply reveal themselves. They must be subject to an analysis in which therapist and client work together to shine a light on the layers of meaning manifest in any dream.

A key element in an analysis is to work with the client to explicate the phenomenology of the dream. Here, we not only approach the dream as it appears, seeking to understand the manifest meaning as given, but we also critically interrogate the dream story itself across what Ashworth (2003a; 2003b) refers to as the 'fractions of the lifeworld'. Ashworth argues that a phenomenological analysis of research data (eg. from an interview) is strengthened by interrogating the text for emergent meaning across a number of 'fractions' or universal structural dimensions of the lifeworld.

> ... these are not independent categories or parameters or perspectives.
> Rather, they are mutually entailed, with overlapping or interpenetrating

meanings. The oddity, the uncouthness, of the term fraction in this context is intended to avoid the user slipping into an easy assumption that lifeworld fractions are strictly distinguishable categories. It gets away from any kind of modelling of the lifeworld in terms of constituent dimensions in a quasi-quantitative way. (Because of the distinct use of the term in phenomenological philosophy, I hesitate to employ the word 'horizon' here, but each fraction is, in a certain sense, a lifeworldly horizon of the phenomenon under study.) (2016: 23)

The fractions are derived from the extant existential literature, drawing on ideas from Husserl (1970), Heidegger (1962), Merleau-Ponty (1962) and Sartre (1957). The fractions are selfhood (identity), sociality, embodiment, temporality, spatiality, project and discourse. In addition, I would argue that we should incorporate from Heidegger (1962) the notions of being-towards-death and mood, which will be ontically apparent through expressions of affect and emotion (especially anxiety). These will, of course, be familiar concepts to most existential therapists. Indeed, as mentioned above, Boss (1957) incorporated the notion of 'bearing' in his own dream work, which is clearly a way of engaging with the concept of sociality. Ashworth (2016) provides detail about each concept, but for those less familiar with them, in brief they are as follows.

- Selfhood refers to our subjective understanding of who we are, our identity if you will.
- Sociality concerns the way that human beings are fundamentally in relation with others, with all situations intrinsically intersubjective.
- Embodiment relates to our embodied state as human beings and how it features in an experience, including consideration of gender, 'disabilities' and emotions.
- Temporality refers to the way in which existence is temporally structured such that we are always 'living in time', and how the sense of time might be phenomenologically apparent within any experience.
- Spatiality concerns a person's understanding of their position in the world through geography, space and place.
- Project is that aspect of a situation that relates to a person's ability to carry out activities to which they have committed and which they believe are central in their life – in other words, our fundamental concerns.

- Discourse concerns the language and terms used to describe an experience and how our experience may be structured through particular discursive structures.

My argument is that we should work with our clients to explore the dream story across these fractions, examining it for the presence of concepts like embodiment or spatiality to see if critical attention to these universal structures helps expand the meaning of the dream for the client. Perhaps the most critical 'fraction' – certainly for those of us engaged in therapeutic work – is selfhood or identity. In many ways, the entire enterprise of psychotherapy is about the struggle to make sense of who we are and our place in the world. I have argued previously that the best way of understanding this concept is through Ricoeur's (1988, 1992) notion of narrative identity (Langdridge, 2006). Ricoeur (1988) himself draws, in part, on the therapeutic concept of 'working through' to describe the process by which we might come to construct a narrative identity. Selfhood is not some fixed (or essential) inner construct that drives our actions but is mutable and reflexive, constructed through the stories we create to make sense of the episodes of our lives. As such, one's identity is continually made and re-made over the course of a lifetime:

> If it is true that fiction cannot be completed other than in life, and that life cannot be understood other than through stories we tell about it, then we are led to say that a life *examined*, in the sense borrowed from Socrates, is a life *narrated*. (Ricoeur, 1991: 435)

It becomes critical therefore to understand the stories of selfhood – a person's narrative identities – being conjured up in their dreams. Who is the dreamer? What do we make of them? What aspect of life does this sense of identity open up and what does it close down? If we accept the argument above about a dream providing a space for imagination and creativity, then it follows that this includes imaginative play with a person's narrative identity. A dream in these terms offers a safe space to come face-to-face with existential limits around selfhood and identity.

Finally, it is worth noting that the presentation of a dream by a client breaks up the dialogue and thus provides a break in the therapeutic encounter that offers an opening for us to work differently with this material. We do not need to disrupt the therapeutic encounter or artificially manipulate the relationship. Rather, we are responding to the gift of a dream story with a different mode of engagement, one that is more structured and directive than usual. When a dream is presented, we have the opportunity to temporarily change the mode of our therapeutic relating. When a client presents a dream, it provides us with a break in the here-and-now of the therapeutic encounter. We can stop and invite the client to make sense of the dream with us, working through it iteratively across the fractions of the lifeworld to gain maximum insight into their ontic concerns and possibly even producing a perspectival shift in their understanding.

> **Client**: I am getting more sentimental as I get older. Funnily enough, I had a dream that relates to this last night.
>
> **Therapist**: That's interesting, would you like us to explore that dream further?
>
> **Client**: Yes, why not.
>
> **Therapist**: Okay, let's focus on the dream together then. I would like you to first tell me the dream as you remember it. Then I will ask further questions about particular elements of the dream to help us to explore it in more detail. Is that okay?
>
> **Client**: Sounds fine.
>
> **Therapist**: Okay, so go ahead and tell me your dream. Try not to miss out any detail and we'll explore it further together by going through it again when you have finished.

Case study – the story of Michael

Michael came to see me some years ago to discuss a 'dilemma' about his relationship. He didn't know whether to continue with it, as he loved his partner a great deal but they often argued and rarely had sex. He felt that, while there could be good times, particularly when they were at home, without any pressures, they ended up arguing more often than not when they did anything together. I said that I was happy for us to work together and agreed an open-ended weekly contract with him that we would review in our sixth session.

With most clients I discuss the possibility of keeping a dream diary in the first contracted session (not the initial assessment), where they can record all their dreams immediately on waking, but I stress this is by no means compulsory. Indeed, the majority choose not to do this and instead bring the occasional dream to our sessions. I decided to introduce the suggestion of keeping a dream diary because I had noticed that few people spontaneously brought dreams to therapy and I wanted to encourage more of my clients to engage with their dream material.

Michael did not actively keep a diary but did bring the occasional dream for us to work on together. At the six-week review it was apparent that there was much more for Michael to talk about than just the relationship, though this remained centre stage, so we decided to continue the work and review again at six months. In the end, he continued to attend sessions for a little over a year before the therapy came to an agreed ending.

Michael was 36 years of age and came from a fairly privileged middle-class background in Scotland. He worked in banking, which did not particularly interest him but provided him with a good salary and lifestyle. Both his parents had worked in the music industry. They divorced when he was a teenager and he recounted this as a horrible time for him, albeit with remarkably little expressed emotion in the sessions themselves. He had a half-brother from his father's subsequent remarriage but was not very close to him. His mother lived alone in London and Michael felt much closer to her than to his father, in spite of his father's attempts to include him in his new family life.

The break-up of his parent's marriage was acrimonious and they no longer spoke to each other at all. Michael told me how he came out as gay when he was at university, where he studied history, telling his mother first and his father several years later. In many ways, it sounded as if his father was more accepting but Michael did not seem to acknowledge this in any meaningful way. I disclosed to Michael that I was also gay, as I do with most clients if it feels appropriate to the therapeutic relationship. Michael was generally pretty happy as a gay man and this did not feature centrally in our work, other than as a structural factor that underpinned his everyday experience.

Michael lived with his partner, Tom, and had done so for six years. Tom was a little younger than Michael but from a similar background. He was also gay, white and middle-class and educated to degree level, but had returned to university as a mature student to study law. Tom had struggled to find what he wanted to do in life but thought law would be a worthwhile career. Michael was supporting Tom financially in the most part. He recalled how passionately he pursued Tom, declaring his love very early on while Tom was initially reluctant to have a relationship. After they had been seeing each other for six months or so, Tom told Michael that he loved him, and they moved in together shortly afterwards. Michael felt that Tom was devoted to him but was worried that the relationship had become rather stale and too argumentative.

I remember seeing Michael for the first time. He was warm and charming and clearly wished to present himself to me in the best possible light. I thought he was handsome – he was quite tall, with piercing blue eyes and a broad smile. He was dressed immaculately, in the latest trend, with hair that was clearly styled to look effortlessly casual. I warmed to him immediately and felt for his dilemma, wondering to myself whether this would involve a relationship break-up or not. This was something that I would need to put to one side (bracket), as it became apparent that this was much more my agenda than his, in spite of him presenting this as his initial dilemma. By the end of the first session, however, I was also a little troubled as it felt as though I had witnessed a well-polished performance – a façade – and I wondered whether this was the 'real' Michael. To be more accurate, I didn't know what version of selfhood I was experiencing and whether it was one that would allow Michael to engage effectively with his current concerns in therapy with me.

Many of the early sessions were given over to discussions about Michael's relationship and how difficult it was to live with Tom, who was permanently stressed or angry. Michael also revealed that he was depressed and had recently been prescribed Citalopram by his GP. Michael was not that keen on taking it but felt it was necessary 'for now'. However, he expressed little emotion and I struggled to see his 'depression' in our sessions, although I was mindful of the need to check in with him about his mood, given that he was taking an antidepressant. Indeed, during the first few months of therapy Michael continued to maintain the sense that he was generally okay. I continued to struggle with the gap between the content of his talk (about the relationship problems, his depression) and how he presented it, in his typically light and charming manner.

Every now and again Michael would let the happy-go-lucky persona drop and reveal more of his emotional life to me. Occasionally he would drop the façade of control to express a terrible rage against all the injustice he felt he received from other people in his world. It was linked to a deep depression about the unfairness of life and how he often felt let down by others. This was not entirely bad for him, however, as it also motivated his personal fights for equality and justice.

Control became a central theme in the therapy, although this was more apparent to me than Michael until much later in the therapy. He also revealed that he had recently had 'a bit of a fling' with another man, which Tom knew nothing about. Michael and Tom had a monogamous relationship that neither of them wanted to open up and Michael felt confused about this 'fling'. He was flattered by the attention, especially because he was being pursued by the other man, but didn't want to do anything to hurt Tom.

The dream

Five months into therapy, shortly after he told me about his 'fling', Michael described a dream from the previous night that had disturbed him. He woke up from it feeling troubled and anxious and actively sought to remember the detail so that he could discuss it with me. Mood was central to grasping the manifest meaning in Michael's dream.

In the dream he found himself in a village with his partner, being pursued by a number of men who were threatening and abusing them for being gay. They were running away from these men, trying to escape and feeling scared. Michael called the police and yet they continued to be pursued; this attempt to control the assailants had no effect. He felt rage inside and started imagining kneecapping the men chasing them, especially when he felt cornered. He gained great pleasure from the violent outburst and relief that it offered from the anxiety of the chase and sense of being trapped.

When Michael presented the dream to me, I suggested that we stop to consider it properly and work together to grasp its full meaning. He agreed and was keen to do this. I asked him to tell me the dream again in the first person another couple of times and to add further detail as it occurred to him. During this process, I sought to be alert to the presence of fractions of the lifeworld in the story. I then suggested some possible fractions one by one that we could use to explore the meaning of the dream, in the order below.

- Spatiality – I noticed the village location immediately as it seemed strange, given Michael lived in London and had never mentioned a village to me previously. I asked Michael to describe the location in more detail and reflect on what this location might mean to him. The only thing that Michael could think of was that it might reflect the location of the man from the recent sexual 'fling' who endlessly complained about living in a small town.

- Sociality – I then wondered about the people in the dream – his partner and the men chasing him. I asked him about the other people to see if he could say more and make any sense out of who they were. He described feeling the need to look after Tom and to try and stop them both being pursued. Then he stopped dead, having just realised that this dream related to his recent 'fling' and his fear that Tom might find out and be 'crushed' by his 'betrayal'. We talked further about this and explored how Tom and him being pursued reflected the sense that the person he had the 'fling' with was pursuing him in a way that now felt out of control.

He felt that this 'mistake' was now putting his relationship at risk and was potentially catastrophic.

- Narrative identity – I then suggested we explore a little further this sense of his 'fling' being a mistake in the context of the dream. I asked about the call to the police. This reflected his attempts to stop the chase in the dream and, in the waking world, to cool things down and get some distance from this other man. He felt that this was doomed to failure as he was weak when drunk and the other man continued to pursue a sexual relationship with him. But this was 'not him', he was a 'good guy' who did not do these things (he was 'faithful') and would never want to hurt Tom.

- Mood – Finally, I sought to explore his mood and particularly the violence in the dream. His violent rage reflected deep-seated anger at being the victim of homophobic violence many years earlier in his life, transformed here into a sense of justifiable anger when being cornered by homophobes wanting to harm him and Tom. He was protecting his partner and that justified the extreme force. The paradox that emerged, however, was that the homophobes were actually representative of the – somewhat out of control – fusion of his desire for another man and this man's desire for him. He wanted rid of this and yet was repeatedly drawn back – when drunk – to engaging in these behaviours.

Epilogue

Michael himself raised the issue of ending our work at about 12 months. As is so often the case, I had also been wondering whether it might be a good time to end the therapy. It felt as if we had covered all the ground that Michael wanted to cover. Michael felt that he had 'talked enough' about his relationship and that he was 'in a better place to deal with it now'. In particular, he had decided to avoid illicit sexual liaisons with others – it was 'not him', after all – and concentrate his efforts on his relationship with Tom. Our work on his dream had been central to this process, as it had provided him with greater insight into the consequences of his actions. He was more hopeful that they could make it work. We had also talked about his rage and his need to exert control over his world, along with his depression. His depression was less acute and he was thinking about coming off the antidepressant. His rage and need for control remained palpably present for him but he now understood a little more about the relationship between these aspects of selfhood and his wider social world.

Discussion with the editor

Simon: I think most existential therapists will identify with your statement that dreams 'offer client and therapist alike unique insight into current ontic concerns', but your suggestion 'that we might understand dreams as an aspect of consciousness beyond the four dimensions of existence – a kind of meta-dimension' – seems to offer something quite innovative in terms of existential theory and practice. Can you say something more about this notion of a meta-dimension and how it relates to the four dimensions of existence model which many of us currently use?

Darren: I guess the first thing I would say is that, while many existential therapists might *theoretically* recognise the potential of dreams as a way of gaining access to our current ontic concerns, I have a feeling that, in practice, fewer actually engage with them to this end. And I think that is a shame. But putting that aside, I'm glad you like the idea of thinking of dreams as a 'meta-dimension', Simon. It is an idea that I have been thinking about for some time and is still probably somewhat under-theorised. It first struck me when I was working analytically on a dream and thinking that, while the material related to the waking world, there was also some separation from that world – a greater imaginative freedom, if you will, where the dimensions did not apply as usual.

Now, given that the four dimensions speak to the waking world and do not necessarily make sense in the dreamworld, I wondered how the imaginative freedom offered by the dreamworld fitted into this theory. I could not see how dreams could be subsumed within the four dimensions and so I thought they must sit alongside them as an additional dimension, a fifth dimension. But it is a special dimension – hence positing it as a 'meta-dimension' – as it allows us to play with all of the other four dimensions freely and creatively, without boundaries and with much less inhibition than in our waking life. It is a dimension like the other four but one of quite a different order.

Simon: I was intrigued by your example of working with Michael. In particular, I was interested in what led you to focus on the four particular lifeworld fractions of spatiality, sociality, narrative identity and mood.

Darren: This is perhaps the key practical question for anyone wanting to use this method in his or her own practice. It is simple to answer but often quite difficult to grasp. The fractions that are focused on in a dream are, in some sense, always prefigured in the dream. The job of the therapist is to attend to the dream with the fractions in mind, and to listen out for those that appear particularly salient. This is sometimes very obvious and quite easy to grasp, but not always. There is then a process of working collaboratively with the client to see whether those fractions help deepen their understanding, whether they provide additional insight or not.

The process is akin to that of the researcher engaged in the phenomenological analysis of some text derived from an interview where they identify the key themes (or 'the essential structure', in Husserlian terms) that underpin the material. The notable difference is that, in the dream analysis, the participant (client) is actually available to engage in dialogue, which means the hermeneutic process can occur collaboratively, with dynamic access to the world of the client. So, while the choice of fractions might be driven by the therapist, drawing on their knowledge and experience, this is always balanced out by the presence of the client and the humility that we must always adopt as therapists when attempting to understand the world of another.

Simon: You talk about dreams providing a space for imagination and creativity and imaginative play with a person's narrative identity. I was curious about this as I think many existential therapists, including me, have conceptualised dreams as narratives that show how the dreamer relates to, and is open to or attempts to avoid, aspects of being human. So, play may be missing and it is in the safe container of the therapeutic alliance that the client is encouraged to play…

Darren: Following Schafer (1992), I adopt a narrative understanding of all therapeutic practice myself. Consequently, I would very much agree with your concept of dreams as narratives that reveal how the dreamer relates to or attempts to avoid aspects of being human, but I think this is not all that they offer. I don't think your understanding of dreams precludes them also being understood as spaces for imagination and creativity. Dreams are frequently metaphorical and – as Ricoeur (1992) argues – it is through metaphor that we see creativity brought into being in discourse. That is, the metaphor allows us to imaginatively rethink (or 'redescribe') reality, much as we might do in fictional writing or our dreamworlds.

Metaphors rupture language and, through this breaking apart, open up space for original thought, rather than simply improve everyday communicative competence, whether that is in dialogue with another person or with ourselves in moments of reflection. Narratives share a creative capacity with metaphors through the process of semantic innovation. Semantic innovation in narratives occurs in the bringing together of characters, action, events and so forth through the notion of a plot, whereby individual episodes are creatively configured into a coherent and meaningful whole. This is the stuff of dreams and this is the kind of play to which I am referring. This can, of course, occur in therapy outside dreams but I think the peculiar quality of dreams allows space for *more* freedom and therefore *more* creativity that may offer *more* possibilities for insight and change.

References

Ashworth P (2016). The lifeworld: enriching qualitative evidence. *Qualitative Research in Psychology* 13(1): 20–32.

Ashworth P (2003a). The phenomenology of the lifeworld and social psychology. *Social Psychological Review* 5(1): 18–34.

Ashworth P (2003b). An approach to phenomenological psychology: the contingencies of the lifeworld. *Journal of Phenomenological Psychology* 34(2): 145–156.

Binswanger L (1963). *Being in the World* (J Needleman trans). New York, NY: Basic Books.

Binswanger L (1958). The existential analysis school of thought. In: May R, Angel E, Ellenberger HF (eds). *Existence*. New York, NY: Basic Books.

Boss M (1957). *The Analysis of Dreams* (AJ Pomerans trans). London: Rider.

Cohn H (1997). *Existential Thought and Therapeutic Practice: an introduction to existential psychotherapy*. London: Sage.

Domhoff GW (2000). *Moving Dream Theory beyond Freud and Jung*. Paper presented to the symposium 'Beyond Freud and Jung?', Graduate Theological Union, Berkeley, CA; 23 September, 2000. https://dreams.ucsc.edu/Library/domhoff_2000d.html (accessed 18 May 2018).

Fosshage JL (2007). The organizing functions of dreaming: pivotal issues in understanding and working with dreams. *International Forum of Psychoanalysis* 16(4): 213–221.

Freud S (1900/1953). The interpretation of dreams. In: *The Complete Psychological Works of Sigmund Freud vols IV & V* (J Strachey ed). London: Hogarth Press.

Fromm E (1951). *The Forgotten Language: an introduction to the understanding of dreams, fairy tales and myths*. New York, NY: Open Road Integrated Media.

Gendlin ET (1977). Phenomenological concept versus phenomenological method: a critique of Medard Boss on dreams. *Soundings* 60: 285–300. www.focusing.org/gendlin/docs/gol_2045.html (accessed 18 May 2018).

Giorgi A (2009). *The Descriptive Phenomenological Method in Psychology: a modified Husserlian approach*. Pittsburgh, PA: Duquesne University Press.

Hall C, Nordby V (1972). *The Individual and his Dreams*. New York, NY: New American Library.

Heidegger M (2001). *Zollikon Seminars: protocols – conversations – letters* (F Mayr, R Askay trans). Evanston, IL: Northwestern University Press.

Heidegger M (1962). *Being and Time* (J Macquarie, E Robinson trans). Oxford: Blackwell.

Husserl E (1970). *The crisis of the European sciences and transcendental phenomenology* (D Carr trans). Evanston, IL: Northwestern University Press.

Jaenicke U (1996). Dream interpretation, the 'royal road' to the dreamer's actual and existential suffering and striving. *Journal of the Society for Existential Analysis* 8(1): 105–114.

Jung C (1974). *Dreams*. Princeton, NJ: Princeton University Press.

Jung C (1963). *Memories, Dreams, Reflections*. New York, NY: Pantheon.

Langdridge D (2013). *Existential Counselling and Psychotherapy*. London: Sage.

Langdridge D (2007). *Phenomenological Psychology: theory, research and method*. Basingstoke: Pearson Education.

Langdridge D (2006). Imaginative variations on selfhood: elaborating an existential-phenomenological approach to dream analysis. *Existential Analysis* 17(1): 2–13.

Loden S (2003). The fate of the dream in contemporary psychoanalysis. *Journal of the American Psychoanalytic Association* 51(1): 43–70.

Merleau-Ponty M (1962). *The Phenomenology of Perception* (C Smith trans). London: Routledge and Kegan Paul.

Ricoeur P (1992). *Oneself as Another* (K Blamey trans). Chicago, IL: Chicago University Press.

Ricoeur P (1991). Life: a story in search of a narrator. In: Valdes MJ (ed). *A Ricoeur Reader*. Toronto: University of Toronto Press (pp425–437).

Ricoeur P (1988). *Time and Narrative, volume 3* (K McLaughlin, D Pellauer trans). Chicago, IL: Chicago University Press.

Sartre J-P (1957). *Being and Nothingness* (H Barnes trans). London: Methuen.

Schafer R (1992). *Retelling a Life: narration and dialogue in psychoanalysis*. New York, NY: Basic Books.

van Deurzen E (2007). Existential psychotherapy. In: Dryden W (ed). *Dryden's Handbook of Individual Therapy* (5th ed). London: Sage (pp195–226).

van Deurzen-Smith E (1988). *Existential Counselling in Practice*. London: Sage.

Vedfelt O (2002). *The Dimensions of Dreams: the nature, function and interpretation of dreams*. London: Jessica Kingsley.

5

The unfinished self: inclusivity in experiential-existential therapy

Greg Madison

The experiential-existential approach to therapy intends to prioritise *experiencing*. *Human experience* in this sense is not itself just another concept, not just our ideas about it. Experiencing is *bodily felt,* fundamental and implicit, not already formed into explicit concepts. From the implicit feeling in the body, new insights can emerge: new understandings of what we are living through, how we are living it, about living itself. '*In* the body' is misleading, as if first there were an interior and exterior. Even the term 'the body' in its usual sense obscures the phenomenologically-derived *body-environment process* that, on reflection, we know from our own living.

What is a 'body'? What is 'living'? It seems ironic to me that we often go to the library to answer these questions. All the while we actually *are the answer* but we rarely pause reflexively and look at *what* we are, what 'living' *is* because I am an instance of it, what 'being embodied' *is* because I am that… Rarely do I directly encounter myself as the concrete instance that explanations about the body can only point to. Experiential-existential therapy is a 'pointing' practice. It does not obsess about pinning down explicit understandings. The assumption is that any understanding is incomplete because any living person is incomplete. Understanding should elaborate itself the more a person lives. Many answers may come, but no conclusions.

Moment-by-moment experience changes who and what we are. Our elaboration comes from our radical openness to world interaction. In therapy, client and therapist can be understood as a mutual body-environmental process. Each person's bodily responses interact as one process (what we call 'the session'). Anything 'that happens' explicitly in the session – reflections, statements, interventions, emotional expression – can resonate as a feeling in the body where this implicit level offers verification, more refinement and further living. This is a claim that can be easily verified in your own practice; you do not need to accept it conceptually.

It is not difficult to begin to notice which interventions have an experiential resonance and which don't. If what you offer to your client resonates, you can then turn to the bodily feeling it evokes in them and follow that path, rather than just the next conceptual or logical step. Soon you will notice that your own body also offers a guide to the level of implicit meanings in the session. Once you find what I am pointing to, you can describe it using any theory or philosophical system, or many. Focusing literature and the work of the existential philosopher Eugene Gendlin describes this process of implicit experiencing (see Madison & Gendlin, 2011) without imposing a whole new conceptual tradition or system onto the process.

In summary, experiential-existential psychotherapy invites a moment-by-moment phenomenological awareness of what occurs 'in' the client and in the interactive flow between client and therapist and how each person becomes bodily different because another person is present. This approach accepts a radically intersubjective stance – client and therapist bodies as 'interaffecting' *environmental processes*, not *skinned objects* with a gap in between (see Gendlin, 1997); diffuse verbs, not discrete nouns. Therefore, the therapist is *personally* (not just professionally) implicated because the therapist's unique being is unavoidably affecting the client's flow, with the ease of movement depending on the therapist's openness as much as the client's, and equally in both directions.

Of course, it is contradictory to begin a chapter about an approach that puts experience first by first laying out all these conceptual principles as if they land from heaven. And the principles above purposely emphasise the 'experiential' aspect of this model because it is perhaps less known among existential practitioners. However, there is also the 'existential' side of this hyphenated approach. This aspect of the approach, while founded on and consistent with the usual existential philosophers who inspire existential practice, is explicitly informed by the work of psychologists from the British school of existential-phenomenological therapy (for example, Spinelli, van Deurzen). This 'continental' influence serves to balance what to me is an overly optimistic (and unnecessarily positive) bias in contemporary focusing-oriented therapy.

I hope the statements above offer enough detail so that you can assess whether you want to read more., If so, there are papers and chapters that tie the practice to the principles (see Madison, 2014a, 2014b). What follows here is a case study – a story of meeting that I hope illustrates something of the *spirit* of an experiential-existential approach.

Meeting Hayri

It was the end of January three years ago when Hayri, a slim 26-year-old graduate student from Turkey, swaggered into my London office. He was dressed fashionably, his expensive jeans hanging low on his hips, designer jacket, trendy glasses; he had curly black hair, a handsome face and an intense gaze. Hayri had called me a week before. Now that we were face-to-face, he smiled and began: 'I recognise you, you bought a computer from me.' I remembered him; he had sold me a laptop six months earlier. He had made an impression on me in the shop: inquisitive, asking me questions that were almost intrusive but he somehow pulled them off as naïve and charming.

But today Hayri seemed on edge. He told me how, in November, he had felt a strange itch in his stomach. He went to his GP, who referred him to a specialist. They found a harmless benign cyst but gave Hayri the option of having it removed. He wanted it out but after the surgery the doctors were shocked to discover that it was, in fact, malignant. They were confident they had removed all the cancerous cells and gave Hayri the option of chemotherapy, just to reassure him that it would not recur. Hayri wanted the certainty, which I later discovered was characteristic of him, so in a few weeks he would start intensive chemotherapy. He was angry and embarrassed that he, a privileged young man with everything going for him, should have this weakness – a disease, an imperfection that had to be hidden from the world. Hayri had told no one he was ill except his family, and now me.

In that first meeting, I let my attention drop down into the trunk area of my body to notice my bodily responses as I listened. He spoke quickly and my body was in a kind of swirl, trying to take in what he was saying and feel the meaning in it. I felt an urge to reflect back certain words, to emphasise facts that I felt were not fully acknowledged, to ask a question or clarify a detail, but it was very difficult to break into his flow. I noticed a tightness in my stomach and realised that this was the strain of trying to interact while being frustrated by Hayri's refusal to pause and allow me to respond verbally. Rather than persist, I took a step back, experientially, and my bodily tension eased, allowing space for both Hayri's and my own experience. It felt right to just be quiet and listen closely to his story, without attempting to intervene.

Much of that first meeting was about his medical condition and especially the injustice that such an illness should 'happen to' him. I also learned that, aged 15, Hayri had migrated alone from his hometown in northern Turkey to the UK, initially to study English and then to proceed to a university course in programming. As I relaxed into the feeling of our being together, I noticed a growing warmth for this young man. I cared about him. I felt some connection to the person behind the 'impression management', behind the 'persona' that he identified with, and I began to sense the loneliness of not allowing anyone to see or touch his vulnerability during that migration and now his illness. When our 50 minutes was up, he smiled nervously and seemed almost on the verge of tears as our eyes met.

Over the next sessions, Hayri began to speak openly about the need to be seen as perfect: always right, confident and without weakness. He would frequently argue with me or take up one of my ideas and say it back to me as if he had thought of it, sometimes with a smirk, suggesting he was aware of what he was doing. He seemed to prize this performance of perfection highly, but in his stomach, where the cancer was, he felt almost constant tension. He was hiding his illness from all his friends, yet paradoxically had high expectations of support from these friends, who were unaware of his need. His body was holding the conflict of his pretence that he was not who he knew he really was. After the first few sessions I began to feel that my interventions might be received differently now.

Greg: Hayri, Hayri, let's slow it down a bit here. Tell me, what would be so wrong with your best friend, Luke, knowing that you've been struggling with this disease?

Hayri: It's embarrassing, it shows me as weak, I don't want to be seen as having a disease or as being a cancer patient, I don't want to be seen that way.

Greg: *[I was feeling my body sense of what Hayri was saying and I wanted to find a way to reflect back the core of it to him.]* You're worried that if anyone knew you were ill then that is all they would see in you?

Hayri: I want to be seen as perfect, in control. If they knew I had cancer, they would pity me or see me as inferior.

Greg: So, for you cancer is like a failure or flaw or something... But Hayri, I know you have cancer. How do you think I see you?

Hayri: Yeah, I want to know, how do you see me? *[Hayri occasionally asked directly for my opinion, advice or response.]*

Greg: Good question Hayri, I'm glad you asked. Give me a minute. *[Surprisingly he did, and I let my focus drop down to my chest and stomach to sense 'How do I see this young man?' Then, after a full minute...]* I kind of object to the question...

Hayri: Oh, come on, Greg, you're just dodging it, you don't want to say.

Greg: It sounds like a dodge. But I feel we're getting to know each other and I want to be as honest as I can. I really see you as a young man who unexpectedly is having to face a very scary situation, and I think you're needing to trust someone so you can begin to show how you really feel inside. *[I find that the body usually responds more clearly to short statements. Longer interventions and questions tend to engage the person's thinking mind and take the interaction away from what is experientially alive.]*

Hayri: *[He was unusually silent for a minute, then looked at me. I felt uneasy. I was not sure if the look was maybe anger...]* I think you are right. I can trust you because you're a professional, you and my family, but I don't want to burden them.

I felt something had shifted in our exchange, despite Hayri's response emphasising my professional status. I felt a slight easing in my own body, as if Hayri recognised that he did trust me, at least a bit, but he could not admit that to me yet.

Hayri had never had a relationship where he could talk about what was happening moment-by-moment in the interaction. He became intrigued and started regularly asking me, 'How do you see me?' I always paused and waited for an honest answer to come from my bodily experience of him in that moment; then I presented this in a way that felt consistent with our relationship. In this way, we gradually became more real to each other, increasingly open in a mutual way. We could begin to feel and see the impact we had on each other.

After Hayri's chemotherapy, his six-month check-up showed the tumour had shrunk to a negligible speck and our conversations switched to other topics: his relationships with fellow students, his strong desire for a girlfriend, and his dreams. However, before long, Hayri began to feel some pain in his back and an investigation confirmed that the cancer had returned. This time, though, he told people. First, he told his closest friends and academic supervisor, and we both appreciated that he could accept more of his inner life in his struggle with this disease, which he remained certain he would recover from. He was proud of this change.

The felt relationship

My rapport with Hayri grew in personal warmth as our guardedness with each other began to soften. He was able to begin to notice how his demeanour shifted moment by moment during our conversations, and indeed we also explored a lot about me and my experience as a foreigner, my experience in academia and Hayri's impression of me, and we shared our perspectives about the meaning of life. I began to feel freer to express myself with Hayri, to pause in a session and wait for the right way to say something to come from my bodily feeling into words. He learned to wait for me, although at first he constantly interrupted. Eventually, Hayri started to pause too, to speak from his experience.

I felt free to present my reality because Hayri could forcefully disagree with me, sometimes scoffing with a hard exhale of breath to indicate how ridiculous my point of view was. But usually, through discussion, his initial rejection softened and we would arrive in the middle, appreciating each other's quirks. Eventually, instead of the 'wall of words' he initially built between us, Hayri became more conversational. There were silent pauses in the dialogue. He gave himself time to check if what I said resonated for him. He gave me time to express myself. I took this as a sign that something had really shifted in his experiencing as he worked to include more and more of his feeling life and the feelings of others. By referring directly to his felt experience, Hayri discovered that experientially his world was much more nuanced than the 'image' and the gross dichotomy of 'right/wrong' that had restricted his living and his relationships. One session, while feeling the tension in his stomach, Hayri got an image of a man tied with rope, sitting in a dark shed, and this touched him. For a moment he felt real compassion for this part of himself that was suffering from the way he treated it.

About halfway into our relationship, when his health was again quite good and he had developed his conversational skills, Hayri met a young woman and they developed a truly loving connection that Hayri allowed himself to trust, for the first time in his life. When he was briefly and unexpectedly admitted to hospital, I asked if I could visit him, and he was genuinely grateful and moved. At the beginning and end of that session, Hayri hugged me tightly, and I was surprised and grateful that he would do that.

The emerging democracy of being

Hayri: I feel tense today, as usual. It's the place in my chest and my stomach, where the cancer is. It feels like there is so much going on.

Greg: Maybe it would help to just name what you're tense about and see if you can get a bit of space from each concern?

Hayri: You know, there's the PhD, trying to buy my flat... *[He was naming these things off cognitively, making a mental list.]*

Greg: Hold on, Hayri, can we take it more slowly? First there is the PhD. Let yourself feel how you carry that inside. What is that concern doing to your body?

Hayri: It makes my stomach tight.

Greg: OK, so just let yourself feel that a bit. Don't try to solve the problem... with a big breath, see if it's OK just to let that whole concern and how it feels inside of you lift out of your body and settle next to us here in the room, so you're no longer cramped up from carrying it 'inside'.

I thought Hayri might ridicule this method but he was willing and able to try it. We followed the same procedure with each concern he felt, until his current concerns were named and he felt pretty spacious inside his body.

Hayri: Now I can feel it right where they operated. It's like a scar in me, a place that feels really alone. I feel afraid to be alone.

Greg: Let me say that back to you, Hayri, slowly, so you can see if it feels right. *[Hayri nodded.]* You can really feel this place in your stomach, right where the tumour is, and it feels really alone in there. Can we just acknowledge that this is how it feels, all alone...?

Hayri: *[After a minute, Hayri opened his eyes and looked directly at me.]* That's amazing. It's relaxed and feels calm inside now. *[He was quiet for another minute.]* This feels so important, why don't we have a manual at birth telling us how to do this?

By integrating focusing moments (Gendlin, 1982), Hayri made connection with more aspects of his own experience and slowly began to express his feelings to others and to notice when he fell back behind the image of 'perfect Hayri'. In subsequent sessions, he spoke about saying 'hello' to feelings in his body and was almost embarrassed that it made a difference experientially. He always thought he was just one thing and now he was realising it was not true;

that he was a community of many strands, moving and changing the more he related to his concrete experience.

The uncertainty of living

Hayri arrived wearing a wig and cap. I thought it looked a bit odd but he was convinced it looked normal. He was in shock. He had received bad news from a scan the previous night and texted me immediately. For the first time he was feeling some peace because he had accepted that he couldn't control the situation, and that *a part of him* would like to. The small tumour could not be operated on. Hayri allowed himself to be silent and at times was too shaken to speak. Me too. He kept asking me about my experience with cancer patients: what should he be feeling? I told him people respond very differently to this news and there was no right way to feel. I suggested we check how he actually *did* feel. He said he felt conscious and grateful for our sessions. He said he wanted to do good in the world. His tumour was in the same place in his stomach where his felt sense of tension came. He felt there was a connection and slowly he was beginning to care for that part of himself.

Hayri began to speak about the likelihood that he wouldn't survive and how much time he might have left and wanting to leave a mark in the world. In the uncertainty about his prognosis he scrambled to find some meaning – the usual question, 'Why has this happened to me?' seemed to have no answer in his case. Hayri felt envious of other young people who were getting married, buying houses and having normal lives while his life was so uncertain and preoccupied with illness.

In the midst of all the uncertainty, Hayri consistently believed that he would recover completely, but one session he turned up feeling particularly dark and sad. He started many topics but did not finish any of them. I asked him if it would be helpful to tune into his body a little – something he knew was helpful but, like all of us, often forgot to do. He closed his eyes and became quiet. I suggested he start by noticing his feet and then just allowing himself to feel whatever was happening in his body; I said he didn't have to think anything for a few minutes. After about five minutes I could see his chest expanding as his breath deepened. In my own body, I felt more settled in my stomach area – open, warm, almost a pregnant feeling, like something was coming. Hayri's chest began to heave and he suddenly burst into crying. He was overtaken by deep sobbing for a few minutes. It subsided briefly and then he erupted in even deeper sobs, as though he were finally allowing all the grief and fear and sadness to move through him. Oddly, it seemed fine for this to happen; although in a way he was overtaken, he did not seem overwhelmed. I was grateful his eyes were closed as it allowed me to let the tears run down my cheeks. Gradually his body settled and, as he opened his eyes, he said: 'I have no idea what all that was… That is the first time I have ever allowed myself to cry in front of another person… or in front of myself. It feels like a cut in my stomach is starting to heal.' He paused for a few minutes as the shift integrated in him, and then continued: 'I feel much better. My whole body is relaxed. When I came in, I didn't feel like I was even a part of the world any more, and now I'm back. I can feel I am here again.'

He was very emotional for a couple of days after this session. He looked different, more open, more handsome. I said it seemed that he had let go of 'the image' and now valued the moment-to-moment realness of his experience. He nodded. We spoke about how he hated goodbyes and would want to die instantly. I made a note that we should go back to that.

The end

Hayri struggled with cancer for all the three years I knew him. Each chemotherapy treatment left him more emaciated and weaker, yet he remained positive that eventually he would overcome the disease that kept recurring, and the normal trajectory of his young life would resume. He planned to marry his young girlfriend and to settle down in the country, far from the concentrations of radio waves and mobile signals that he thought might have caused his condition. Hayri was obsessed with understanding why he contracted such a rare form of cancer.

Hayri had suffered a series of indignities that no one, and certainly not a 27-year-old who prized personal perfection, should have to endure. Though he had lost weight and muscle, he still bounded with bravado into our sessions, typically still a few minutes late. The only sessions he ever missed were the ones immediately after commencing a new chemotherapy treatment, when he was initially too sick to leave home. Otherwise he attended with interest and enthusiasm.

Then, when I was away, teaching abroad, I received a text from Hayri saying, 'Can we talk? I'll call you tomorrow. What time?' It was unusual for us to have contact between sessions, except for updates on side effects to his treatment so we could plan to resume our sessions. The tone of the text caused me to remember our last session, when he had broached the subject of his own death. I texted back that I was away. 'Hi Hayri. Very good to hear from you. I'm in Lisbon lecturing at the moment but I'm back in London on Monday. I hope we can connect then? I've been thinking about you. Best wishes, Greg.' Monday came and went but no word from Hayri. This wasn't so unusual; I assumed he was struggling with the side effects of treatment and would get in touch when he was feeling a bit better. On the Tuesday I texted again, inviting him to make contact, wondering if he had taken offence that I was not available over the weekend.

I waited until Thursday, our usual session day, and texted again, this time more insistent that I wanted to hear from him. Around 4pm I got a reply, but from his sister Ruby. I was shocked to hear the news that I had been dreading: Hayri had died Tuesday night in a London hospital. I let the news sink in slowly, in little waves between the last clients of the day. Later, I texted Ruby, could I call her at the end of the day? She agreed. I had never had any contact with Hayri's family and I wondered about the protocol for a therapist to speak to the family of a deceased client. All I knew was that I needed to know more about Hayri's last days, to make it real.

Ruby told me that Hayri was asking for morphine at the end. He was trying to protect everyone, so there was no open discussion about him dying. During the call we both broke down. Ruby said the family were very appreciative of my work with Hayri. When I got off the phone, I cried some more. The next day I broke down again with my supervisor and couldn't speak. As I write this, months after Hayri's death, my throat still restricts. Am I supposed to make our relationship into a 'case'? Distance myself enough to present some professional account of our connection? I have tried.

This chapter is written despite the despair that erupts in me when mortality senselessly rips apart the veneer of life and practising therapy seems like a tawdry distraction. The Sunday night after Hayri died, I awoke around 3am with a question clearly typed across my mind's eye, like a ticker tape: 'HOW MUCH LONGER DO I WANT TO LIVE?' The question rang like a gong through my whole body. A genuine question – what is the point of continuing to live? What is going to happen between now and my death that will make the next couple decades (presumably) meaningful? All I know is that I am learning something about my own life from accompanying Hayri. Somehow, we were good for each other.

Discussion with the editor

Simon: Can you say a little about the genesis of experiential-existential therapy?

Greg: Experiential-existential therapy arose from integrating the practical implications of Gendlin's philosophy, the experiential method of focusing and my existential-phenomenological training. At the same time, Professor Les Todres (retired from Bournemouth University) and I began to collaborate and started using the name. Since then, I have learned that there are a few continental and North American therapists who are also integrating forms of existential therapy and focusing. It is a subset of the community of focusing-oriented therapists (FOTs), who are mostly person-centred, integrative or eclectic in practice. These other FOTs tend to be more 'positive' and individualistic in their stance.

Simon: I am intrigued by the extent to which experiential-existential therapy represents something new and the extent to which it perhaps 'just' introduces a slightly different emphasis to ways of working as an existential therapist. When I read about the notion of a moment-by-moment relationship, it seemed to me to describe the aim of many existential therapists seeking to be in the here-and-now. One thing that did strike me forcibly was that the therapist seems to be quite active in the relationship and, consequently, perhaps risks more and maybe is also open to gaining more himself or herself. This seemed to me to be particularly so with regard to your client, since the focus of the therapeutic approach and his own focus are both on the body – in this instance, a body that is impacted by serious illness.

Greg: It strikes me as quite unique. For almost 20 years, I've been teaching this integration to therapists, most of them existential, and the constant checking with the body feeling is quite radical, relational and intimate. One begins to trust that there is a process of being that guides and corrects our concepts and descriptions of experience and, while doing so, the person undergoes palpable, small steps of change. Most existential therapists I've met remain at the conceptual level, ignoring how the body responds to whatever is happening in the session. This approach does require the therapist to also be very bodily aware and to use her or his responses as a guide to what is happening in the client and in the relationship. If 'here-and-now' means what is bodily alive in that moment, yes. The session develops around what feels alive for the client in the moment.

Simon: I'm not sure if my feeling here is accurate, but it seems to me the focus in experiential-existential therapy is largely on the present. I know in my own practice I find it very helpful to explore the past as it is unfolding in the present and shaping the future, not in order to ascribe causal relationships but simply as a reflection of the way in which clients – all of us – embody in a complex way past, present and future. As I say, I may not have quite grasped the experiential-existential approach, but I guess I would have been interested to explore the meaning of the client's image of perfection, and the way in which that came about.

Greg: Where are the past and the future if not in the present? If by 'the present' we mean what currently feels alive for the client, then that could be a past relationship evoking feelings now, as the memory of it is crossed with the client's present being. It could mean anxiety about what is coming up later that week, if that anxiety is presently felt. *The felt body is the past, as it is crossed with the present, impelling itself forward to make a future.* The meaning of Hayri's 'perfection' would certainly be explored, watching for avenues that evoke a felt response and pursuing them. The case study here can't be taken as a general example, unfortunately, as each instance of this therapy can look very different and, of course, much was left out of this account.

Simon: Finally – and this may or may not be a useful question – as I read I wondered whether some therapists might find your approach quite difficult, either because they are more cerebral or because of their own relationship with their bodies. I have ME and I am constantly aware of my level of fatigue and the extent to which I am physically present. Paradoxically, on occasion it seems to help facilitate an encounter, but there are times when it doesn't.

Greg: Absolutely. Some therapists find this approach difficult. It is fundamentally quite a humble approach, where the therapist sets aside what they think they know in order to be explicitly guided by the felt sensing of the relationship and the client's dilemmas. The bodily experience is prioritised. But that assumes the therapist can also access their body and some need a lot of practice to do that, especially when so much of our therapy training prioritises theoretical interpretation and cognitive analysis. However, every person, no matter what state their body is in physically, does have this kind of living-forward process accessible to them. This way of working usually requires less energy, rather than more, and changes the definition of 'body' from physical 'machine' to an experiential aliveness that extends beyond the physical boundaries.

References

Gendlin ET (1997). *A Process Model*. Unpublished manuscript. [Online.] New York, NY: The Focusing Institute. www.focusing.org/gendlin (accessed 3 January 2016)

Gendlin ET (1982). *Focusing*. New York, NY: Bantam.

Madison G (2014a). Exhilarating pessimism: focusing-oriented existential therapy. In: Madison G (ed). *Theory and Practice of Focusing-Oriented Psychotherapy: beyond the talking cure*. London: Jessica Kingsley (pp113–127).

Madison G (2014b). The palpable in existential counselling psychology. *Counselling Psychology Review* 29(2): 25–33.

Madison G, Gendlin ET (2011). Palpable existentialism: an interview with Eugene Gendlin. In: Barnett L, Madison G (eds). *Existential Therapy: legacy, vibrancy and dialogue*. London: Routledge (pp81–96).

6

'Three's company, two's a crowd': working existentially with couples presenting with issues of addiction

Simon du Plock

Relatively little has been published from an explicitly existential-phenomenological perspective about the nature of addiction and how it can be worked with therapeutically. The literature that is available has largely been generated by a small number of writers over the past 10–15 years (Wurm, 1997; du Plock, 2000, 2002, 2009; du Plock & Fisher, 2005). Working with couples has attracted even less attention; Spinelli was a pioneer in this field when he described his own way of working with couples in 1997, but it was not until van Deurzen and Iacovou's edited text appeared in 2013 that other practitioners made a contribution to the literature. It is not particularly surprising that existential therapists have written little about addiction, since we largely reject thinking in terms of specific treatment modalities for fixed client groups. We are, instead, 'concerned to engage with process and with blocks to process and strive to avoid seeing clients in terms of treatment labels' (du Plock, 2009: 109). It is rather more surprising that we have written little on couples therapy, as Spinelli remarks:

> This seems somewhat startling to me not only because quite a few existential-phenomenological therapists offer couples therapy, but also since it is apparent that this approach provides a unique and novel perspective… I have found the experience of working with a couple to be both stimulating and illustrative of the importance given by existential-

phenomenological theory to the idea of *being-with-others*.' (1997: 101, original emphasis)

I intend, in this chapter, to outline my way of working with a couple who presented with issues relating to addiction. As will become evident, my method owes much to what Spinelli calls his 'tentative and idiosyncratic' approach (1997: 101).

My approach to working with couples is distinct from my work with individuals. When I meet an individual client, my focus is primarily on the relational field that the client and I inhabit, and on the way in which we co-create this. My object is always to attempt to meet my client with what May (May, Angel & Ellenberger, 1958: 37) has termed 'Here-is-a-new-person' in mind. My intention in doing this is to create the optimal conditions for authentic encounter with the other. Such an authentic encounter, one in which my personal preconceptions and biases are minimised, enables me to meet the client with genuine curiosity and naïvety about their way of being in the world. This optimises the opportunity for the client to notice that another approaches their being with care and encourages them, in turn, to take their being seriously – May's (1983: 99) 'I am' experience. I believe that my approach reflects Nietzsche's attitude of encouraging people to become objective towards themselves, rather than getting lost in subjectivity. Greater objectivity may help clients take renewed responsibility for making active choices to author their own lives.

Clients frequently describe themselves as addicts, drawing terms from the language of the world of addiction that suggest they are in some sense 'ill' and not fully responsible for their lives – 'life' is something that happens to them, not something to actively shape according to their values. Human being is inevitably being in relation: as Cohn (1997: 33) expresses it, we never meet *only* the client, we are 'always and inevitably in a context with others'. It follows that couple therapy provides an opportunity to work at greater 'depth', since the relational world presented in the consulting room is far more richly textured. This is not least because in individual therapy the therapist assists the client to reflect on the ways in which they create meaning in their world, while in couples therapy the therapist has the opportunity to observe how two people attempt to create meaning, both as individuals and in common. Clients' ways of being in relationship are not just reported and reflected in their ways of relating to the therapist; they are present in the room in the real time interactions of the two members of the couple with each other and with the therapist.

The therapist's role changes when one or both clients present with an issue related in some way to addiction, since embracing the identity of 'addict' functions to reduce an individual's sense of responsibility and agency in the world. The member of the couple describing themselves as an addict may resist exploring their way of being other than via the selective lens of addiction. Their partner may also subscribe to the notion that the 'addict' is defined by this label. One or both may seek 'treatment' to remove the addiction or help with symptom reduction or management. An ethical existential-phenomenological practitioner needs to be clear that they are primarily offering an opportunity to help the couple clarify their way of being in the world, rather than a specific treatment for addiction. It is helpful, though, to indicate this clarity will enable them to proceed with more confidence, regardless of the direction they decide to take.

My practice is influenced by the move in the British and North American literature, in the past decade, away from concentrating on addiction as a state characterised by a sharp reduction of the capacity for voluntary behaviour in relation to specific substances (generally termed 'drugs'), towards the notion that people can get caught up in ordinary activities when they become invested with special meaning. Following Shaffer's (1994) contention that 'anything can be addictive which powerfully and quickly and predictably changes how you feel', I view the addict as one who self-medicates. The addiction can be a substance or an experience: shopping, gambling or eating (or abstaining from eating) may all fulfil this definition. Reflecting on my own clients, perhaps as many as half present, either directly or indirectly, with problems related to substance abuse. Another quarter bring issues connected with obsessive compulsive behaviour, such as obsessive exercising (this has become increasingly common with the proliferation of private health clubs and the constant media coverage promoting the attainability of physical perfection, for both genders). Others present because they find themselves working obsessively and are constantly on their mobile phone, iPad or other gadget outside designated office hours, to the extent that non-work relationships or leisure become impossible. If I also include those who complain that they are caught up in emotional situations in which they experience themselves as externally determined, addiction touches the great majority of my clients. Beyond this, I find I am increasingly working with clients who present with issues connected to being partners or family of people experiencing some aspects of addiction.

The degree to which these phenomena fit the classical notion of addiction varies, but I find Walters' (1999) definition of addiction a useful yardstick in my work. Walters defines addiction as 'the persistent and repetitive enactment of a behavioural pattern' that includes four elements:

1. progression (or increase in severity)
2. preoccupation with the activity
3. perceived loss of control, and
4. persistence, despite negative long-term consequences.
(Walters, 1999: 10)

Working with couples presenting with issues of addiction

I find the most facilitative way I can explore issues of addiction with clients in couple therapy is via the concept Spinelli (2007: 198) has called 'the couple-construct'. This concept has grown out of his earlier notion of the 'self-structure' (1994: 348), which directs our attention to how each of us assembles, over time, a set of beliefs, values and aspirations about who we believe ourselves to be. An exploration of the individual's self-structure will clarify the role of the addiction in providing them with a sense of structure in their life that they might otherwise not have. A key element of existential couple therapy is the clarification of the extent to which these beliefs, values and assumptions about addiction are shared by both partners, if at all.

Much of my work with couples focuses on the particular ways in which their unique couple-construct functions to both open up and limit their way-of-being-in-the-world as a couple. I engage in this process of clarification with them not with the intention of helping them 'move on' in some way, but to enable them to engage as fully as possible with me so that we can all 'see what is there'. This is especially important with addiction, where denial of a wide spectrum of ways to live can be a key feature. When both clients can genuinely see the way they have constructed their 'way-of-being-in-the-world' as a couple, they may elect to modify it. This is not, though, to underestimate how difficult this is likely to be, nor how much support they may need from the therapeutic alliance: as Spinelli makes clear, the couple may decide to separate if they discover that their individual understandings of being a couple are too divergent.

I generally use the following template for exploring the couple-construct. Sessions are 75 minutes, rather than the 50-minute 'therapeutic hour' of one-to-one work, as I have found this necessary, given the complexity of the dynamics in the room.

> **Session 1**: I meet the couple and we explore what brings them into therapy and the extent to which the emerging couple-construct is characterised by fluidity or the rigidity that may signal issues of

addiction. It is important, I feel, to provide a safe enough container for the couple to feel a connection with me and to begin to tell their story. While I tend to begin the initial session by welcoming them and asking them to tell me something about what has brought them to see me, much as I begin an individual therapy, I also ensure that there is time towards the end of the session for me to describe how I work; how, typically, sessions will be structured, and the rationale for this particular structure. I also take this opportunity to check whether, on the basis of our work so far, they wish to commit to further sessions. If they are able to confirm this, I reiterate that I will meet with them individually for the next two sessions.

Session 2: I meet one member of the couple on their own, with the objective of focusing on their experience of being with their partner in the couple-construct that they have created. This also provides an opportunity for us to reflect on the values and beliefs they hold with regard to being in a couple and the extent to which these are realised in their current couple-construct.

Session 3: I repeat this process with the other member of the couple.

Session 4: I meet with the couple together and we reflect on the experience of the previous two sessions and relate what was explored in each session to their couple-construct.

Section 5: I meet with the couple to clarify the extent to which their individual constructs and couple-construct remain the same or have changed and to consider whether they wish to continue to work with me or leave therapy at this point.

During Session 5, I offer the opportunity to continue to work for a further cycle of five sessions. In the second cycle we use the first session to review their objectives for continuing in therapy. The next four sessions generally follow the pattern of the first cycle of therapy. We may repeat these cycles until the couple feel that they have sufficiently addressed the issues that brought them to therapy. I have found that most couples are able to complete this work in two or three cycles.

In my meetings with each individual, I typically invite them to reflect on the follow points.

1. Their individual sense of who they are, what is important to them, what they hold to be fundamental to their identity and, where addiction is a concern, the extent to which it impacts on identity and the degree to which this includes being an 'addict'.

2. The same, but as they imagine their partner might respond to the question.

3. How their couple-construct supports and/or destabilises their sense of self and what they hold to be important for themselves.

4. The same, but as they imagine their partner might answer the question.

5. As a result of this reflection, how do they feel about their partnership? What is their 'felt-sense'? Are they clearer about aspects that feel satisfying, and aspects where they might want to work towards making a change? If addiction is a feature of the partnership, in what ways is it shaped by this phenomenon?

6. If there are areas where they might like to make changes, how do they feel this might impact upon the couple-construct? How do they feel this might change the quality of their partnership?

Working with Luke and Mike

I resonate with Spinelli's view when meeting couples in conflict that:

> ... our first task together will be that of clarifying the underlying assumptions, biases, values and beliefs of the currently existing couple-construct. Via such descriptive clarification, the couple's inter-relational sedimentations and dissociations can be highlighted... descriptive classification can reveal not only poorly perceived defining aspects of the existing couple-construct, but also those poorly perceived defining aspects that each member of the couple maintains with regard to his or her own self-construct or to the 'other-construct' of his or her partner. (1997: 104–105)

He goes on to assert that each member of the couple makes sense of the conflict that besets them by viewing it through the lens of their own worldview. They are likely to assume that this perspective is shared by their partner and, given this assumption, they are likely to hold it without checking that it is, indeed, the case.

Luke and Mike sent me a jointly-signed email requesting an appointment as they both felt that their relationship had run into difficulties. It seemed from their email that they shared the view that they were drifting apart after being together for six years, having met when they were both in their early 30s. They said they had got my contact details via a colleague of Mike's (he was a nursing manager in a London hospital) who was a past student of mine. They asked for a meeting as soon as possible as they felt they had 'hit a wall' and were no longer able to communicate with each other. I was struck that it appeared they were in agreement about the state of their relationship, even if they were not able to agree about much else, and I wondered if this would provide some foundation for our work together, should they wish to work with me. I also had a sense of urgency – that they were in crisis. I offered them an appointment later the same week and received an acceptance almost immediately.

Session one

They arrived together, although I noticed they seemed awkward with each other and made little eye contact. I went into my usual routine, welcoming them both and inviting them to tell me what brought them to see me. The atmosphere seemed to become more relaxed as they launched into a description of how they had met 'on the gay scene', and how what both thought would be a one-night stand developed into an ongoing relationship. When I asked them what they thought was the reason for this, they both said that they had recognised something in the other that was important for them. Luke felt that Mike was a real 'buddy', while Mike referred to their relationship as one of two 'soul mates'. I wondered what these two terms, at first hearing so different, might mean for each of them, but at this early stage in the meeting decided to sit back and listen to more of their story.

They told me that they had found themselves drifting apart over the past 18 months, and that this sense of drifting had accelerated recently, to the point that they were no longer emotionally or sexually intimate and constantly argued. When I asked them if anything in particular had happened 18 months ago, Luke immediately said Mike had started a mental health degree, and six months later had been promoted to a nurse manager grade, and that he had received a further upgrade in the past few months. Mike agreed that the more successful he became, the more their relationship suffered. He felt this was a real puzzle, since Luke was very successful – he was a company executive with a high income who frequently travelled abroad on business.

When I asked them to tell me more about themselves, Luke described how what he experienced as a very happy childhood had abruptly come to a halt when he was 12 and his parents divorced acrimoniously. He and his sister were 'packed off' to separate boarding schools and he quickly had to learn to fend for himself. Being good at sports, he became popular, but he was aware of avoiding close friendships through his school years and later at university – a wariness he attributed to a fear of being hurt again, as he had been when his parents split up.

Mike also seemed something of a loner: he grew up in a blue-collar family in the Midlands, and said he was always aware of feeling 'different' and not fitting in. He had little sense of what he wanted to do for work and had trained as a nurse because a careers tutor had said he would be 'good with people'. Once qualified, he took the first opportunity he could to transfer 'down south' and had only became career-minded after he took some internal training and realised he had a flair for managing a drug addiction unit.

Luke broke in at this point to say that he had initially been very pleased when Mike began to take his job more seriously: they were living together and their income disparity was starting to feel like an issue. But he thought Mike's addiction studies had led him to change his social habits and this, in turn, impacted on Luke. Now Mike avoided drugs and drank less, and rarely wanted to go clubbing at weekends. Mike retorted that Luke needed to look at his own drug use, and that if he (Mike) could change his behaviour in a more healthy direction, then so could Luke. Luke shifted uneasily in his seat on hearing this and, looking directly at me, said, 'You see? *This* is the problem – Mike's changed and now he's trying to change me. But I don't need to change. I'm comfortable with who I am and if that involves recreational drugs, that's up to me.' Mike came back saying, 'If we really are a couple then it isn't just up to you. You should be glad I have your interests at heart, and the more I work with addicts the more I worry about you.' Luke looked exasperated at this point and, throwing up his hands, said, 'I don't need anyone worrying about me, I'm just fine. Maybe you need to think about how sanctimonious you're getting with all your academic wisdom!'

I was aware at this point that we were drawing towards the end of our time, so I reflected back to them what I thought I was hearing and asked them to correct me if this was not their sense of the situation. It seemed to me that they had originally felt drawn together on the basis that they had a lot in common. I wasn't too sure at this point what this had involved, and thought it would be interesting to explore this further if they decided to work with me. Part of this, though, seemed to be a shared perspective on the value of having an 'open relationship', which perhaps other potential partners had not favoured. I had not heard much about what this 'open relationship' involved, but it did seem to include regular drug and alcohol use. This relationship had worked well for several years but when Mike began to be more involved in his own career and started to change his drug and alcohol use, it seemed to threaten the continuation of the relationship. Similarly, Luke's wish to continue acting as he had at the beginning of the relationship felt unacceptable to Mike. Their relationship seemed to some extent to be defined by its 'openness' and I wondered what else was important to them, or whether, if this 'openness' were threatened, the relationship itself might not survive. In any case, it appeared that they were no longer in agreement about what they wanted from their relationship, and they had not found a way to communicate successfully with one another about this.

I remarked that what at first appeared to be a very relaxed and flexible way of being in a couple now looked surprisingly rule-bound and brittle. I suspected that I was taking a gamble in offering them this feedback so early in our encounter, but it seemed important to give them a sense of how I was experiencing them, even if this might feel challenging, so that they could correct me if they needed to. In fact, they both agreed that what I had observed did indeed feel accurate. I reflected back to them that this agreement about the situation might give us a useful platform for further discussion, and we ended the session with their enthusiastic agreement to continue to work with me.

After they left the office I made my customary brief notes in the 10-minute gap before the next session. I noted down my impression of the couple-construct that Luke and Mike had created. It seemed to me this was characterised by an agreement to have an open relationship. At this point, it was not clear to me the extent to which Luke and Mike shared the same motivation for this or were equally happy about how this worked in practice. I was struck by how easily Luke's status as the high-achiever in the couple seemed to have been undermined by Mike's growing confidence in his own career. I wondered about the extent to which their couple-construct could embrace change, and whether Luke and Mike would be willing to change. It seemed significant that their interactions in the room with me had been mostly conflictual and they had not evidenced much appreciation of each other's world-view. My sense was that both were more heavily invested in following their own interests rather than finding new ways to be a team and, if my hunch were correct, our meetings might allow them to recognise that and decide whether to continue as a couple or end their relationship.

Session two

At the end of the previous session we had agreed that Luke would come alone to the next meeting. He seemed very eager to express his feelings about being in couples therapy, saying immediately, 'You know I really hate that's it's come to this, that we end up talking to a therapist. It's so far from where we started.' I asked him to tell me more about where they started and in what ways now was so different, and our conversation began.

Luke: Well, in the beginning we had a lot in common. You wouldn't have thought it looking at us. Mike's a bit younger than me, but not by much, and I suppose I had a relatively privileged upbringing, with private schooling and university, so I went straight into a good job and I've been financially successful. And he had a tougher time and fewer advantages. But he's really bright and successful in his own way. I work hard and play hard and he's the same. As it happens, he's more sociable than me – in fact, it's surprising how well he gets on with anyone; he has a gift for making friends. People think I'm gregarious but really, I've always been wary of ties. I never had any hang-ups about drugs and getting about, and the good thing about Mike when we met was he was up for anything. We had a pretty open relationship from the start and it worked well for a long time. I think it's only really the last year or so he's become clingy and possessive. I don't like it when he's possessive: I feel like I'm being controlled and that really presses my buttons!

Me: So, it sounds like, when you met, Mike very much complemented your lifestyle, he fitted in well and you had fun together?

Luke: Yes, I think that's right.

Me: But as time has passed, he has developed more of his own interests, and he has created his own career, and it seems he makes more demands on you?

Luke described how he was very supportive of Mike's efforts to improve his qualifications but had not foreseen the extent to which it would involve him in his own circle of friends from the hospital and the college. It sounded, I reflected, as though he felt excluded from this new circle of friends.

Luke: Yes, in a way. I feel Mike keeps them away from me and on the odd times I've met them, I feel they judge me: I'm just the guy who earns the money, while they take the moral high ground with all their psychobabble. Which is crazy really, 'cos I got a degree years ago.

Me: It sounds like you feel they disapprove of you?

Luke: Well they don't exactly say it, and Mike doesn't say it, but I get the sense they look at me as some sort of reprobate! You know – this middle-aged druggie. And since Mike got involved with this addiction course, he's been different too. I mean, he's still up for a drink but we do less of the drugs now. And when I get home on a Friday night, there are always these sort-of questions in the air: where did you go, who were you with, what did you do? Not just interested, but more like I'm reporting to matron! So that's when I decided to push back and I raised the idea of opening up our relationship more. I figured, if I'm feeling stifled, let's let some air in, let's bring a third guy in. We talked about 'threesomes' right at the start when we met but decided against. But this seemed like the right moment to raise it again.

Me: So, in response to Mike getting closer to you…

Luke: More invading my space!

Me: OK, so in response to that, you proposed bringing in a third person with the aim of reducing the pressure on you?

Luke: Yes, but it backfired big time. He really didn't go for it, started shouting at me that I couldn't handle intimacy, that I didn't care about anyone except myself… and then he came right back and said if I really cared we would get a civil partnership! I really didn't see that one coming… smart move!

I reflected to Luke that listening to him talking about his relationship, and especially his last remark about Mike making a 'smart move', created for me the image of two boxers in a ring, sparring. I said this sat oddly for me alongside the close relationship he had described at our first meeting.

Luke: That feels really sad… and I get the mental image of keeping back from him so I don't get punched. It feels important somehow, this sense I've always had of holding myself back. With Mike, I thought I could get involved just enough to keep us ticking fine, but it seems like he wants more of me. And he wants me to change. Not sure either is an option!

He looked crestfallen and sat silently for a while. It felt like we had reached a serious point, but we were also nearly at the end of our time so I reflected that I felt he had helped me get a much fuller picture of his experience of being in a relationship with Mike. I also felt we had been able to reflect together on what being in any intimate relationship meant to him, and I had the impression he found it challenging to let others get close. His use of drugs and casual sex seemed to fit with this in the sense that they functioned to keep him busy and stimulated but did not make emotional demands on him. All the time Mike was happy to be part of this way of being, Luke could see him as a 'buddy', but now that he wanted a more exclusive relationship, Luke did not know how to respond. Luke agreed that this was broadly accurate, and also said that it helped just to get his difficulties out in the open so he could have a look at them: 'I don't know where to go from here, but at least it's a relief to let it all out.'

Session three

Mike needed little prompting from me to begin talking. He had clearly used the time since our first session to come to some conclusions, and he hit the ground running.

Mike: You know, I've been thinking a lot since our first meeting and it seems to me we never really have been a proper couple. I mean, call me old-fashioned if you want, but it's never really been like the song – just the two of us. There's always been the dope, or the coke, or the booze. I can't remember more than the odd couple of days when we haven't been high on something, or coming down off something, or planning the next party. And I count myself in on this; I take my share of the responsibility. When we first met, one of the things I found most attractive about Luke was there was never a dull moment, there was always the next thing coming along. Being with Luke was a real rollercoaster of fun.

I think in the first couple of years I just enjoyed the ride. It was a change for me to go with the flow. My background is all hard graft and money was tight when I was growing up, so being with Luke was a real contrast. And then over the next couple of years I started to find it hard to keep up. I mean, there were my studies, and I needed to take them seriously if I was going to move up the nursing ladder and not get stuck at the bottom. So, I had to make time and devote the energy to them. But it was still pretty much fine because Luke was travelling most weeks, so we partied at the weekends, and every weekend was like starting over together.

But eventually I realised the weekends for him were just an extension of the week. Don't get me wrong, he's very professional, very good at what he does, but in the evenings, wherever he is, he hits the bars, and so far as he's concerned, I'm nowhere and he does what he wants, takes what he wants. So, the weekends really aren't that special, just more of the same, except I'm there to keep the flat tidy and do all the food and the laundry and that.

[*He paused for a few minutes.*] God, I sound like a golf widow, don't I? And I hate hearing myself sound like this – it isn't really me. Luke's favourite saying is something from Warhol, 'One's company, two's a party and three's a crowd.' I'm not sure what Warhol meant, but I think Luke says it to emphasise how much he likes a good time!

Me: It sounds quite ambiguous to me. I think the more usual phrase might be, 'Two's company, three's a crowd.' If you say 'One's company', perhaps it means you're self-sufficient? How do you understand it?

Mike: That's weird, I never thought of it before. It sounds like the exact opposite of how he is – I mean, he just never behaves as though he's self-sufficient; he always seems to have someone in tow... if not me, then some casual pick-up. And he's always in a crowd, in the sense that he's never happier than when he's in a disco or a nightclub.

I reflected that I was feeling a bit puzzled too, but one of the things I was picking up was that perhaps there were some aspects of Luke he didn't know a lot about, just as there were aspects of Mike that Luke wasn't aware of.

Mike: And I'm not just having a selfish moan here. I'm also worried for him. I mean, he doesn't see it this way, but I think he's running all kinds of risks. He tells me he's in control, but it's obvious to me that if he's on his own and taking God knows what, and in any kind of combination, and then going off with people he's never met in his life... And when I say any of this to him direct, he just says, 'Oh, this is your nursing training coming out, you used to be so much more chilled,' so I feel he's pushing me away and trashing me as a professional at the same time.

Me: How do you feel about Luke meeting other people when he's away?

Mike: Well, I used to be pretty much OK with it, and in fact we prided ourselves on not being jealous and being able to have a kind-of open relationship.

Me: You used to…?

This seemed to pull Mike up short, and he reflected that, thinking about it now, this open relationship idea was more Luke's than his.

Mike: I mean, I didn't object and we were going around with a group where that was the norm. We were very clear about boundaries: no sex with friends, and no overnight stays. But Luke always took advantage of this arrangement more than me. I never said anything because I liked the feeling that I could play around a bit if I wanted, but I hardly ever did. And Luke's always had more confidence than me. He can pick people up without trying, so on some level I thought this was a good deal – better to agree to some playing away than risk losing him altogether.

Session four

I generally use this session to meet with the couple together, reflect with them on their experience of their previous two sessions, and relate to their couple-construct what was explored in each session. Rather to my surprise, given their limited level of interaction in our first session, I discovered that they had spent a considerable amount of time during the past two weeks discussing what had happened in their individual sessions with me. It seemed their curiosity about these sessions had enabled them to move away, at least to a degree, from their recent conflictual way of relating.

Mike: I mentioned that odd thing about 'One's company, two's a party and three's a crowd' to Luke and we figured out it really should be 'Three's company, two's a crowd'.

I reflected that it seemed they had managed to talk about some quite sensitive issues in a constructive way, and I wondered how they had done this. They responded that it was only in our sessions that they had realised how close they were to breaking up and this realisation encouraged them to risk being more honest with each other than they had been previously. Mike said that he discovered how angry he was with Luke for pushing them into an open relationship, but that this had been quickly replaced by the realisation that he had agreed to this, and so was equally responsible for their situation. Luke told Mike how he felt Mike increasingly judged him for his drug and alcohol use, but he also reflected that part of his anger about this was that he feared he was increasingly using substances to help him cope on a daily basis. He had been able in our individual session to acknowledge the extent to which he used drugs and recreational sex to avoid intimacy.

Luke: I don't feel great admitting this, but I'm happiest on my own. Or maybe not happiest, but least stressed. I'm not good at intimacy, so if it's not just me, then the next best thing is a crowd, after that being with a casual trick, and the most challenging thing of all is being a couple. There, I've said it and I'm not proud of it. But I can't take it back.

Session five

I was pleased that both recognised that they had made a start on re-inventing their relationship but said there was considerably more work ahead if they were to continue as a couple. They both acknowledged that they did not know if they would be able to refashion their relationship to the extent that would offer them enough reason to stay together. Luke seemed to have moved quite a long way already and said that he felt motivated for his own sake to reach a deeper understanding of his use of drugs and recreational sex. At this point, though, he admitted that he could not tell how this might impact on his relationship with Mike. Mike, for his part, recognised that he had to some extent excluded Luke from his new life and had fallen into the habit of relating to him in the way he related to substance users in his workplace. He felt shocked that he had done this, and, at the same time, was not sure how Luke could be part of this new life; if Luke really did think 'two was a crowd', perhaps he did not actually want to be with Mike at all.

Though both were clearly daunted by the issues their new perspective on their relationship threw up, they agreed at the end of the session to contract for five more sessions. I was not particularly surprised that Mike attended our next meeting alone. He told me that they had agreed to take a break from their relationship and they both intended to pursue individual therapy. As he explained, they had come to the realisation in the course of their work with me that their relationship no longer provided them with the freedom they had initially sought. The fact that they had taken their relationship for granted seemed, on reflection, indicative of the way they had fallen into the habit of taking each other for granted. In couples therapy, they had first thought that this realisation alone might provide a solution to their dilemma, but when they discovered that this insight was the beginning of a journey rather than the destination, they realised they were not motivated enough to continue.

The experience of couples therapy had, though, provided them with motivation to continue in individual therapy. Luke had no previous experience of therapy and now wanted to work on his reliance on drugs and recreational sex. Mike had been shocked to discover the extent to which he had distanced himself from Luke and had attributed all their difficulties to Luke's 'addictions'. With regard to their relationship, it seemed both had arrived at an enhanced appreciation of the challenges of creating a flexible couple-construct and a greater understanding of what each meant by the word 'freedom'.

Concluding reflection

I have outlined my way of working with couples (and in this case a couple presenting with issues of addiction) in the hope that this may assist other existential-phenomenological practitioners to clarify their own approach in this area. I have drawn on theory and practice that I have developed over a number of years (2000, 2002, 2009; du Plock & Fisher, 2005). I am indebted to Spinelli (1997, 2007) for his investigation of relational dimensions of therapeutic encounter. My own approach in this area is grounded in the understanding that it is only in the course of careful clarification of their couple-construct that the members of a couple can obtain the sense of agency that will enable them to decide whether they wish to continue or change their way of being in relationship.

This clarification can enable the couple to generate a more sustaining couple-construct, but it may also, as it did for Luke and Mike, lead them to decide that their individual needs cannot be met within the existing couple-construct. We might conclude, in this case, that the therapy has in some sense 'failed', but this would be a mistake, since the realisation by the partners of the ways in which their current couple-construct is untenable can also provide them with the possibility to part on the basis of greater insight, which may provide a resource for future personal relationships. Privately, I reflected that, while much of our work had focused on their different views on addiction, perhaps the true addiction was a shared one: an addiction to the concept of an open relationship that never really existed.

Discussion with Zack Eleftheriadou

Zack: You talk about the need to expand the 'therapeutic hour' to 75 minutes in order to accommodate the complexity of the dynamics in the room. I wonder if you can say something more about this complexity?

Simon: Well, I think there are a number of things that can be said here. First, my sense from talking to other existential therapists, and from my own work as a supervisor of therapists working with couples, and indeed with families and groups, is that colleagues often find themselves extending their practice into these areas with little preparation. Often they are responding to need – either because an existing client asks if the therapist can see them with their partner or because a potential client gets in contact requesting this. And I have been struck a number of times by the readiness with which colleagues or supervisees have agreed to work in this way. I think it's good that we respond to need, and at the same time I think it's important to at least have some knowledge of existing theory and practice, much of it not ostensibly 'existential', before plunging in. At the very least I think anyone contemplating couples work needs to ensure their supervisor has experience of this, and undertaking some specific couples training and reading widely should be requirements for anyone who intends to offer such therapy on a regular basis. While there is much to be said for 'learning on the job', this must not be at the expense of clients. It's tempting to assume couples therapy is just an extension of one-to-one therapy, and I hope my example above goes some way to countering this assumption.

Zack: I think I pick up an interesting tension in what you have written between how challenging couples therapy can be and your evident enthusiasm for it.

Simon: That's a very accurate observation – I do feel that couples therapy, and all forms of working with groups, brings its own challenges, and at the same time I think it is an area that probably should receive far more attention and be greatly expanded. When I teach existential group therapy, I invariably show Yalom's classic DVDs, because even though he uses actors, they capture the complex dynamics unleashed in the consulting room. And it's the same with couples therapy – we are able to see in the here-and-now how the clients are in a particular relationship. This is tremendously powerful and enables us to really engage with not just the *accounts* clients give their therapists about how they are in the world but with how they *actually* relate. In the process we at least begin to do justice to the fundamental tenet that *Dasein* is always situated *Dasein*, that people are always in relation and can only be understood in relation. The data are much more complete.

At the same time, my sense is that facilitating a therapeutic alliance where there may be conflict, where clients may talk over each other, interrupt each other and perhaps seek to undermine or be confrontational with the therapist, asks a lot of us. We should not necessarily assume that every existential therapist either wants, or is able, to provide couples therapy.

References

Cohn HW (1997). *Existential Thought and Therapeutic Practice: an introduction to existential psychotherapy*. London: Sage.

du Plock S (2009). The world of addiction. In: van Deurzen E, Young S (eds). *Existential Perspectives on Supervision: widening the horizon of psychotherapy and counselling*. Basingstoke: Palgrave Macmillan (pp67–77).

du Plock S (2002). Some reflections on an existential-phenomenological approach to addiction. *Existential Analysis 13*(1): 83–90.

du Plock S (2000). Gifts of life: an existential-phenomenological approach to shopping addiction. In: Baker A (ed). *Serious Shopping: essays on consumerism and psychotherapy*. London: Sage (pp73–94).

du Plock S, Fisher J (2005). An existential perspective on addiction. In: van Deurzen E, Arnold-Baker C (eds). *Existential Perspectives on Human Issues: a handbook for therapeutic practice*. Basingstoke: Palgrave Macmillan (pp67–77).

May R (1983). *The Discovery of Being: writings in existential psychology*. New York, NY: WW Norton & Co.

May R, Angel E, Ellenberger HF (eds) (1958). *Existence: a new dimension in psychiatry and psychology*. New York, NY: Basic Books.

Shaffer HJ (1994). Denial, ambivalence and countertransferential hate. In: Levin J, Weiss R (eds). *The Dynamics and Treatment of Alcoholism*. Northvale, NJ: Jason Aronson.

Spinelli E (2007). *Practising Existential Psychotherapy: the relational world*. London: Sage.

Spinelli E (1997). *Tales of Un-knowing: therapeutic encounters from an existential perspective*. London: Duckworth (republished 2006 by PCCS Books).

Spinelli E (1994). *Demystifying Therapy*. London: Constable (republished 2006 by PCCS Books).

van Deurzen E, Iacovou S (eds) (2013). *Existential Perspectives on Couple Therapy*. London: Palgrave Macmillan.

Walters GD (1999). *The Addiction Concept: working hypothesis or self-fulfilling prophesy?* Needham Heights, MA: Allyn & Bacon.

Wurm C (1997). Deciding about drinking: an existential approach to alcohol dependence. In: Du Plock S (ed). *Case Studies in Existential Psychotherapy and Counselling*. Chichester: John Wiley & Sons (pp141–156).

7

Stoking the flames: coaching towards authentic and impassioned change

Sasha van Deurzen-Smith

At the time of writing, I am, as far as I know, one of only five people in the world to have a master's degree in existential coaching. Most practitioners will have trained either as an existential therapist or in some other coaching modality before deciding to explore this field. As such, I feel a particular devotion to the subject, and I am delighted to be able to share this, and to continue to develop existential coaching as a profession in its own right. Over the course of my studies, private practice and subsequent teaching, I have seen many differing takes on existential coaching, and I continue to be fascinated by the diversity that an existential approach allows. In this chapter, as well as giving an overview of what existential coaching is and how one might apply it, I am also sharing my own, unique style.

The concept of coaching is sometimes difficult to tie down. This is partly because coaching is still in its youth and partly due to the diversity of its scope. The concept is largely attributed to the work of Timothy Gallwey in his 1974 book *The Inner Game of Tennis*, in which he explores a more holistic approach to sports coaching and the value of looking at psychological aspects of the player rather than just focusing on the practical elements of their athleticism. It was not long before the concept was adopted by the corporate world and coaching diversified into various strands, such as career coaching, executive coaching and leadership coaching. This led eventually, with the aid of self-help books, to life coaching. The International Coach Federation (ICF, 2018) defines coaching as:

...partnering with clients in a thought-provoking and creative process that inspires them to maximize their personal and professional potential.

This sense of 'maximizing potential' is key in differentiating between coaching and psychotherapy, which in many ways are very similar. Coaching is specifically concerned with forward movement, working in a focused way on a particular goal, concern or area of life, whereas psychotherapy might be described as a more general dialogue, with the intention of healing emotional problems (van Deurzen & Hanaway, 2012). For this reason, the client groups of the two professions are significantly different. In some cases, a client might be suitable for either coaching or psychotherapy, but the expectations around each choice differ.

Although the field is still largely unregulated, the more robust coaching approaches are rooted in psychological and psychotherapeutic knowledge. Of course, in the case of existential coaching, it is also underpinned by philosophical insight. This is most obviously achieved by adopting a phenomenological approach (Husserl, 1931): a method of enquiry in which the enquirer stays, as best she can, with the experience of the respondent. The result is a greater understanding not only of the specific experience being explored but of what this reveals about how the client finds herself in relation to the world. For example, part way through a session, the sunlight shifts and a rainbow is created in the room. The client notices, and immediately shifts focus from the original dialogue to an appreciation of the rainbow. On exploration, the client describes how she sees this as a good omen, some sign from the Universe that renews her faith in her ability to come through her difficulties and find the 'pot of gold' at the end. In this example, the client reveals a distinctly spiritual worldview, and seems to thrive on a sense that she is receiving guidance and reassurance from an outside source. In contrast, my own experience is an immediate desire to identify the source of the rainbow, revealing a preoccupation with understanding how the world works.

By searching for this insight into the unique perspectives we carry with us throughout our lives, we begin to understand how to work *with* rather than *against* ourselves. As such, a philosophical understanding of our own lives is invaluable, and takes both client and coach beyond the next goal or target and into something far more profound and self-sustaining. Where traditional coaching approaches focus on applying tools and strategies in order to help the client towards their next goal, existential coaching teaches the client to think philosophically about their life, with the understanding that this insight will not only give greater momentum but will ultimately allow them to make more considered, authentic and personally meaningful choices. If we can get in touch with our values and understand how to work with them, while adopting the existential attitude of not shying away from difficulties or shirking responsibilities, we create a much more robust outcome for the work. This can transcend many different scenarios we might find ourselves in, and thus acts as a strategy for living rather than a strategy for a specific set of problems.

Phenomenology and intuition

There are many aspects of a phenomenological approach that are worth exploring in more detail but I have chosen to focus here on the notion of intuition within phenomenological work, as it's something that I value greatly in my own practice.

The term 'intuition' has often been attributed some mystical quality, as if it gives access to knowledge that is not directly available, by way of some oracle or spiritual awareness. Yet the role of intuition is important, particularly when working phenomenologically. Husserl (1931), Heidegger (1962) and Kant (1965) were significantly at odds with one another regarding their definitions of intuition, and each of their interpretations has some insight to offer. Husserl believed that intuition goes beyond purely sensory phenomena and included *eidetic* or *categorial* intuition in his phenomenological method. Heidegger was sceptical of the use of such intuition of essence in philosophical interpretation, and argued that it could never be free of presuppositions. I am wary of the common assumption that there is a chain reaction between intuition and imagination. Husserl defined them very clearly as separate processes. Often, when we have an intuitive sense about something, we start to create an imagined story around it. For example, a woman walks into her house and immediately has a strong feeling that something is 'off'. She begins to imagine the scenario that has caused this experience: for example, by supposing that there has been an intruder. Unbeknownst to her, she has picked up on subtle changes in the environment, such as the faint smell of cigarettes in her non-smoking household, or a breeze from an open window. Although her intuition may have led her to a correct assumption, it is an assumption created by her immediate flight of imagination. The intuiting, however, was gained from a pre-reflective observation of immediate facts.

The role of intuition for a coach, therefore, is to alert us not to the potentiality raised by this awareness (in the form of our capacity for imagination), but to recognise the metaphorical signpost and identify the information that has led us to that point. If we can detach intuition from imagination and trust its significance, we can also use it to forge a greater capacity for empathy. When we intuit the significance of a particular statement made by a client, a flight of imagination about its emotional context reduces our understanding to guesswork. An acknowledgement of our intuitive sense and a careful checking of the steps that have led to this awareness can allow the emotional content to emerge. This is not a solo activity but one that must be conducted with the client, and can reveal their own internal misinterpretation of their emotional responses, often because they have reduced them to more simplistic, unambiguous feelings rather than appreciating the complexity of their emotional life. In recognising the inherent ambiguity and intertwining nature of emotion, we open ourselves to a greater understanding and the reasons for our 'stuckness'.

Attunement and the four dimensions of existence

To be an effective coach is to be able to attune deeply with the client to a point where they feel understood and heard, and also to put the coach's own uniqueness into the relationship. A client might have a very good understanding of their problem. They may have wrestled with it on a cognitive level and understand where they are going wrong, but this has not yet solved it. What they have not yet done is grappled with it on a broader scale in order to gain a holistic understanding of their situation. An application of the four dimensions of existence, as developed by Binswanger (1963) with further additions and conceptualisations by van Deurzen (1988), is an invaluable resource for opening up our insight into the client's perspective. These dimensions are classified as *Umwelt* (the physical dimension); *Mitwelt* (the social dimension); *Eigenwelt* (the personal dimension), and *Überwelt* (the spiritual or philosophical dimension).

The client's understanding of their presenting issue is usually rooted in one particular dimension and a skilled existential coach will be able to lead an exploratory dialogue in order to investigate the hitherto less examined dimensions. The goal is not to root the focus of the predicament by pinning it down to one level of experience but to adopt a holistic attitude that accounts for the delicate and complex interplay between all four dimensions, to create a shift in the client's approach to the problem and, thereby, find a solution.

The coaching relationship often begins with an assumption that the coach has managed either through hard work or through some natural gift to have rooted themselves so firmly in a state of confidence, productivity and achievement that they have become a being-in-itself (Heidegger, 1962), unflappable in their ability for self-actualisation. The client is seeking a mentor who can guide them through their current difficulties and into a state of perpetual success, at which point they will know that they have 'arrived'. This is common territory in the coaching world, which thrives on notions of goal-setting, achievements and target-driven work. Yet, to someone with an existential perspective, this is clearly flawed. That is not to say that I do not consider coaching to be an essentially goal-orientated process, designed to accomplish the best possible outcome within a given situation. In many ways it is this property that defines it as a helping profession. An existential perspective to coaching simply broadens our understanding of what the goal is. It understands that, although change of a practical nature is a common outcome of coaching work, a change of perspective or a moment of insight is likely to be more valuable to the client.

This insight may in turn create progress towards a particular goal. It may also change the goal altogether. Yet this is a secondary concern. My main interest when working with a client is how to empower them to think philosophically about whatever faces them in life. I am always focusing on the psycho-educational aspect of coaching, on enabling clients to become more aware of their thought processes, and on examining the complexities of their decision-making and the forces at work both inside and outside their locus of control. The presenting issue is simply a microcosm for exploring this, and if we merely find solutions towards a practical endpoint, the client will take away no understanding of how to replicate this is in the myriad other aspects of their world. If we can become philosophical thinkers, we can learn to face our challenges and choices with authenticity and insight.

Naïvety, curiosity and the use of metaphor and imagery

Of course, it would be dishonest to imply that this process of attunement is solely reliant on the client accepting our mutual status as thinking partner, rather than expert and mentee, for the coach's own journey is also crucial. That is not to say that I consider myself to be the 'expert', but when beginning with a new client – or even at the start of a session with an ongoing client – it is easy to use this assumed status as a safety net. To be able to lay out our own naïvety, sometimes dubbed un-knowing (Parsons, 1984; Casement, 1985; Spinelli, 1997), and accept that we do not know how best to help or, indeed, necessarily what the problem at hand is, demands vulnerability as a practitioner. It can cause the client to feel thrown if they are not yet used to this way of working, and it can cause the coach to feel insecure. Yet, if we continue to try to hide behind a formula, framework or sense of a right or wrong way of facing life's challenges, we ultimately cheat the process. The moment we surrender these is the moment that the real work can begin.

This openness to the reality of our mutual lostness allows curiosity and possibility into the relationship. It also allows the coach to learn from the client's experiences, rather than insisting on being the teacher. In this space, we work together to unravel the intricacies of the client's thoughts, emotions and assumptions about the world and the reasons behind their decisions. We then use this insight to co-create a new way of living that works with the specific strengths and weaknesses of the client.

I am a great believer in the power of metaphor and imagery as an aid to facing both our own and the client's sense of un-knowing. When we choose to explore an experience through the use of imagery rather than language, we immediately detach from our pre-established narrative. We begin to explore the nuances and pre-reflective senses of the predicament at hand, and come up with new solutions that are not apparent within the limited confines of our specific language and vocabulary (Glouberman, 2010). There is an immediacy to image work, largely informed by the intuitive capacity of which I spoke earlier. If a client volunteers an image or sensation to describe their experience, it is an opportunity to delve into new territory and explore their world in a uniquely revealing way.

A working metaphor

When a client walks into my private practice, they usually know what they want to get out of the coaching relationship. This is because, for the most part, they have chosen coaching rather than psychotherapy in order to address some specific block in their lives. They have a goal, or a challenge that needs to be overcome. It might be a clearly defined target (for example, they wish to lose weight) or something vaguer (perhaps they just feel that something is missing from their lives and they want to find it). I imagine their lives as a ball of mixed wool – different colours and textures all tangled up, each thread an aspect of their life. To be able to create something from this, we cannot focus on one strand in isolation; we need to understand how each relates to the other. This will not only help us to untangle the current situation; it will enable us to weave something robust and unique.

This is not about cherry-picking the best and discarding everything else, but about understanding the interplay of each of these threads in our lives. So, the client who wants to lose two stone does not simply focus on their desire to fit into that old pair of jeans and their knowledge of how to do so. If this were enough to instill change, they would have done it long ago and would not need a coach to aid the process. Instead, they begin to understand the intricacies of the situation: how they struggle with the experience of turning down a colleague's homemade cake, for example. Or how the process of cooking a luxurious meal makes them feel a sense of self-care that they do not experience in any other aspect of their lives. This insight is invaluable because it takes us out of the pre-established narrative that the client knows unthinkingly and into uncharted territory. If the client in this example attempts to simply remove that thread of self-care, the new reality that they have been weaving will eventually fall apart. They must find a way to fulfil this need in a more reflective way, so that it supports rather than hinders their newly emerging sense of self. Likewise, they must develop a readiness to adapt and an acceptance of the inevitability of upset and challenge. No matter how beautiful and robust our garment may be, it cannot remain a good fit forever; it is ultimately at the mercy of the wear and tear of living.

Case study

Narin came to the UK from Turkey in her late teens. She was now in her mid-20s and worked as a receptionist. She was impeccably dressed, extremely well-mannered but rather shy and withdrawn. When I first spoke to her on the phone, Narin's voice had been so quiet and wavering that I had misspelled her name. Now, in front of me, I saw the full impact of her timidity. Under her dark, finely tailored suit was a small, fragile frame. Her subtle make-up and naturally beautiful features gave her the kind of appearance that many women would find enviable. Yet Narin's eyes projected a sort of vacant sadness that betrayed her put-together look. She rarely made eye contact, and her perfectly symmetrical fringe acted as a buffer between her gaze and mine.

After introducing myself and explaining my approach, I invited her to describe what had brought her to coaching and what she hoped to get out of it. Narin proceeded to give me a long list of goals, which seemed to cover almost every facet of her life. As she spoke, I was struck by what I perceived to be a combination of vulnerability and strength. It was as if she had a great untapped power that was currently only manifesting as a desire for self-actualisation and greater control over her life. I suppose this duality is what had drawn her to coaching. The tension between these two facets of Narin fascinated me but I sensed that she was not herself aware of it. I decided to set this aside initially; I didn't want to make an assumption about her experiences of herself and of her world. However, I knew that, if my intuition was right, this might become a theme in our work.

She told me that her goals were to quit smoking, to recover her social life, to change career and to find a greater sense of passion in her life. I began to feel tense as I listened to her long list of expectations and demands of herself, and I wondered if I would be able to help her to navigate this process effectively and how willing she was to put in the work. As if she understood my qualms, when she came to the end of the list, she looked me straight in the eye and declared, 'I know that this will take me a long time and that it will require a lot of effort. I am prepared for that commitment.'

The question now was where to begin. I asked Narin if she had a sense of a natural starting point, or whether this was something we needed to explore. She told me that she felt so overwhelmed by the amount of changes she wanted to make that she found it difficult to reach any clarity and begin the work. I reassured her that there was no pressure to be certain of her first steps and encouraged her to start by simply talking me through her thoughts. I said that, in doing so, something was likely to emerge. I got the sense that Narin felt a heavy burden of responsibility, and I was keen to allow her to use our relationship as a means to claim a greater sense of freedom.

It often shocks me how imbalanced we can be between responsibility and freedom, and how pronounced this tension can be in the simple dynamics of a session. Some clients feel it's necessary to monitor the time so closely that they are the ones who take responsibility for bringing the session to a close; others rely on me to provide a five or 10-minute wind-down period before the end or they would never stop. I have been known to ask clients in the latter camp to be in charge of time-keeping for one session as a point for exploration. There was no need for this with Narin; she was staunchly in the former category.

As we delved into her life, it quickly became apparent that Narin felt that her desires for change stemmed from the same basic issue. She did not feel that she was living authentically. This was particularly relevant with regard to her career. Since moving to the UK, she had been working as a receptionist and, although she felt capable in the job, she was more and more aware that her passions lay in the world of fashion. Narin told me that she felt most motivated and most engaged when she was shopping, styling outfits or looking after her clothes. Indeed, when she spoke of these experiences, she radiated a sort of energy that rarely showed itself in our sessions.

I was amazed how something that I considered to be mundane, such as ironing, evoked such a wholehearted and warm response in her. Yet this engagement was unsustainable for Narin; she would quickly interrupt her explorations by dismissing them as shallow. It seemed that, no matter how passionate she was about the subject, she could not help but shut it down with a self-deprecating statement about superficiality. At this point, I began to look at the problem using the four-worlds model. Narin was firmly rooting her passion at a physical level when she talked about shallowness. In fact, she had a tendency when discussing it to stick only to the practical elements. She would describe in intricate detail the way a garment looked, or the process of how she looked after it. I began to wonder about a more well-rounded picture of this part of her life that was obviously so important to her. I knew that there must be a deeper meaning to this in order for it to have such an impact.

In the hope of encouraging her to investigate the intricacies of her experiences, I invited her to tell me what it felt like when she styled an outfit for herself, how others responded to her fashion sense and how it felt to care for something so lovingly as she cared for her clothing. We explored the pleasure it brought her to buy a new item, how she would search for months for the 'right' pair of boots and how her mother had taught her as a child to tailor clothing in order to perfect and personalise it. Soon, a bigger picture emerged. The threads of her experience began to form a web, mapping her perspective as illustrated in Figure 7.1.

Figure 7.1: Narin's web of experience

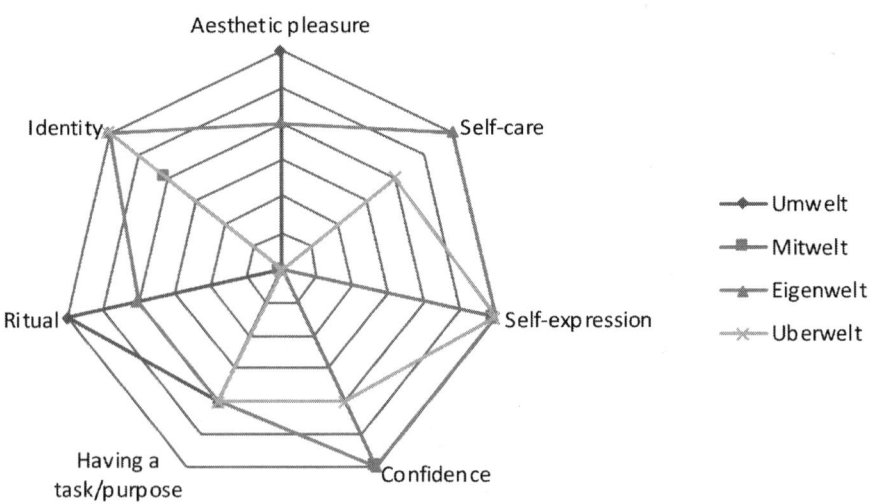

It became clear that the power of fashion for Narin was far more complicated than simply an aesthetic pleasure. She was passionate about the way fashion offers people a means for self-expression. For her, it was a way of putting one's best foot forward, no matter what the circumstances; a way of showing the world who you are and what you are made of. It was also profoundly about self-care, something that she struggled with. In fact, although this was clearly deeply personal for her, Narin actually wanted to share this experience with others, and to help people to explore this power for themselves. This was where her passion was emanating from, and I thought it was essential for her to remain in touch with this, so that she could no longer dismiss it as mere superficiality.

When we were not discussing fashion, there was something very cold and disconnected about Narin. I was not sure if this was purely my own perception, a response that she somehow triggered in me, or whether this was indicative of something outside our specific dynamic. As we began to explore her social life in more detail, it became apparent that this reaction was not unique to me. She described several friendships that had turned sour because she had felt that people were taking advantage of her. The same was true of her close family. Although in some ways her relationships with her parents and siblings might be considered close, they were peppered with resentment. She saw them frequently but felt unable to connect with them. This, she explained, stemmed from deep resentment about how they spoke to her and how she had been treated as a child. As I listened to her stories about this treatment, I was at times shocked by the cruelty of it and felt deeply moved as I connected with Narin's distress. Her childhood experiences of physical chastisement, the unsupportive tone that her parents took with her on a day-to-day basis and the overriding sense of humiliation that they evoked in her all formed a picture of why she had become so disconnected in her communication. For the first time, I felt that I actually empathically understood something of Narin's aloof nature. As she recounted her experiences she wept.

Traditionally such a display of 'negative' emotion is not encouraged in the coaching environment (Duffell & Lawton-Smith, 2015). This is partially because practitioners and professional bodies are wary of the fine line between coaching and therapy, but it is also because there is a perception of such emotions as disempowering. As an existential coach, I am acutely aware of both the inevitability of such emotions and the importance of working with them rather than struggling against them and upholding this taboo. I knew that if I had dismissed these explorations as more strongly associated with psychotherapeutic terrain, I would have cheated us both out of this deeper recognition of her internal world. I would have further cemented her need to disconnect if I refused to engage with her vulnerability.

It was allowing this distress into the coaching relationship that created the biggest catalyst for change. As we began to explore Narin's struggle, she started to conceptualise it as a darkness that she felt was ever present and oppressive. Whenever something made her more aware of this darkness, she would become self-destructive, picking fights with people, showing up late for work and sacrificing basic elements of self-care – for example, neglecting to eat regular meals. It was as if this darkness took her over and she became unable to connect with her desire for change. Yet we both knew that the desire was there. It was this desire that had brought her to coaching in the first place and had kept her coming regularly.

I reminded her of this, of how strong this part of her could be when the shadow that she spoke of was at bay. I asked her what happened to this fire when the darkness crept in. She told me that the fire all but disappeared, leaving a faint glow of light in the blackness, a single flame. In describing it further, she told me how fragile it became in that moment, how she could see it dancing, as if it were about to be snuffed out by some passing breeze. I asked her what she would need to do to keep the flame going, and she replied that it needed her protection. We devised a plan that Narin would focus her attention on the flame when she felt disconnected from her passion and her drive, and that she would do what she could to protect it. I suggested to her that the light of the flame is more powerful in its contrast to the darkness; that you cannot have a concept of light without a concept of dark. Although Narin agreed with this on an intellectual level, she told me that that the fear of the light being vanquished altogether stopped her from being able to connect with this understanding in a wholehearted way.

Over the next few sessions we frequently revisited Narin's metaphor. We continued working together in long-term coaching, often dubbed 'transformational coaching' (a term derived from Mezirow's (1975) concept of transformational learning due to the focus on co-creating a profound shift in perspective, usually over a long period of time), and she told me that the notion of protecting her light had been extremely useful. She was able to take charge of difficult situations in a way that she did not previously feel capable of. She felt more in touch with her passions and with her desire for change. She began to make some courageous moves – applying for entry-level positions in fashion retail and eventually entering the industry. She contacted an old friend and arranged a photo shoot, which she styled, to form part of a portfolio of her work. I can see now, Narin had moved from protecting the light to stoking the flames.

Although Narin had come to me with a range of goals she wanted to work on, I did not place particular significance on one or the other. A non-existential coach may have honed in on one at a time, in order to keep that traditionally target-driven thrust to the work. As an existential practitioner, I stayed with exactly what Narin brought to the work, which was a profound sense of yearning for change, peppered by a lack of self-compassion and general misunderstanding about her own motivations. Narin had become her own saboteur, and by addressing this with me, in a gentle, practical and heartfelt way, she began to find her stride.

Discussion with the editor

Simon: I felt quite intrigued, as I read your chapter, about the extent to which existential coaching is similar to, and distinct from, existential therapy. When you stated it is 'essentially a goal-orientated process', I wondered how this could be reconciled with a phenomenological attitude and, in particular, with horizontalisation. When you talked about using the four dimensions of existence as a useful guide, it seemed to me existential coaching and existential therapy have a lot in common. And then I recalled my own experience of working in a broadly coaching capacity for employee assistance programmes where the presenting problem generally morphed into a philosophical discussion about meaning and ethics and values, and it seemed to me that the relationship is quite complex. I wonder how you see these similarities and whether you feel there is a creative tension here?

Sasha: This is an interesting question, and I do think that existential coaching and existential therapy are largely similar. This is, though, the main way in which they differ and, as you identify, it filters into the actual process of working and not just the outcome itself. For me, personally, there is a huge creative tension. I come from a family totally embedded in the therapeutic world and have a tendency to get very absorbed in the more psychotherapeutic elements of existential coaching. However, it is important to remember the contract between coach and client, and therefore the expectations. It is incredibly easy to get seduced into falling down the 'rabbit hole' of these sorts of phenomenological explorations.

In coaching, the expectation and contract are that we are working towards some sort of practical end-point or concrete change, and this must be kept in mind throughout the work. As I touched on in this chapter, for me there is a distinction between psychotherapeutic and psycho-educational aspects of both therapy and coaching. Coaching focuses on psychoeducation with elements of therapeutic work and therapy is usually the reverse ratio. Both of these can be done in a phenomenological way, though perhaps the phenomenology of psychotherapeutic work is more recognised as therapy is an older profession. We probably need more exploration of what it means to work phenomenologically in coaching in a practical way.

Simon: Following on from my previous question, I wonder if you can say a little more about what it means to empower clients 'to think philosophically'? In asking this, I am mindful of the position of philosophical consultancy, which seems to advocate teaching clients (or 'visitors') how to apply the theories of specific philosophers to problems of living. Obviously, any practitioner setting out to do this needs a detailed knowledge of academic philosophy, and I am assuming this is not your own intention.

Sasha: The application of philosophical consultancy is an interesting one, and certainly, as you suggest, different from my assertion that clients can be empowered to think philosophically. Before I address the differences, let me start by explaining that I am not opposed to some philosophical education as part of existential coaching, should the coach be able to deliver this and the client explicitly ask for it in relation to a particular dilemma. What I am suggesting in thinking philosophically, though, is not about learning how to apply specific philosophical concepts but rather how to foster a philosophical attitude to one's life. By this, I mean that clients can learn to develop a more reflective, enquiring and insight-driven approach to living. This is quite distinct from applying academic philosophical concepts to one's life. It is in fact based on the notion that we can develop the capacity to think deeply, and in our own way, about our lives, the way we think, and life more generally. The aim is to empower people to use this kind of deep thinking in order to develop their own ideas about their lives and in turn to figure out how best to move forward.

Simon: At the beginning of this chapter you wrote enthusiastically about the development of existential coaching 'as a profession in its own right', and I wonder how you see the future for this relatively new field and what will need to be established for it to have a vibrant future?

Sasha: My belief is that existential coaching is a good answer to the current lack of focus on psychoeducation in society. My hope is that existential coaching will also become a sort of antidote to the current distrust around life coaching generally. If we have robust training and regulation in place, existential coaching can fill the gap that currently exists between psychotherapy (which people often seek after or during trauma, crisis or a severe mental health issue) and life coaching (which has a tendency to over-simplify human issues and suffers from minimal training and poorly established professional regulation).

This sort of psychoeducation is, I think, essential and should be accessible to everyone before they fall into the kind of crisis that unexamined living can lead to. This would undoubtedly require greater public awareness about the field of coaching generally, as well as the specific contributions of an existential approach, and the importance of empowering people through self-reflective practice. It also requires more robust professional regulation and training. It is an exciting time for those who are keen not only to participate in formalising the profession but to act as ambassadors, translating the somewhat esoteric world of existential philosophy into the lived experience of an existential attitude that should, and can, be highly relatable and accessible.

References

Binswanger L (1963). *Being-in-the-World*. New York, NY: Basic Books.

Casement P (1985). *On Learning from the Patient*. London: Routledge.

Duffell P, Lawton-Smith C (2015). The challenges of working with emotion in coaching. *The Coaching Psychologist* 11(1): 32–41.

Gallwey T (1974). *The Inner Game of Tennis*. New York, NY: Random House.

Glouberman D (2010). *Life Choices, Life Changes*. Shanklin: Skyros Books.

Heidegger M (1962). *Being and Time* (J Macquarrie, E Robinson trans). Oxford: Blackwell Publishing.

Husserl E (1931). *Ideas* (WR Boyce Gibson trans). London: Allen & Unwin.

ICF (2018). Frequently asked questions. [Online.] *International Coach Federation*. https://coachfederation.org/faqs (accessed 30 July 2018).

Kant I (1965). *Immanuel Kant's Critique of Pure Reason* (N Kemp Smith trans). New York, NY: St. Martin's Press.

Mezirow J (1975). *Education for perspective transformation: women's re-entry programs in community colleges*. New York, NY: Centre for Adult Education, Teachers College, Columbia University.

Parsons M (1984). Psychoanalysis as vocation and martial art. *International Review of Psycho-Analysis* 11(4): 453–462.

Spinelli E (1997). *Tales of Un-Knowing*. London: Duckworth & Co (republished in 2006 by PCCS Books).

van Deurzen E, Hanaway M (2012). *Existential Perspectives on Coaching*. Basingstoke: Palgrave Macmillan.

van Deurzen-Smith E (1988). *Existential Counselling in Practice*. London: Sage.

8

Existential group therapy

Rimantas Kočiūnas

This chapter discusses principles that existential group therapy may be based on. It argues that any model of existential group therapy is informed by an understanding of existential therapy in general and also by the specific theory of group therapy to which that particular model relates. Referring to existential therapy, I suggest that its essential element is not so-called existential themes raised in the process of therapy, but the existential philosophical lens through which any issues or problems are discussed.

Many paradigms of psychotherapy (psychoanalytic-psychodynamic, cognitive-behaviour, Gestalt and so forth) attempt also to apply their theoretical principles to therapeutic work in groups. Thus, there are many different models of group therapy, though their variety is less than for individual therapy. This is because the work with a psychotherapeutic group is much more complex. Also, training programmes for group therapists are much less available. In recent years, more and more popularity has been gained by support groups of various formats that require, in fact, only knowledge of universal principles of group dynamics, unrelated to any particular theory.

Existential therapy also strives to apply its principles to psychotherapeutic groups. It is important to note that the existential understanding of human life could be an adequate foundation for the development of existential group therapy. This is expressly mentioned both in the philosophical conceptions that this understanding is based on Martin Heidegger's concept that '*Dasein* ist *Mitsein*' (1926/1962: 155) and by many theories of existential therapy (van Deurzen, 2012; Spinelli, 2015). In the existential sense, a human being is viewed as a complex and multidimensional entity, inevitably interconnected with the world of other living beings and objects, as a unique process of life developing within the intersubjective context.

However, there are few publications in English discussing possibilities of existential therapy in groups (Hora, 1968; Mullan, 1978, 1992; Cohn, 1997; Jacobsen, 1997; Kočiūnas, 2000, 2015; Ventegodt, Andersen & Merrick, 2003; Tantam, 2005; Witemb, 2012). Occasionally one can find some publications on the application of the existential approach (although its underlying theory is not always immediately clear) when working with homogeneous groups, such as clients/patients suffering death anxiety (Garrow & Walker, 2001), cancer patients (Kissane et al, 2004) and patients with chronic illness (Spira, 1997). On the other hand, Irvin Yalom, for example, one of the most prominent figures in group psychotherapy, who is sometimes seen as belonging to the existential therapy realm, speaks about existential group therapy as something incomprehensible: 'I do not practice "existential group therapy" – in fact, I don't know what that would be' (2002: xv).

Hans Cohn once wrote that 'unfortunately, existential thinkers and therapists have not yet concerned themselves, in any detail, with group phenomena' (1997: 57), and in fact nothing has really changed up to now. So the question of how to formulate the most important principles on which the practice of existential group therapy is based is still relevant. It is this question that I attempt to answer in this article, drawing on my own considerable practical experience in working with groups.

Theoretical assumptions of existential group therapy

The nature of existential group therapy would depend on how we understand existential therapy and group therapy, and where we see their main focus.

The discussion initiated by Mick Cooper and Ernesto Spinelli in 2012/13 in the virtual space of the existential therapy community, which reached its peak activity following the First World Congress for Existential Therapy in London in 2015, revealed a wide variety of understandings and definitions of existential therapy. Although any universal definition of existential therapy is doomed to be a compromise of multiple different views, with some oversimplification, two approaches might be identified, one being more superficial or 'thematic', and another a deeper one, based on 'existential position'.

The first is obviously represented by Irvin Yalom (1980), whose attitude might be expressed as follows: existential therapy is the upper storey of any psychotherapy, where it turns to universal existential concerns and givens faced by any person. Thus 'existentiality' of psychotherapy depends on discussion of the so-called existential themes or issues. In the context of group therapy, such approach is illustrated in the phrase by Bo Jacobsen:

> Existential-analytic group therapy... with a special focus on existential issues, and sometimes with a special initial selection of clients, pointing towards common existential problems. (1997: 159)

Another approach links existential therapy with the existentiality of the therapeutic worldview of the therapist, with his system of depth attitudes towards human life and the world, and with the relating of the client's problems to wider perspectives of his or her life and its socio-cultural context and the phenomenological stance of the therapist (see, for example, the writings of Rollo May, Emmy van Deurzen and Ernesto Spinelli). The understanding, adhered to by the therapist, would determine what will get more attention in therapy, and so too in group therapy: the analysis of 'existential issues and problems' or development and support of the existential therapeutic process.

Speaking of group therapy, three notions are most often encountered: a) the group as a context or background, used for dealing with problems of individual participants (ie. Gestalt therapy, psychodrama and so forth); b) the group as a whole, 'a collective individual' (ie. psychoanalytical models, especially the theory of Wilfred Bion); c) the group as a process of interpersonal interactions reflecting participants' problems in life, most of all in relationships. These problems are explored in the context of interactions between participants and between participants and the therapist, and the therapist is involved in this process more as an assistant or helper – interpersonal group psychotherapy by Irvin Yalom, existential group psychotherapy by Hugh Mullan, group analysis by Siegfried Foulkes.

It seems that the latter understanding of a therapeutic group and the conceptions of group therapy related to it come closest to the existential understanding of a human being as *Mitsein* and could serve as important base points for contemporary models of existential group therapy that are currently under construction.

The core of interpersonal group psychotherapy, according to Irvin Yalom (Yalom & Leszcz, 2005), is continuous work with interpersonal interactions in the group, striving to understand them in the context of the participants' and the group's life, and exploration of emerging feelings and emotions. It is supposed that, in the group, the content (what is discussed) is not so important; what matters is the process (how an issue is discussed and what consequences, as a result, are brought to the relations in the group). The process of therapy evolves with the group moving through different stages of maturity, somewhat similarly to the ontogenetic development of an individual.

As Irvin Yalom has put in one interview: 'Therapy is not really life *per se*, but it's a dress rehearsal for life' (Overholser, 2005). It is crucial here that the therapist's position would be based on openness, genuineness and spontaneity. In the same interview, Irvin Yalom elaborates:

> If you're going to be a good group therapist, you tend to be much more open with yourself and more disclosing. You can't use your professional title in the group and yet call people by their first name with everyone else in the group. You want the group to be engaged and informal and so you start being on a first name basis with patients, you tend not to play the expert.

Closely related to such understanding of group psychotherapy, another American psychiatrist and psychoanalyst, Hugh Mullan (1978, 1992), has also attempted to apply the ideas of existential philosophy and phenomenology to group therapy. He also stresses the importance of interpersonal relations and emotional experience in therapy, allowing only secondary roles to interpretation. Interactions between the participants' and the therapist's experiences are seen by Mullan as crucial: the patient cannot change without the therapist also undergoing changes. In his opinion, the therapy must stand on three principles, as follows.

1. Subjectivity. This is the very essence of therapy, and on the part of not only the participant in the group but the therapist as well. Therapy is impossible without the therapist's personal involvement and personal development. The therapist must be open and sincere, not seeking shelter behind his/her role or status. Any system of therapy, when relying on schemes, inevitably remains inauthentic. It is important to keep in mind that the group is not a simple and direct reflection of 'outer' life; its life is unique, intensive and multi-layered, due to the subjectivities of all taking part in it.

2. Mutuality. This principle means that subjectivity is inseparable from intersubjectivity. Both the participants and the therapist face the same challenges and paradoxes in life. The work in therapy always involves mutual self-disclosure in the process of joint search for the meaning of an experience.
3. Non-rational experience. This means that sessions of the group are not planned in advance and interactions between the participants are not 'pre-programmed' in any way. Spontaneous reactions of the participants and the therapist are considered the most significant. To be better prepared to accept new experience, one has to learn to be 'un-knowing', unaware of what might come into being – ie. able to tolerate uncertainty. Special value is assigned to spontaneous associations, dreams, phantasies and unexplainable feelings.

Some representatives of existential therapy (Cohn, 1997; Jacobsen, 1997) suggest that existential work with psychotherapeutic groups is possible using the principles of group analysis, with some modification, and introducing an 'existential dimension' to the understanding of group processes.

Hans Cohn (1997) has formulated the most important reference points of an existential-phenomenological approach to group therapy. These statements, to a certain extent, define the theoretical foundations of the 'existential therapeutic group', its basic assumptions, the dynamics of the therapeutic process and the therapist's stance in such work.

- If 'being-in-the-world' always means 'being-with-others', if the world is essentially a 'with-world', or a relational field, then the 'individual' [...] can only be understood in a context of mutual disclosure.
- What we see as 'psychological' disturbances are then disturbances [...] of 'relatedness' and communication.
- The therapeutic group provides a context in which these relational and communicative disturbances can be observed, [...] experienced, and the possibilities of different ways of relating and communicating can be explored.
- The group therapist is a member of the group, with a specific task – to assist in the process of clarifying relational and communicative disturbances and potentialities of the group.
- Interpretations of group events are essentially the task of group members [...] Group phenomena have, of course, past roots and

future possibilities – but these are inevitably part of the present experience [...].

- The reliving of past relationships in the present group situation [...] is not primarily focused by the therapist but dispersed among members within the group [...].
- There is no reason why the therapist should not contribute his/her own understanding and feelings to the group process [...].
- Some group therapeutic approaches stress the necessity to focus on what happens 'within' the group and ignore what members bring into it from 'outside' [...] In an existential-phenomenological approach, with its emphasis on context, the possibility of such a division does not arise [...]. (Cohn, 1997: 55–56)

Such theoretical premises, while 'borrowed' from some other theories of group therapy, might serve very productively to describe specifically existential aspects of the process of a therapeutic group, of the sharing of responsibility by the therapist and the participants, and of the therapist's role and 'work' in such group.

Before discussing the model that I myself have developed – the Existential Experience (EE) group (which reflects the premises mentioned above) – it is important to mention at least briefly the radical version of existential group therapy, Intensive Therapeutic Life (ITL), that emerged in Lithuania some four decades ago and is still actively developed up to the present.

Aleksandras Alekseičikas, psychiatrist and psychotherapist, started to develop the model of Intensive Therapeutic Life as a therapeutic group in the 1970s. Due to its originality, deeply philosophical content, uncommon and emotionally very potent methods and the charismatic personality of its originator, this model quickly became and still is very popular in Lithuania and its neighbouring countries. It is used with groups of usual format but is often applied when working with large groups, and also as a therapeutic community model in the psychotherapy department of a psychiatric clinic (Alekseičikas, 1999, 2008, 2011).

The main element in the concept of Alekseičikas' psychotherapy is 'life' as the primary process, which encompasses everything in the very meaning of the word, including nothingness and non-life. It means activities by an individual, where everything – organic processes, senses, desires, memories, thinking, will, intuition, soul and spirit – are inextricably blended, thus growing into common being with other people and the world in general. In a therapeutic group, Alekseičikas creates specific circumstances that encourage the actualisation of the healing powers of life itself and reveal previously unnoticed possibilities of a freer and more realistic way of living day to day. Another important category is the time that specifically delineates our being – the limits set by time force us to plunge into life now, without delay. The 'time' of a group's life is conceived as progressing through human life periods – childhood, adolescence, maturity and old age. In fact, it fits with the natural stages of development of any psychotherapeutic group.

Another basic element of this group therapy model is action or activity that gives life its necessary intensity. All this is precisely and aphoristically summarised in a phrase, 'We live only once, but every day', which points to the necessity of filling every moment of life with deeds that have real outcomes. Living in the world means living and acting. The organising principle of the shared life of the group's participants is 'We'. Alekseičikas (1999: 12) quotes the Russian philosopher Levitsky, who maintained that 'I is not a part of We', but 'We is a part of I' – that is, I am not a part of the world but the world is a part of I.

Authentic relations in the group are determined not by the hours spent together but by the degree to which the other participants, all the group, 'settle to live' inside every participant. An extremely important condition of therapeutic group life is freedom. According to Alekseičikas (2008), neither freedom nor human being can be infinite. In psychotherapy, practising 'life' starts from a reminder that the psychotherapeutic group is not here to give anything to participants but demands their efforts and urges them to 'work' for (and in relation with) others, share, help and, through this, gain valuable experiences.

In this model of group therapy, the process involves thorough and realistic exploration of participants' values, meanings and worldviews, along with the knitting of the 'net' of the therapeutic process. This 'net' provides both growth of the group as an integral 'organism' and therapeutic changes in individual parts of this 'organism'. In the life of a group, considerable attention is given to the participants' understanding of possibilities arising from the very human nature offered by life (or lying dormant) in the participants themselves, as well as of restrictions, some of which are related to individual imperfections or limits, while others depend on the individual context of life or are determined by the same nature of human being. This is also one of the most important and universal aims of existential therapy.

This model of existential group therapy made a lasting impact on the development of existential therapy in Lithuania and its neighbouring countries. It also influenced significantly the variant of existential group therapy that is discussed in this article.

Existential experience and group therapy

In the model of Existential Experience (EE) in group psychotherapy that I developed (Kočiūnas, 1991, 1999, 2000, 2009, 2015), its theoretical foundations are evidently related to the ideas of Alekseičikas, Yalom, Mullan and Cohn that are discussed briefly above. The evolution of this model was also greatly influenced by almost 30 years of experience of practical work with psychotherapeutic groups of different character and format.

So, what does EE mean in this context? The notion of 'existential' represents understanding of a psychotherapeutic group as a process of life that is finite in time but indefinite in its content and that has no predefined regulations. Such a group may be characterised as a minimally structured life situation, in which participants, with their unique life histories and experiences, interact with each other and with the therapist and, in this way, create their 'group life'. This 'life', being a concentrated manifestation of the everyday lives of the participants and the therapist, reflects the complexity of life in general, with all its controversies and inconsistencies, possibilities and limitations. The participants' issues discussed in the group are viewed as resulting from their habitual ways of 'being-in-the-world', which prove to be insufficiently realistic and inadequate to the demands of specific life situations, as they lack connectedness with others and involve distorted or strained individual relations with the existential givens.

All these difficulties are revealed and discussed within the context of the relations and interactions of the participants of the group. Ultimately, what is happening between participants in the context of the ever-changing situations of the life of the group is more important than the analysis of the life of an individual participant. Here is how the participant D describes the lasting impact of his experience of this 'between' – of the group's focus on relations:

> Even after a few months there is still a very vivid impression that all the work in the group was an intensive and mutual experience of the tiny group life, far, very far exceeding just something being done with the problems of each participant. No, it was the time when relations between all the participants of the group were being knitted, spun as threads, and continuously deepened. With some, those connections were becoming stronger; with others, they tended to break, and then new possibilities – for new relations – continued to emerge. In this group, I faced all my problems with the relations in the 'larger' life. The boundary between what was going on in the group and my immediate reality beyond the group was becoming so impalpable that it was possible to fully capture

the texture of my life in its complete entirety. The experience of life in
the group was both sobering and healing, first and foremost due to the
openness and honesty of the participants. As one lady told me at the group,
'I will promise you nothing here, just to honestly say what I feel.'

The notion of 'experience' emphasises drawing on the participants' unique personal experience, which is revealed in the process of building the shared group life. In later stages of the group's development, the focus turns to explorations of the experience of being in a group with others. Here, any aspects of experience are considered important: conscious, rational, irrational, emotional, interpersonal, intrapsychic or transcendental, all of them being phenomena of real life. Experience in the EE group is not judged as either good or bad, valuable or worthless, meaningful or meaningless. Any life experience may be important, and it is even more important what a person does with it. Understanding one's own experience is extremely significant in achieving psychotherapeutic change. Moreover, interactions between the individual experiences of the participants possess extremely strong powers for transformation and ultimately determine the therapeutic impact of the group process.

Participant B describes her experience as follows:

Life in the group is like walking on the sharpest edge of reality. When I
manage being open with another person, it seems that my soul becomes
more sensitive, there is extreme subtlety added to all of my senses.
Touching something that is real causes me to shiver inside myself.
Sometimes this touch brings a lot of pain, while at times it happens
that this pain is less because what I feel and experience uncrowns
omnipotence of my own suffering and expands my field of vision...
For the group to be effective, the important thing is the participants'
willingness, ability and courage to share their painful issues, traumatic life
experiences, all immediate feelings that arise in the group.

Group purposes and goals

The main purpose of an EE group is to help participants understand the possibilities offered, and restrictions imposed, by life. The specific goals of the group's participants are directly related to the nature of their life problems and may differ widely. On the other hand, certain universal goals of the group are also present, such as:

- to extend boundaries of one's own feelings, ways of thinking, behaviour, understanding of values
- to help participants understand deeper and accept their own uniqueness in the context of universal conditions of human existence
- to encourage participants to accept responsibility for all that happens in life, also including difficulties (experience of the authorship of one's own life)
- to encourage realisation of one's own inevitable relatedness with others, to develop abilities to start and maintain close and long-term relations
- to develop abilities to choose freely and take risks in life, along with accepting inevitable experiences of anxiety and guilt
- to practise continually raising issues of meaning in daily life and seeing unconditional meaningfulness of life, in spite of its never-ending challenges and crises
- to practise integrating past experiences and future expectations for realistic and productive activity in the present.

These common goals serve as a certain context providing participants' problems with a deeper existential dimension.

Group dynamics

The work of a psychotherapeutic group implies group dynamics, which may be defined as the entirety of events and interactions in the group. Three levels of group dynamics may be distinguished:

- an individual participant with his/her intrapsychic dynamics
- interaction between the participants of the group and their interaction with the therapist
- development of a group as a whole.

The psychotherapeutic group works at all these levels simultaneously; their dynamic interactions provide conditions for the psychotherapeutic potential of a group to reveal itself.

The following conditions are mentioned in the EE group: 1) the desirability of openness and sincerity in sharing personal experiences and feelings, expressing thoughts arising in the 'here-and-now'; 2) choosing a way of being in a group, along with acceptance of responsibility for it;

3) the sharing of responsibility for the nature of life in a group. These conditions equally apply both to the participants of the group and to the therapist.

It is also very important to bear in mind the 'age' periods throughout the life of the group. They may be named figuratively as 'childhood', 'adolescence', 'maturity' and 'old age'. A group in its 'childhood' phase is characterised by immaturity, discrepancy between wishes and reality and helplessness when encountering difficulties in building common life of a group. Participants desire to do a lot, but appear to be able to achieve much less, and therefore feel dissatisfied and tend to blame others. They have difficulties in accepting 'the givens of life', and desperately strive for support from the therapist, while their ability to maintain 'being-with' is rudimentary.

The period of 'adolescence', or 'youth', is dominated by the search for one's own identity, along with perceiving the necessity to build relations with others and efforts to find a compromise between one's own interests and those of others. All this is accompanied by the participants' disagreements and conflicts while they try to find their own place in the group and learn to accept the 'otherness' and 'awkwardness' of other people. In this period, some participants often attempt to question the therapist's ways of working, and even his or her way of being in the group, demand their right to free self-expression (along with ignoring responsibility and the inevitable 'cost' incurred by such freedom), and resist the settled order of life of the group. Thus, through this quest for identity and related conflicts, the group as a whole is really born.

The 'mature' stage of group life allows the participants to draw on accumulated experience. One of the important aspects here is the ability to accept what has already happened as an integral part of self and as a valuable experience, notwithstanding its emotional background.

The final stage of the group – its 'old age' – allows participants to look back at the collective life that has been experienced by the participants and which is about to finish, and each participant also has an opportunity to review their own path in that group life. An important task at this stage is for participants to come to terms with the fact that the group's lifetime is finite, with their own imperfections and with those of other participants. This is the time when the participant comes to a deep understanding of their responsibility for their life and admits humbly that it is impossible to have or implement everything they might wish for.

This is a concentrated review of the process of the group growth by participant G:

> Summarising all the way that the group had travelled, it seems that we were growing very quickly, though sometimes got frozen in this growth, but sometimes surged up swiftly. While in the beginning the group life was more reactive (for me it meant open expression of spontaneous reactions of anger or exasperation along with checking out how these reactions were perceived by others), later on all of us grew from spontaneous egocentric reactions to mature relations. This growth took us from clarifying relations to building them, along with learning how to not forget about our 'inner child' while building relations of grown-up people. We grew from building relations with those whom we liked to making and maintaining contacts with those who were difficult to accept or understand. We grew from the ability to condescend and forgive towards the ability to forgive and ask for forgiveness, and then to the ability to feel gratitude.

Another participant, K, reflects here on the group process as whole:

> The group process is some kind of 'condensed' life, where, due to limited time, every word uttered, every action weighs a lot more than usually… It may remind one of a meditation of sorts on life – one is both relaxed and tense at the same time, both concentrated on events and feelings and flexible, depending on what is going on in the group and inside every participant. There is little control in this life, so it is lively, dynamic, unpredictable and intensive. And one has to stay continuously in the present, to learn 'to be present in the moment'. One of the most essential things in the group process is that it is created by ourselves through participation and involvement, or refusal of such, through our own responsibility for our way of involvement, for our own interventions and pauses. All this means a lot of freedom – choosing what to respond to and how, what to do at any specific moment. The therapist's role in this is far from being the most important or domineering; his is just another place, but a certain 'contour' of life is drawn by every one of us.

The therapist's stance

In an existential group, crucial importance lies in the therapist's stance – his/her existential thinking based on their belief system and aimed at understanding a person in his/her existential reality. The existential nature of a therapeutic group is determined to a great extent by the therapist's way of being in the 'here-and-now', by his/her ability to reveal existential dimension in his own life and the life of a group. He/she should not be 'playing the role' of a therapist, or 'taking the position of a therapist', but should remain a real person, a live human being, but with specific responsibilities and duties within the group. A most important feature of the EE group is the harmonious blend of the therapist's empathy and neutrality. Empathy helps the therapist to understand how participants experience their life and allows him/her temporarily to identify with their worries and concerns. Neutrality implies a therapist's striving to be impartial, to avoid judging participants' behaviours, characters and attitudes to life as either good or bad, appropriate or inappropriate.

The task of the group therapist is not to provide participants with explanations of the process in the group, based on some theory, but to be permanently and actively involved in this process and offer personal reactions. It is important that the therapist 'phenomenologically' reflects the processes and the events of group life. This helps participants to assess these processes, feel clearer about their own position and discover their own 'truths' in the process of therapy. To ensure this phenomenological reflection of the life of a group agrees with reality and is of therapeutic value, the therapist should be able to understand what is going on in the group.

From an existential perspective, what is most important is that the therapist sees every participant in the context of his/her life world, which comprises his/her life history, relations with close people and friends (with participants and the therapist in the group), professional and working environment and other aspects of 'being-in-the-world'. These aspects should be 'revived' in the group, since (most often) they constitute part of the participant's psychological problems. The therapist needs to see how the individual participant has arrived at a difficult situation in life, how he/she perceives it, what stance he/she takes regarding it, and how he/she attempts to find a way out. On the other hand, the therapist should always be aware that his/her hypotheses about the participants' possibilities and restrictions cannot be absolutely precise, so he/she should use these with caution. Participants are, no doubt, the best experts with respect to their own problems. Therefore, working in an EE group, the phenomenological attitude of the therapist gets so much attention because it allows the group dynamic to bring forward the experiences of the participants as they themselves perceive them.

Uncertainty

Uncertainty is one of the most important and most difficult 'givens' to accept (Spinelli, 2015), and for this reason permeates all the life of the EE group, raises its tension and intensity and sustains anxiety and pressure. The content of meetings of an EE group cannot be planned in advance and, almost inevitably, remains unstructured. It depends on interpersonal situations born in the 'here-and-now' and their relatedness to the therapeutic goals of participants. The therapist refrains from giving any instructions to participants about what they are to do or how, thus promoting uncertainty, which means participants must search for their own place in the 'therapeutic space' of the group. In this way, the EE group 'materialises' one of the conditions of human existence – that of being 'thrown-in' into the world – which is often not easy to accept and therefore participants tend to ignore it. Unwillingness to accept reality sometimes becomes transformed into anger and the therapist is often accused of 'not explaining anything', 'doing nothing' and that 'it is not clear at all why everybody has come here'. However, this is exactly the starting point from which to solve the essential issues of life in the EE group: 'What is the purpose of the group?'; 'What is the purpose of my presence in the group?'; 'What does the therapist want?'; 'What do I want?'

Uncertainty is not specific only to the introductory stages of the group; it accompanies the group through all its life. While uncertainty is ever-present in the group process, the participants' relation to it undergoes considerable changes. This may be illustrated by the account of the participant E:

> I was overwhelmed by what ensued between me and T. Even now I am not able to fully comprehend what happened... Perhaps, there is much more to it than I am capable to understand right now. The therapist just rubbed my nose into the possible source of my loneliness, when we had managed to become so close to each other and to experience mutual 'togetherness'. For me that was the greatest gift: to understand that I am always in a hurry to escape complicated relations or to simplify them...
> I perceived with such clarity what *terra incognita* is presented to me by human relations in which so many contradictory wishes, feelings, actions are entangled. I am stunned to realise that there are so many conflicting feelings within me at every single moment... I crave so much for clarity, certainty, but this is impossible, or if it happens, most probably it is fictitious, because one cannot 'simply' love or 'simply' hate; it is not only me or only you; it is not possible to be just like this... For me, to discover this complexity and multi-sidedness of relations, to see how indefinite and uncertain they might be, was the greatest result of the group.

'Here-and-now'

One of the fundamental features of existential therapy is its direction towards the present. This is why – in the EE group – it is most important to refer to processes happening in the here-and-now. This means that the group's attention is kept focused on what is happening at the present moment between the participants and with each of them. Any past experiences are considered within the present context by discussing in what ways events, experiences, and feelings that happened in the past are meaningful or significant now.

The principle of 'here-and-now' means encouragement to check abstract reasoning and theorising against concrete acts. Participant S describes one situation in the group:

> One participant responded very emotionally to her neighbour in the group circle and slapped her on the knee rather aggressively and with force. Somebody became very indignant about that and started a heated 'fight for justice', demanding the culprit to punished. However, he did not take or suggest any actions, appealing instead for some punishing act by the group or a more resolute reaction by the therapist. The therapist suggested that he should put his indignation to life, thus bringing the offender to justice. There was a feeling as if something heavy had fallen on our heads. All the group sank into a pause that was full of silent tension while awaiting what would happen next. The 'prosecutor' himself was lost; it was obvious that his inner tension was also skyrocketing. He attempted to organise a vote for exclusion of the delinquent member but gained no support from the group at all. It appeared that it is not so easy to take responsibility for one's words; it is much more comfortable to fight for justice in words.

Self-disclosure

Shared life in an EE group is built through the self-disclosure of participants (Kočiūnas & Dragan, 2008). Self-disclosure is important as a way of open communication towards helping participants understand each other. Two types of self-disclosure appear most valuable for a group: 1) continuously sharing immediate experiences in group situations, and 2) sharing one's own inner conflicts, unresolved personal issues, painful feelings, weaknesses, hopes and expectations.

The great power of deep self-disclosure is evidenced in the experience of the participant L:

> This is a real revolution in my life. It is like a wake-up after 30 years of slumber. It is only now that I realised what is happening around how and where I live and what I do. It seems that I do not know how to be with people, though I have always considered myself a very communicative

person. After the chaos of 30 years, of never-ending tornadoes, that unexpectedly ceased here, in the group... to start tidying things around myself, to throw away everything that proves unnecessary... A very wide array of feelings... Tears, self-pity, a wish to have somebody's attention and compassion – childish, all childish and nothing else... Now I realise that it is unwise to flounce about in search of a warm and safe nook. I am still living through the story of my relationship with a man that I revealed in the group, but now I understand why I allowed violence and humiliation towards myself. Entering his life, I thought I had found a haven, complete with stability, material wealth and comfort. I had supposed that all this would provide emotional comfort as well. However, there appeared to be a high price to be paid. And a lot of suffering. Now I feel willing to revive my own space, and there are no 'childish games' in this, no competition for attention or recognition, but a real life, the life of my own. It is scary, I must admit, and feels very insecure. Though I feel very beautiful inside – a beautiful young lady. I want to build my future life consciously, without haste and with care for myself.

Silence

The path towards authentic life in an EE group often passes through periods of long, tense and even painful silence. While enduring this silence, participants experience existential anxiety and learn to endure it. Difficult periods of silence also reveal the phenomenon of boredom as a mode of meaningless existence. Thus, participants eventually come closer to authentic communication between them. Experiences, caused by silent pauses, may be seen as a form of purification preceding real, sincere and open communication.

Here are some impressions of participant N:

> The experience of silence proved to be especially valuable. When pauses happened in the session, there was a possibility in them, while being silent, to face something powerful and authentic inside myself. At some moment, I started to knowingly accept the possibility of silence, to learn to experience it. It seems to me that the more grown-up the group was, the more it could accept silence, while words emerging after such pauses weighed much more and were much more meaningful.

Therapeutic change

In existential group therapy, and in existential therapy in general, changes are understood as a natural and inevitable part of life, as a mode of human existence. A therapeutic group often only facilitates building the foundations for changes in life; it only starts the process of therapeutic change, which gets 'grounded' in the periods between the sessions as well as after completion of the therapeutic group. Since life itself is a process of continuous change, the participants of the therapeutic process have to find their own place in this process and search for appropriate ways to bring particular changes to their lives. Therefore, the therapeutic group most often does not solve difficult issues but opens doors for their solution in life and enables their 'rehearsal' in a safer environment.

After the group was finished, participant P wrote about the changes that she related to her participation in the group:

> Now, in life, I try to learn to wait and to be patient, and this is noticed both by my family and by colleagues. I try to learn to wait for my son to be ready for changes, instead of trying to push him, and I enjoy watching him grow. I get lessons from him as well – to refrain from running at a crazy pace but slow down and live in a more conscious and reflective way. I try to learn to wait for the man I love to get ready for changes in our relationship. Now I share my grievances with my parents more often, and together we slowly recreate our relations anew. I was surprised and welcomed hearing from my mum about her own wounds – these were important things for me to know about my behaviour with her. Having chosen to live my own life as it seems best for me, I pay for it sometimes with loneliness, sometimes with guilt for my choices. Or with anxiety and tension. And the more I respect myself, my life and my choices, the more respect I feel for the life and choices of others.

Conclusion

Among psychotherapists, individual work with clients is much more popular than practising with groups. Many reasons might be mentioned here, but it is clear that working with a group offers a unique possibility to understand clients' (participants') difficulties in the real context of creating a life-world with others, of being-with-others. For existential therapy, one of the most important things in understanding clients (participants) is seeing their problems in the context of their life and, first of all, in the inevitably intersubjective environment. Achieving this task in a psychotherapeutic group proves to be easier and requires less effort. Thus, existential group therapy is not only possible, but it might also constitute an important part in the landscape of existential therapy.

Discussion with the editor

Simon: You write that individual therapy with clients is much more popular than practising with groups, and I think that is something I can certainly recognise. It puzzles me a little though, especially since it provides us with a way of getting beyond the stories clients tell us and our own sense of them in relation with us, so that we can see how clients actually engage with the world. In this respect we might almost argue that, in the context of existential practice, group therapy should take precedence over individual therapy! I wonder if you have any thoughts on this?

Rimas: Actually, I agree but, as I have mentioned above, the problem lies in the training of group therapists and the limited enthusiasm of therapists to engage in group therapy.

Simon: You write with such insight and authority on existential group therapy that I am naturally led to wonder about the personal and professional motivation that has led you to be active and innovative in this particular area of therapy. I'm curious about whether political and cultural factors play a part – I'm thinking here about the broadly 'individualistic' ethos of the West (if such broad categorisation is helpful at all) versus perhaps a more 'collectivist' tradition in Eastern Europe… this comes to mind for me especially in relation to Yalom's apparent rejection of even the notion of existential group therapy.

Rimas: It might make some sense to speak about the 'individualistic West' and the 'collectivist East' (although there is a considerable danger to get drowned in ungrounded speculations). For me, working with a group – as opposed to working with an individual client – is a much greater challenge, demanding fuller and more complex involvement of myself as a therapist. To be with everyone and for everyone and at the same time to be with all of them, with the group, is a fantastic human and therapeutic 'adventure'. I believe that these two formats of therapeutic work match very nicely – regular work with groups helps to span much wider the relational horizon of an individual client, while ongoing individual work allows much better and deeper awareness of each participant of the group. Yalom's position appears to be more related to his understanding of existential therapy – it being not a separate school, but just a 'higher', 'existential' level of any therapy. It seems that he sees a group purely as reflecting participants' usual lives and their interpersonal interactions, thus underestimating, or even tending to overlook, a separate and independent life that is born and keeps evolving in the group.

Simon: You provide a fascinating account of ITL and compare it with your own EE model of group therapy. I can see that they have much in common, but I find it more difficult to identify exactly how they diverge, both in theory and practice. My sense, perhaps rather unfocused, is that your own approach places less emphasis on a specific group task and more on the co-creation of meaning and so is more explicitly 'existential', but I may not be correct.

Rimas: I would concur with such impression. Also, I have responded accordingly to your reactions in the text above.

Simon: You are obviously very active in promoting existential group therapy in Eastern Europe – how do you see it developing in the future?

Rimas: If we keep talking about existential group therapy more and also showing how it works, and if there are more colleagues willing to leave the more common framework of individual therapy, prospects for this therapy are certainly good. I am quite often invited to neighbouring countries to give demonstrations of intensive existential groups and, besides, our training programme for group therapists proceeds quite successfully.

References

Alekseičikas A (2011). *Arbeitsplatz Seele: psychotherapie durch das Leben*. Regensburg: EWK-Verlag.

Alekseičikas A (2008). Gydyti gyvenimu. In: Kočiūnas R (ed). *Gydyti Gyvenimu: Aleksandro Alekseičiko intensyvus terapinis gyvenimas*. Vilnius: Humanistinėsir Egzistencinės Psichologijos Institutas.

Alekseičikas A (1999). Intensyvus terapinis gyvenimas. In: Kočiūnas R (ed). *Grupinė Psichoterapija Lietuvoje*. Vilnius: Via Recta.

Cohn HW (1997). *Existential Thought and Therapeutic Practice: an introduction to existential psychotherapy*. London: Sage.

Garrow S, Walker JA (2001). Existential group therapy and death anxiety. *Adultspan Journal* 3(2): 77–87.

Heidegger M (1962/1926). *Being and Time* (J Macquarrie, E Robinson trans). Oxford: Blackwell.

Hora T (1968). Existential psychiatry and group psychotherapy: basic principles. In: Gazda GM (ed). *Basic Approaches to Group Psychotherapy and Group Counselling*. Springfield, Ill: Charles C. Thomas (pp109–148).

Jacobsen B (1997). Working with existential groups. In: du Plock S (ed). *Case Studies in Existential Psychotherapy and Counselling*. London: John Wiley & Sons (pp157–173).

Kissane DW, Love A, Hatton A, Bloch S, Smith G, Clarke DM, Miach P, Ikin J, Ranieri N, Snyder RD (2004). Effect of cognitive-existential group therapy on survival in early-stage breast-cancer. *Journal of Clinical Oncology 22*(21): 4255–4260.

Kočiūnas R (2015), The existential approach in group psychotherapy. *International Journal of Psychotherapy 19*(1): 95–104.

Kočiūnas R (2009). Egzistencinis požiūris grupinėje psichoterapijoje. *Psichologija 40*: 7–20.

Kočiūnas R (2000). Existential experience and group therapy. *Journal of the Society for Existential Analysis 11*(2): 91–112.

Kočiūnas R (1999). Egzistencinis patyrimas ir grupinė terapija. In: Kočiūnas R (ed). *Grupinė psichoterapija Lietuvoje*. Vilnius: Via Recta.

Kočiūnas R (1991). Egzistencinio patyrimo grupės principai. *Psichologija 11*: 20–30.

Kočiūnas R, Dragan T (2008). The phenomenon of self-disclosure in a psychotherapy group. *Existential Analysis 19*(2): 345–363.

Mullan H (1992). 'Existential' therapists and their group practice. *International Journal of Group Psychotherapy 41*(4): 453–468.

Mullan H (1978). Existential group psychotherapy. In: Mullan H, Rosenbaum M (eds). *Group Psychotherapy: theory and practice* (2nd ed). New York, NY: The Free Press (pp377–399).

Overholser JC (2005). Group psychotherapy and existential concerns: an interview with Irvin Yalom. *Journal of Contemporary Psychotherapy 35*(2): 185–197.

Spinelli E (2015). *Practising Existential Psychotherapy: the relational world* (2nd ed). London: Sage.

Spira JL (1997). *Group Therapy for Medically Ill Patients*. New York, NY: Guilford Press.

Tantam D (2005). Groups. In: van Deurzen E, Arnold-Baker C (eds). *Existential Perspectives on Human Issues: a handbook for therapeutic practice*. London: Palgrave Macmillan.

van Deurzen E (2012). *Existential Counselling and Psychotherapy in Practice* (3rd ed). London: Sage.

Ventegodt S, Andersen NJ, Merrick J (2003). Holistic medicine: scientific challenges. *The Scientific World Journal 3*: 1108–1116.

Witemb SA (2012). Existential thinking and its influence on group therapy. *Group 36*(2): 107–119.

Yalom ID (2002). *The Gift of Therapy*. New York, NY: HarperCollins.

Yalom ID (1980). *Existential Psychotherapy*. New York, NY: Basic Books.

Yalom ID, Leszcz M (2005). *Theory and Practice of Group Psychotherapy* (5th ed). New York, NY: Basic Books.

9

Trans and non-binary genders

Christina Richards

Trans people are those people who are not content to remain the gender they were assigned at birth. They may identify within the gender binary of male or female and wish to move into a different binary position from that assigned at birth, or they may identify outside of that binary as a *non-binary* or *genderqueer* person. These groups of non-binary or genderqueer people (which are roughly analogous terms and I shall use non-binary people here for ease of reading) may have aspects of masculinity and femininity, be fluidity gendered and so moving between masculinity and femininity, or may not identify as any gender at all (Richards & Barker, 2013, 2015; Richards, Bouman & Barker, 2017). These terms, and indeed the social understandings of the practices and identities associated with these terms, are constantly evolving, which creates something of a minefield for therapists working in this area, and certainly for authors seeking to write about it. Nonetheless, I shall venture to use *trans* here, as an umbrella term, to refer to all those groups of people who are not content to remain the gender they were assigned at birth – both those who identify within and without the gender binary.

These identities have previously been pathologised (Dickinson et al, 2012), but it has recently been recognised that trans is not, in itself, a mental illness (APA, 2013a), primarily due to the fact that trans people have no higher rates of psychopathology than the general population (Cole et al, 1997; Colizzi, Costa & Todarello, 2014; Haraldsen & Dahl, 2000; Hill et al, 2005; Hoshiai et al, 2010; Kersting et al, 2003; Simon et al, 2011). Of course, this does not include minority or marginalisation stress, which is stress caused by being in a minority group that is discriminated against and which may therefore lead to psychopathology. However, in this case it is the discrimination, rather than the demographic one belongs to, that is psychopathogenic. Consequently, trans people should not be expected to come to therapy simply because they are trans, and especially not with the intention of 'curing' their being trans. Indeed, any such therapy is likely to be ineffective (Seikowski, 2007) and may be harmful (Lawrence, 2003; Loewenberg & Krege, 2007). For this reason, professional therapeutic associations state that such 'reparative' or 'conversion' therapies are unethical and that members practising them will be subject to censure (eg. British Psychological Society, 2012).

While trans people generally do not wish to have therapy for being trans (Lev, 2004) (although some may be sent for therapy and for some there may be other coercive factors involved), they may come for a variety of other reasons, including all those that bring cisgender[1] people, such as bereavement, job losses, relationship problems and so forth. In this case, the most effective intervention is generally to proceed much as one would with the cisgender client, without becoming sidetracked by the fact the person is trans – just as with any other demographic, such as sexuality, ethnicity, age and so forth. Of course, these issues should not necessarily be ignored; rather, the therapy should not be inappropriately biased towards them simply because the therapist assumes they must be of relevance, when in fact they are not.

This chapter, however, focuses on trans-specific issues, rather than those of a general nature – particularly that of clients seeking therapy to help them decide which gender presentation and physicality is most congruent with their sense of internal gender identity. To aid in this endeavour I will examine a case study of a young person who was assigned a female sex at birth but who does not identify as female or feminine. This person, whom I have called Kai-Bo, is an amalgam of the varying presentations, identities, practices and issues I have seen in my work as an NHS therapist and psychologist, over many years. It is most certainly not an individual I have seen. However, the issues arising should aid in understanding this most important work.

In terms of my day-to-day work, I am in an interesting position in that the people I see come from many different backgrounds – including, for example, teachers, people who have spent many years in forensic psychiatric settings, asylum seekers, doctors and lawyers, and from just about any group

---

1. Cisgender people are people who are content to remain the gender they were assigned at birth.

or demographic you might imagine. The single linking characteristic is that there is some aspect of their gender and/or sexuality they wish to address. Naturally this heterogeneity means that clients will affect me personally in different ways as they differ or share my own sexuality, gender, ethnicity, age, educational background and so on. I should note, though, that is it not similarity *per se* that affects me, as intersectionality works in complex ways (see das Nair & Butler, 2012). Therefore, the things that may trigger me to personal reflection or to consideration in supervision (or, no doubt, that trigger responses of which I am unaware) may be to do with an apparently less salient characteristic – for example, my gender may be superficially the same but my experience of coming to it may differ; my sexuality may be similar, but its expression in my cultural group may differ. Such things can matter more than broad 'tick-box' labels for single demographic characteristics. I consequently always try to keep a weather eye on that which disturbs me – and in positive ways, too (always an easy one to forget), as feeling warm towards a client can be a good thing but feeling overly so can lead to misjudgement – just as feeling overly cold can.

The majority of the clients I see wish to have physical interventions, such as hormones and surgeries, and this necessitates multidisciplinary team working. I struggle with the tension here between the rigidity of the more medical discourses I am engaged with and the necessary fluidity and 'unknowing' of the psychotherapeutic ones. Naturally, the temptation is to flee to the margins – to hide behind the *Diagnostic and Statistical Manual of Mental Disorders* (DSM) or the *International Classification of Diseases* (ICD) as what is 'known' and so eschew discomfort with the messy complex reality of clients' worlding. The allure of the other pole is equally strong, however: to hide in 'unknowing' or 'being-with' and never make an intervention or decision, but simply listen and never hear or say or do. And I am called upon to do all these things. I must make decisions as to whether people should have hormones or surgeries; I must liaise with forensic services about risk, sometimes serious risk, and these things require action that does not allow for sitting and simply 'unknowing'. Naturally, the sweet spot is somewhere between the hard and the soft – for example, I need to know the nature and action of the hormones I recommend on psychological grounds, but I also need to know what they mean *for this client*. It's not always an easy path.

To help, I think a lot. I put my feet up on my desk, look at my books and plants and consider things – how are my feelings and intuitions affecting my more reasoned thoughts about this? What is my clinical impression? What would my colleagues from various disciplines do? What is the philosophical basis for my thoughts here? And what does the literature say? This last is important, and is, in my opinion, often overlooked in therapeutic practice. Consequently, it is this to which we now turn.

The literature

The literature on trans people has been rather heated. Historically, of course, what we now term trans has mainly been viewed in Western idioms and religious traditions as 'sin', although globally and in pre-Roman times many people who identified outside of the gender binary were accepted and even revered (Herdt, 1996). As medical discourses took over from religion, 'sin' turned into 'perversion' and was seen as something to be (unsuccessfully) treated (eg. von Krafft-Ebing, 1886; Ellis, 1919; Hirschfeld, 1952). More recently, however, the literature has been split into that which considers trans – especially binary trans people – to be something that unnecessarily reinforces the gender binary through over-adherence to gender stereotypes, and (especially for non-binary trans people) something that necessarily troubles the gender binary through transgressing it. These stances, of course, avoid directly enquiring of trans people what their position is, as they draw on a theoretical, rather than a phenomenological, basis (see Richards, 2017).

With the exception of my own brief work (eg. Richards, 2011, 2014a, 2014b), the existential literature has been remarkably silent on the topic of trans, and even on gender itself, aside from de Beauvoir's oeuvre (eg. de Beauvoir, 1949/1997). Perhaps this is because it is primarily written by men, who are in the main white, relatively affluent and apparently heterosexual and cisgender. I wonder if this group felt that there was nothing to investigate as gender appears so unproblematic as to not invite enquiry? Certainly, it is telling that it is a woman – de Beauvoir – who is most linked with gender in the existential canon.

Notwithstanding this, the main thrust of what work there is has been scholastic argument concerning whether gender and sexuality are existential givens (see Milton, 2014). The therapeutic importance of this argument rests on whether we are doing our clients a disservice if we stick to a strict philosophical understanding of the existential given – that, because gender and sexuality vary, they cannot be considered to be in the same class of changeless, inviolable philosophical entities that existential givens are, such as death (see Rodrigues, 2014). In contrast, authors such as Medina (2008) argue that for many gay people there is an inviolable sense of oneself as gay – that, while the choice of androphilic attraction varies, the attraction itself does not and, further, feels fundamental to the person's self. While these arguments have not been extended in the literature to trans (aside from Leighton's 1999 brief assertion that trans people should expand their notions of the birth-assigned gender categories instead of transition, and my own oeuvre suggesting they should not), the arguments concerning the nature of existential sexuality and gender are analogous.

Beyond this argument concerning givens, there are many existential positions that can usefully be considered in trans work: the fact that we have a sometimes uncomfortable degree of freedom to choose, that some people choose not to choose, and that some people choose to be in the act of choosing (in that they delay the discomfort of having made a choice through continuously telling themselves they are 'doing something' because they are [still] choosing – see Richards, 2011). Additionally, we can use the notion of a *leap to faith* (Kierkegaard, 2009) when clients are considering the momentous matter of whether to transition or not, as, even with all the thought (and therapy) available to them, there may still be no safe intermediate steps between where they are and where they want to be. Parents, partners and employers must be told, bodies will change, and so on. Finitude too – being towards death – can lead many people, especially those who are older or who have passed a significant birthday, to re-evaluate their gender position; the death of one's parents in particular can focus the mind, as clients realise they are next on the escalator and wish to live their remaining time in a (more) authentic manner. This authenticity is, of course, the *sine qua non* of trans work as, above all, trans people are searching for an authentic expression of a – sometimes ephemeral – internal sense of themselves. Determining the precise expression of this and accommodating and addressing the world they are thrown into are at the very heart of therapeutic work with trans people. Indeed, on a personal note, I find it an immense privilege to be a part of that work. Just occasionally I have had a client come out to me about their gender or sexuality before they do to others, and it touches me deeply (an overused term I use advisedly, truthfully, here) to be so trusted.

This therapeutic work is very often conducted within pragmatic bounds. For the private client, these may be rather more flexible in terms of choice of therapist, appointment times and so forth but there will nonetheless still be bounds on session length, location, cost and the like. Within nationalised healthcare, there are necessarily further restrictions, due to resource issues, and these restrictions are especially profound when patients ask to be evaluated for irreversible physical changes that will be paid for by the taxpayer. It is this therapeutic milieu – the place of the bulk of my own therapeutic work – to which I now turn, as the pros and cons of working in such a setting are many.

Current National Health Service practice

When the fact that the patient is trans is irrelevant or incidental to their presenting concern, current NHS services for trans people are naturally provided in all of the same places as for cisgender people. Only when specialist assistance is sought for trans matters are referrals made to specialists in the field. These specialists come from a range of disciplines, including endocrinologists, surgeons, psychologists, psychotherapists, counsellors, psychiatrists, nurses, speech and language therapists and more. Most commonly, these professionals will work in a multidisciplinary team or network and will endeavour to engage in truly multidisciplinary teamworking, due to the fact that so many aspects of trans care overlap. For example, I work closely with an endocrinologist, as the psychological effects of hormones may impact a patient alongside the physical effects. Indeed, we also publish together (eg. Richards & Seal, 2014), which I find extremely useful in marshalling our various thoughts and approaches.

When patients are first seeking assistance for their gender dysphoria, they are likely to be referred by their primary care physician (their general practitioner (GP)) to a gender clinic – a secondary or tertiary service in the UK's National Health Service (NHS). No counselling or other intervention is required for referral; however, due to funding issues, there is usually a rather protracted wait to be seen and many patients elect to go private and/or (if they wish for physical changes) to self-medicate with hormones bought from the internet, with all the attendant risks associated with that (see Seal et al, 2012). This wait is, as you might imagine, exceptionally trying for clients, and I do feel a great deal of empathy for people coming to me after so long. It is hard to be the representative of a 'system' that is so under-resourced as to make such waits necessary. I try not to just blame the system, however – it's too amorphous and impersonal, and indeed I am a (very small) cog in it. I am aware that I try to change things through my work with the wider NHS as the representative of the British Psychological Society (BPS), but this means little to the client who is having to endure the wait. In some sense, if only by association, I am guilty too, and I feel it is important to acknowledge that with the client and to take such blame as is coming.

Once people have arrived at a gender clinic, they will be assessed, usually by a psychologist or a psychiatrist, who will use the *Good Practice Guidelines for the Assessment and Treatment of Gender Dysphoria* (Royal College of Psychiatrists, 2013),; the *Standards of Care for the Heath of Transsexual, Transgender and Gender Nonconforming People* (7th ed) (World Professional

Association for Transgender Health, 2011), and the *Interim Gender Dysphoria Protocol and Service Guideline 2013/14*[2] (NHS England, 2013). Patients may wish to have physical changes to align their bodies with their identity, which may necessitate hormones and/or surgeries, but by no means all do and it is therefore important that I do not assume a single pathway for all those who are not content with their gender. Of course, this does not mean that, because some people are content without physical interventions, then others should be also. This is because endeavouring to dissuade people does not work (Gelder & Marks, 1969; Gijs & Brewaeys, 2007; Mukaddes, 2002; Raymond, 1969); as we have seen above, it is unethical and, ultimately, there is nothing wrong with being trans – a point worth reiterating freely and often (as I do here, and elsewhere in my work).

Those people who do want physical interventions will be counselled about their various options (see Ettner, Monstrey & Eyler, 2016) and a staged approach is usually taken, with more reversible interventions such as social role transition preceding hormones, which in turn precede any surgeries. Hormones are often given at the point of documented social role transition, with any chest surgeries six months later and any genital surgeries after about a year. Of course, prior to this, differential diagnoses and/or formulations that would not invite physical treatments will have to be considered and it is here again that I must address the tension between the different models I work within. These diagnoses and/or formulations might include such things as psychosis; difficulties with development into the adult world; autistic special interests centring on gender; a purely sexual motivation for transition and the like. In the vast majority of cases, these things will not apply, and so a discussion must be had in which the patient or client must evaluate whether the interventions, especially those of a permanent nature, will benefit them. Sometimes factors such as unsupportive family and partners, unsupportive school or work, or a general fear of rejection and/or abuse, can make trans people have difficulties with transition, although the fear of such things is often greater than the reality. Nonetheless, trying out living in the preferred gender can be an important part of determining which interventions, if any, are right for any one particular patient and here, perhaps especially, I endeavour to get alongside the client to support and assist this sometimes difficult process.

Alongside such real-world lived experience, counselling and psychotherapy can usefully aid in exploring thoughts and feelings about gender and sexuality,

---

2. This is still extant at the time of writing in 2018 due to political difficulties with the increased funding needed to implement the necessary changes.

and especially in unpacking any fears that the client might have about living in their preferred gender role, or indeed about their gender identity itself. As seen above, these matters of the freedom to be oneself authentically, the practical, social and psychic blocks to this and the struggle to find the solutions to these are, of course, fundamental to existential philosophy and practice. Let us now, therefore, consider how this works in contemporary NHS practice by means of a case study.

Case study

Kai-Bo was a 20-year-old, birth-assigned female who was unhappy with their[3] gender. They had always felt that they didn't fit in, both at school (where they were bullied) and at home, and they reported a rather tempestuous relationship with their parents – especially their father. They suffered from depression from around the age of 13, which in retrospect they attributed to their periods starting, but they recounted being isolated prior to that. Although quite intelligent, Kai-Bo struggled during their A-Levels and found that they were getting anxious when away from the family home. At 17, they refused to go to school and spent time in their room playing computer games and watching Anime – a form of predominately Eastern animated film. They felt unable to go to school, college or work, but were able to see friends and attend cosplay conventions in other towns, where they would dress as their favourite Anime characters. They saw their GP about anxiety and were prescribed 20mg of the antidepressant Citalopram daily, secondary to a diagnosis of 'social anxiety', but found this to be of limited help. They refused CBT on the basis that 'nothing works'.

Having become involved with various internet cosplay groups, they came across a trans group and felt something 'click'. They recalled not liking dresses as a child and preferring to wear tracksuits or jeans and a T-shirt. They felt distressed about their breasts as they developed and remembered being teased about them at school. Aged 20, Kai-Bo attended the NHS clinic where I work because they wished to have 'top surgery' (a bilateral mastectomy and associated chest recontouring to effect a masculine chest). In the first appointment, they presented in an androgynous role, with a cartoon character on their T-shirt, trainers and tracksuit trousers. I noticed various plastic keyrings hanging from their backpack.

---

3. *They*, rather than *he/she*, is the preferred term used by people who identify outside the gender binary, as it does not presuppose that binary.

My key task with Kai-Bo was to get inside their worldview in order to establish the exact nature of their request for top surgery; what this would mean for them intrapsychically, and whether such surgery would realistically fit within their current life. At this early stage, I had a nascent formulation – predicated on the fact the onset of their difficulties apparently predated their gender dysphoria – that their request for surgery might be more a search for an identity and a hope that a physical change might effect a psychological one so they would feel less anxious and more able to engage with the adult world of work, adult relationships and so forth. Of course, as a formulation, it would be constantly open to revision in light of new information, and at that early stage it could be nothing more than a tentative direction for therapeutic enquiry. Personally, I am aware that non-binary identities are an emerging field and, as such, there is less established practice and less literature than I usually like to have at my disposal. Consequently, I have to consider what little literature there is (eg. Richards, Bouman & Barker, 2017), my philosophical stance as it applies to these matters – especially with regards to the degree of intervention it is appropriate for me to make and how I impact upon the client's freedom, and, following from that and most importantly, *ethics* – what is morally right for me to do here?

My main method with the client is that of phenomenological enquiry, although an enquiry that is bounded by the pragmatic realities of NHS practice as detailed above. I have limited time and am in the unenviable (paradoxical) position of needing to make a recommendation on surgery as well as explore the client's worldview. While this is a rare circumstance for a psychotherapist or psychologist, these dual roles are increasingly common for our profession, as we are increasingly called upon to be expert witnesses, to influence child custody cases, and even to section people under the Mental Health Act 2007. Many psychotherapists may not have these statutory duties but will still have a (perhaps unacknowledged) influence on their clients' lives and so the moral aspect of such work should similarly be attended to. It is paradoxical and immoral for us to claim both that, if we do our work properly, we only provide a space for exploration and have no direct impact on the client's decision (and so the client takes all the responsibility), while at the same time claiming full professional (expert) status (and pay packets). I am not speaking here about the practitioners with independent means who are able to volunteer open-ended, free therapy of the kind that offers only 'space' – except to ask them to measure their outcomes or to test the philosophical stance that suggests that important outcomes are unmeasurable.

In general, my process of phenomenological enquiry is actually more a series of contiguous enquiries as I seek information on a certain series of questions concerning family structure, sexuality, sexual abuse, gender, substance (mis)use and so forth. I endeavour to do this in as open and phenomenological a manner as the pragmatic bounds allow. This is the process I followed with Kai-Bo. After three sessions, my basic assessment was complete and I recognised a degree of gender dysphoria but I was still concerned that Kai-Bo's gender identity was not necessarily coherent across their interior world and the outer world, as they had not tested it in any wider environments. Put philosophically, I was concerned that their being-in-the-world was split, if you will, into a possibly bad faith position that would not stand and was causing (existential) anxiety. However, I could not tell the nature of this – if it was their lack of gendered expression in the wider world that was the cause (and so surgery would be a useful part of the solution), or if they thought they needed to have surgery but in fact the root of their anxiety lay in an instability of identity rather than gender, and this was the problem. Of course, I needed to also be reflexively aware of the part my own identity played in my thought processes and I would have taken the matter to supervision if this had been marked.

One option would have been to continue to phenomenologically explore Kai-Bo's interior world, but the time allotted to us precluded that and, indeed, I am not convinced that such an exploration would have yielded useful results. Instead, I suggested some CBT methods, without couching them as 'therapy', centring around graduated exposure in social situations, which is a proven treatment for anxiety such as they were experiencing (Hawton et al, 1989). Kai-Bo agreed, seeing the wisdom of this approach, and reported that they felt respected as they were not instructed to undertake the methods, but instead they were discussed as a range of options to be taken up and used as they deemed appropriate. Of course, I am deviating from the strict existential-phenomenological approach here in that graduated exposure as a technique (and perhaps especially as a suggested one) apparently presupposes one course of action in a certain direction as being more useful than another (in this case, in addressing their social anxiety). In the strict philosophical sense, the anxiety may be grounded in angst, which could be addressed through more psychological interventions aimed at the underlying cause of this – perhaps finitude or nauseous freedom. However, in my view, what is best for the client must be central to my interventions, irrespective of my own philosophical stance and provided it forms a coherent overarching approach that fits with the formulation (see Cooper & McLeod, 2010). Given the time constraints of the therapy, graduated exposure seemed to offer the most benefit within the resources available.

After Kai-Bo had practised graduated exposure, they reported feeling more confident. We discussed what that meant for them and they told me they were able to 'be me more' and 'not bother with what everyone thinks about me all the time' – that is, they were able to exert more of a *will to power* in regards to their authentic self. Building on the self-esteem that accompanied this wider-world expression of self, we considered whether some voluntary work would be useful. They were initially reticent, having been pushed into occupations such as this before, but told me that they would like to work with animals, and we discussed the possibility of their working in an animal rescue shelter. In a deviation from strict phenomenological practice, I encouraged them in this and they decided to go for it. It transpired also during this discussion that, while they were now happier to express themselves in wider situations, they were nonetheless extremely concerned about what their father might say about them having surgery. In effect, the removal of the more immediate pragmatic barrier of the possibility of engaging with the wider world opened space to consider the more psychological concerns about their father's reaction.

In the sessions that followed, Kai-Bo continued to flourish, especially after they got a voluntary position at the shelter, where they found that many of the fears they had previously held proved unfounded and so abated. In the following sessions we worked on the psychological processes underlying these changes, endeavouring to explore what they meant for Kai-Bo (and with me trying to fit these within a theoretical framework and formulation, although only occasionally out loud). As the months passed, it became clear that Kai-Bo was able to articulate their gender at their voluntary work and elsewhere, and this was reflected in a formal change of name and documentation. I queried how their father had taken this and they replied (with a wry grin) that he hadn't liked it much, 'but it's my life, not his'.

Is Kai-Bo a person with a non-binary gender, then? They say they are and it works in the world – really, that is all there is to it. They certainly met the diagnostic criteria for gender dysphoria in the *DSM-5* (APA, 2013b), and so I was happy to diagnose them and refer them for treatment (you'll notice that this is the only part that diagnosis plays here). They had their surgery and, after recovering, continued to grow in confidence – speeded, most likely, by the surgery. In this case, my original formulation was likely wrong – that's why we update them. Should we have treated Kai-Bo surgically earlier? Perhaps, but while they may have found their anxiety easier to bear, they may also have found that it did not abate with surgery alone and might have been crushed by that outcome. As more people are treated earlier – and as therapeutic endeavours become refined in combining philosophy, the real world and medical interventions – we will know better how to proceed with clients like Kai-Bo – and, if we are wise, will adjust our interventions accordingly.

Discussion

Therapy with people with trans and non-binary genders will vary greatly according to context, as we have seen. However, the fundamental principles of attending to the client's lived experience – both intrapsychically and in the wider world – will remain paramount. Additionally, notions of gender vary cross-culturally and sub-culturally and consequently nuances may escape even the most *au fait* therapist – a reminder that we should question our own as well as our client's assumptions. Beyond simply being respectful of varying understandings, intersectionality – a consideration of the intersections of other demographics such as age, ethnicity, (dis)ability and so forth – are vital to consider, as these matters will inflect client's understandings of their gender and (as we have seen above, with regards to social anxiety) how clients may realise their gender in the wider world. It can be tempting for those in an intersection of privileged positions (as many people who have been able to pay to become therapists are) to assume clients are afforded a greater degree of latitude by their thrown world than is, in fact, the case. When working with clients then, it is important to consider that the vast bulk of the work will be carried out *out there* – whether through thinking in the line at the grocery store or in the bath, or in practically meeting some real-world challenge. We need to be mindful that we are a part only of our clients' (bounded) lives, and that those lives must be lived and not just thought about.

Key points

In summary, it is important to remember that trans and non-binary genders are an emerging field and, as such, the theory is rapidly developing. Consequently, ethics and an ethical approach to practice must trump these (as yet not fully formed) theoretical concerns – whether derived from the academy or elsewhere. Further, the lived experience of the client is paramount – both client and therapist assumptions may fall down when real-world tested, and meanings of confirmed assumptions may change. As formulation will necessarily not be based on literature and the lived and experienced discourses of the person's life will still be forming, it is useful to be reflexively aware what discourses both we and the client are drawing upon when engaging in formulation. Similarly, while a pure existential-phenomenological approach may prove beneficial in some cases, a well applied, pluralistic (or other) approach that takes into account the practical constraints of the setting is likely to be of more benefit to the client than a truncated 'pure' approach only.

Afterword

We can see that trans and especially non-binary genders are very much an emerging field that will no doubt continue to excite debate and political change for the foreseeable future. Future directions will include a continued tension between the rights and freedom of self-determination balanced against the need for a safe, considered approach towards irreversible interventions, especially if they are paid for by others. This will be coupled with the recognition that some people may not have a fully formed notion of who they are or what they want associated with that – and consequently can benefit from therapeutic space in which to consider this.

Nonetheless, the move from pathologisation to acceptance has been hard won and should be cherished. Hopefully the open and nuanced approach offered by enlightened thinkers within the existential-phenomenological tradition can continue to play a part in assisting people with diverse sexuality and gender forms.

Discussion with editor

Simon: I was struck, reading your chapter, by the complexity and nuances of work with trans clients, and I wondered what motivated you to engage in this field, what training was available, and how a therapist might now find their way into this area of clinical practice?

Christina: I think my motivation was one of great interest in such an intersectional field. In my daily work, issues of law, surgery, endocrinology, philosophy, social science, natural science and a great deal more interweave to create a complex but never boring challenge. Until recently, training in this area was by informal apprenticeship – you qualified in a discipline and then worked with others in a clinic until specialised in trans and non-binary work. With the exponential growth in referrals of trans people, that is changing, with formalised training slowly becoming available in the high GDP global West.

Simon: Like many existential therapists, I have had the experience of working in multidisciplinary teams in the NHS and have needed to devise ways of functioning effectively with these colleagues while retaining my therapeutic identity. My sense is that, even in private practice, few of us are able to provide 'pure' existential therapy – in fact, I suspect that the need to establish professional relationships with a range of practitioners may help us hone our own particular way of working more readily than splendid isolation ever can. Do you think your own struggle to hold 'medical discourses' and the 'unknowing' of existential therapy in a creative tension offers some helpful insights for other existential therapists?

Christina: I think it all boils down to recognising that no one way is 'right' – whether existential, phenomenological, medical or any other. All have something to offer and all have costs associated with that. The difficulty, issue or, indeed, practicality in front of me suggests which discourse to draw on. I do think we need to be robust in our thinking, however – we need to be able to defend our positions, especially when they are not part of the prevailing power discourse, whatever that is. For example, if we are to argue against diagnosis, we need to know what those diagnoses are. It's not enough just to dislike them on principle. Similarly, when in multidisciplinary settings, it behoves us to have a basic understanding of neuro-anatomy, psychopharmacology and the like, in order to integrate them as necessary and to eschew them properly otherwise.

Simon: You say 'literature is often overlooked in clinical practice'. I am curious about this – can you say more about what you mean?

Christina: I think people, often rightly, go with what is happening in the room at the time and ignore the literature. That's fine, that's congruent, and that's personal – it doesn't reduce the person to an idea or a theory. But it also doesn't fit what is happening into a wider frame, a wider set of ideas that might offer avenues for exploration or even a reason or a truth or two – a reason or truth that must be coloured by the client's reality, to be sure. The thing is, it's really hard to do – to be listening, really listening hard to a client, while *at the same time* fitting in what they are saying (and its meaning) with what they have already said, your formulation based on that and the literature supporting the formulation – a whole world of abstract and personal ideas. But then it's meant to be hard – it's people's lives and, after all, we *are* therapists and that means something.

References

American Psychiatric Association (APA) (2013a). *Gender Dysphoria*. Washington, DC: American Psychiatric Association.

American Psychiatric Association (APA) (2013b). *Diagnostic and Statistical Manual of Mental Disorders* (5th ed). Washington, DC: American Psychiatric Association.

British Psychological Society (BPS) (2012). *Guidelines and Literature Review for Psychologists Working Therapeutically with Sexual Minority Clients*. London: British Psychological Society.

Cole CM, O'Boyle M, Emory LE, Meyer III WJ (1997). Comorbidity of gender dysphoria and other major psychiatric diagnoses. *Archives of Sexual Behavior* 26(1): 13–26.

Colizzi M, Costa R, Todarello O (2014). Transsexual patients' psychiatric comorbidity and positive effect of cross-sex hormonal treatment on mental health: results from a longitudinal study. *Psychoneuroendocrinology* 39(1): 65–73.

Cooper M, McLeod J (2010). *Pluralistic Counselling and Psychotherapy*. London: Sage.

das Nair R, Butler C (2012). *Intersectionality, Sexuality and Psychological Therapies: working with lesbian, gay and bisexual diversity*. Oxford: Wiley-Blackwell.

de Beauvoir S (1949/1997). *The Second Sex* (HM Parshley trans). New York, NY: Vintage.

Dickinson T, Cook M, Playle J, Hallett C (2012). 'Queer' treatments: giving a voice to former patients who received treatments for their 'sexual deviations'. *Journal of Clinical Nursing* 21(9–10): 1345–1354.

Ellis H (1919). *Studies in the Psychology of Sex: modesty, sexual periodicity, auto-eroticism* (3rd ed). Philadelphia, PA: FA Davis Co.

Ettner R, Monstrey S, Eyler AE (eds) (2016). *Principles of Transgender Medicine and Surgery* (2nd ed). New York, NY: The Haworth Press.

Gelder MG, Marks IM (1969). Aversion treatment in transvestism and transsexualism. In: Green R, Money J (eds). *Transsexualism and sex reassignment*. Baltimore, MD: John Hopkins Press (pp383–413).

Gijs L, Brewaeys A (2007). Surgical treatment of gender dysphoria in adults and adolescents: recent developments, effectiveness, and challenges. *Annual Review of Sex Research* 18: 178–224.

Haraldsen IR, Dahl AA (2000). Symptom profiles of gender dysphoric patients of transsexual type compared to patients with personality disorders and healthy adults. *Acta Psychiatrica Scandinavica* 102(4): 276–281.

Hawton K, Salkovskis PM, Kirk J, Clark DM (1989). *Cognitive Behaviour Therapy for Psychiatric Problems*. Oxford: Oxford University Press.

Herdt G (1996). *Third Sex Third Gender*. New York, NY: Zone books.

Hill DB, Rozanski C, Carfagnini J, Willoughby B (2005). Gender identity disorders in childhood and adolescence: a critical inquiry. In: Karasic D, Drescher J (eds). *Sexual and Gender Diagnoses of the Diagnostic and Statistical Manual (DSM)*. New York, NY: The Haworth Press (pp7–34).

Hirschfeld M (1952). *Sexual Anomalies and Perversions* (revised ed). London: Encyclopaedic Press.

Hoshiai M, Matsumoto Y, Sato T, Ohnishi M, Okabe N, Kishimoto Y, Terada S, Kuroda S

(2010). Psychiatric comorbidity among patients with gender identity disorder. *Psychiatry and Clinical Neurosciences 64*: 514–519.

Kersting A, Reutemann M, Gast U, Ohrmann P, Suslow T, Michael N, Arolt V (2003). Dissociative disorders and traumatic childhood experiences in transsexuals. *Journal of Nervous and Mental Disease 191*(3): 182–189.

Kierkegaard S (2009). *Concluding Unscientific Postscript to the Philosophical Crumbs* (A Hannay ed & trans). Cambridge: Cambridge University Press.

Lawrence AA (2003). Factors associated with satisfaction or regret following male-to-female sex reassignment surgery. *Archives of Sexual Behavior 32*(4): 299–315.

Leighton T (1999). Existential freedom and political change. In: Murphy JS (ed). *Feminist Interpretations of Jean-Paul Sartre*. University Park, PA: Pennsylvania State University Press (pp149–173).

Lev AI (2004). *Transgender Emergence*. London: Haworth Clinical Practice Press.

Loewenberg H, Krege S (2007). *Follow-up of 107 Male-to-Female Transsexuals after Sex-Reassignment Surgery*. Presented at the World Professional Association for Transgender Health Biennial Symposium, Chicago, September 8th 2007.

Medina M (2008). Can I be a homosexual please? A critique of sexual deliberations on the issue of homosexuality and their significance for the practice of existential psychotherapy. *Existential Analysis 19*(1): 129–142.

Milton M (ed) (2014). *Sexuality: existential perspectives*. Ross-on-Wye: PCCS Books.

Mukaddes NM (2002). Gender identity problems in autistic children. *Child: Care, Health and Development 28*: 529–532.

NHS England (2013). *Interim Gender Dysphoria Protocol and Service Guideline 2013/14*. London: NHS England.

Raymond MJ (1969). Aversion therapy for sexual perversions. *British Journal of Psychiatry 115*: 979–980.

Richards C (2017). *Trans and Sexuality: an existentially-informed ethical enquiry with implications for counselling psychology*. London: Routledge.

Richards C (2014a). Trans and existentialism. In: Milton M (ed). *Sexuality: existential perspectives*. Ross-on-Wye: PCCS Books (pp217–230).

Richards C (2014b). Group therapy and sexuality. In: Milton M (ed). *Sexuality: existential perspectives*. Ross-on-Wye: PCCS Books (pp265–284).

Richards C (2011). Transsexualism and existentialism. *Existential Analysis 22*(2): 272–279.

Richards C, Barker M (eds) (2015). *The Palgrave Handbook of the Psychology of Sexuality and Gender*. London: Palgrave-Macmillan.

Richards C, Barker M (2013). *Sexuality and Gender for Mental Health Professionals: a practical guide*. London: Sage.

Richards C, Bouman WP, Barker MJ (eds) (2017). *Genderqueer and Non-Binary Genders*. London: Palgrave-Macmillan.

Richards C, Seal L (2014). Reproductive issues for trans people. *Journal of Family Planning and Reproductive Health Care 40*(4): 245–247.

Rodrigues VA (2014). Are sexual preferences existential choices? *Existential Analysis 25*(1): 43–52.

Royal College of Psychiatrists (2013). *CR181 Good Practice Guidelines for the Assessment and Treatment of Gender Dysphoria*. London: Royal College of Psychiatrists.

Seal LJ, Franklin S, Richards C, Shishkareva A, Sinclaire C, Barrett J (2012). Predictive markers for breast augmentation and a comparison of side effect profiles in transwomen taking various hormonal regimens. *The Journal of Clinical Endocrinology & Metabolism* 97(12): 4422–4428.

Seikowski K (2007). Psychotherapy and transsexualism. *Andrologia 39*: 248–252.

Simon L, Zsolt U, Fogd D, Czobor P (2011). Dysfunctional core beliefs, perceived parenting behavior and psychopathology in gender identity disorder: a comparison of male-to-female, female-to-male transsexual and nontranssexual control subjects. *Journal of Behavior Therapy and Experimental Psychiatry 42*(1): 38–45.

von Krafft-Ebing R (1886). *Psychopathia Sexualis: eine klinisch-forensische studie* (Sexual Psychopathy: a clinical-forensic study). Stuttgart: Ferdinand Enke.

World Professional Association for Transgender Health (WPATH) (2011). *Standards of Care for the Heath of Transsexual, Transgender and Gender Nonconforming People* (7th ed). Minneapolis, MN: WPATH.

10

Living ME: a case study of the experience of being diagnosed with a chronic 'psychosomatic' illness

Simon du Plock

Existential-phenomenological therapists have tended to approach the notion of 'research' with a degree of suspicion. The existential-phenomenological tradition has until recently been located, for historical reasons, largely outside academia. There is, consequently, more concentration on dissemination through pedagogy than on accumulation of knowledge via research, as has been the case for psychology since 1879, when Wundt founded the first laboratory for experimental psychology at the University of Leipzig. It may be that, in the past, existential-phenomenological therapists were mainly to be found in private practice where there has been (relatively) less pressure to produce research. Over and above this, though, existential-phenomenological therapists have been critical of forms of research that, in concentrating on observable, measurable behaviour, are unable to capture the subjectively lived experience of clients.

Good psychotherapy research is, I would suggest, a living thing: it should illuminate some aspect of what it means to be human, and it should leap off the page to revitalise some aspect of our way of being as therapists. In doing so it mirrors a key characteristic of good therapy, that there is a genuine connection between the meaning worlds of client and therapist and, in meeting, some sharing of experience. I have long argued (du Plock 2004, 2016, 2017) that we existential-phenomenological therapists should, in considering the value and relevance of research in our specialism, make use of the philosophical attitude that underpins our client work. It seems to me that an inquiring mind is the *sine qua non* of psychotherapy and there need be no radical break between this attitude and its rigorous channelling when undertaking case study research. McLeod points out that we are constantly engaged in 'research' as we go through life and in our clinical work:

> A counselling session with a client can be seen as a piece of research, a piecing together of information and understandings, followed by testing the validity of conclusions and actions based on shared knowing…
> (2003: 4)

I believe that existential-phenomenological therapists are ideally positioned to generate case study research grounded in first-person experience and naïve inquiry – this is, after all, remarkably similar to what we aspire to generate in the course of our practice with clients. When McLeod writes that:

> A useful working definition of research is: a systematic process of critical inquiry leading to valid propositions and conclusions that are communicated to interested others. (2003: 4)

he might easily be describing the phenomenological perspective as it is deployed in existential-phenomenological therapy.

In what follows I will outline the preliminary stages of a piece of case study research in order to illustrate how this subjective experience and the specific research trajectory it entails provide a source of thick description and hypotheses that can be explored further with co-researchers. The early stages of such an inquiry are not dissimilar to the process of reflection and analysis typical of existential therapy. While what follows reflects Ellis' definition of a clinical case, in that it is 'research, writing, story and method that connect the autobiographical and personal to the cultural, social and political' (2004: xix), it is not a narrative account of therapy, written from the therapist's perspective. Instead, I have attempted to explore a phenomenon – my own experience of being diagnosed with a chronic 'psychosomatic' illness – using the phenomenological method that I would normally apply when engaging as a co-researcher to explore a client's way of being in the world. As I am the primary researcher in this instance, I would term this enquiry 'an autoethographic case study of self'.

Being diagnosed with myalgic encephalomyelitis (more commonly known as ME or chronic fatigue syndrome) has encouraged me to think more deeply about the nature of enquiry and has added substance to my assertion (du Plock, 2004) that the researcher's identity – their sense of who they are – is as crucial a factor in what it can illuminate as it is in the practice of therapy. The notion of the neutral, objective researcher is as absurd as the notion of the neutral, objective therapist. In both cases, the illumination they can provide depends upon who they are – or perhaps *where* they are – in relation to either the client or the research topic. I have found it helpful to conceptualise this 'whereness' (following the logic that asking a client *where* they are is more revealing than asking them *how* they are) in terms of 'research trajectory', by which I mean the angle at which the researcher enters into an explorative process. The angle at which one enters the field of inquiry determines what is illuminated and also what is cast into shadow. I say 'cast into shadow' because there is neither light nor shadow prior to the advent of the enquirer. As this trajectory serves to privilege some aspects of the phenomenon under consideration and will obscure others, it is important for the case study researcher to be aware of their subjective stance from the outset.

So, rejecting the possibility of being a neutral investigator, I need to describe clearly my own trajectory of inquiry in relation to the experience of being diagnosed with a chronic illness. In some respects, I am attempting no more than to take seriously the axiom of existential-phenomenological investigation that the 'prime researcher' – a term used to indicate the co-constructedness of 'reality' entailed in both therapy and research – should pay appropriate attention to the meanings they bring to the phenomenon under consideration. Ruth Behar, writing in a classic text about 'humanistic anthropology', makes clear that researchers who locate themselves in their own texts forfeit the defensive position of 'scientific observer':

> Writing vulnerably takes as much skill, nuance, and willingness to follow through on all the ramifications of a complicated idea as does writing invulnerably and distantly. I would say it takes yet greater skill… To assert that one is a 'white middle-class woman' or a 'black gay man' or a 'working-class Latina'… is only interesting if one is able to draw deeper connections between one's personal experience and the subject under study. That doesn't require a full-length autobiography, but it does require a keen understanding of what aspects of the self are the most important filters through which one perceives the world and, more particularly, the topic being studied. (2014: 13)

Change of personal identity

The impact of the experience of illness on sense of self and identity has received considerable attention, particularly from the symbolic interactionist perspective (Bury 1991; Charmaz, 1983; Corbin & Strauss, 1987). A number of writers (including Clark & James, 2003) have used their findings to explore the specific problems presented by chronic illness, including ME. None, though, have been in a position to explore first-hand the experience of chronic illness via a case study. My own diagnosis in 2007 presented me with a radical challenge to my sense of identity in a number of ways, some of which are relevant here.

Diagnosis typically entails an 'expert' of some kind making a judgement about another person who, generally, is considered a 'non-expert'. In medical terms, a doctor tells their patient that they 'have' a certain illness or condition. When the patient is a psychologist and the condition generally thought to be at least partly psychosomatic in nature, the authority and power in play become complex and problematic. This is perhaps particularly so given existential-phenomenological critiques of diagnosis. It may also be that my previous way of constructing a sense of self heightened the challenge of this diagnosis: as Aujoulat and colleagues argue in their research into the experience of chronic illness:

> People who had previously enjoyed being in control of things and who describe themselves as having a managerial type of personality appeared in our study to be at greater risk of experiencing a feeling of loss of their sense of identity. (2007: 9)

I found myself thrown into a process of enquiry in which I was not merely the prime researcher but was also the primary subject, as I sought to engage with questions such as: how do I feel about 'having' an illness? How might ME impact on my sense of identity? What does it mean to be a psychotherapist with a chronic, debilitating condition? As a psychologist, I found it natural to reflect on this challenge by reading in depth about ME and keeping a diary to structure what initially seemed a situation over which I could exercise little control. At the outset, I did not specifically frame as research the literature search I undertook or the diary in which I recorded my subjective experience of both the condition and my interaction with healthcare professionals. When I rose above the situation to take a helicopter view, I conceptualised them as subjective strategies adopted in response to my personal situation.

In the case of diary-keeping, I was informed by my knowledge of the therapeutic effects of writing structured accounts of stressful experiences (Hunt, 2000; Hunt & Sampson, 2002; Pennebaker, 1993; Philips, Penman & Linnington, 1999). I soon noted, though, that I found both activities therapeutically useful and I began to make connections between this insight and my existing professional knowledge. As an example, following my diagnosis, I visited NHS and other websites that offered information on ME and CFS, and felt reassured to discover how precisely the ME label mapped my symptoms, even though these websites invariably emphasised the limitations of the few available treatments. This reminded me of how therapy clients often seek a label for their condition and can be dismayed rather than relieved when therapists cannot or will not provide one. Similarly, I found I kept increasingly detailed verbatim accounts of my meetings with healthcare professionals. Writing these records assisted me in debriefing. It also helped me to gain an enhanced sense of mastery, as I was able to identify their different relational styles.

From naïve to systematic enquiry

This movement from subjective experience towards more general (I would not say objective) experience meant that soon my idiosyncratic questions were reframed as:

- What does it mean to 'have' an illness?
- How might a diagnosis of ME impact on sense of identity?
- What is it like for a psychotherapist to be diagnosed with a possibly psychosomatic condition?

I found relatively little has been written – or at least published – addressing these questions. This led me to further hypothesise that there is something about the identity of 'psychotherapist' that makes it difficult for us to engage with our own experience of illness. It is difficult for us to consider ourselves as a 'case'. In this connection, I noted that Bayne (1998), writing in *The Needs of Counsellors and Psychotherapists*, writes about emotional self-care, but does so primarily in terms of using strategies to cope with stress.

Without necessarily doing so in full awareness, I found I had taken my diagnosis and actively sought to understand it as 'a continual transformative process' with which I developed a close relationship, rather than accepting it passively as a victim. I also found, paradoxically, that, in closing with it to make it my own, my enquiry became one of more than just personal significance. In the wider enquiry that I undertook, I found I journeyed from a descriptive self-analysis of the type with which phenomenological enquiry often opens to a consideration of the co-constitution of relationship in the course of professional consultation. In the process of this I moved from naïve enquiry – the quotidian acquiring of information – towards research enquiry. Barber, distinguishing between naïve enquiry and research says:

> ... to qualify as research, your inquiry must involve a careful searching, your method of collecting information must be located within a recognizable methodological tradition, and you must demonstrate systematic investigation and critical reflection upon both what you are doing and how you are doing it. You need also to illuminate both your motivation and rationale and what influences you at the time. (2006: 89)

The diary in which I recorded accounts of my meetings with each of the health professionals involved in my treatment provided a way of keeping track of a complex process, since five professionals played a role: two general practitioners, a practice nurse, a medical herbalist and a clinical psychologist. While my thinking was that maintaining a record would allow me to 'stay in the driving seat' in a pragmatic sense, I soon noticed that writing functioned as a way of debriefing. I moved from recording primarily factual information to a more comprehensive reflection on my feelings prior to, during and following each meeting. I found I looked forward to meetings with the clinical psychologist and medical herbalist, although each involved a fatiguing journey of several miles. In contrast, I generally felt apprehensive about meetings with the GPs and practice nurse, even though the surgery was nearby. I also noticed that I wrote verbatim notes after visits to the surgery, but often recorded only a summary of my meetings with the psychologist and herbalist. This structured enquiry had clear therapeutic functions for me in helping me make distress and confusion meaningful. I agree with Sousa (2007) when he argues that existential-phenomenological therapy and research should not be conflated. I would also suggest that, while it is often important to conceptualise them as distinct activities, research can be therapeutic and therapy involves exploration akin to research.

Emergence of an organising theme: 'openness to relationship'

Within the first month of treatment the theme of 'relationship' surfaced to link these observations. As an existential-phenomenological therapist, I am constantly aware of ways in which I can hold myself open to, or close down possibilities of, being-with-the-client. I know that a number of factors are involved in this, including my willingness or otherwise to hold myself open for the experience that May (1958: 37, 38) describes as the experience of 'here-is-a-new-person'. Our ability to encounter the other in this open manner is a prerequisite, according to May, for the other to have an 'I-am' experience (1958: 42–46).

While I have sometimes become aware of the I-am experience as a therapy client, I had not previously had this experience within a relatively short time of working as a client with five different healthcare professionals. I found it instructive to reflect on the ways in which each health professional embodied a relational style that to some extent determined their availability for relationship. These reflections became a major organising theme in my research diary. Typically, (and I had numerous meetings with these five professionals), I found I felt less unwell after meetings with the herbalist and psychologist.

The herbalist, medically trained but without a counselling background, tended to present as interested and available for encounter. Her focus was holistic: she would ask me open questions and discuss various options and recent research in a relatively democratic way, generally free of jargon. She did not attempt to hide herself but, equally, did not disclose inappropriately. She presented smartly but relatively informally in terms of dress, and sat to the side of her desk while taking notes. I found it interesting and reassuring that she was transparent in this way, permitting me, for instance, to follow her train of thought when she was considering the merits of various prescriptions. Her boundaries were flexible but holding, and my felt sense was that her style of engagement was broadly similar to that to which I aspire in my own clinical work.

I found my therapist, a senior male clinical psychologist approaching retirement, was generally open to a relationship based on mutual understanding. It was disarming, especially as an existential practitioner, to be greeted at our first appointment by 'I've Googled you, and I feel I know you already!' My response – 'Well, I've done the same to see what you've published' – left us in a curious position. I think our mutual agreement that therapy would not be possible but that administering various tests and providing fortnightly conversations could be helpful and supportive was accurate. Perhaps the most helpful aspect of our meetings was that he disclosed his frustration with the shortcomings of the GPs and supported my referral to a specialist clinic. I noticed that I looked forward to our meetings and did not need to use my diary to debrief to the extent that I did after visiting the GP surgery.

In contrast, the female nurse at the surgery made little eye contact and was concerned to take blood samples as quickly as possible. She disclosed nothing of herself or her training and her mode of relationship was of the 'doing-to' type. Frustrated at our first meeting that I admitted a fear of needles, she responded, 'You're my second needle-phobic so far this morning – it's not my day!' Perhaps unsurprisingly, I felt 'unseen' in these encounters, except insofar as I fitted the category of 'difficult patient' and was labelled 'phobic'.

The senior of the two GPs, a middle-aged man, stayed behind his desk most of the time and kept his eyes on a computer screen. His mode of relationship was to use the computer as intermediary. Having typed information into it, he would share the 'factual' information it generated. One of his most puzzling announcements was: 'How would it strike you if I told you that you have a 20% chance of heart attack in the next 10 years?' I found this style of relating to me as if I were an audience for medical technology alienating; not only did I not feel seen, I felt that I had somehow failed to appropriately appreciate the technology with which the doctor was so clearly enamoured.

His colleague, a younger man perhaps in his late 30s, took pains to demonstrate his willingness to treat me as an equal by maintaining constant eye contact. So relentless was this that I began to fantasise that he had taken an intensive course in advanced empathy techniques. He explained in some detail what was known about ME. He seemed to thus invite my compliance with a long-term antidepressant drug prescription and was baffled and defensive about what to suggest beyond this when I indicated I was not willing to take this route. While he agreed to refer me to a specialist clinic, he did so with the caution, 'A lot of people expect a cure but there isn't one.' As I had explicitly stated I was seeking ways to manage a chronic condition, this seemed to confirm that, regardless of the amount of eye contact, once again I hadn't been seen, but had been categorised as one among 'a lot of people'. Moreover, this category, 'a lot of people', was clearly viewed as problematic.

My experience, while I frame it in the context of being 'seen' by the other, reflects the findings of studies that have focused on patients' sense of self-determination and power. Such studies indicate that the key features of an empowering patient-medical practitioner relationship include continuity, patient-centredness, mutual acknowledgement and relatedness (Chang, Li & Liu, 2004; McWilliam et al, 1997; Paterson, 2001). McWilliam and colleagues found that patients experience empowerment in the process of telling their story if the healthcare professional is able to facilitate a mutual exploration of their situation and situatedness. In doing so, they argue, patient and practitioner collaborate to add to or create meaning from the patient's experience. In contrast, Paterson (2001) finds that, where the healthcare professional discounts experiential knowledge and provides inadequate resources, particularly in terms of time and continuity, the patient is likely to feel disempowered.

'Relationship' reframed in the context of the case study

Up to this point, my observations were focused on the extent to which each healthcare professional was able to be in relationship with me, according to my sense as an existential-phenomenological therapist of what the phenomenon of relationship might mean. I had noted how I felt more or less ill according to the extent to which each was able to encounter me. My feeling was increasingly that there might be a link between the experience of being 'seen' and feeling ill. As Charon asserts:

> The healing process begins when patients tell of symptoms or even fears of illness... These narratives, or pathographics as they are sometimes called, demonstrate how critical is the telling of pain and suffering, enabling patients to give voice to what they endure and to frame the illness so as to escape dominion by it. Without the narrative acts of telling and being heard, the patient cannot convey to anyone else – or to the self – what he or she is going through. More radically, and perhaps equally true, without these narrative acts, the patient cannot grasp what the events of the illness mean. (2006: 65, 66)

As the enquiry widened, a further cycle of research evolved – I began to think about these communication difficulties more systemically, as it seemed to me that the various health professionals were not able to hear *each other*. My impression was reinforced by the wording of the King's College Chronic Fatigue (CFS) Research and Treatment website, where I found this cautionary note for prospective patients (Deary, undated):

> The perpetual battle for validation that most sufferers of CFS are caught in is, literally, physiologically exhausting, depressing and dispiriting. It affects the course of the illness. No other sufferer of chronic disease has

to fight this bizarre battle to have the facts that they live with every day legitimized by a hostile authority. As long as CFS has to prove itself, that much longer will sufferers suffer. As therapists, our first and last concern is to take the suffering of clients seriously. All this involves is listening.

While this message seems to be directed towards patients, it is obvious that such a 'battle for validation' is primarily one between healthcare professionals themselves. As the website expressed it in 2007, when I accessed it for information (the site's content has since been reworded):

> Some GPs are sceptical about the existence or treatment of CFS/ME. If you are having problems getting a referral for these reasons, *you could perhaps try another GP in your practice*. (my emphasis)

The casual wording of the highlighted phrase belies a serious problem: such a request will probably be interpreted as a challenge to the power structures of many GP practices. A healthy person might find making such a request daunting, and it is likely to exacerbate the symptoms of an ME sufferer.

Concluding comments

So, to summarise the journey I have taken, I have – however briefly and sketchily – suggested that existential-phenomenological therapists should ground their research in subjective experience and naïve enquiry. My personal and professional experiences led me to an enhanced awareness of the 'self' of the researcher at the core of a reflexive process. A wealth of thick description surfaces when we attend to the researcher's individual journey into the field. The thick description I obtained in the early stages of my research journey provided a resource for reflection on later stages of enquiry. There is considerable overlap between the mode of enquiry that I used in this research and that which I use in therapeutic practice. As Fishman states:

> the practitioners know that therapy knowledge always starts with the contextually specific, qualitatively rich case that is naturalistically situated, that deals with real persons (not statistical composites), and that generalizes via induction from the specific. (2010: ix)

My own experience of a diagnostic process was the catalyst for personal identity questions and therapeutic activities that led to more general enquiry and the emergence of an organising theme – in this particular instance, that of health professionals' openness to being in relationship with patients. This, in turn, led me to hypothesise about their openness to be in relation with each other, and the implications of systematic communication patterns for the patient's sense of self. While it is not always the case that the researcher is prompted by direct personal experience to embark on their enquiry, the resulting study is impoverished and, I would argue, less informed by phenomenology if the self of the researcher is not reflected on. We might, in fact, speculate such reflection is even *more* important when the researcher's motivation for exploring a phenomenon is unclear or is 'hidden' behind the adoption of a 'phenomenological method'.

Discussion with Zack Eleftheriadou

Zack: Reading your chapter, I had the sense that you found writing up your experience as a case study to be very therapeutic.

Simon: I'm glad that comes across as I think that one of the most important things for me in this long and rather traumatic process was discovering how helpful it was to resist adopting ready-made labels or identities that might lead me to see myself as the passive sufferer of an illness. What helped me in this situation was holding fast to my identity as a clinician and as a researcher, and viewing my situation through this lens. I want to say the crucial thing for me was to adopt the attitude I bring to bear when I am working with a therapy client – an attitude of curiosity. I attempt to bracket what I know (or might think I know) about something or someone, in order to arrive at a position of naïve curiosity: what is it like to be this person, with these attributes, skills, cultural background, and what is it like for this person to encounter this particular phenomenon? You can see, I think, that in engaging in this way, the phenomenon becomes interesting rather than just crushing or debilitating or dominant. And this way of engaging also mirrors what happens when we write a case study. I also found, in reflecting on my experience and especially in regularly writing about it as I would write when I am constructing a case study, I was able to impose order and structure on what might otherwise have felt like a rather chaotic experience.

Zack: Treating yourself as your own case study seems to have given you a way of engaging with your experience and making sense of it, rather than becoming its 'victim', but I wonder if there are any potential dangers in doing this?

Simon: It might be objected that looking closely at our own subjective experience could become self-indulgent, and I'm sure this is something to bear in mind. This is why I think Behar's work is so important, in that it reminds us to ask ourselves why we are reflecting so closely on something in our own awareness. As she reminds us, the purpose of writing vulnerably and closely (as against invulnerably and distantly) is to enable us to draw deeper connections between our personal experience and the phenomenon under study. I have taken care to ensure that my own experience is only a catalyst for a rigorous inquiry. This is what I mean when I talk about moving from subjective experience towards more general experience and reframing my idiosyncratic questions to explore what it means to 'have' an illness, the implications of diagnosis for sense of identity, and what it is like for a psychotherapist to be diagnosed with a psychosomatic condition.

I am not sure that I would have looked at any of these questions if I had not been moved to do so by my own experience of being diagnosed. To hold back from exploring this would have felt quite odd, really a rejection of the exhortation to reflexivity that we find increasingly throughout the psychotherapy training and research literature. In many ways, I think what this approach to case study research does is enable us to take the role of what Costley and colleagues (2010) have called the 'insider-researcher' and find valid ways of exploring phenomena and situations about which we have intimate knowledge. I think my understanding of phenomenology came together with my experience of diagnosis and 'treatment' to enable me to say something valid about the different ways medical professionals open up or close down the possibility of being in relationship with those who consult them, and also about the implications of these different degrees of encounter for the wellbeing of their patients.

Zack: What do you think you have gained from writing this case study that you can use in your own clinical practice?

Simon: That really is the crucial question, I think. I feel that, in the process of making myself the object of my own case study, I came to a far greater appreciation of the importance of 'being-with', rather than 'doing-to' in my engagement with clients. Like most existential therapists, I have read quite a lot about this. Of course, Heidegger writes about the medical approach to treating individuals as objects or tools that break down and need to be fixed, but the impact of this on the individual's sense of identity becomes immediately evident when we are, ourselves, subject to this dehumanising mode of treatment. So, I am left with a much enhanced understanding of how to facilitate authentic encounter in my clinical work.

References

Aujoulat I, Luminet O, Deccache A (2007). The perspective of patients on their experience of powerlessness. *Qualitative Health Research* 17(6): 772–785.

Barber P (2006). *Becoming a Practitioner Researcher: a Gestalt approach to holistic inquiry.* London: Middlesex University Press.

Bayne R (1998). Survival. In: Horton I, Varma V (eds). *The Needs of Counsellors and Psychotherapists: emotional, social, physical, professional.* London: Sage (pp183–198).

Behar R (2014). *The Vulnerable Observer: anthropology that breaks your heart.* Boston, MA: Beacon Press.

Bury M (1991). The sociology of chronic illness: a review of research and prospects. *Sociology of Health and Illness* 13(4): 451–468.

Chang LC, Li IC, Liu CH (2004). A study of the empowerment process for cancer patients using Freire's dialogical interviewing. *Journal of Nursing Research* 12(1): 41–49.

Charmaz K (1983). Loss of self: a fundamental form of suffering in the chronically ill. *Sociology of Health and Illness* 5(2): 168–195.

Charon R (2006). *Narrative Medicine: honouring the stories of illness.* New York, NY: Oxford University Press.

Clark JN, James S (2003). The radicalized self: the impact on the self of the contested nature of the diagnosis of chronic fatigue syndrome. *Social Science and Medicine* 57(8): 1387–1395.

Corbin J, Strauss A (1987). Accompaniments of chronic illness: changes in body, self, biography, and biological time. *Research in the Sociology of Health Care* 6: 249–281.

Costley C, Elliott G, Gibbs P (2010). *Doing Work-Based Research: approaches to enquiry for insider-researchers.* London: Sage.

Deary V (undated). *CFS and the Facts of Life – an article for clinicians.* [Online.] King's College Chronic Fatigue (CFS) Research and Treatment Unit. www.kcl.ac.uk/ioppn/depts/pm/research/cfs/health/index.aspx (accessed 3 September 2007).

du Plock S (2017). Philosophical issues in counselling psychology. In: Murphy D (ed). *Counselling Psychology: a textbook for study and practice.* Chichester: Wiley-Blackwell (pp36–52).

du Plock S (2016). Where am I with my research? Harnessing reflexivity for practice-based qualitative inquiry. *The Psychotherapist* 62(Spring): 16–18.

du Plock S (2004). What do we mean when we use the word 'research'? *Existential Analysis* 15(1): 29–37.

Ellis C (2004). *The Ethnographic I: a methodological novel about autoethnography.* Lanham, MD: Rowman & Littleford.

Fishman D (2010). Foreword. In: McLeod J. *Case Study Research in Counselling*. London: Sage (ppix-xi).

Hunt C (2000). *Therapeutic Dimensions of Autobiography in Creative Writing*. London: Jessica Kingsley.

Hunt C, Sampson F (eds) (2002). *The Self on the Page: theory and practice of creative writing in personal development*. London: Jessica Kingsley.

May R (1958). Contributions of existential therapy. In: May R, Angel E, Ellenberger HF (eds). *Existence: a new dimension in psychiatry and psychology*. New York, NY: Simon & Schuster (pp37–91).

McLeod J (2003). *Doing Counselling Research*. London: Sage.

McWilliam CL, Stewart M, Brown JB, McNair S, Desai K, Patterson ML et al (1997). Creating empowering meaning: an interactive process of promoting health with chronically ill older Canadians. *Health Promotion International* 12(2): 111–123.

Paterson B (2001). Myth of empowerment in chronic illness. *Journal of Advanced Nursing* 34(5): 574–581.

Pennebaker JW (1993). Putting stress into words: health, linguistic and therapeutic implications. *Behaviour Research and Therapy 31*: 539–548.

Philips D, Penman D, Linnington L (1999). *Writing Well: creative writing and mental health*. London: Jessica Kingsley.

Sousa D (2007). From Monet's paintings to Margaret's ducks: divagations on phenomenological research. *Existential Analysis 19*(1): 143–155.

11

Finding meaning: cross-cultural existential therapy with a young refugee

Zack Eleftheriadou

In this chapter I will present a case study of a young person who became a refugee and experienced profound trauma in the context of multiple cross-cultural conflicts. The chapter draws inspiration from both existential and psychodynamic theoretical frameworks to make sense of such a life-changing socio-psychological experience. Both theoretical viewpoints place emphasis on the relational nature of the therapeutic encounter and therefore assign greater importance to the relationship than do other theoretical aspects. Both view the individual as always being 'in relationship' with others (the therapist, their family and culture, among many other layers), rather than viewing the individual in isolation. For the purposes of this chapter, the focus will be on pertinent aspects of existential thinking such as the therapist's phenomenological stance, which is to understand the client's subjective experience or 'being' by setting aside dogma or any preconceptions in order to let the client's narrative story unfold. This stance facilitates the client to find new possibilities and to discover the unique meaning of their experience.

Theoretical links and bridges

The theoretical backdrop of this case is a bridge between (relational) psychoanalytic and existential/phenomenological thinking. Although these two theoretical frameworks may be seen as contradictory, pluralistic thinking (where numerous theoretical approaches are held in mind at the same time) in this context is important for a number of reasons. First, I would argue that the state of becoming a refugee, experiencing trauma and losing so many aspects of one's familiar experience warrants more than one theoretical framework. My view has always been that it is such a complex experience that one framework cannot possibly even begin to address the richness of the human experience; we require more than one lens. Second, in order to work cross-culturally and across contrasting value systems, we need to have more than one framework in mind. For reasons that will become clear below, my experience indicates that these two approaches provide a helpful way to understand the complexity of a person's experience and how they make sense of it within their cultural value system.

There are many points where psychoanalysis and existential thinking differ, but a greater degree of convergence has been evidenced recently with 'relational psychoanalysis' (as interpreted by psychoanalysts such as Stephen Mitchell (Mitchell & Aron, 1999) and Daniel Stern (2004)), which has rejected the overemphasis on the intrapsychic (from or within the self) and instead emphasises the interpsychic (the relating of one person with another). This is particularly helpful in working with cross-cultural populations because the therapist strives to understand not only the individual's meaning but also the nature of their relationships within and outside their psychosocial context (which includes the therapist).

The central aspect of my work is to create a trusting therapeutic relationship that is experienced as real (as opposed to a clinical, distant one). Stern and colleagues (1998) have named the most charged and pivotal aspects of the therapeutic relationship as 'moments of meeting'. In order to create these connections, the therapist adopts the following stance: 'cannot be routine, habitual or technical' (p913) and 'requires a response that is too specific and personal to be a known technical manoevre' (p911). In contemporary relational psychoanalysis, such moments may be met from the therapist in different ways: by an interpretation (linking emotional experiences and events) or a verbal comment that acknowledges their narrative or affective state but allows the client to make the connections. However, the important aspect here is that even a non-verbal response can be equally affective and meaningful. These are complex concepts, but for my current purposes what is vital to understand is that 'the application of habitual technical moves will not suffice' (p912). If something different and authentic takes place, it can offer food for thought and even provide an opportunity for change in our clients.

It is important to start by saying that existential thinkers, such as Heidegger, May or Yalom, do not all share the same assumptions. For example, they differ in whether they believe some of the major questions of existence can be answered, and some hold a more positive view of human nature than others. Therefore, I shall draw on some of the shared assumptions that are especially useful in cross-cultural therapeutic work. An existential framework offers a creative way of seeing the person, rather than simply offering another theory. In fact, I think that existential ideas, such as a person's uniqueness, are invaluable for all therapists to consider, regardless of their theoretical orientation. Existential theory accepts that most of us experience traumatic events in life and moves away from the medical (and often pathologising) model of treatment. It 'does not seek to cure or explain, it merely seeks to explore, describe and clarify in order to try to understand the human predicament' (van Deurzen-Smith, 1997: 3).

According to existential theory, there are certain events in our life that are out of our control, that are 'givens' of existence (Yalom, 1980). First, there is the given that our death is inevitable. This brings the paradox of life and motivation to life while knowing that one day it will all end. This is brought forcibly to the fore for young refugees. Suddenly there is loss and abrupt separations and endings from their family, friends, religion, familiar environment and, of course, language (Gonsalves, 2014). Second, existential writers such Yalom (1980) talk about the concept of isolation: however much we seek to relate to others, ultimately we are alone and cannot possibly share all the richness of our experiences. Of course, cultural displacement can push us into an extreme position of isolation. There can be a feeling of becoming disconnected from oneself because one's cultural and most personal identity is experienced as lost. Here the existential idea that there is no fixed sense of self (Spinelli, 2015) can provide valuable insight into the migration experience as it impacts in unpredictable ways.

The experience of trauma can further intensify this feeling of being disconnected. In this context, trauma refers to being part of and/or witnessing experiences of war, death and injury or torture that are emotionally overwhelming for the individual to process. These experiences are so stressful for the individual that they can feel as if one's most fundamental sense of what it is to be human has gone. When such experiences are pushed out of mind because they are too painful, we therapists have to find a way to support people to re-connect with these, themselves and others. Trauma is a profound, life-changing experience.

In many cultures there are strong overt and subtle moral codes of thinking, behaving and acceptable interpersonal communication. According to deVries (2007), culture can act as a protective and supportive system when one is faced with the unfamiliar or human distress:

> ... culture thereby buffers its members from the potentially profound impact of stressful experiences. It does so by means of furnishing social support, providing identifies in terms of norms and values, and supplying a shared vision of the future... it locates experience in a historical context and forces continuity on discontinuous events. (2007: 400–401)

Every relationship and emotion is embedded in a particular socio-cultural context. Meanings and concepts (see Eleftheriadou, 1994) change in the new cultural context and they need more scrutiny. For a refugee who suddenly loses their familiar context, life can seem meaningless. Meaninglessness in the new environment can leave them with a sense that the usual boundaries have become diluted and they are confronted with a new-found but uncomfortable freedom. For many people, it is tempting to cling on to any of the known cultural pathways, which seem to offer certainty and may bring some comfort.

Existential thinking emphasises the importance of our context and can provide a useful framework, whatever our theoretical modality. Spinelli (1989) writes about human existence as being embedded in a 'being-in-the-world'. The philosopher, Heidegger (1927/1962), in his influential *Being and Time*, refers to 'thrown-ness', or being placed in a particular context about which we have no choice. Observations of and research into cross-cultural development have shown how such 'being-in-the-world' always takes place in a relational context (Spinelli, 2015). This view is shared by May (1958), who stated that a person can only be understood in the context of their complete being. Similarly, Stolorow, a psychoanalyst and philosopher, states:

> ... trauma is constituted in an intersubjective context in which severe emotional pain cannot find a relational home in which it can be held. In such a context, painful affect states become unendurable – that is, traumatic. (2008: 2)

This idea suggests not only that trauma is embedded in a context but that, in order to manage the experience, we need to find a way to reconnect with others.

In consequence, the notion of a 'worldview' is helpful because it encompasses the physical, spiritual and social world and how these three all come together to form our private world. According to van Deurzen-Smith (1988), the 'four dimensions of human experience are interlinked and interrelated. It is not possible to work exclusively in one sphere and neglect all other aspects' (p102). If the therapist adopts this open stance they are more likely to be able to gain an understanding of the client's philosophy of life, rather than fitting them into the Western psychotherapeutic framework.

Every moment is full of possibilities and choices and yet it becomes so difficult to be in touch with this, especially if you hold the belief that you knew how your life path was destined to unfurl. The goal of existential psychotherapy is to support the client to explore all the different connections of their worldview (or lack thereof) and understand the meanings they hold. The creation of meaning is a personally constructed process, largely influenced by cultural values. It can be difficult to separate personal and cultural elements. It is important that any exploration is anchored into the 'here-and-now', especially for those who have experienced trauma, since the temporal aspects of the experience can be lost. Commonly, when a person undergoes trauma, they cannot move away from the past and experience dissociation (Bromberg, 2003). Dissociation is the experience of confusion between the past and present; memories/events are re-experienced as if they are recurring. Such constant intrusions into the present may prevent the person from even conceiving of a future. The work of psychotherapy is to eventually transform these intrusions into recollections that are more manageable.

The therapist's role is to make an emotional contact by being authentic. It is a stance that owes much to the relational school of psychotherapy, which emphasises the interpersonal nature of the therapeutic encounter and process as they occur in the present moment. The quality of the relationship between client and therapist remains central to the work and takes precedence over theoretical aspects or technique. Stern (2004) describes the therapeutic space as a 'co-creation', which represents a more contemporary (relational) psychoanalytic view. The two participants create something through their unique interpersonal relationship.

There are three phenomenological 'rules' (originally discussed by the German philosopher Husserl (1962) and more recently by contemporary existential thinkers such as Spinelli (1989)) that are helpful throughout the process. First is the 'rule of epoché', or the process of stepping back from the therapist's assumptions. When we have experience with a particular client group, we can hold preconceptions of what they are likely to bring. Spinelli (2015) discusses how we describe ourselves in terms of self-constructs that are challenged by our experiences. The therapist helps the client examine and challenge these constructs and understand possible limitations. The process is facilitated though the therapist practising a state of 'unknowing', or openness.

The therapeutic alliance is far richer if we can remain open and let the story and dialogue take their course. This is especially evident with refugees who feel lost and have lost their familiar structure. Therapists have to caution themselves not to provide too much of a structure or to go into a rescuing role. Of course, what I am referring to is a process of striving towards this, as it is impossible to achieve such a stance completely. However, it gives us a chance to stand back and reflect before providing any response that may be reactive.

Second, the rule of 'horizontalisation' asks us to view all of the material the client brings as having equal significance. We all formulate views about what is important for the client to explore right from the beginning. This rule reminds us that there are many issues and they may unfold differently. Clients, of course, often bring 'presenting issues' or are referred because someone perceives they have a particular problem, but when we have worked with them for a while, other issues emerge. Both the intrapsychic and interpersonal experiences of trauma survivors also vary tremendously, so we can never know how trauma will impact on them.

Third, the 'rule of description' urges us to stay with the 'here-and-now', with the immediate behaviour/emotions being conveyed, rather than seek causal links in the past and present or positioning where the person 'should be'. This also implies that there is not one correct interpretation but the material they are conveying is part of multiple issues and can change, depending on where the person is. The 'rule of description' is especially important in the beginning of the therapy and can open up new possibilities.

Clients are often confused about what they are feeling and in trauma work they are often overwhelmed by the emotional intensity. Van Deurzen-Smith suggests that:

> what is needed is the understanding of what the emotion is indicating about the way in which one is conducting one's life… it sets out to help clients in learning to read the message of their emotional experience, so that they can master it rather than suffer it. (1988: 139)

Furthermore, van Deurzen-Smith states that 'raw feelings, once recognised, need to be translated into understandable messages. These messages need to be deciphered and turned into constructive action' (1988: 140).

There are many theories and classifications about trauma (see van der Kolk, 2007). I will not address the psychiatric classifications, as I believe it is preferable to view the concept of 'trauma' as widely as possible and to move away from medical/psychiatric categorisation. Trauma is a process, rather than a state or set of symptoms to be overcome. It 'cannot be easily integrated, so we shut down instead or resort to self-blame and flounder in hopelessness' (van Deurzen, 2011: 119). No matter how secure our attachments have been, the trauma of losing everything around us can have a profound impact. Nevertheless, many people do find creative ways to cope with even the most adverse circumstances. Trauma is not simply the experience that one undergoes; it is much more about how it is experienced and the sense one makes of it and who it is experienced with. Hence, there is a 'narrative truth' but no external historical 'truth' to uncover. Although the traumatic experience is often pivotal to one's identity and future life journey, it is imperative that this does not remain the only defining factor. The therapist's task, then, is to assist the client to incorporate traumatic experience and conflicting emotions into other aspects of their life, in order to rebuild their shattered identity.

The refugee experience is often one of detachment. It can feel as if one is leading a life that one did not choose and that is suddenly unpredictable. The exploration of cultural and familial attachments is a complex process that challenges the notion of a straightforward linear 'adaptation' process. This is in line with the existential idea that we may share social experiences but, as I have argued, we each follow a unique path. My case study below illustrates that there are many cultures where there is not a separate stage of 'adolescence' where you can explore and experiment and even delay entry into adulthood. Young people, particularly from more collectivist hierarchical cultures, have different guidance from their parents or elders, as will become evident.

Case study

Some years ago, a 17-year-old Eritrean man, whom I shall call Samuel, was referred to me by his youth worker. He was having problems sleeping and experiencing flashbacks and was described as 'depressed'. My first impression was that he had a frozen expression that made him look much older than his years. I appreciated having an open-ended therapy contract with him because trauma work needs time. It is important to avoid stereotypical meanings and to create a space to explore the different meanings of events and situate them in a socio-historical and political context. However, this is not a purely factual knowing, as the impact of socio-political factors is woven into our clients' lived experience. I learnt that Samuel had fled his country after the capture and suspected death of his father and eldest brother because of their political activities. His mother, two sisters and his youngest brother had gone into hiding. He was also detained and tortured but then released. Shortly after these events, he was urged to leave the country by an uncle (living in the UK) who helped him find the means to travel.

This level of torture and loss leaves people in shock, particularly when it takes place over a prolonged period of time. It is simply far too overwhelming to be integrated into our experience and hence many aspects are pushed out of our memory. Retrieval cannot be hurried as it can be too much to bear, so it takes time to process. Here is an example of the narrative between us.

Samuel: They [*referring to a group of peers at college*] see refugees as poor and stupid and won't get very far.

Therapist: [*I try to encourage him to rephrase generic terms using the 'I' pronoun and to translate experiences into what they make him feel.*] Can you tell me more about that? I wonder how does it make you feel?

Samuel: Annoyed, but then I have bad days and can't get out of bed to go to college. I worry and I think maybe they are right.

Therapist: So, let's look at it from your perspective. At times you get annoyed with their perception of you and the racism you have encountered [*it was vital to validate this*], but during other times, when you are having a bad day, you think they might even be right?

Samuel: It all plays on my mind… but I want to finish my studies. [*Touching his neck*] I had a sore neck again… It was a bad night. I had to have the light on. I should go to the doctor.

Therapist: I am aware that you are talking about how your sore neck is really worrying you but at the same time how you are viewed here in the UK [*bridging between the body and mind*]. Take me through what was going on last night that prevented you from sleeping. [*Sleeping difficulties for refugees have to be validated; many are on 'hyper-alert' mode for considerable time after the trauma(ta) has occurred (van der Kolk, 2007)*]. Can you make other connections?

Samuel: I don't know, just too much thinking… Well, I knew my roommate was watching the news. I didn't want to watch it but couldn't help it. I saw a young boy in Syria suffering.

Therapist: It sounds like that boy really stayed with you [*bracketing my assumptions*]…

Samuel: Yeah, I didn't hear much… I thought the boy had no parents. Just like my brother… I wish I knew where he was.

Therapist: It's so hard not to know.

Samuel: You, Dr Eleftheriadou, are not like the other doctors, you are different.

Therapist: Can you tell me what's different about us and the way we talk here.

Samuel: I feel you are listening, not judging me.

Stern (Stern et al, 1998) highlights how, even in one small exchange, there can be different layers of meaning and that they are all important. As illustrated by the dialogue, the meaning is often unclear to the clients themselves and this is why it needs creative facilitating from the therapist, with some mirroring/paraphrasing (key) elements and reframing. When timed appropriately, open questions such as 'I wonder what this means to you?' or 'How does that make you feel?' can be helpful to open up the dialogue. The therapist's role is to be alongside the client, facilitating exploration. Hopefully the client can learn to do this exploration by themselves and continue it, even after the therapy finishes.

The above narrative demonstrates the clarification or opening up process on many levels, what it meant to try to get to know his culture and history and yet not perceive him as only the 'traumatised' or 'refugee person'. It enabled us to examine the tremendous guilt he had about his family. For a long time, he only wanted to think about the past, in order to hold onto his family. He could not bear to think about a future without them. Another significant issue highlighted in the narrative is how people who undergo torture can experience a type of objectification of their body (Bromberg, 2003; May, 1958). Van der Veer (1998) provides compelling evidence to support the notion of the existence of bodily memory of traumatic events. Storolow (2008) describes a client who exhibited somatic manifestations of trauma, writing of how 'the traumatized states actually underwent a process of transformation from being exclusively body states into ones in which the body sensation came to be united with words' (p3). We have to take on board this split between the body and mind and address all the various communications – in other words, to facilitate a cohesiveness between the body and mind.

Samuel's bodily symptoms were communicating his reaction to extreme fear. He had been threatened with shooting, blindfolded and kicked, especially along his neck and upper back. He had consulted a doctor in the UK, which was necessary in order to discuss these physical symptoms, and there was no apparent underlying physical cause. Linking words with his body's language was incredibly painful for him, but it was a significant part of Samuel's healing process – to begin to slowly remember his experiences of torture, at his pace, in a safe setting, and, crucially, for this to be witnessed with compassion by another human being. The paradox in this type of work is that you are supporting clients to remember, which is just as important as helping them to forget other aspects, such as the intrusive memories (or the re-experiencing of a traumatic event through thoughts, images or dreams). In other words, they are supported and encouraged to think about other aspects of their lives and regain emotional and body regulation, including sleep.

There are many situations in our lives where the dilemmas present us with conflicting emotions. Decisions made in times of greatest upheaval may also bring about a huge sense of uncertainty and anxiety. When I first met Samuel, he was still in shock; I had to earn his trust as he had little faith in people. He found himself in this unfamiliar therapeutic venture and he also did not know how to relate to me, as a non-African, older woman, who held less authority in his culture (and family). Coming from a more hierarchical culture, he often referred to me as a doctor. In existential philosophy, the therapist is not the expert in another's life, but it can take some adjustment for clients who are used to age hierarchies.

Samuel felt anxious about making choices as there was 'no father to guide him' any longer. He also struggled with the different kind of existence he was now faced with in the UK. He was living in a hostel and exposed to many cultural viewpoints. Because of his age and cultural background, he had been discouraged from questioning the family value system, especially his father's political activities. At times, he was still feeling overwhelmed and uncomfortable about the choices he had to make on his own, but slowly he began to experience days when he was no longer so guilt-ridden about not following what his father would have wished for him. After a year in the UK, he also managed to make a few friends through college, and decided to specialise in science. This provided him with a structure, which can be invaluable for young refugees and can support the healing process. Overall, his days felt like they had started to have a sense of purpose again and the past had its place.

Conclusion

I have emphasised in this chapter the significance placed on the therapeutic relationship by both the relational school of psychoanalysis and existential theories. Existential theory highlights how each client creates a unique co-created space with the therapist, which in turn allows for the client's unique meanings to emerge. The 'rules' outlined by phenomenology are especially useful in trying to view the client's experience from a fresh, questioning angle. Although the case study cannot capture all the complexity of Samuel's experience, I hope that it illustrates some of the most intense existential dilemmas and emotions accompanying this profound cultural and personal identity challenge and how we explored the 'thrown-ness' he experienced following his arrival to the UK. This chapter also shows how the givens of existence (Yalom 1980) can become more powerful when one changes cultural environments and basic trust in others is violated through war and torture experiences.

I have sought to demonstrate the importance of creating a safe space to explore traumatic experiences in the presence of a witness. Working with refugees mainly requires compassionate human presence, rather than analysis or attempts to fit their experience into any particular theoretical framework. The client's sharing of their experience, or simply telling their story (with much necessary repetition), can support them to re-integrate with themselves and reconnect or make new connections with different aspects of their worldview. As Stolorow (2008) suggests, the therapist's capacity to provide attunement and understanding can support the client to get to know their rich emotional life and gain some necessary distance from their place of trauma, isolation and terror.

Finally, it is important to say that a vital precursor for undertaking any work with trauma survivors and refugees is that the therapist has gone through their own therapeutic process and addressed their own existential concerns. We need to be able to tolerate our own feelings about death, isolation and meaninglessness before we can tolerate another person's. Work with refugees and trauma can be difficult, if not impossible, to bear without extensive work on ourselves (Eleftheriadou, 2010). It is also important to challenge our own cultural and Western training and to be open to the clients' dilemmas in the context of their unique psychosocial worldview. This stance becomes even more significant when working with someone who is young, psychosocially vulnerable and comes from a completely different cultural system.

Discussion with the editor

Simon: Existential philosophy emphasises that ultimately we are alone. The chapter highlights the experience of isolation. Why is this experience intensified for a young refugee?

Zack: Across the lifespan, we create deep connections with familiar references (for example, the landscape). These connections create a familiar structure that is predictable and safe. However, a young refugee has to cope with the fact that these familiar references disappear and this can create a deep sense of loss and disorganisation. A high level of anxiety is often experienced and they may actively seek these familiar cultural and highly evocative references in the new cultural context in order to diminish the pain of isolation.

Simon: You emphasise the idea of 'reconnecting with other compassionate human beings' as more important than the theoretical aspects of our work. Please explain why this would be the case in existential thinking.

Zack: The existential model is a more flexible way of working than other models. It acknowledges that, when we are faced with high levels of anxiety, we may resort to theoretical understanding. However, a purely conceptual understanding of the client's situation and emotions can take us away from an emotional connection and push the client into further isolation. A distressed person requires authentic emotional connection with another human being who is capable of deep compassion.

Simon: How do you view 'co-creation' from an existential perspective?

Zack: We all have a deeply subjective experience of our social worlds. When a person enters therapy, a unique intersubjective dialogue is created with that particular therapist. The therapist brings their own subjectivity and psycho-cultural values. The therapy takes a certain route and process because of that particular duet between that particular therapist and that particular client within that temporal space.

Simon: Can you describe the process of 'unknowing' in cross-cultural work?

Zack: The process is relevant to cross-cultural work as it takes an open stance of not taking any concept for granted. This is vital in cross-cultural communication as meanings differ, so we have to retain openness and questioning to ensure that we have a shared understanding.

Simon: What do you think best equips the therapist to work in such an emotionally challenging area?

Zack: Extensive personal (alongside professional) development work is vital. I cannot emphasise enough the importance of exploring our identity and connections with our culture and those from other cultures. Work with refugees and torture survivors brings to the fore many of the existential givens (isolation, meaningless and death) and therefore it is significant to explore and subsequently to become comfortable with them. This does not mean that we are 'immune' to them when they are raised by the client, but hopefully that we can become more able to tolerate the client's material.

Simon: You state that, however securely attached we are, trauma can have a profound effect. Please explain.

Zack: Trauma is a profound and life-changing experience and it is limiting to view it purely through a psychiatric diagnostic lens. Existential thinking supports the need to move away from the notion that refugees have 'psychopathological' emotions. A minority of people may develop more long-lasting 'mental health issues', such as depression, but my belief is that anyone who undergoes trauma(ta) is likely to exhibit shock, among a plethora of other emotions. These are 'normal' reactions under the abnormal and extreme socio-political circumstances of war.

References

Bromberg PM (2003). Something wicked this way comes: Trauma dissociation and conflict – the space where psychoanalysis, cognitive science, and neuroscience overlap. *Psychoanalytic Psychology 20*(3): 558–574.

deVries MW (2007). Trauma in a cultural perspective. In: van der Kolk BA, McFarlane AC, Weisaeth L (eds). *Traumatic Stress: the effects of overwhelming experience on mind, body and society*. London: Guilford Press (pp398–413).

Eleftheriadou Z (2010). *Psychotherapy and Culture: weaving inner and outer worlds*. London: Karnac.

Eleftheriadou Z (1994). *Transcultural Counselling*. London: Central Books.

Gonsalves C (2014). *The Refugee Journey: from homeland to mid-way-to-nowhere*. Amazon.in

Heidegger M (1927/1962) .*Being and Time* (J MacQuarrie, ES Robinson trans). New York, NY: Harper & Row.

Husserl E (1962). *Ideas: general introduction to pure phenomenology*. New York, NY: Collier.

May R (1958). Contributions of existential psychotherapy. In: May R, Angel E, Ellenberger HF (eds). *Existence: a new dimension in psychiatry and psychology*. New York, NY: Basic Books (pp37–91).

Mitchell SA, Aron L (eds) (1999). *Relational Psychoanalysis: the emergence of a tradition*. London: The Analytic Press.

Spinelli E (2015). *Practising Existential Therapy*. London: Sage.

Spinelli E (1989). *The Interpreted World*. London: Sage.

Stern D (2004). *The Present Moment in Psychotherapy*. London: Norton.

Stern D, Sander L, Nahum JP, Harrison AM, Lysons-Ruth K, Morgan AC, Bruschweilerstern N, Tronick EZ (1998). Non-interpretive mechanisms in psychoanalytic therapy: the 'something more' than interpretation. *The International Journal of Psychoanalysis* 79(5): 903–921.

Storolow RD (2008). The contextuality and existentiality of emotional trauma. *Psychoanalytic Dialogues* 18(1): 113–123.

van Deurzen E (2011). *Skills in Existential Counselling and Psychotherapy*. London: Sage.

van Deurzen-Smith E (1997). *Everyday Mysteries: existential dimensions of psychotherapy*. London: Routledge.

van Deurzen-Smith E (1988). *Existential Counselling in Practice*. London: Sage.

van der Kolk BA (2007). The body keeps score: approaches to the psychobiology of posttraumatic stress disorder. In: van der Kolk BA, McFarlane AC, Weisaeth L (eds). *Traumatic Stress: the effects of overwhelming experience on mind, body and society*. London: Guilford Press (pp214–241).

van der Veer G (1988). *Counselling and Therapy with Refugees and Victims of Trauma* (2nd ed). Chichester: Wiley.

Yalom ID (1980). *Existential Psychotherapy*. New York, NY: Basic Books.

12

Spirite equus: what we can learn from equine-facilitated therapy

Julie Scheiner

As a youngster I was fascinated by animals. I found them very healing to be around and they made me feel secure. My dog, Bruce, was as much a part of the family as any other member. I also spent many hours at my local stables, enamoured of the horses. Being with Bruce and the horses calmed me whenever the world felt too much.

Bruce appeared to be able to sense if something was not right with any member of the family and was always there with a Labrador 'smile' and a look that to me conveyed a sense that 'everything will be ok'. Just being in his company made me feel that he was right and I immediately felt better. My relationship with horses was very different. For a start, I had an inherent respect for these gentle giants, because of their sheer size. But I also noticed that they appeared to want to engage with me. When I began my training as a psychotherapist, I wanted to find out more about how to work therapeutically with them, and I wrote my doctorate thesis on this subject.

I trained with EAGALA (the US-based Equine Assisted Growth and Learning Association) and became a fully-fledged equine-assisted therapist. They are just one of a number of associations and organisations offering a variety of models of equine-assisted therapy. I wanted to work with horses in a way that felt I was in equal partnership with them, rather than what I felt was a 'master and slave' relationship.

My own training as a counselling psychologist and the helpful therapy I received during training for my own difficulties (I was diagnosed with dyslexia while I was training) enabled me to understand my own blind spots. Initially I trained in CBT, which felt patchy at best. I never felt the connection with CBT as a way of working with clients. However, I then came across existential therapy, and at once felt at home with its ideas and concepts. I finally felt that I had a way of thinking about and working with clients that I could relate to.

Equines and therapy

Documentation of the use of animals in mental health treatment appears as early 1792 (Trivedi & Perl, 1995). Research has demonstrated positive results in the treatment of psychological and physical symptoms in various populations where pets are used as part of the therapy (Klontz et al, 2007). During the 19th century, the presence of animals in mental institutions was quite common. For example, in the 1830s, the British Charity Commissioners suggested that mental health institutions should be filled with animals such as sheep and goats, in order to create a more pleasing environment and alleviate the appalling prison-like conditions. Clearly, such recommendations were taken seriously; an article in the Illustrated London News in 1860 described how, in male and female wards alike, patients could be seen pouring out their tales of woe to a variety of animals, and were more cheerful as a result (Alldridge, 1991, cited in Fine, 2001).

For many thousands of years, mankind has interacted with horses in a wide range of contexts. The existential philosopher Martin Buber (1947/1970) described spending a summer at his grandparent's estate when a boy, and recalled an 'I-Thou' encounter with 'my darling, a broad dapple-grey horse'. He recollected that, while stroking the horse's mane, 'what I experienced in touch with the animal was the Other, the immense otherness of the Other'. Jung (2002) wrote that horses embody one of humanity's deepest mythological archetypes. Horses have often been referred to in ancient myths and described as companions to the gods and messengers between humans and the divine. Hannah (1992) wrote of Pegasus, the famous winged horse in Greek mythology, that he 'is himself a symbol that united the opposites – a chthonic animal, absolutely of the earth and yet with wings belonging to the spiritual realm'. The merging of divine with mortal human and animal figures appears to be an effort to capitalise on the strength of both. Chiron, the Greek centaur, half man, half horse, was famed for his knowledge and skill with medicine, and so may represent the very first conscious link between human, horse and healing.

Historically, equine-facilitated psychotherapy (EFP) developed from therapeutic riding. Its roots may be traced back over two centuries, when two German physicians, Gerard van Swieten (1700-1772) and Anton de Haen (1704-1776), recommended horseback riding as a treatment for mental illness (cited in Connor, 2018). They felt it had a soothing effect on the fibres of the muscles, and that this could reduce 'hypochondria' and 'hysteria'. The Swiss physician Tissot, in 1782 (Riede, 1988: 35), described the psychotherapeutic effects thus:

> As riding becomes a source of pleasure for a patient, it will be a truly desirable distraction that becomes very helpful to the physician. The greater the impact of fear and sorrow on a disease, or the greater the likelihood that these factors actually caused the disease, the more eagerly we grasp for ways to disperse these moods, or to prevent them. One such way is exercise on the horse which can encourage both patient and physician, and which afterward can affect the best results.

Connor describes in detail the development of EFP through the 20th century in two distinct camps: the Equine Facilitated Mental Health Association (EFMHA), which emerged in the 1970s as part of the North American Riding for the Handicapped Association (NARHA), and EAGALA, which was developed in Utah by horse trainer and counsellor Greg Kersten and social worker Lyne Thomas, in the 1990s.

Therapeutic riding tends to focus on grooming, handling and riding horses. Activities and games depend on the rider's capabilities. This can be seen as a form of occupational therapy rather than a primarily psychotherapeutic activity. Research has evidenced the benefits of this interaction for a wide range of groups (Bates, 2002).

EFP goes beyond traditional therapeutic riding for the disabled; indeed, riding rarely comes into it. Rather, it may be understood as a field of science and practice in which horses act as a container for the client's difficult feelings and projections, thereby enabling emotional growth and learning. EFP uses tasks such as caring for the horse as a means of forming bonds and establishing trust, respect and responsibility. A limited number of studies demonstrate these benefits (Cawley, Cawley & Retter, 1994; McCulloch, 2001; Preusch, 1997), and EFP has grown remarkably since its inception, with steadily increasing access to training and a growth in practice-based evidence and research.

As previously stated, there is a wide range of models and approaches to practice, some more formalised than others. For example, EAGALA has developed a replicable framework, code of conduct and standards of training and practice). Its model:

> ... embraces the science that humans learn best by doing. The model prescribes a hands-on approach where clients are given the space to project and analyze their situations, make connections, and find their own solutions. Since the solutions are personally experienced in conjunction with intellectual understanding, they tend to be deeper, more profound, and longer lasting. (EAGALA, undated)

In the EAGALA model, a team approach is often used, with the psychotherapist, an equine specialist and the horses working with the client together. The work always takes place 'on the ground':

> ... the horses [are] front and centre, deliberately unhindered and never ridden, and allowed to interact with the client as they wish. This creates the space for the client, with the support of the professional facilitators, to reflect, project, and make deep connections. (EAGALA, undated)

In an actual session of EFP, clients are first introduced to the herd, which can number from two upwards. Sessions can be individual, for groups or for families. Once the clients are introduced to the herd, they are encouraged to interact with the equines as much as they wish and feel able. For some clients, just being around horses can be quite an overwhelming experience, either because they are afraid or because something deep within them has been triggered.

By working with equines, who provide clear and immediate feedback, clients begin to notice how they are with others and perhaps also how they are generally in the world. While working with a horse, a client may experience a variety of feelings associated with differing aspects of their lives. Some clients may experience an equine as 'stand-offish' and it may be that a client has experienced this from his/her peers in his/her own life. For example, for some clients, simply being able to 'be' in the world, to 'be' in therapy, may be experienced as challenging. The intensity of two people in a therapeutic relationship may be experienced as painful for some clients. Clients who find it difficult to connect with their feelings in the presence of their therapist and who find this experience intimidating, painful or exciting (to name but a few feelings), may find being with an equine less pressured, due to the non-verbal nature of the interaction.

EFP is about facilitating the client to learn about him/herself by participating in activities with horses. The activities are mainly designed to help the client attain their goals. The process mainly takes place between the equine and client. The therapist is there as observer and interpreter, reading and feeding back to the client what they observe from the client and horses' interactions and behaviour. The belief is that horses, because they can be prey and are, consequently, herd animals, have a particular sensitivity and immediacy in their reading of and response to body language and signals. How they interact with a client can reveal ways that the client commonly relates with others and behaves in their life. This information can be fed back to the client who will, in any case, have their own perceptions of the interaction with the horses, and can help them identify and address what is blocking them from achieving their goals and living the life they want.

Because all EFP takes place in a natural setting, this allows a more natural interaction with an equine and encourages a more 'organic' experience. Equines by their very nature are curious animals and collaborating on the ground facilitates a more natural interaction for equines to 'feed back' to clients. The activities that take place in EFP are experiential and involve the equine as an active facilitator. The activities are designed to push clients out of their comfort zones so that they create different kinds of relationships, with both equines and people. They are also intended to encourage clients to think about alternative ways of relating to others and other ways of getting their needs met. Although there may be some rules (depending on the type of training and model), these are there to stop clients falling into their usual, destructive patterns of behaviour in relationships.

Linda Kohanov, who has done much to advance the theory underpinning EFP, writes (2001: 73):

> The men and women I counsel have a terrible time admitting their true feelings to themselves, let alone to others, because they've been taught to disregard their emotions by the authority figures in their lives. They're caught in this vicious circle of feeling confused and threatened around incongruent people, yet not being able to act congruently themselves. The horses are able to break this cycle by showing people what they're really feeling without sugar-coating it, yet somehow it's not so threatening when these animals see through you. I think it's because horses don't have any theory and motives. They're just responding honestly in the moment.

Where clients feel unable to truly be open with their feelings, the use of metaphors can greatly aid the process. Clients may feel safer using metaphors while they are building a trusting relationship with their therapist. Metaphors are an important element of EFP. Freud wrote that 'in psychology we can only describe things by the help of analogies; there is nothing peculiar in this' (1926/1961). Fine (2001: 186) cites Kopp's observation that metaphors are useful in therapy because 'they are similar to mirrors in their ability to reflect inner images within people'. She continues:

> Metaphor therapy relies on the position that people in general structure their reality metaphorically. Both the client and the clinician can apply metaphors as a method of discovering and understanding the client's concerns. The imagery generated from the metaphors can be used to help the client uncover how she or he is coping or feeling.

Moreover, 'clients may develop therapeutic gains when the metaphors applied also suggest a resolution [to their internal conflict]' (p187). The presence of animals within therapy provides additional opportunities to use metaphors within sessions: for example, when observing herd behaviour and hierarchies, people often identify their own position within the human herd.

Equine therapy and ecotherapy

Arguably, horses are an important link to our natural surroundings, which are widely recognised as vital to our mental wellbeing and as a means to treat mental distress (see, for example, Bakolis et al, 2018; Barton, Griffin & Pretty, 2012; Ryan et al, 2010; Perkins, 2018; Natural England, 2016) and which are increasingly under attack by the modern world and digital life (Chawla, 2015). Jung (2002) believed that modern man's disconnection from the natural world is 'largely responsible for the pathological condition of contemporary culture', stating that:

> Civilised man is in danger of losing all contact with the world of instinct – a danger that is still further increased by his living in an urban existence. In what seems to be a purely man-made environment, this loss of instinct is largely responsible for the pathological condition of contemporary culture. (Jung, 2002: 15)

He goes on to argue that, in 'primitive society, whether or not people were more intimately connected to their environment, there was less evidence of conflict between consciousness and emotions and instinct'.

The basic notion of ecopsychology is that mental health cannot be solely conceptualised through the medical lens but is dependent on and influenced by our relationships with other humans and other species and ecosystems. These relationships have a deep evolutionary history, suggesting humans are dependent on nature not only for physical sustenance but for our mental health, which Wilson has termed the 'biophilia hypothesis' (Wilson, 1995; Roszak, 1996).

As stated above, working with nature is an important part of ecopsychological practice. Taking psychotherapy out of office buildings and homes and into the open air (such as fields) allows the beneficial effects of interacting with nature to be applied and experienced.

Existential psychotherapy

Existential psychotherapists often make use of the so-called four-worlds model when working with clients. The notion that there are three worlds or dimensions to human living – the physical *(Umwelt)*, social *(Mitwelt)* and psychological (*Eigenwelt*) – originated in Ludwig Binswanger's elaboration of Martin Heidegger's work. Emmy van Deurzen has argued for a fourth spiritual (*Überwelt*) dimension. These ideas can be useful in clinical work in guiding the therapist to generate a description of the client's engagement with being and the extent to which they are able to relate freely across each of these dimensions. As van Deurzen (1990: 15) expresses it, if we use this model:

> ... it becomes possible to listen to the client's account of herself as revealing her preoccupations with particular levels of her existence. A systematic analysis of how the client expresses her relationship to the natural, public, private and ideal dimensions of her world can provide much insight into imbalance, priorities and impasse. An impression can be formed this way of where on the whole territory of human existence the client is struggling for clarity.

EFT can contribute to existential therapy in each of these areas:
- physical
- social
- spiritual
- psychological.

Physical dimension

On the physical dimension (*Umwelt*) we relate to our environment, which includes attitudes towards our bodies, our physical surroundings, the climate, our possessions, our own bodies and our mortality. Although we struggle for security within this dimension, recognising our limitations can perhaps bring a release of tension. Taking this a step further in relation to EFT, awareness of our existence within a physical space and attempting mastery over this in relation to our own struggles can be helped by an equine partner. An equine may help us recognise our own shortcomings within this domain and release further tension through the realisation that the end goal is being in the moment, not mastery.

Social dimension

On the social dimension (*Mitwelt*), we relate to others in the course of interacting with the public world around us. These are the ordinary, everyday encounters we have with others. These encounters are characterised by an interplay of struggle for dominance and submission and between aggressive individualism and humanitarian, unselfish co-operation. Feelings of failure and aloneness typify the social dimension, as each person strives to dominate the other and avoid being dominated by the other. In this volatile situation, partnership with an equine may alleviate this sense of loneliness, allowing a sense of connectedness to other, if only temporarily.

Spiritual dimension

It is on the spiritual dimension (*Überwelt*) that we find meaning by putting all the pieces of the puzzle together for ourselves. The contradictions that have to be faced on this dimension are often related to the tension between purpose and absurdity, hope and despair. People's values represent something that matters enough to live or die for, that may even have ultimate and universal validity. Perhaps meaning and validity can be found in those moments with equines where there is unconditional acceptance by another and the tension of having to create may diminish in the presence of ultimate and universal validity.

Psychological dimension

On the psychological dimension (*Eigenwelt*), we relate to ourselves and in this way create a personal world. People search for a sense of identity, a feeling of having substance and a self. Inevitably, events will confront us with evidence to the contrary, plunging us into a state of confusion or disintegration. Facing death might bring anxiety and confusion. Perhaps it is here where EFP comes into its own. Reflection of our sense of identity by the equine's behaviour towards us may validate our sense of self and encourages us to self-reflect on our place in the world, helping alleviate the sense of confusion and lack of importance.

The work of Martin Buber (1947/1970) offers some theoretical basis for EFP. His distinction between two ways in which human beings can relate to the world – the 'I-It' relationship, in which the other is objectified and met as an object to be examined and analysed, and the 'I-Thou' relationship in which the other is met in a holistic and fulfilling way – provides inspiration for therapists wishing to work with EFT. Both parties are transformed by the experience of being accepted as they truly are.

Bella – a case study

Bella, a woman in her mid-30s, had been seeing me for therapy for some time. Initially she attended because of what she described as a depressive episode that she felt unable to move forward from. She explained that these feelings were not unusual for her and that she was keenly aware of how they manifested but did not know why they kept happening. Bella had previously attended therapy while at university but said it had not shed any light on her continued feelings of depression. She had also seen previous therapists but felt 'undernourished' by them. She was interested in existential therapy, having taken some philosophy courses while at university and read several popular existential therapy books – in particular, the works of Yalom, whom she immediately felt a kinship with. She talked about how he tended to explore themes and meanings within therapy and thought that this way of working would finally enable her to understand her place within the world and explore her feelings and thoughts more freely.

Initially our therapy sessions focused on what had brought Bella into therapy and what she needed and wanted from it. Bella felt that she understood her symptoms but wanted to explore the reasons for her continued sense of hopelessness. I let Bella lead our work and dictate the pace as I didn't want to direct her in ways that she may not have wanted to go. She always attended her sessions on time, was always well dressed and always had a smile on her face. I was constantly struck by her smile when she entered the room and wondered what it meant. She mentioned that she often felt nervous on first entering the room and we reflected on this. I felt the smile was a kind of mask that she wore to hide her 'true' feelings, whatever they might be. She agreed and said she often found it difficult to talk about her feelings.

She was always open in therapy, and we talked about various issues that had brought her into therapy and what she was finding difficult in her life. She described a happy childhood, although when I asked further she described some issues with her mother that she felt had affected her confidence for a number of years. She said that, as a consequence, she often experienced feelings of shame and not being good enough, and that, whatever she did to address her apparent shortcomings, she could never to do enough to be loved by her mother. My sense was that Bella wanted to be a 'good' client; she wanted to please me. At times I felt that, by attempting to be the 'good-enough' client, she had placed me in a role where I was the expert and the 'good-enough mother'.

After a while it appeared that we were becoming 'stuck' in a loop. Bella understood at one level why she felt so ashamed and unloved and why this had such a profound effect on her relationships, but somehow we didn't seem to progress, which made her feel frustrated at times. This was when I began to wonder if a different form of therapy might enable her to move forward. Supervision was invaluable to me at this point, as it enabled me to recognise my own feelings of frustration with Bella's stuckness. My supervisor helped me realise that sometimes stuckness in therapy is a symptom of something deeper: a reflection of Bella's own process and how frightened, fragile and vulnerable she could be feeling.

When I suggesting using the equines in therapy, Bella at once felt that this would help. She had a natural affinity with animals and was keen to see if working with equines would move things on. She had ridden as a child and was used to being around equines. I explained to her the process of EFP and that it wasn't like riding, and she immediately became more inquisitive and excited, but also a little apprehensive.

I felt that using the equines in therapy might not only help Bella but also change the tempo of therapy. I was all too aware of the 'mask' I felt Bella sometimes wore in therapy. Her use of humour to distract us from her difficult feelings could also be an obstacle. I had addressed this with her and she admitted that at times therapy was challenging and painful and she used these techniques to avoid this, but that she also recognised the potential benefits.

In practical terms, the introduction of equine therapy meant changing the contract in terms of time – the therapy sessions extended to an hour and a half from the traditional 50 minutes – the venue, and the cost. It also introduced a high degree of uncertainty for both of us. I was not sure what to expect and to an extent I was taking a leap of faith, as was Bella. She and I had established a high degree of trust, but I do not always know how the equines will react to clients. However, many therapists have said to me over the years, 'trust the process' in my work with humans, and I feel that the same could be said for equine therapy.

Bella's previous relationship with equines was that of a rider but she also recalled enjoying a sense of a kinship with them. Bella clearly enjoyed the smell of the equines, the natural surroundings and being outside of the therapy room, and the tension leaving her body was almost palpable. I noticed immediately how her shoulders relaxed, a genuine grin appeared on her face and her evident feeling of joy at seeing the herd.

She stood still, as if in awe. I waited as she watched the herd for a while, and then asked her what she had noticed. She turned to me and said that seeing the equines grazing together made her feel overwhelmed with emotions. Part of her wanted to run towards them but another part wanted to stand and just watch these magnificent animals in their own environment. The herd ambled over to meet Bella, and she seemed overjoyed. An important part of working with equines is recognising that we are in their environment and it is their choice whether they work with our clients. Horses, by their size alone, can be a lot for anyone to take in, and having six of them coming to meet her was not only exciting but overwhelming for Bella.

The herd surrounded Bella, sniffing at her to check whether she was friend or foe. One of the most pertinent aspects of working with equines is their ability to fundamentally know which member of the herd is most suited to the client. Equines have the ability to 'resonate' with each other and communicate on all matters, whether it is where to graze, social hierarchy or safety. It is this innate ability to see what is beyond our own understanding that makes equine therapy so effective. As the others drifted away, one of the herd members stayed with Bella, allowing her to stand close to her and interact with her. What was interesting to notice about this particular equine was her history. She had only recently come to live with the herd, having been sold on, and had not yet fully bonded with the others, and so lived as an outcast. It was noticeable how quickly this equine took to Bella. In fact, I noticed that she was standing on Bella's feet. I asked Bella what was going through her mind at this particular time. She turned and laughed. She said that she had often been considered 'flighty' by previous partners and unable to commit to relationships, and that at this moment in time she felt totally and literally 'grounded' in her body. The equine's willingness to be intimate with her and the way she stopped Bella moving away was fascinating to watch. Bella later said that this was a pivotal moment when she felt accepted by another being without question.

This is one of the known factors in EFP. Equines do not judge and do not have an agenda, although they are able to provide direct feedback through the therapist, who interprets what they may be reflecting back to clients. The equines are not interested in false selves; they cut through the projections and, through their stance, position and subtle, non-verbal cues, reflect directly back to clients what they are experiencing. For example, an equine may stand with their ears pricked and tail swishing. A client may experience this as a frightening stance; some may feel that the equine is looking at them in an aggressive manner. Exploration of these responses through the use of interpretation can open up the door to further investigation of a client's inner world. The most important aspect is that the equines respond to clear, honest feedback and see through a false presentation. This is due to the fact that equines are prey animals and live in herds for protection. They have an acute ability to notice subtle changes and may spook easily and therefore need clear feedback to ascertain whether an object is a threat to themselves and the herd. This is partly what makes equine therapy so successful, as the equine provides quick and accurate feedback as they seek to ascertain risk and read subtle cues, for their own safety.

Bella was able to have several more sessions of equine therapy. We introduced exercises that she worked on either on her own or with the herd, depending on the mood of both. The sessions were designed to give Bella a sense of self and ownership of her feelings and also to put her in touch with the feelings that had initially bought her into therapy and how these had impacted on her. For Bella there were several pivotal moments in therapy, which were generally when she felt the herd had accepted her without question. She did not always find it easy to put into words why or how equine therapy had worked for her. She felt that at times the feelings went beyond words and translated into moments of pure joy, and these would always stay with her as a snapshot. Those moments of pure joy and a feeling of acceptance lifted Bella from the dark place she felt she was in and perhaps freed her.

EFP enabled Bella to see how she might have been in the world, how she reacted to her surroundings, to people, and how they reacted to her. She came to recognise that all she needed was to be herself, that she could be loved just as she was, without having to compromise herself or her ideals. We moved away from the stuckness in therapy that for so long had blocked us both. Bella felt that existential therapy opened up a lot of avenues for exploration and questions that needed answering, but also the idea of taking responsibility for, and ownership of, her feelings. She recognised how vulnerable she felt in the room but also that she inherently trusted our therapeutic relationship. It was her fragile sense of self that kept her stuck in the room: she felt frightened and vulnerable but also wanted to be in relationship with me.

We both took a leap of faith by agreeing to work with the equines but, because I trusted them, Bella trusted me, and I trusted our therapeutic relationship was strong enough for us to work outside the conventional therapy space.

Bella has since left therapy, after a successful ending. She keeps in touch with me on occasion and has a picture of herself with her favourite horse. She said she felt able to be vulnerable with the equines because of their size and also because of the strength they showed her in allowing her to be close to them. Their non-judgemental acceptance of her enabled her to recognise her need to be loved and to realise that she could be loved unconditionally for just being herself. This is what released her from her stuckness and this is what she took from therapy when our work together came to its natural finish.

Discussion with the editor

Simon: There seems to be an enormous growth in introducing a wide range of animals into the therapeutic environment, and research studies increasingly provide evidence for the efficacy of such initiatives. I know first-hand how, in my private practice, my cats have brought an extra dimension to my work with clients. Of course, animals have been around in the consulting room for many years – famously, Freud had a dog that was often present in sessions – but the more formal and systematic involvement of animals is relatively recent. I wonder what you think may be the reasons for its growth, and what you think the longer-term future of animal-assisted therapy may be?

Julie: Having researched this topic not only for this chapter but also for my doctoral thesis, I have, like you, identified an increase in use of animals in therapy. I remember while I was in therapy, during a particularly difficult session, my therapist's colleague had her dog in the office and my therapist said to me quite strictly, 'Julie, stroke her dog, you'll feel better' – that, coming from a psychotherapist, did make me chuckle. But she identified how bad I was feeling after the session (it was a good session) and I remember the huge sense of relief, a letting go and exhaling, when I sat down to stroke the dog.

Part of the popularity of animal therapy is that, when we're in the presence of animals and stroking them, oxytocin is released in both animal and human.

Oxytocin is also known as the happy hormone, so, simply put, it is beneficial for animal and human to interact. Aside from the scientific side of things, I think that animals can be a source of comfort and joy. Imagine when you come home, the excitement of your pets and their joy at your return. I know that this is probably seen in dogs more than in most other animals, but the sheer outpouring of love and affection shown by one's animals can feel intense and immense. I also think that the modern world can feel like a lonely place at times, and with animals it's hard to feel lonely. Look into an animal's eyes; at times they can look at you as if they're looking into your soul. Animals, especially those we have regular contact with, such as cats and dogs, can provide such unconditional love and affection, unlike humans, where love at times can feel conditional. I also think that therapy itself can be a tough process for some, especially when sessions are challenging. When an animal is in a therapy room, they can add an extra dimension to therapy, as well as a distraction, and it can be comforting just to have another presence in the room. Animals can offer a safe space to hide but also offer comfort, as they appear to have a sixth sense when people are in a dark place.

Simon: I was interested that you say there may be some rules, depending on the type of training and model of EFP used, and these are there only to stop clients repeating unhelpful behavioural patterns in relationships. I wonder if you can say a little more about the nature of these rules and the extent to which they either support or challenge what we might typically regard as an existential-phenomenological therapeutic alliance?

Julie: I think that, with any type of therapy, there may be elements of clients wanting to please their therapists or saying what they feel therapists may want to hear. Taking this into consideration, the power play and dynamics that can get played out in therapy may colour the therapy itself. I think that, with existential therapy, we may definitely see a lot less of this particular dynamic, and the added intervention of equines reduces this interplay still further, as horses tend to reflect our truth. For example, I have seen clients who say that they're feeling okay and, once with the horses, have seen the horses interact with them in a way that shows they clearly are not. When asked, the client will often reply, 'I thought I was okay but to be honest I've been feeling such and such.' So, clients may be masking their feelings with me but they are very clearly reflected in their interaction with equines. I suspect that with other types of therapy, such as CBT, where there are a lot of ground rules, it can be easy for clients to tell therapists what they think they want to hear.

Simon: I am trying to get more of a sense of the extent to which EFP actually involves physical contact with horses. The impression I have is that the human therapist has a major role in introducing the idea, accompanying the client, and then assisting them to reflect on the experience. It feels as though the word 'facilitated' is key here – and that the animal contact can facilitate a client to get in contact with their feelings in a more direct way than perhaps a human therapist can. So EFP might be particularly appropriate for some presenting issues, but may be less so, or even contra-indicated for others? And it may be introduced at specific stages within another therapy? If so, it seems to me that the human therapist will need to be very skilful in assessing how and when to use it.

Julie: EFP does involve physical contact with horses, that is true. However, I always think it best to give a client free rein in the sessions and to be around as much or as little as a client wants. The wonderful thing about EFP is that it is an emerging field, with no rights or wrongs. I will always go at a client's pace. I don't necessarily view my role in EFP as particularly major; the equines are the all-important reflector and container for the client's feelings. My role as a therapist is to introduce the idea, accompany the client and help them reflect on their feelings. However, the actual therapy is the relationship that can develop between human and equine and bond them in a short space of time. I think that the therapist's role in EFP is to stand back and allow the equine the space and time to work with the client. It can be a quiet time of reflection for all involved. It can also be a challenging time but what is so wonderful about equines is that they don't lie; they reflect what they see in the client. I think that some therapists may feel that they need to be more involved, to ask more questions, but I take a view that less is more. In everyday life, we may be subjected to lots of noise, and what I love about EFP is that it allows for quiet time, for reflection, for observation and for contemplation.

I'm not sure if EFP can ever be contra-indicated. It can be as much or as little as someone wants or can put in. This also goes for the equines. We have to be aware of how much they're holding, as they're sensitive animals, which is what makes them especially good for therapy. I don't know if EFP has ever not worked with anyone.

Simon: You say that Bella was 'used to being around equines'. Perhaps a very obvious question, but it occurs to me that some clients might feel anxious or even frightened at the prospect of EFP.

Julie: You're absolutely right, some clients are anxious and frightened about the prospect of EFP. I think that there is a parallel between being frightened and anxious about being in therapy and being frightened and anxious with horses. For example, asking the questions about what frightens people about horses can be a metaphor for what frightens them in life. I understand people's fears, as they are very real, but the great thing about EFP is that clients can interact as much or as little as they want to with the equines. Facing their fears about being with horses can also be a game changer. Those that are frightened can really face those frightening thoughts and feelings head-on within a safe environment. Horses are more likely to be frightened of us, so that also creates a different playing field. We have to be respectful of horses' environment and understand that feelings can be difficult to deal with, just as in conventional talking therapy. Therapy is a big deal and can be frightening. It takes real guts on many levels to enter into a therapeutic relationship and it is the same when working with animals, especially horses. I always say to clients, have courage, believe in the process and together we can achieve.

Simon: I am fascinated by the notion that animals are in some sense 'truthful'. It is clearly a very important aspect of EFP and I wonder what this actually means for you as an existential practitioner.

Julie: I sometimes wonder, am I seeing the version of the client that they want me to see? In other words, is the client being wholly authentic with me, and even if they feel they are, is there something that they're trying to hide? I know that therapy can be very challenging at times. I also know that my clients try to be honest and truthful when they can. A lot of pets can tune into our tone of voice but equines are also watching out for non-verbal cues, which is how they read us and how they convey to me whether a client is being honest with themself. Equine therapy is about clear, open and honest communication because, with the horses, we can never lie.

Simon: Finally, what do you see as the future for EFP?

Julie: In terms of the long-term future of animal-assisted therapy, I hope it grows and grows. There is a growing evidence base for using animals therapeutically in care homes and hospitals. I'd like to see more use of animals in healthcare environments in the NHS.

With specific reference to EFP, what we need is more research studies exploring its efficacy and perhaps one day, even its inclusion in the NICE guidelines for treating depression and anxiety. As it stands now, without that evidence base, I can only see it being used as an adjunct to talking therapy for the present.

References

Bakolis I, Hammoud R, Smythe M, Gibbons J, Davidson N, Tognin S, Mechelli A (2018). Urban mind: using smartphone technologies to investigate the impact of nature on mental well-being in real time. *BioScience* 68(2): 134–145.

Barton J, Griffin M, Pretty J (2012). Exercise, nature and socially interactive based initiatives improve mood and self-esteem in the clinical population. *Perspectives in Public Health* 132(2): 89–96.

Bates A (2002). Of patients and horses: equine facilitated psychotherapy. *Journal of Psychosocial Nursing and Mental Health Services* 40(5): 16–24.

Buber M (1947/1970). *I and Thou*. New York, NY: Touchstone.

Cawley R, Cawley D, Retter K (1994). Therapeutic horseback riding and self-concept in adolescents with special educational needs. *Anthrozoos: a multidisciplinary journal of the interactions of people & animals* 7(2): 129–134.

Chawla L (2015). Benefits of nature contact for children. *Journal of Planning Literature* 30(4): 433–452.

Connor C (2018). *The silent therapist: a review of the development of equine assisted psychotherapy*. [Online.] Marley's Mission. www.marleysmission.com/pdf/silent_therapist.pdf (accessed 6 August 2018).

EAGALA (undated). *Professional experiential therapy that drives change*. [Online.] EAGALA www.eagala.org/works (accessed 29 May 2018).

Fine AH (2001). *Handbook on Animal Assisted Therapy: theoretical foundations and guidelines for practice*. San Diego, CA: Academic press.

Freud S (1926/1961). Inhibitions, symptoms and anxiety. In: Freud S. *The Standard Edition of the Complete Psychological Works of Sigmund Freud, vol 20* (J Strachey ed & trans). London: Hogarth Press (pp77–175).

Hannah B (1992). *The Cat, Dog and Horse Lectures and 'the Beyond'* (D Frantz ed). Wilmette, IL: Chiron (pp55–129).

Jung CG (2002). *The Earth Has a Soul: CG Jung writings on nature, technology and modern life* (M Sabini ed). Berkley, CA: North Atlantic Books.

Klontz BT, Bivens A, Leniart D, Klontz T (2007). The effectiveness of equine-assisted experiential therapy: results of an open clinical trial. *Society & Animals* 15(3): 257–267.

Kohanov L (2001). *The Tao of Equus*. Novato, CA: New World Library.

McCulloch L (2001). The combination of therapeutic horse riding and psychological rehabilitation in the successful treatment of a boy with traumatic brain injury: a retrospective study. *Journal of Psychological Practice* 7(1): 50–53.

Natural England (2016). *A Review of Nature-Based Interventions for Mental Health Care* (NECR204). London: Natural England.

Perkins BL (2018). A pilot study assessing the effectiveness of equine-assisted learning with adolescents. [Online.] *Journal of Creativity in Mental Health.* https://doi.org/10.1080/15401383.2018.1427168 (accessed 15 September 2018).

Preusch P (1997). *Therapeutic Riding and Self-esteem.* Doctoral dissertation. Buffalo, NY: D'Youville College.

Riede MR (1988). *Physiotherapy on the Horse.* Washington, DC: The Delta Society.

Roszak T (1996). The nature of sanity. [Online.] *Psychology Today*; 1 January. www.psychologytoday.com/gb/articles/199601/the-nature-sanity (accessed 29 May 2018).

Ryan R, Weinstein N, Bernstein J, Brown K, Mistretta L. Gagne M (2010). Vitalizing effects of being outdoors and in nature. *Journal of Environmental Psychology* 30(2): 159–168.

Trivedi L, Perl J (1995). Animal facilitated counseling in elementary school: a literature review and practical considerations. *Elementary School Guidance and Counselling* 29(3): 223–233.

van Deurzen E (1990). *Existential Therapy.* London: SEA Publications.

Wilson EO (1995). *The Biophilia Hypothesis.* Washington, DC: Island Press.

13

Out of it: addiction and recovery as lived phenomena

Ryan Kemp

There is no doubt that existential therapists are ambivalent about the use of labels, diagnoses or disorder categories (du Plock, 2009). And yet these ways of describing persist in the general imagination and are useful clinical heuristic devices. So, while this chapter will use the term 'addiction' and 'addict' repeatedly, it should not be interpreted as any sort of reification of this condition or as a denigration of the individuals so described. I am also going to use 'drugs' to describe pharmaceutical drugs, alcohol and any other substance (or process) that gives pleasure.

So, if we were to apply an existential-phenomenological description to addiction, what would emerge? This chapter will set out such a description, making the case that this adds an exciting new perspective on addiction that is directly clinically relevant.

The harms of addiction are often invisible but are significant when quantified. It is estimated that 25 million people in the world are drug dependent (World Health Organization, 2010). The World Health Organization (WHO) estimates that drug use accounts for the loss of two disability-adjusted life years and 11 for alcohol (World Health Organization, 2010). In the UK, it is estimated that there are approximately 262,000 problem heroin users, 1.6 million people in the UK with mild, moderate or severe alcohol dependence (HM Government, 2010) and 451,000 problem gamblers (Wardle et al, 2011). These are not small numbers and they do not include an emerging number of other addictions, now broadly described as behavioural addictions.

Before exploring an existential understanding of addiction, it may be worthwhile briefly surveying how addiction is understood by other therapeutic traditions. Almost without exception, conceptions of addiction focus on cause. Thus bio-psychiatric conceptions centre on the brain – either its architecture (the so-called pleasure pathways) or the neurotransmitters that flow in these pathways (the so-called dopamine hypothesis). In their definitions, both the DSM and the ICD psychiatric diagnostic manuals focus on symptoms related to physical tolerance, withdrawal, cravings and being unable to stop even if this is desired. There is no sense in which actual livings humans are involved. The descriptions used could apply to rats (from which much evidence underlying the descriptions are derived) as much as to humans.

Psychological theories are more focused on the whole human but are, again, often also centred on causal factors. So, cognitive-behavioural theories emphasise the reinforcing (pleasure again) qualities of drugs. Psychoanalytic theories tend to emphasise either the sexual parallels (pleasure again) or the attempt at self-medication (Khantzian, 1999). I would not want to contend that these theories are wrong, only that they fail to describe what it is like to be an addict. The lived, worlded experience of addiction is absent. How can we respond to addiction if we don't know what addiction is like for the addicted person?

Phenomenological contribution

A central claim I will make is that 'addiction' is a way-of-being, a form of existence that is lived at all times, not just when satiating certain impulses, and that this way-of-being reflects our modern times. Modern life is fast, ever-changing, saturated with technological solutions and invested with an individualistic, consumer ethic. Even though life is crowded, many feel alone, alienated and unhappy. Individuals are encouraged to seek satisfaction through pleasure, in whatever form it arises. This is regarded as a matter of personal choice, and the best way to exercise this choice is to buy what makes you happy. This modern self has therefore been accurately described as empty (Cushman, 1990).

The entry point into addiction is disputed, but a phenomenological analysis would suggest that the entry into drug use (before addiction) is in the pursuit of pleasure or the relief of pain (Kemp, 2009a). Pleasure and pain point us immediately and dramatically in the direction of the body. For phenomenologists, the body is not the biological entity studied by physical science but the lived vehicle of our existence. In its most primordial state, the body is lived as a semi-hidden background to our experience of the world (van den Berg, 1952). When I am absorbed, say, in typing a letter, my experience is the keyboard and the screen on which I see movement. Only when my back aches am I drawn back to my body as a thing. Thus, the body can be reflectively experienced as an object itself. So, I might rub my back to ease the tension felt there. When the body fails, as in illness, then the body is foregrounded in experience. The most significant moment at which the body intrudes for addicts is when they start to crave and suffer withdrawals, both of which are painful. For those suffering significant addiction, this intrusion is constant and compelling.

Thus, for the addict, the body is constantly intruding and changing on its own terms. This has an alienating effect; the body is no longer 'me' but experienced as an alien other that seeks its own ends. In cases of significant physical addiction, this leads to a hatred and distrust of the body as an inconsistent and dishonourable host. The body then becomes an object-body, a site of instrumental intervention (Kemp, 2009a). When the addict is in pain, this is not merely a bodily reality, it is also a withdrawal from the world, which is also lived as a place of pain. It is easier to withdraw from the world, consume your drugs and limit contact with people.

'World' or 'lifeworld' is an existential term that describes the matrix of meanings inherent in the things, space and relationships that are our lives. Based on my clinical observation (see Kemp, 2011), the addict's lifeworld has common features: a) withdrawal from the world; b) very little contact with others; c) very little movement or physical activity; d) excessive leisure activities (usually TV watching), and e) monotony. The emotions that accompany this life are negative, unpleasant, persistent and pervasive. These addictive existences are described as *narrow*, with very little breadth or depth. In addition, addicts move into a *withdrawal* from others and all things. The addict then becomes the embodiment of modern individualism, alone and trusting only themselves. The ambiguity, complexity and challenge of the world cannot be faced. Instead, the world is simplified – 'I only need to buy drugs'; contained – 'I won't go out unless to score', and inoculated – 'I don't feel anything bad when I am high.' Meaning steadily fades out of these unlived lives. Our current times are deeply technocratic, industrial and consumption-orientated, with a growing ideology of individualism. The addict is thus perfectly suited to our world and our world is perfectly suited to addiction.

This ethic of individualistic consumption without end might now be seen as normal. Note the number of brands that use 'addict' as a label and the number of television shows portraying consumer consumption or the addiction industry.

Another feature of modern life is its culture of immediacy. Addicts are also very 'now' orientated and so are drugs (Kemp, 2009b). Drugs call out to the addict to be used now. Drugs do not last and therefore have no future. This distortion of temporality has its source in active addiction, with this effect becoming prototypical. The 'now that lingers' extends into the entire existence of the addict, which means they do not live as though they have an open future. Addicts are often described as impulsive, but perhaps impulsivity is less about impulse control than about how the individual temporalises their existence. With a closed future, the relation of addicts to death is also undermined. Addicts thus often put themselves literally closer to death, but this is not a simple attempt at self-destruction. This is death as a mediating, limiting, meaning-giving experience. In lives that are progressively stripped of significance, encounters with death serve a crucial function in insisting the addict constructs some meaning.

Addiction can also be described as a completely technocratic state of being that seeks to instrumentally change emotional states (Kemp, 2009c). Thus the 'high' of drugs is temporary and unreal. I might drink two glasses of wine after a difficult day, but this only delays my having to face whatever has upset me, unless, of course, I keep drinking and drinking. Addiction is therefore by definition emotional untruth; it is a 'closing' of the subject to the truth of their life. The untruth of addiction can then extend into lying as a primary mode of relating that also acts to keep the human other 'out' and is a form of interpersonal closure. Addicts can struggle to maintain relationships because there is a form of fundamental distrust in their relating that undermines the natural functioning of interpersonal trust. In addiction, relationships can become chronically alienated and foreclosed, because the 'drug' becomes the primary other. The work of therapy as a way of truth, acting against this closure, seeks to create an openness to being. In the case of addiction, the issue covered over most often is that of shame. This shame is multiple, related to personal transgressions, doubts about value of self and how society regards the addict.

Addicts often feel 'out' of society; they often have fantasies of forming their own alternative communities. This alienation is both literal, political and symbolic. The word addiction itself derives from the Latin for 'assign, award or devote' and is linked to the word 'diction'. Ad-diction implies a structural constriction of possible expression both through speech and action. If we were to look at other words connected to addiction (see Kemp, 2012), what emerges from these etymologies is an inherent *ambivalence*. Drugs pull both towards the good and towards the destructive (Derrida, 1981). In addition, Western society has moved from a work ethic to a production ethic and now to a consumption ethic (Reith, 2007). Addiction is quite literally a process of consumption without limits. The creation of pathological identities allows the alcohol and gambling industries to legitimise their expansion by designating those who are harmed by this expansion 'pathological gamblers' or 'alcoholics'. Therefore, the addict is constructed as either bad (criminal) or sad (sick). This masks the fact that the addict is following an ethic of consumption-in-itself (Kemp & Butler, 2016) that is inherent in our modern capitalist societies. The addict thus functions as a societal symptom that haunts and hinders the illusion of social and ethical cohesion. This explains to some extent why addicts are so commonly vilified, for they reveal the hidden danger of a consumption ethic.

This very brief phenomenological description of addiction suggests that addiction is characterised by a pursuit of pleasure or the termination of pain and by an ethic of consumption; is focused on immediacy; is technocratic, individualistic, ambivalent and alienating, and is a form of existential deception. Modern society draws us all into these ways of being, but the addict is especially captivated. As such, the addict mirrors society, or is perhaps the exemplary contemporary subject. Nonetheless, addiction is a form of suffering, both for the individual addict and for our addictive society. This phenomenological understanding of addiction opens new ways in which to engage and understand both addiction and the recovery from addiction.

Case study

Like many of the people I have treated over the years, Al came into therapy after having had many detoxifications – in this case, his fifth. However, there seemed to be something different about Al at this point and I felt this from the beginning. Although alcohol was the current problem, Al had suffered from drug abuse in his late teens and into his 20s. He dabbled with most drugs but heroin had been the great seducer. It had occupied and dominated his life for almost a decade. However, after a period in hospital where he almost lost his legs to amputation, he had managed to stop. Unfortunately, he had started drinking almost immediately after this, and this had continued for the past 15 years.

Al described his early years as disrupted; he never knew his father and his stepfather had been an unloving disciplinarian. He grew up not knowing who he was and became a 'chameleon' who adapted to social situations by becoming what was needed. He also described feeling like he was trapped in a body that was not his but that he could neither escape from nor fully inhabit. He dropped out of school and formed friendships with people he admired, all of whom were either using drugs or selling them. What followed was a 25-year drug and alcohol career. He married, but deception and crime interfered and the marriage ended in divorce. There followed a string of broken relationships, many jobs and seven periods in prison, interspersed with brief periods of abstinence and attempts at recovery. While many people told Al he would come to harm if he continued in this way, he said this never hit home as a reality. Instead, he only worried about where he would get money from, how to avoid those that he owed money to and where he would get his next score. Solutions were focused on getting drugs and drink, not on any other problem.

In the early years of trying to recover, Al said he was convinced he could take drugs or drink, he just had to find the right way to do it. He never seriously contemplated that he could live without it. Later, he reported feeling trapped in a 'no-win situation', where he both wanted to use (desperately) and wanted to stop (reluctantly). Like many individuals attempting to find recovery, Al sought help from many quarters, including formal treatment from my own NHS team, but also from AA and other mutual aid organisations. Al knew he had 'personal issues' as he put it, but felt AA also offered him something unique. It was a place where he felt safe and understood. Yet he didn't get the 'spiritual stuff' and, although he went to meetings, he didn't feel he worked the steps in a proper way.

Much of our early therapeutic work was on issues of self, identity and narrative cohesion. It was about Al telling his story and coming to understand why he had made the choices he had, many of which were very destructive. This was all positive, but Al was still struggling with relapsing and after seven months required another detoxification. Having previously contracted Hepatitis B, his liver was in poor health and a short stay in hospital was again required. A short time after this, Al said he 'finally understood AA' and why there was only one mention of alcohol in the 12 steps. When he had asked about this at a meeting, he was told that alcohol was not the issue, he was the issue; all the remaining 11 steps were about self-transformation. Despite all our sessions, this seemed to strike the right chord with Al. Suddenly our work took on another momentum and pace. He no longer sought to stop drinking and understand his addiction; instead he sought to transform his sense of self.

He also started something very new – he volunteered in a local soup kitchen. This would prove to be the most crucial transformative move Al was ever to make, because it shifted his attention from himself to others. His chronic, now obviously destructive, self-obsession fell away and he began to speak about others and to appreciate what life was capable of giving him and what he could give to others. Very quickly, he no longer craved alcohol because the unease that had haunted him for so many years faded away. He was at ease in himself and, strangely, alcohol was no longer an issue.

Reflecting on this story, several issues stand out for me now. The initial work on the self was important (du Plock, 2002) but was not the solution. It clarified the meaning that the drugs played in Al's life, but did not lead to any real change. On reflection, however, I believe it created a platform upon which the actual change could take place. So it was necessary, but not sufficient. What was crucial was the move out of an obsession with himself and with drugs and towards others. At first this was practical – the volunteering gave him structure and purpose – but later it became foundational and a way of life.

The second thing that strikes me is that Al embodied the modern capitalist subject. He was a self-made man, desperate to fit in and prove himself. He never bemoaned his circumstances or what life gave him. He wanted something and went about seeking it in all the wrong places for many years. What stands out is that Al never used any political or social language. It would have shocked him to learn he was playing such a role. The fact that he was reflecting the social world around him was completely unknown to him.

Al has been abstinent for several years now. He continues to struggle with physical health issues but is looking forward to some newly developed Hepatitis B treatment. His psychological health appears stable and his recovery seems well established. As he now works helping others with addiction problems, I see him from time to time.

Discussion of the case study

This case example illustrates that the phenomenological description of addiction helps to radically change our conceptions of what addiction is. It shows that Al suffered from a number of distortions to his lifeworld: he was unable to maintain any significant relationships; he chose short-term ends over longer-term consequences; he used his body as an object rather than as a host; he was unable to see the existential truth of his predicament, was deeply ambivalent about his drug decisions and was shaped by the social world he inhabited. He had to transcend all of this for any meaningful recovery to take place. This transcendence happened, not in one flash of insight (even though Al himself might say this), but in a sequence of moments. So, the decision to seek treatment, the decision to take methadone, the decision to attend AA, the move from drugs to alcohol, the frequent detoxifications, the start of therapy, the decision to start working on himself (rather than on drugs) and the decision to start volunteering were all moments where Al moved a little into a new world that eventually led to an abstinent recovery. Some of these moments are clearly more significant than others, but they all contributed towards the momentum that eventually carried him into a new kind of existence.

What is clear from Al's story is that he suffered a strained relation both to himself and to the world in which he lived. You could say he was too much 'in' himself and too little 'out' in his world (Weegmann & Khantzian, 2011). It was probably like that before drink and drugs arrived, but they perpetuated this state of affairs for decades. It probably hindered or curtailed any natural change that might have brought about a resolution of this impasse. Al described being confused about his relation to himself. To some degree, this could be seen as a self-fascination to which he was inexorably drawn but from which he also suffered. The self never faded into the background of his experiential life, so allowing the world to be 'the there' of existence; rather, it whirled around directly in front of him, haunting him. Authentic being is not one in which one constantly reflects on every issue. This is debilitating and, in a sense, painful. It also means the world is excluded and, therefore, Al could not settle in relationships, hold a job long or play any part in community life. He could not 'be' in his world; it felt like a drama and he felt like an actor playing a part. While drugs brought suffering, they were an attempt to solve a problem that Al could not solve alone. Thus, drugs are an attempt at a fix, but often they are rather closer to a fix-ation, a stasis. And drugs brought more loneliness and exclusion.

One of the paradoxical truths of addiction is that stopping is easy; it's the staying stopped that is the problem. As was noted above, addiction is an existence, a way of being in the world. The biggest challenge for the recovering addict is to 'get out' of this existence and into an existence that can sustain a recovery. What sparks this change is extremely varied, but the move, whatever that is, must transcend addiction. For a meaningful recovery to take place, the addict will need to move beyond their previous narrow existence and to embrace life in its fullest sense. The real danger is that, when addiction ends, a void opens up in the life of the addict, which they often fill again with drugs.

Once abstinent, the easiest way for the addict to live is as before, avoiding life and human relations. This withdrawal has a protective function; it protects the addict from any temptation. But if the world is addictive, if our contemporary times are addicto-genic, there is no avoiding temptation. Life is an ongoing temptation. So temptation must be borne and ultimately transcended.

Experience suggest to me that a recovery-existence requires broadening and reaching out. *Broadening* is living a life, which embraces several aspects of the lifeworld. *Reaching out* is towards the others who were previously systematically avoided, but also towards the things of the world. In the process, the self is also broadened and expanded, for the self is nothing more than our relations with the world and the other beings therein.

It is here that mutual-aid organisations can be extremely useful. Twelve-step traditions emphasise the mutuality of recovery, a set of personal relations (to the meeting, their sponsor, other members) and also a relation to a transcendent power (as the member conceives it). Thus, the 12-step member is never alone in recovery but is always in a dependent relation to 'an other', whether actual or transcendent. Twelve-step traditions never create processes that force change. Rather, they emphasise waiting for the moment of change (often called 'rock bottom') to occur and the acceptance that comes with that moment (Kemp, 2013). Even through many years of trying, Al was not abandoned by this support. But a point came where Al realised that it was not drugs he was fighting; rather, he was fighting himself. Then he needed to get 'out' of himself, back into the world. So, he started volunteering, building new relationships and mending old ones. Rather than seeking to receive, he sought to give. All these changes were inversions of his previous existence. He was 'in' another world. It is in this sense that the world does the transforming and, in equal measure, the world itself is healed to become a place in which recovery might be lived.

There is plenty of research to show that trying to force change in addiction treatment, often through confrontation, does not work (White & Miller, 2007). To do so would be to 'act as the other', rather than be 'open to the other'. To hand over your recovery to others requires enormous courage and it is, again, completely counter to the ego-driven control agenda that characterises many addictions. Recovery, as it is described here, requires a humble acceptance of the limitations of human subjectivity. In existential terms, it is to accept the finitude of human existence.

In summary, to accept one's finitude is to dwell in truth, even if this means to suffer one's lack; to deny one's finitude is to dwell in untruth and constantly battle to maintain an illusion.

Discussion with the editor

Simon: I would be interested to know a little more about you, how you came to work in the field of addiction and what motivated you to develop your own particular perspective and model.

Ryan: When I qualified as a clinical psychologist, I had ambitions to do work with adults, hopefully doing long-term therapy. When I applied for my first job, I was unsuccessful, but they offered me instead a job in an NHS drug and alcohol team. I thought that I would give it a try and if I didn't like it I could always move later. It turned out to be a super team, very innovative and open, and it also coincided with an expansion of drug treatment in the UK. Beyond this, I also realised I was well prepared for the work. There was alcohol abuse and addiction in my family and I had spent eight years working in the gambling industry while at university. I was comfortable around addicts and, although that could be a shortcoming, it was an entry point.

I spent my early years just learning the usual approaches – mainly CBT, DBT and motivational interviewing. I was also very interested in psychoanalysis, but this had little place in the field. Somewhere around 2004, I re-read JH van den Berg's brilliant little book *A Different Existence* (1972). It is an existential-phenomenological description of a young man probably going through a psychotic depression. But it demonstrates, in lovely, simple ways, how to understand suffering and describe it. I remember thinking that I wished I had an addiction book that was similar. Then the thought occurred to me that perhaps I needed to write that book. I vividly recall thinking about the issue of temporality at that time. One of my clients was late and I was sitting at my desk trying to work out how time is involved in addiction. I gave up and decided it was impossible. Then I thought, 'Where is that client and why is he always late?' And then I was 'in' the problem and a small part of the solution was in front of me.

Simon: It's rare that I read something and feel so immediate a sense of recognition of my own experience of working with clients presenting with issues of addiction. The notion of addiction as technocratic, individualistic and characterised by a form of existential deception all reflect my own experience. If, though, addiction is characteristic of an alienated society, I wonder if you could say something more about how addicts are 'especially captivated'?

Ryan: Your comments are very kind. I would contest that the rise of addiction is directly involved and a result of the way our world is at this point in history. Our lives are flooded with injunctions to 'enjoy', 'just do it', 'trust your desire' and so forth. Both our society and addicts believe that pleasure is a right, a solution and a moral good. It is coupled with a post-modern sense of freedom. As long as you are not hurting anyone else, then you should be free to do whatever you want, enjoy whatever you want. It is reinforced by neoliberal capitalism, which wants all citizens to be super-consumers. Thus, the commodification of everything. Even spirituality is for sale. Addicts are especially captivated because their experiences and values are congruent with this ideology.

Simon: I agree with you when you identify that the move from self-obsession to an openness to others may be the crucial shift that enables an addict to lose their thrall to a substance, but I think this step follows on from a greater understanding of the meaning they ascribe to the substance, insofar as they begin to understand how it functions as a way of making the world narrower, less complex. Is this your understanding too, I wonder?

Ryan: I would agree that understanding the meaning of the substance is crucial. You see this element in all the different forms of therapy for addiction. Often this is called the 'function' of drugs, which is slightly different but is aiming at the same understanding. However, I would add that getting at the meaning is necessary, but not sufficient. I have had many clients who could tell me all about their childhoods and how their parents had failed them. They understood why they started taking drugs and how this was sustained. But they were still constantly relapsing. In my opinion, it is this shift that opens the addict to the world that is the crucial added dimension.

Simon: I am interested when you say, 'the world does the transforming and, in equal measure, the world itself is healed to become a place in which recovery might be lived.' I like the way this takes seriously the existential notion of a co-created world, and implicit in this seems to be something political – perhaps a way of moving beyond the 'ethic of consumption-in-itself'?

Ryan: If we are to take the notion of being-in-the-world as truly ontological, then there is no individual and no world. Individual and world are just aspects and reflections of the same process, which is existence. When the addict authentically engages with their world, when they escape from a pleasure drive or pain phobic orientation, the world is opened as an incredible expansive arena of possible meanings. The narrowness of addiction, its inwardness and self-obsession, is overturned. The paradox is that the world does this and is equally transformed. Perhaps the metaphor of being a therapist is similar. There is no way to avoid being affected by the work we do, even if that is not our intent. Obviously, I am not claiming that one addict in recovery changes all of existence. Yet I have heard families say that, when their son/daughter/husband/wife is in recovery, they live life differently. Our ways of being, of relating and loving are deeply worlded and worlding. It is a fundamental reciprocity that greater minds than mine have struggled to articulate.

As I have developed my work, it has increasingly seemed more political. It was not my intention to head in this direction, but I was led by the experience of the research. I see constant parallels between addictive behaviour and consumer behaviour, and between our culture's relation to the environment and what we 'want'. Yes, let's save the planet, but I can't do without my coffee in a paper cup. Here, again, our relation to the truth 'as lived out' is exposed. 'It shouldn't happen,' but 'I still want it.' Desire triumphs over all other values. Hopefully our society doesn't get as close to 'death' as many addicts have to before transformation occurs. It is my existential prayer.

References

Cushman P (1990). Why the self is empty: toward a historically situated psychology. *American Psychologist* 45(5): 599–611.

Derrida J (1981). Plato's pharmacy. In: Derrida J. *Dissemination* (B Johnson trans). Chicago: University of Chicago Press (pp67–122)

du Plock S (2009). The world of addiction. In: Van Deurzen E, Young S (eds). *Existential Perspectives on Supervision: widening the horizon of psychotherapy and counselling*. London: Palgrave Macmillan (pp109–120).

du Plock S (2002). Some reflections on an existential-phenomenological approach to working with addiction. *Existential Analysis* 13(1): 83–90.

HM Government (2010). *Drug Strategy 2010. Reducing demand, restricting supply, building recovery: supporting people to live a drug free life*. London: HM Government.

Kemp R (2013). Rock bottom as an event of truth. *Existential Analysis* 24(1): 104–116.

Kemp R (2012). The symbolic constitution of addiction: language, alienation, ambivalence. *Health* 16(4): 434–447.

Kemp R (2011). The worlding of addiction. *The Humanistic Psychologist* 39(4): 338–347.

Kemp R (2009a). The lived-body of drug addiction. *Existential Analysis* 20(1): 120–132.

Kemp R (2009b). The temporal dimension of addiction. *Journal of Phenomenological Psychology* 40(1): 1–18.

Kemp R (2009c). Relating to the other: truth and untruth in addiction. *European Journal of Psychotherapy and Counselling* 11(4): 355–368.

Kemp R, Butler S (2016). *We are all vampires: the burden of consumption-in-itself on western subjectivity*. Unpublished manuscript.

Khantzian EJ (1999). *Treating Addiction as a Human Process*. Lanham, MD: Jason Aronson.

Reith G (2007). Gambling and the contradictions of consumption: a genealogy of the 'pathological' subject. *American Behavioral Scientist* 51(1): 33–55.

van den Berg JH (1972). *A Different Existence: principles of phenomenological psychopathology*. Pittsburgh, PA: Duquesne University Press.

van den Berg JH (1952). The human body and the significance of human movement. *Philosophy and Phenomenological Research 13*: 159–183.

Wardle H, Moody A, Spence S, Orford J, Volberg R, Jotangia D, Griffiths M, Hussey D, Dobbie F (2011). *British Gambling Prevalence Survey 2010*. London: National Centre for Social Research.

Weegmann M, Khantzian EJ (2011). Envelopments: immersion in and emergence from drug misuse. *American Journal of Psychotherapy* 65(2): 163–177.

White W, Miller W (2007). The use of confrontation in addiction treatment: history, science and time for change. *Counselor* 8(4): 12–30.

WHO (2010). *World Health Statistics 2010*. Geneva: WHO Press.

14

Ontological insecurity: the case of Henry James

Simon du Plock

In this chapter I will consider the Jamesian novel as an attempt on the part of Henry James to create ontological security. My interest in this area (leaving aside personal experience of ontological insecurity) was kindled some years ago when I was researching the French writer Marcel Proust. I found myself looking at the relationship between literature and existential philosophy and, specifically, considering the extent to which Proust's *À la Recherche du Temps Perdu* (1954) constitutes an exercise in confronting existential anxiety. In this chapter, I will examine James' method of maintaining a relationship with the world via the novel form and its implications for the psychotherapist's understanding of the schizoid process.

Ontological insecurity

The reader who wishes to consult the principle sources for the elaboration of the concept of ontological insecurity may refer to Sartre's *Being and Nothingness* (1943/1958), (in particular, Part 1, Chapters 1 and 2), and Chapter 3 of RD Laing's *The Divided Self* (1959). Laing used the term 'ontology' not in the philosophical sense of Heidegger or Sartre but, as he later put it, 'in its present empirical sense as it appears to be the best adverbial or adjectival derivative of "being"' (1967: 39). It is in this sense that I intend to use the term in this chapter.

Laing also wrote on ontological insecurity in his 1967 work *The Politics of Experience*, and with Esterson three years earlier in *Sanity, Madness and the Family* (1964). Further useful consideration of this concept may be found in psychoanalytic literature, in particular in the writings of Guntrip and of Winnicott. In addition, Ernesto Spinelli provides a lucid account in Chapter 7 of *The Interpreted World* (1989), while Emmy van Deurzen-Smith has argued for a notion of ontological insecurity as not just a description of psychopathology but, rather, as a characteristic of ordinary human experience (van Deurzen-Smith, 1991). Expressed simply, as human beings are thrown into an absurd world and are in a constant state of becoming, they are never able to feel secure with regard to their ontology – the general conditions of their existence.

Nevertheless, RD Laing argued in *The Divided Self* that some people experience a profound and debilitating degree of ontological insecurity:

> The individual in the ordinary circumstances of living may feel more unreal than real; in a literal sense, more dead than alive; precariously differentiated from the rest of the world, so that his identity and autonomy are always in question. He may lack the experience of his own temporal continuity. He may not possess an overriding sense of personal consistency or cohesiveness. He may feel more unsubstantial than substantial and unable to assume that the stuff he is made of is genuine, good, valuable. And he may feel his self as partially divorced from his body. (1959: 42)

While writers do not invariably concur on the characteristics of ontological insecurity, it is possible to state that, in essence, the ontologically insecure, unlike the ontologically secure, are said to lack a sense of their presence in the world as real, alive, whole and temporally continuous. As such, it is difficult for these people to live out into the world. They experience a major split in their relationship with the world – a split that extends into main relational dimensions: first, a split within their self, such that a rent is experienced between aspects of the self that have been accepted and aspects that appear to be alien and must be denied; second, a split between self and others who are perceived as a threat to self-autonomy. As Shaffer has said, for the individual who feels this level of insecurity, the experiences of life become 'a matter not so much of gratifying oneself as of preserving oneself' (1978: 52).

Symptoms of withdrawal such as anti-social behaviour, extreme timidity and aloofness become much more comprehensible once we are aware of the level of threat experienced by the individual. This threat is perceived, according to Laing, in terms of engulfment – being swallowed up, stifled or taken over; of implosion – being filled with something alien and dangerous, and of petrification – disconnection from the dangerous world of others and, as a result, finding oneself isolated and depersonalised. Because, of course, humans are only really fully human in relationship.

As Spinelli points out (1989), these three fears are highly reminiscent of the archetypal themes of the horror story, a genre in which Henry James was prolific and to which he returned repeatedly throughout his career. Anyone who has read the most famous of his stories, *The Turn of the Screw* (1898/1990), will recognise how the main protagonist, the governess (who in the Victorian class system is neither servant nor master, child nor adult), experiences the slow destruction of her sense of self, is engulfed not merely by other characters but by the house in which she works and is filled with terrors that are nameless but seem related to repressed sexuality. She can never rest but must constantly labour to 'fix' things and she knows what the reader only discovers at the close of the tale – that the looks of others can kill.

How, then, have I used the concept in terms of my own study of the relationship between psychotherapy and literature?

The relationship between ontological insecurity and literature

Literature seems to serve a multiplicity of functions. In earlier stages of civilization, it was connected with magic and ritual. The earliest definable function was a communal one: communal listening to the recital of a professional bard. Even the most self-expressive of Romantic poets committed to the theory that the object of poetry is simply to give expression to the poet's feelings in the way that best satisfies him or herself, by the fact that he or she uses the communicative medium of language, concedes the desire to communicate.

Some commentators have found disturbing the question, 'What is the function of literature?' Welleck and Warren suggest it steers us towards a utilitarian position from which we will naturally stress the 'use' rather than the 'delight' of literature, and semantically equate its 'function' with its extrinsic relations. If they must use the term 'function', they say that its 'prime and chief function is fidelity to its own nature' (1970: 37).

A further theory of literature is that of diversion and amusement, or to relieve us – either writers or readers – from the pressure of emotions, but the debate (which began with Plato) continues between those who support and those who deny the anti-catharsis doctrine. Does literature relieve us of our emotions or excite them? And, in any case, are our emotions wrongly discharged when they are expended on poetic fictions?

Freud (1959: 146) subscribed to the notion of literature as diversion. He regarded the author as an obdurate neurotic who, by his creative work, keeps himself from breakdown but also from any real cure. The writer, then, is a socially-validated daydreamer. Instead of altering his character, he perpetuates and publishes his phantasies.

But Freud was not entirely comfortable with this position, as we find from a reading of his earliest psychoanalytic work:

> Like other neuropathologists I was trained to employ local diagnoses and electroprognosis, and it still strikes me myself as strange that the case histories I write should read like short stories and that, as one might say, they lack the serious stamp of science. (Breuer & Freud, 1893–95/2000: 160)

While he was attempting to behave like a scientist, then, he could not help but remark that the resultant works were literary and artful, quite the reverse of the outcome a scientist might predict. Was Freud's own literary imagination, his own humanism, infiltrating his work? Not so, he answers: 'I must console myself with the reflection that *the nature of the subject*, rather than any preference of my own, is evidently responsible for this' (my emphasis). While scientific methods, Freud concluded, led 'nowhere', a 'detailed description of mental processes such as we are accustomed to find in the work of imaginative writers' resulted in 'at least some kind of insight' (pp160–161). Each of these suggested functions – aesthetic pleasure, diversion, catharsis and the partial relief of neurosis – hints at but fails to elucidate a further, perhaps specifically existential function. In each instance, the question seems to be aesthetic pleasure as an alternative to what? Diversion from what? Neurosis emanating from what?

Eagleton (1988) and other Marxist literary critics have attempted to explain the rapid increase in literature's popularity and status in the 19th century as a function of the comparative decline of religion. This thesis of literature as social cement is strikingly expressed in reductionistic form in the inaugural lecture of George Gordon, one of the first professors of English literature at Oxford, when he wrote:

> England is sick… and English literature must save it. The churches having failed and social remedies being slow, English literature has now a triple function. Still, I suppose, to delight and instruct us, but also, and above all, to save our souls and heal the state. (Eagleton, 1988: 23)

This increasing promotion of literature on a societal level to replace the failing ideology of religion was matched on an individual, psychological level by its use by a new class of professional novelists and a greatly increased number of amateur diarists in the place of, or in conjunction with, religious faith as a tool for making coherent sense out of the now apparently random moments of particular lives.

Which brings me back fairly and squarely to ontological insecurity. I was encouraged, on re-reading *The Divided Self*, to see that Laing makes use of literature in his explanation of the concept of ontological insecurity. Right at the opening of his discussion, Laing uses the worlds of Shakespeare and Keats on the one hand and Kafka and Beckett on the other to point up the contrast he wishes to make between the basic existential positions of ontological security and insecurity. And we can immediately see that the dates of these writers fit in well with the Marxist view of literature briefly outlined above.

If Laing felt that it was helpful to use literature in this way, it did not seem a great leap for me to suggest that a writer's output might, in itself, be viewed as constituting an attempt to create ontological security. Of course, in making these observations, I had a particular writer in mind. I have recently been reviewing the work of Henry James, and especially the form of the Jamesian novel, as a series of experiments in ways of being-in-the-world – a perspective that I will elaborate below.

Laing, in his presentation of ontological insecurity in *The Divided Self*, introduces two brief case studies – Mrs R and Mrs D. If we amalgamate these, we find they provide a fair example, or operationalisation, of the responses of those with a low threshold of security to the three forms of anxiety said by Laing to be encountered by the ontologically insecure person – engulfment, implosion and petrification. Laing (showing his psychoanalytical orientation) is able to offer a deeper understanding of the behaviours of Mrs R and Mrs D by conceptualising them as a defence against extreme anxiety.

It might be argued that we cannot replicate this procedure in the case of Henry James, since he is not available to us in the same way as a client. And that is quite correct, but he is available to us in another way, in his literary canon. It has for many years been unfashionable among literary critics to subscribe to the view that you can locate a writer in his/her work. Writers themselves have taken a quite different view, as Edel notes (1985). He cites Edgar Allan Poe, who repudiated the view that 'the work of an author is a thing apart from the author's self', while for Joseph Conrad, 'The writer of imaginative prose stands confessed in his works', and James, in the same vein, states: 'The artist is present in every page of every book from which he sought so assiduously to eliminate himself' (1985: xiii–xiv).

So, what happens when we look at James in the way Laing looked at his cases? Let us, as it were, take his biographical details.

The case of Henry James

Henry James was born in 1843, in Washington Place, New York, His parents, Henry James senior and his wife Mary, were wealthy nomads who lived in hotels in whichever country they chose to inhabit. By the time Henry James was 21 the family had lived in New York, London, Albany, New York again, Geneva, London, Paris, Boulogne, Newport, Rhode Island, Switzerland, Germany, and then back to America, to Boston and finally Cambridge.

James was taken to England when he was six months old and to France a year later. He was, from his earliest years, disturbed about his sense of place. The earliest memory he records – of the Place Vendôme at six months of age – is so elaborate as to be highly improbable. Even when the James family settled for a few months, 'The possibility' (he wrote later) 'of going to one place to another was always in the air' and there was always a feeling of 'the absence of plan or continuity' (Edel, 1985: 47) – an absence we might consider a source of ontological insecurity.

We can see from his diaries that the need to fix himself, to record himself in one place he could 'own', was strong – so strong, in fact, that he includes an autobiographical digression in the early pages of his novella *Washington Square* (1880/1982). This a digression unique in his entire canon and, in fact, most unusual in the schema of the novel at this time, which was some years before Proust began to publish his own immense autobiographical journey through time. James seems to have wished to make sure that his frail identity and that of the Square would be merged:

> It was here that you might have been informed on good authority, that you had come into the world… it was here that your grandmother lived in venerable solitude… it was here that you took your first walks abroad, following the nursery-maid with unequal step… (1880/1982: vi)

He was always to be seen following, unequal, in the footsteps of another, whether his father or brother. At other times he seemed to live in the shadow of his mother, whom he described in his notebooks as the 'keystone of the arch' (Edel, 1985: 11). She comes down the years to us as a phantasmal form who, nevertheless, infuses the young Henry with intense fears of close relationship. Mary James, variously described by Henry James as 'sleepless', 'soundless' and 'selfless' (Edel, 1985: 11), is impressed upon us as a suffocating martyr to whom homage must constantly be offered up; a bloodless creature to be propitiated by the lifeblood of her children. William James, Henry's older brother, seems to have experienced his mother quite differently. He writes of her in middle life: 'Mother is recovering from one of her indispositions, which she bears like an angel, doing any amount of work at the same time, putting up cornices and raking out the garret-room like a little buffalo' (Edel, 1985: 12). The unintended humour appears to indicate that he did not feel smothered with maternal solicitude, unlike Henry, who was to write of his 'sense of her gathered life in us and of her having no other' (p13).

The mother envelops him: 'she was each of us', she had a 'complete availability', James wrote after she had been dead 30 years. This 'complete availability' was reflected also in the young boy's experience of religion and education. For most children of the period, church and school served as twin institutions, ordering their lives and casting shadows, for good or ill, across their adult years. Henry senior, remembering a joyless childhood, shrank from anything that would be 'narrowing' for his children and when little Henry's schoolmates challenged 'What church do you go to?', he was as bereft of an answer as he was when asked to name his father's profession. The elder Henry's reply was that:

> We could plead nothing less than the whole privilege of Christendom, and that there was no communion, even that of the Catholics, even that of the Jews, even that of the Swedenborgians, from which we need find ourselves excluded. (Edel, 1985: 35)

But, as young Henry recorded, to have all the churches and all the religions was really to have none and to belong nowhere again. Henry James senior's theory of education was similarly unstructured. He feared pedantry and rigidity; he had a horror of dogma and of moral judgements. His solution was to throw his sons into numerous schools and let them find their own feet. He reasoned that there was divine truth in the world and the children were bound to discover this through divine guidance. This 'theory' produced in young Henry the feeling that he had no standard by which to judge the facts of the life he saw around him. His father gave him, he felt, no sense of values. He saw his father as living only by his mother. Indeed, after his mother's death, his father was incapable of going on without her: 'He passed away or went out…

for the definite reason that his support had failed' (Edel, 1985: 14). However, much Henry senior was an individual in his own right, what struck the small boy was his dependency.

From the daydreams recorded in his notebooks, from his tales, from his observations in his memoirs, we can fathom the effect on the young Henry James of this view of the parental relationship, which remained with him throughout his life. At some stage, the thought came to him that men derive strength from the women they marry, and that, conversely, women can deprive men both of strength and life. We might note, as Henry James seems not to have noted, that apparently, if men do not marry, the same applies to their mothers…

This view of marriage led to further considerations. What happens to a man who gives himself to a woman? Does that person not renounce himself? As I will argue below, this fear of emotional involvement forms the keystone of James' work, just as his mother formed the keystone of his life. We might note a sort of free association: in a list of names he set down in his notebooks when he was 50, James included 'Ledward', on which he improvised several variants: Ledward – Bedward – Dedward – Deadward. This appears to be a casual rhyming of led – bed – dead. It is also, in effect, a highly condensed statement of the themes of many of his works. To be led to the marriage bed was to be dead. In fact, to be led to any sort of bed for a sensual purpose might lead to death. The *petit mort*, or 'little death', (of orgasm) was for James not momentary but permanent.

Henry James was named Henry after his father, as his elder brother had been named William after their grandfather. For the next 40 years he was destined to be known as Henry James Junior. All his works, up to and including The Portrait of a Lady (1881), bore the 'Junior' label. Throughout his life, Henry volubly protested against the parental failure to let him have a distinctive name and (by the same token) an identity of his own. As later generations of Jameses carried on the dynastic confusion, he continued to argue that the name given to a child can affect his whole life. As late as 1882, the year of the elder Henry's death, the father and son were being taken for one another, since they both wrote and published and on occasion appeared in the same table of contents of the *Atlantic Monthly*.

But what agitated James was not so much the confusion of names, or even his identification by others with his father, but his need in a family of competing egos to find any identity at all. Reading James' novels, we discover at every turn the writer's predilection for second sons. Sometimes he kills off elder brothers or turns them into villains; sometimes his hero is an only son, usually with a widowed mother. He confers on them an ideal fatherless and brotherless state. For Henry, life in the James family was a state of inexhaustible younger brotherhood, as if William 'had gained such an advantage of me in his 16 months' experience of the world before my life began that I never for all the time of childhood and youth in the least caught up with him (Edel, 1985: 17). William 'was clean out before I got well in' (p17). He had 'cleaned out' and there was nothing left for the impoverished Henry.

A Small Boy and Others (1913) and *Notes of a Son and Brother* (1914/2011), both intended to be about William, are, in fact, about Henry. It is almost as though the younger brother is setting the wrong right and correcting the record. In *The Portrait of a Lady*, the young Isabel Archer's revolt against attending school is unexplained. We might get some hint from *A Small Boy and Others*, where the rage of the five-year-old Henry on his first day is due to the discovery that William is there ahead of him and 'in possession' (Dupee, 2014: 48). Henry was subsequently to find in adolescence that, if he could paint, William could paint far better and, when at 20 he entered Harvard, 'of course I was to find my brother on the scene and already at a stage of possession of its contents that I was resigned in advance never to reach' (Edel, 1985: 18). He goes further and talks about living 'on the echoes' of William's life; of wishing to live, if only 'by the imagination, in William's adaptive skin' (p18).

As we have seen, Henry turned into the depths of himself to fashion a fictional world based on the realities around him in which elder brothers are vanquished, fathers made to disappear and mothers put in their place; a world of wishful thinking in which he did not have to face reality. In turning to writing novels, at which William had no skill, Henry might be thought to have chosen the observer's role rather than that of the actor, which had already been appropriated by William. Henry longed for a condition of the self that would consist in looking without being looked at and would protect him from the dangers of unregulated encounter – a state of being that a writer's life appeared to offer.

Henry James' experience here may be usefully likened to that of the schizoid client. Unable to wrest an identity of his own within his talented, nomadic family, he ceased to attempt to make direct connections with others and withdrew into a world of his own devising. Realising that his brother and father had already claimed those areas of life in which he hoped to make his own mark, he gave up entirely. This scenario frequently obtains for the schizoid person who, faced with difficulties in their attempts to live out into the world, believes that there is no room for them anywhere and close more and more doors on themself until they collapse into themself. James, though, differs in a crucial way: while he, like them, withdrew further and further into his own world, he was able to construct a safe place for himself there; he relinquished the possibility of unmediated contact with the world but recognised that there was still something left for him.

The literary canon that he constructed continues to bear witness to this. As a successful failure, James has a great deal to teach us. Our clients, on the other hand, often fail to carve out a pleasant place for themselves in the face of their difficulties; they are unable to stand in that paradox and say, 'I can still choose to construct something worthwhile and sustaining for myself' and, having done so, make it available to others as a means of communicating with them. In *Roderick Hudson* (1875/1986), James dramatises at great length another paradox: the eternal paradox of art. While life is all passion and heat and indulgence, art is, he states, all coolness and abstraction and detachment. How should the artist, then, conduct himself so that, while remaining in the element of art, he transcends its limitations? James has no answer for this question and can only offer the cold consolation of art, as opposed to the misery and conflict of life. In Roderick's fate, James sees the defeat of art by destructive passion and is therefore wary.

In each story, the chief protagonist must struggle to wrest their values from the darkness and chaos around. At an existential level, it is clearly a struggle for identity, but it might be suggested that it is a struggle whose result is predetermined. This 'struggle' has something of a paraphrenic quality about it. In paraphrenia, a term first introduced by Freud in the Schreber analysis (1911/2003) to denote a condition located on the borderline between hysteria, multiple personality and schizophrenia, individuals create themselves into a constellation of different characters who constantly vary. James populates his imaginary world with extensions of himself. Several commentators, including Edel (1985) and Poole (1992), have judged this to be true of both his male and female characters. It is not absurd to suggest that, in the hundreds of characters we find in his canon, we meet only the author and perhaps three or four of his family. He creates himself out into this imaginary world and in each novel presents, rather as one might set out a problem in a game of chess, a question about a particular aspect of how he should live his life. Since, though, each character or chess piece on the board is constructed as an extension of himself, James is able to position them in such a way that certain outcomes become impossible. In each novel he considers a different way of living as an artist directly out into the world, and in each he concludes that art and life are mutually incompatible.

All of the works – novels, novellas and short stories – centre on the existential question of whether emotional contact with another might be survivable; all, in different ways, conclude that it is not, until we arrive at the late works, and in particular *The Sacred Fount* (1901/1995), *The Wings of the Dove* (1902/2008), *The Ambassadors* (1903/1986) and *The Golden Bowl* (1904/2009), in which it seems that the self-defeatingly complex style of the text ensures that the question is no longer fairly put. It is as though James finally glimpses the possibilities that have passed him by as just that, and he resolves the anxiety this realisation generates by retreating further into his interior world. Before he does so, though, he allows Strether, in *The Ambassadors*, full awareness of his error. In a poignant soliloquy, he states: 'Live all you can; it's a mistake not to. It doesn't so much matter what you do in particular so long as you have your life' (p5). Much later, he adds: 'If you haven't had that, what have you had?' (p215).

Towards the end of his life, James experienced something that he called a 'breakdown' and he consulted a well-known psychiatrist, who prescribed warm baths and electric shock treatment. We can only wonder what might have resulted had James been able to consult an existential therapist. It might be that he would have begun to live his life out into the world. His future readership would, of course, have lost the novels that were originally the products of his autotherapy and later constituted his frantic attempts to maintain his interior world.

These exercises in autotherapy can be seen in some respects as acts of bad faith, since the question 'How can I live my life?' is increasingly framed in a manner that will not permit the response 'Directly, freely and without compunction'. James might voice regrets, as he does when tempted by sensuality in Venice in 1872. His wistful observation, 'Verily nature is still at odd with propriety' (Kaplan, 1992: 4) might be read as more personal than political.

It is necessary, however, as an existential therapist, to sound a notion of caution at this point. Van Deurzen-Smith (1991) has stated that ontological insecurity should properly be understood not as psychopathology but as a characteristic of ordinary human experience. We might opine that James sacrificed a life of action for one of passive contemplation as a writer; we might suggest that, had he had the 'benefit' of therapy, particularly our own brand of therapy, and the encouragement to challenging self-reflection that it entails, he might have moved from this position. However, to do so is clearly to commit two major assumptions: that to write is not to act out into the world and is not, in some way, a valid mode of being-in-the-world, and that to write and to act out into the world are mutually exclusive. A moment's reflection should convince us that to write with a view to publish constitutes a very public way of acting out into the world, of being-in-the-world – a form of exposure of which Henry James was acutely aware, as his private notebooks testify. But even the outright failure of his play, *Guy Domville,* in 1895 – a narcissistic wound that James referred to as 'the most horrible of my life' (Edel, 1985: 425) – did not persuade him to stop publishing, although he turned his attention away from the theatre.

A number of commentators have understood James' development of the novel form in terms of a flight from 'real life' into deeper and deeper obfuscation.; Indeed, Levey (1991) has described James' increasingly complex 'working up' as a 'distancing of actuality'. As an example, he cites James' attempt to capture in words an object of desire he was unable to capture in actuality: an encounter, during one of his many visits to Italy, with a near-naked Torcello urchin, whom he turns, by a reversal of the Pygmalion process, into a statue – 'This little unlettered Eros of the Adriatic Strand'. Levey notes what he considered this distancing technique is also found in letters to friends:

> He later attempted to give an account of activities by Miss Bronson (an American philanthropist) which seem – as far as they are discernible through his verbal veil – to have been both imaginative and practical. She bothered herself over a section of this population he alluded to as 'the very small folk' of Venice. They were gondoliers and such, whose piety, for instance, she took seriously. She even took what he calls 'cognizance' of their wives and children. If his case of emotional atrophy were less grave, it might be the subject of a Max Beerbohm cartoon: 'Mr Henry James is induced by Mrs Brown to take cognisance of the little people of Venice'.
> (Levey, 1991: 16)

This 'verbal veil' is increasingly evident in the Jamesian lexicon too. James criticism has recognised three phases in the novelist's journey from complexity to complexity. The youthful style of the early period (up to and including *The Portrait of a Lady*, written in 1881) develops from the stilted and clumsy first novel, *Watch and Ward* (first published serially in *The Atlantic Monthly* in 1871), to what Maini calls 'the expansive, felicitous, opulent and luxuriant prose of achieved graces and sheltered values' (1988: 147), redolent of what was to come.

An alternative reading of Henry James

What if we choose not to follow the conventional wisdom that the Jamesian lexicon develops until it becomes a screen behind which the ontologically insecure writer could observe the world he dared not enter? An alternative reading of James' 'tortured prose' may be indicated by Conrad's description of him as 'the historian of fine consciences' (Armstrong, 1988: 3). As James wrote in *The Future of the Novel*, 'it is of all pictures the most comprehensive and elastic… for its subject, magnificently, it has the whole of human consciousness' (1900/1956: 17). For James, experience is never limited or complete, but is rather an *'immense sensibility*, a kind of huge spider-web of the finest silken thread suspended in the chamber of consciousness, and catching every airborne particle in its tissue' (my emphasis) (p25).

James came to understand – even though his oeuvre may appear to be firmly rooted in the classic Victorian and Edwardian themes of inheritance and titles – that human and social reality is bewilderingly complex and all human beings can do in response is try to make their own truths as they negotiate the turns and twists of life. The search for personal identity sits at the heart of each of James' novels. As Hyacinth, in *The Princess Casamassima* (1886/1987), expresses it:

> … nothing in life had such an interest or such a price for him as his impressions and reflections… Everything in the field of observation suggested this or that; everything struck him, penetrated, stirred, he had in a word more *news of life*, as he might have called it, than he knew what to do with.' (p10; my emphasis)

James' lifetime of writing may thus be understood not as a journey away from using writing to 'fix' himself in one place (as in the semi-autobiographical section of *Washington Square* discussed above), or as a screen behind which he could hide from direct experience, venturing out to explore and then reject various modes of living in the world. Rather, it can be seen as a movement towards a fascination with the fragmentary nature of life and an acceptance of the impossibility of ontological security.

Therapeutic implications

What can the therapist take from a case study of Henry James that will assist them in their own practice, and not just practice with clients who are artists of one sort or another? James illustrates what can follow when we are totally self-absorbed and narcissistic. His work attracts people who have similar traits: the reader has to work hard to follow his clues and gain access to his world. Having gained entrance to the inner sanctum, they can look out from a privileged position. There is something almost erotic about this: the notion that the reader's taste is so nice, so honed that they are able to truly appreciate such eccentric work. And this is the trap of which James, perhaps, was a victim and one in which some of those who are attracted to the work find themselves enmeshed.

Nobody could satisfy James and even the small circle who were willing to approach the master were never permitted to be fully present with him. Indeed, the dead were permitted to enter James' life more fully than the living, as we find in his somewhat disturbing reaction to the death at 24 of his cousin Minnie Temple, one of the very few women for whom he admitted a deep affection. On learning of her death, he wrote to his mother: 'Twenty years hence – what a pure eloquent vision she will be.' Minnie alive was a creature of flesh and blood to be loved, and also, for Henry, a threat, as all women were. Minnie dead was an idea, a thought, like a character in a novel who might be worshipped in complete safety. He wrote to his brother William:

> She represented, in a manner, in my life several of the elements or phases of life at large – her own sex, to begin with, but even more Youth... It's almost as if she had passed away – as far as I am concerned – from having served her purpose.' (Edel, 1985: 109)

These observations on James may be extrapolated to clients in general. People can do as he did; they can turn themselves into art objects that become rarefied and isolated and, perhaps, highly precious – like James' *The Ivory Tower* (1917). This mirrors what occurs in psychosis when people turn in upon themselves further and further, in a closed system cut off from the outside world. In poverty of affect, such people receive no nutriment from the outside world and cannot renew themselves or allow any connection with others. This was the situation of Henry James, with one important distinction – he continued to create his art and was, therefore, still connected to the outside world. He was still putting up signs saying, 'If you want to reach me, follow this road. Here is my art, read it if you can and, if you are able to understand it, you can find me.' By contrast, the psychotic individual loses contact with others because they give out messages that are so intricate, so distorted, that no one can gain access to their inner world. The approach to their inner world resembles a maze set with traps. If we try to approach them, the individual throws us something that is disconcerting and leads us off in the wrong direction. They are afraid of what will happen if another does come near, so they constantly set riddles and tests, each of which we must pass to be allowed to enter. Thus, the work of Henry James offers us an interesting path to greater understanding of the schizoid process. It is possible to investigate it by investigating Henry James' process, since he is more than simply schizoid: he does something with this state; he tries to connect, he evidences and articulates what psychotic people can only enact. He connects back to the world so that we can use it; we can say he lets out a 'silken thread' that, if we follow it, will lead us to him. In following this thread, we can, I argue, investigate the schizoid process more effectively than we can by observing clients who have, so to speak, cut the connecting cord.

The secret of Henry James' relative mental health is that he maintains this connection, albeit in an esoteric way. This is not to suggest that he needed psychotherapy. Rather, I am suggesting that he is poised on the edge, on the borderline; he goes through the psychotic process but in doing so he transforms it into art and illustrates and expresses it so that the reader is invited to connect with him and learn from him – and it is this that makes him sane and not purely psychotic.

Clayton, in his work on the relationship between fiction and psychological wellbeing, makes an important point when he recognises the role of the Jamesian novel as a psychological strategy in the face of ontological insecurity, as experienced by not only the author but by his readership too:

> James served as the Master for a literary culture that needed, as he did,
> to valorize an aesthetic defense against psychological chaos. But they are
> not merely 'defenses'. And he was truly a master, able to shape in language
> a contemplative space that he used as a refuge, but that extended beyond
> refuge, too – a place of transformation, of healing, making whole. It
> wasn't simply a place in which creativity was possible but a representation
> of the creative imagination in its war with chaos. (1991: 147)

The James scholar swiftly leaves the novels of the early phase behind in favour of the middle and last. At this point, the reader must approach the London edition, James' immense revision of almost every sentence of his oeuvre. This is all the more fascinating in that it was a critical failure in his lifetime and remains today a constant source of debate among critics, who are undecided as to whether it represents the apogee or a falling off of the master's genius. If, as van Deurzen-Smith states (1991), 'Authenticity is the ultimate goal' (of existential therapy), 'not that of being adequate at copying other people's work', it is clear that those who become enmeshed in James' world and fail to create of their own accord become mere copyists.

Clayton realises this when he writes that James:

> ... flees the impinging mother, he flees turbulence and competition as his father did...he turns his disability into a position of moral as well as aesthetic authority, then teaches this (unconscious) strategy to his spiritual followers, who need it for much the same reason as James himself. (1991: 150)

While James' art seems to have had a therapeutic function and to have provided him with a certain sort of autotherapy, it becomes less and less a blueprint for anything to do with what psychotherapy, and certainly existential therapy, is intended to be.

James is poised on the borderline between psychological health and illness, but does his case indicate anything about the assistance that therapy might be able to offer others in this situation? Returning to the suggestion that suffering is a necessary condition of creativity, and that its relief in any way, including via psychotherapy, would destroy the artist's talent, certainly, as Storr (1989) has acknowledged, the image of the isolated, angst-ridden artist has wide currency. While a case might be made that a psychiatric or behavioural-based therapy that aims to cure might deaden creativity, this objection need not hold for existential therapy. We might argue that it is possible to move away from the dichotomy of being either chaotic and in pain and an artist or conformist and deadened. Might there not exist a third possibility that would hold the tension between acknowledging the reality of other people while living fully and challenging prevailing norms? Such a way-of-being-in-the-world might open up the possibility of creativity at a more productive level – for the general good as well as for the individual who dares to attempt it.

Moreover, to accept the challenge to live more fully out into the world is not to abandon art. Psychotherapy is a discipline that seeks to help people become aware of how they author their lives and how they might author their lives. In this sense, it can be conceptualised as a tutorial for living in which clients reflect on what sort of book of life they are writing by their actions, beliefs and commitments. It is not coincidental that people talk about opening a new chapter in their lives, or of turning over a new leaf: living and writing are not mutually exclusive. Life itself is art: the more intensely we are willing to enter into the flow of it, the more stimulus for thought and for writing we obtain. It may be the case that those who open themselves up to this flow in order to be inspired may feel overwhelmed and reinforce the popular perception that art is invariably connected to neurosis or psychosis, but this need not be so. It may be that writing and living can be mutually supportive – writing might help us author our lives more effectively and we do not need to either bury ourselves in our lives or in our novels. Rather (and perhaps this is where existential therapy may come into its own), a person can become expert at linking the two.

But can we ever have non-neurotic art? To hold the view that we cannot is to be caught up in the medical model, for there is nothing necessarily neurotic or psychotic about art. Existential therapists can help their clients find their own way to have some control over reality as it is shared with others so they are able to find ways to be flexible and resourceful when engaging with the 'immense sensibility' of life and not lose themselves in its vastness and complexity. The existential therapist is, to paraphrase Stevie Smith (1957/1975) one who learns to swim out into the stream of life and wave encouragement to the client who flounders in the shallows. This willingness to become immersed in life is quite distinct from the position James espoused in his novels, as exemplified by Strether in *The Ambassadors* (1903/1986), who, 'half ashamed of his impulse to plunge and more than half afraid of his impulse to wait' (p63), turns in on himself to divert the immediacy of these impulses and transforms them into yet one more piece of the rare substance that forms James' ivory tower of art.

Discussion with Zack Eleftheriadou

Zack: The idea of using the work of a writer as a case study is an interesting one. This is not the typical way of creating a case study.

Simon: I am enthusiastic about thinking about the notion of case study as widely and creatively as possible. In some respects, treating artistic output as a guide for clinical practice is not a new idea at all. I have regularly lectured in the Baltic states and Russia, and there it is common practice to take inspiration from novels. The classics in particular are held to be repositories of wisdom about how to live, and therapists there have told me how they have introduced ideas from Bulgakov, Dostoevsky and Tolstoy in their work with clients. We might take the view that working phenomenologically rules out such a direct use of literature. Nevertheless, if we ask ourselves why we read at all, we will recognise that we very frequently do so as much because we seek guidance, or even instruction, as we seek diversion or entertainment. So, we do know that literature is a source of 'case studies'!

Coming back to the West, I have noticed how often people applying to train as existential therapists cite reading existential literature – Camus, de Beauvoir, Kafka etc – as their initial inspiration for doing so. They resonate with the image of the human condition they find in these writers. Their work speaks to us in powerful ways, yet fiction quickly cedes to theoretical works once they get on a training programme. Mary Warnock (1970) makes what I think is an important distinction between 'philosophical Existentialism' and 'non-philosophical Existentialism'. As an academic philosopher, she is concerned, as you might expect, to distinguish between literature that rigorously addresses existential themes using Husserlian phenomenology and literature that does not attempt a systematic account of man's connection to the world. I think it is pretty clear that Henry James falls into the latter camp, but he is still fundamentally concerned to rigorously address the question 'How shall we live?' And he does so via a series of very detailed 'cases' that reward close attention. Paradoxically, much of the work that Warnock would admit into the category of 'philosophical existentialism' – what Sartre calls 'littérature engagée' – loses its ability to engage the reader as it strains to instruct: the analogy might be with directive versus non-directive therapy.

Zack: The concept of 'ontological insecurity' is rather strange if, as you say, human beings can never be ontologically secure.

Simon: It is indeed a strange concept and one that had an extraordinary impact when RD Laing introduced it in *The Divided Self* way back in 1959. Van Deurzen-Smith, in her seminal paper published in the *Journal of the Society for Existential Analysis* in 1991, attributes its impact less to its accuracy in describing a psychopathology and more to the way it captures a characteristic of 'ordinary human experience' (p38). Ordinary people, not just those struggling with psychosis or schizoid phenomena, were able to recognise themselves when they read Laing's description of ontological insecurity. It seems to me that a measure of ontological insecurity, along with a degree of existential anxiety, is necessary if we are not to fall back into the false security of Heidegger's *das Man*. The difficulty and the challenge are to craft a life that vibrates with this awareness of insecurity and is not shattered by it.

Zack: How have you used insights from literary cases in your own clinical practice?

Simon: James Hillman wrote: 'Case history is a fiction in the sense of an invented account of the imagined interior processes of a central character in a narrative story' (1983: 12). It seems to me that the novelist is in at least as good a position to create such an account of the human condition in action as is the therapist. Writers such as James, Joyce, Proust and Woolf devote many hundreds of pages to such analysis in a way that is not available to even the most expansive case history.

I have found it as helpful over the years to reflect on my client work through the lens of 'cases' drawn from literature in general as it is to read the case studies assigned to the psychotherapy literature. The insights of either are rarely, if ever, directly transferable to my client work; rather, both can encourage the intense curiosity about the human condition that is the *sine qua non* of existential therapy. Sartre, Camus and de Beauvoir set out to explore anxiety, alienation and absurdity in a way that can inform practice. Clients frequently bring books to me (sometimes literally) and we explore together what makes the text significant for them.

References

Armstrong PB (1988). *The Phenomenology of Henry James.* Chapel Hill, NC: UNC Press.

Breuer J, Freud S (1893–1895/2000). *Studies on hysteria* (J Strachey ed & trans). New York, NY: Basic Books.

Clayton J (1991). *Gestures of Healing: anxiety and the modern novel.* Amhurst, MA: UMP.

Dupee FW (ed) (2014). *Henry James: autobiography.* Princeton, NJ: Princeton University Press.

Eagleton T (1988). *Literary Theory: an introduction.* Oxford: Basil Blackwell.

Edel L (1985). *Henry James: a life.* New York, NY: Harper & Row.

Freud S (1959). Creative writers and day-dreaming. In: Strachey J (ed & trans). The *Standard Edition of the Complete psychological Works of Sigmund Freud vol 9.* London: Hogarth Press (pp143–153).

Freud S (1911/2003). *The Schreber Case.* Harmondsworth: Penguin.

Hillman J (1983). *Healing Fiction.* New York, NY: Station Hill Press.

James H (1934). *The Art of the Novel: critical prefaces.* New York, NY: Scribner.

James H (1917). *The Ivory Tower.* New York, NY: NYRB Classics.

James H (1914). *Notes of a Son and Brother.* Charlottesville, VA: University of Virginia Press.

James H (1913/2011). *A Small Boy and Others.* Charlottesville, VA: University of Virginia Press.

James H (1904/2009). *The Golden Bowl*. Harmondsworth: Penguin.

James H (1903/1986). *The Ambassadors*. Harmondsworth: Penguin.

James H (1902/2008). *The Wings of the Dove*. Harmondsworth: Penguin.

James H (1901/1995). *The Sacred Fount*. New York, NY: Barnes & Noble.

James H (1900/1956). *The Future of the Novel: essays on the art of fiction*. New York, NY: Vintage Books.

James H (1898/1990). *The Turn of the Screw*. Harmondsworth: Penguin.

James H (1886/1987). *The Princess Casamassima*. Harmondsworth: Penguin.

James H (1881/1990). *The Portrait of a Lady*. Harmondsworth: Penguin.

James H (1880/1982). *Washington Square*. Oxford: Oxford University Press.

James H (1878/2012). *Watch and Ward*. London: Barzun Press.

James H (1875/1986). *Roderick Hudson*. Harmondsworth: Penguin.

Kaplan F (1992). *Henry James: the imagination of genius*. London: Hodder & Stoughton.

Laing RD (1967). *The Politics of Experience*. Harmondsworth: Penguin.

Laing RD (1959). *The Divided Self*. London: Tavistock.

Laing RD, Esterson A (1964). *Sanity, Madness and the Family*. Harmondsworth: Penguin.

Levey M (1991). Venice within Venice. *Times Literary Supplement*; 20 December.

Maini DS (1988). *Henry James: the indirect vision*. Ann Arbor, MI: UMI Research Press.

Poole A (1992). *Henry James*. Oxford: OUP.

Proust M (1954). *À la Recherche du Temps Perdu*. Paris: Gallimard.

Sartre J-P (1943/1958). *Being and Nothingness* (H Barnes trans). London: Methuen.

Shaffer JBP (1978). *Humanistic Psychology*. Englewood Cliffs, NJ: Prentice-Hall.

Smith S (1957/1975). *Collected Poems*. Oxford: Oxford University Press.

Spinelli E (1989). *The Interpreted World*. London: Sage.

Storr A (1989). *Solitude*. London: Flamingo.

van Deurzen-Smith E (1991). Ontological insecurity revisited. *Existential Analysis 2*: 38–48.

Warnock M (1970). *Existentialism*. Oxford: Oxford University Press.

Welleck R, Warren A (1970). *The Theory of Literature*. Harmondsworth: Penguin.

15

Time-limited existential therapy and counselling

Alison Strasser

One of life's constants is time. There is no life without time. We are born in the knowledge that our life is limited, that we will inevitably die, irrespective of any spiritual or religious beliefs we may hold; time will continue its own inexorable march towards infinity, regardless.

> Time represents more vividly than any other category the necessity of accepting limitation as well as the inability to do so, and symbolizes therefore the whole problem of living. The reaction of each individual to limited or unlimited time betrays his deepest and most fundamental life pattern, his relation to the growth process itself, to beginnings and endings, to being born and to dying. (Taft, 1933)

Sixty years after Taft (a student and colleague of Otto Rank) wrote these words, time-limited existential therapy (Strasser & Strasser, 1997) was born. As brief therapy and short-term counselling began to be more widely used, my father, Freddie Strasser, and I realised that the theme of time itself could become a catalyst for therapeutic change. In simplistic terms, this particular existential approach understands that the awareness of ending evokes emotional responses from both the client and therapist. Generally, anxieties will emerge sooner and more explicitly than in longer-term therapy. Since anxiety is another of the ontological givens, it too becomes integral to the process of change.

Many agencies and therapists in private practice work with their clients within a specified number of sessions. This is usually defined as brief therapy or counselling. Within the spectrum, there are numerous modalities, ranging from psychodynamic to solution-focused approaches, that encompass a range of different solutions to working within a specified time frame. The existential approach discussed in this chapter uses the limitation of time and the inevitable end, working with what arises from the resulting pressure that is elicited for both the therapist and counsellor. Once there is knowledge of an end, of a limit to the process of therapy, a different atmosphere emerges. It heightens the anxieties and intensifies the tension for the client, who expects to be 'cured', and for the therapist, who wishes to help the client.

This chapter will explore the journey that a client and I undertook over 12 sessions as an illustration of working within a brief, time-limited existential frame. Time and its passage through our lives will be discussed in relation to how it is applied as a major *therapeutic* focus.

The original Wheel of Existence was published in *Time-Limited Existential Practice* (Strasser & Strasser, 1997) and I will use an updated Wheel of Existence (Strasser, 2016) as a diagrammatic representation of the interplay between key existential and phenomenological concepts and as a philosophical attitude when working with clients.

The Wheel of Existence

As Freddie and I started to develop our ideas about the significance of time in therapy, the Wheel of Existence (Strasser & Strasser, 1997) emerged as a schema for understanding how the different elements of existential philosophy are integrated into a whole, rather than split into divisions of mind, thoughts, body and emotions.

The Wheels of Existence are versatile and serve multiple functions in that they can be used as a specific structure for teaching but also provide a background frame that can be drawn on when reflecting about a client either in the session or later in supervision. Since 1997, many different versions of these wheels have been developed and used for a variety of teaching programmes, including supervision, coaching and mediation. This current Wheel of Existence (see below) was developed to simplify the concepts and methods into one unified frame that illuminates the movement of flow and integration that is essential to existential philosophy and practice.

Figure 15.1: the Wheel of Existence (Strasser & Strasser, 2016)

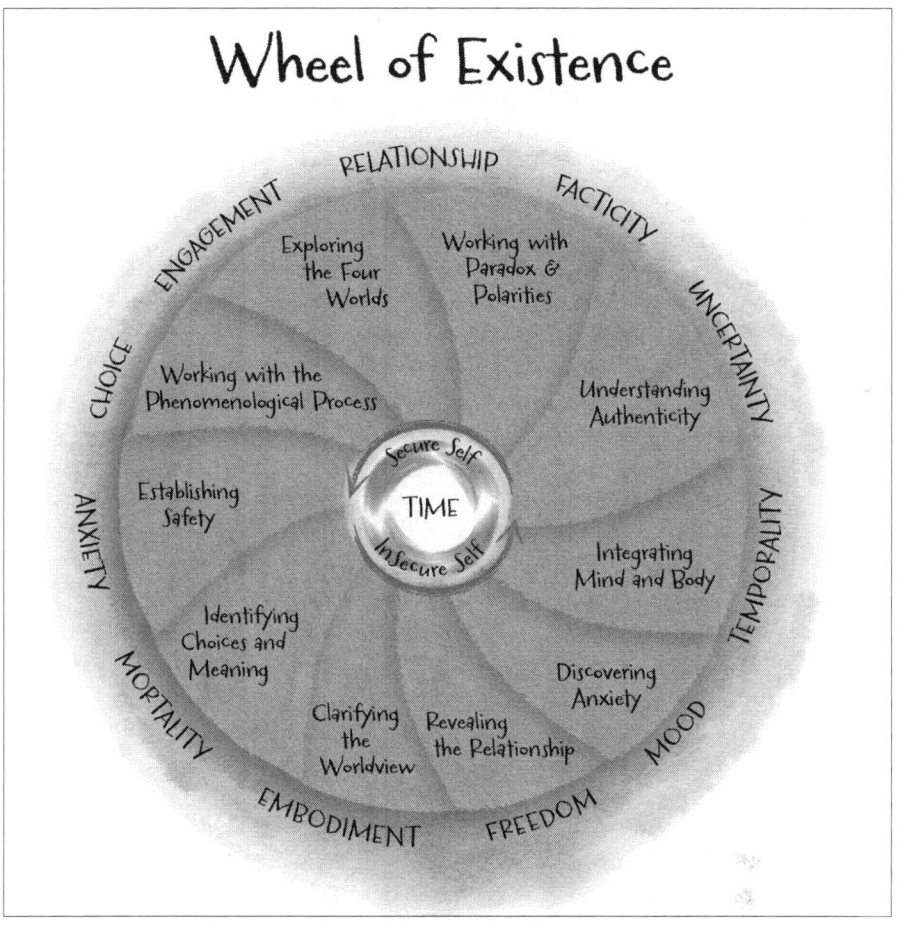

The elements chosen for inclusion in this new version of the wheel are subjective and open to variation. In other words, another existential practitioner might work with a series of different existential givens and themes.

In my Wheel of Existence, the segments revolve around the core, the theme of time, which is placed in the middle to denote its centrality of meaning and intent. There is physical clock time, partly determined by seasonal fluctuations and the rhythms of day and night. There is our personal, subjective relationship to time, sometimes described as existential time, which is how we treat time and how we imagine it treats us. At a concrete level, it emerges in our time-keeping habits, the manner in which we relate to our past, present and future, and how we leap into the unknown. Time is never stagnant and will morph as our moods change, seeming to gain speed when we are happy and slow down when we're not.

Circling the inner core of time are the secure and insecure 'self'. This refers to the self as not fixed or entity-like but as a process that continually reinterprets and reshapes its identity from the multiplicity of derived experiences. We move incessantly from feeling secure, good, ok, hopeful and so forth to being thrown into disarray and feeling insecure, bad, not ok and pessimistic about everything.

Even though these ontologicals are set in stone, they cannot determine our humanness in that our freedom arises out of our responses to these universal facts.

'What is most personal is most universal' (Rogers, 1961:10) provides the link that unites the ontological (outer section) and the ontic (inner section) of the wheel. Our personal experience is universal, in that the story the client may tell is their individual story and in its essence is also universal and familiar. Disclosing and listening elicits a shared, felt sense that is uniting and bonding. As therapists, we are attuned to these shared stories and our resonating response helps form the trust that is essential for good therapy to occur.

The inner segments of the wheel around the central core represent the dynamics of the therapeutic process in the discovery of how we each, individually and uniquely, respond to the ontological givens. These are known as our ontic responses and give flavour and depth to our personal being-in-the-world. As an example, the given of anxiousness is universal but our responses are unique to us. In the case study below, my client Graeme responded in various way, including running away, hiding his head in the sand and, in other situations, using the excitement of anxiety as his creative edge. This is represented as 'Discovering Anxiety' and some, but not all of the other segments in both the inner and outer circle will be described as Graeme's world is revealed.

The interplay, as depicted by the perforated lines between the ontological and ontic, is important in that, on the one hand, the therapist and client are sharing in the commonalities of being human and, on the other, both are responding in their distinctiveness and carving personal and particular pathways.

Working with Graeme

Graeme appeared a very confident young man as he walked into the room. Yet he came with low expectations. He had seen numerous psychologists, counsellors, psychiatrists and other types of therapists since the age of 12 and was very doubtful that anyone could help him overcome the anxiety that stalked him night and day.

He described himself as over-analytical and as someone who was quite capable of thinking himself into any kind of situation in which he was the person that was bullied, picked on and ultimately rejected. Rejection was his greatest fear and he did everything he could to be liked and accepted. For him, this required him to be constantly charming, polite and interested in others.

Although we contracted for 12 sessions, Graeme initially came for just two, after which he lost his job and disappeared. He came back to see me three years later, after a series of panic attacks and a succession of medical appointments that resulted in the suggestion that his condition required psychotherapy rather than medication. He had saved enough money for 12 sessions, so we again contracted for that space of time.

Aged 31, Graeme felt he had developed a variety of strategies for managing the anxiety that had plagued him since childhood. His child sense of self was shy and always in the shadow of his elder sister, Molly, whom he both admired and feared. Although they were now good friends, as a child his memory was of Molly ridiculing him and pushing him away when he tried to be included in activities with her friends.

His first trip to the local GP was at eight years old, when he was crippled with stomach cramps. He was admitted to hospital and eventually released when no cause could be found. As an adolescent, he had several sessions with a psychologist, who gave him some useful strategies to help reduce his overall anxiety, and especially his interminable propensity for imagining worst-case scenarios.

Graeme described his parents as having a close and intimate relationship. They had spent their youth travelling before finding a house, job and having children. He felt strongly that his father had compromised his personal dream of becoming a pilot because his mother forced him into a life of certainty and stability. A big shock for Graeme was finding out, two years before coming to see me, that his father had been diagnosed with a slow-growing but terminal cancer. He couldn't bring himself to spend time with his father and repeatedly admonished himself for his cowardice.

Although appearing confident, Graeme described himself as perpetually anxious. He confided that symptoms of a fluttering heart and nausea would appear most often when he was worried about work and that he would try to address these concerns by working longer hours and without a break.

He lived with his girlfriend, Kate, whom he understood wanted more commitment from him; to get married, have children and live in a house with the proverbial 'picket fence'. He said he loved Kate and knew he should settle down but that he also had other aspirations he wanted to satisfy, such as working in New York and London to develop his career as a music producer. He was currently working as a sessional music engineer, supplementing his income with bar work, but revealed a sense of wanting to achieve more.

Establishing the frame – the first session with Graeme

Uncertainty as an existential given (see its place and its relationship in the wheel in Figure 15.1) is the concept that, however much we attempt to make life certain, we also understand that certainty is unattainable. Our attempt to counter this 'given' is to create some kind of certainty and we do this in numerous ways, such as creating beliefs, values, coping strategies and behaviours to survive and distract us from the inevitability of uncertainty.

A common therapeutic strategy is for the therapist to create at least an artifice of safety by setting firm boundaries and establishing, as much as possible, a safe, reliable and consistent framework. In our first session, Graeme and I established our 'rules' around our weekly meeting. These included a 24-hour cancellation notice period that, if not adhered to, would mean the missed session counted towards the total 12. Unlike in other time-limited models, such as solution-focused therapy (de Shazer et al, 2007), we discussed expectations rather than goals. My experience has shown that, as depicted in the wheel, our issues do not exist in isolation but are interconnected to other elements of our life and living as a whole. Working with goals has the potential to drive both the therapist and client towards a particular destination, to the detriment of the totality. It is also important for the therapist to outline his or her expectations. This sets up the parameters that therapy is relational – that there are two people in the room, not just the client.

I set up a discussion with Graeme around the possibility of him taking responsibility for his own recovery. He saw himself as a hard worker; he had taken on the responsibility of two jobs and was working six days a week to pay the rent and save for times when he might be without work. As a budding music producer, he had to supplement his income with the bar work. The long hours he worked impacted on his relationship with Kate and gave rise to fractious arguments. In essence, he had taken up the mantle of financial responsibility in his life but had not addressed other important issues. His anxiousness around how others perceived him, his unwillingness to move forward with (or out of) his relationship with his girlfriend and his inability to face his father's illness were parts of his life that Graeme chose to ignore. He had found it easier to take an antidepressant or rely on professionals to find a solution than to delve into his own psyche and come up with his own answers.

As our first session unfolded, Graeme admitted that he had been running away from his feelings about mortality and the emotional turmoil of confronting the terror of his father's terminal cancer and ultimate death. He said he wanted to rekindle his passion for his music-production career, to be inspired and to inspire others. Graeme was adamant that he did not want to reach the end of his life with regrets; he didn't want to be like his father, who he felt had missed out on his dreams, compromising instead with the quarter-acre plot, house, family and secure job. He wanted to ensure that he lived life to the full but his anxiety was pulling him backwards, almost freezing his capacity for growth.

In that first session after the three-year hiatus, Graeme seemed more present and aware of his concerns than I remembered from our previous time together. He was passionate about making changes and exploring his anxiety rather than medicating for its disappearance. At 31, he now had a glimpse of what he could achieve in the musical world and did not want to lose his relationship with Kate.

The 12 sessions we agreed on sat comfortably with both of us in that it was within Graeme's financial budget and, from my perspective, it was a stretch of time that both permitted our relationship to develop and allowed for the ending to play an integral part of the therapeutic journey. Congruent with a time-limited approach, it is important to bring in the ending in the first session. Graeme admitted that he didn't like endings and he generally dealt with them by disappearing, as he had done after our first two meetings.

Discovering anxiety

Graeme's presenting issue was anxiety (as shown on the wheel and its relationship to self and the other givens in Figure 15.1). In existential terms, this anxiety is not fear but a background sense of something that is indefinable: a 'nothing and nowhere'. According to Heidegger, 'nowhere does not mean nothing', for '[t]he threatening thing, thus, cannot approach out of a definite direction within the vicinity, it is already "there" – and yet "nowhere"; it is so near that it stifles one and steals one's breath – and yet it is nowhere' (Heidegger, 1962: 186).

The mood of anxiety or anxiousness is central in the existential language for understanding and resonating with our client's world. Unlike fear, which is tangible and specific, anxiety is unspecific and indeterminate. Anxiety and the feelings it evokes gives access to our ontological being-in-the-world – our worlding (Spinelli, 2015), the place where we live in the uncertainty of being, in that, if we pause and look, we can peek into the existential nothingness of our world. Thus, anxiety can be understood as a threat to being where 'being' is who we are, our grounding in our identity. This anxiousness is both a threat to self and, ultimately, the threat of non-being or death. 'A paradox of death is that on death we are completed in our incompleteness' (Adams, 2013: 116). Yet we also have to *live* our life. Taking Kierkegaard's evocative 'leap of faith' (jumping into the unknown) (1846/2009) is both necessary and life affirming. Anxiety is the instigator for this, the means by which we can be propelled out of the darkness and into action.

The desire to push away anxiousness and be sage had dominated Graeme's whole life. He would take to heart what he heard people say or think about him, sensing strongly that he wasn't good, clever or nice enough. As a child, he felt bullied by his older sister, who had everything he didn't have in terms of being intelligent, sporty and sociable. He always felt like the outsider – the shy little boy who was judged, criticised and rejected. His playground memories were of keeping safe by waiting at the edges, watching and wishing to be included in the games but anxious about being ridiculed and rejected.

Graeme used to disappear into his imagination. It was an excellent strategy for keeping himself safe and at a distance from his anxiousness. Good memories were of weekends fishing with his father, when few words were exchanged but there was a sense of camaraderie. In contrast with these happy memories, he often felt dismissed and he experienced these rejections as a form of death or annihilation. Others, including his sister, teachers and boys at school seemingly had the power to create in him feelings of being cut off and dismissed in his entirety. Interestingly, he had a push/pull relationship with his parents, sometimes experiencing them as strong but more often as weak and powerless – a place that Graeme was afraid of acknowledging within himself.

As with all the ontological givens, our relationship to time and how we respond reflects our overall stance towards how we live in the world. One place where time would appear to stop and his feelings of annihilation would disappear was when Graeme was in the music studio, fully immersed in what he was hearing and what could be created. He loved this space and when he left it would experience a descent as he crashed back into the everyday world of time, similar to the effect of coming off drugs. Then time would stretch towards an anticipated but anxious future where an internal voice, the 'what if?', plagued his whole sense of being. Sitting by himself in this present moment would conjure up feelings of helplessness, of not wanting to take responsibility for his girlfriend, his father, mother or even himself.

Between our sessions, I began to ponder about the ways in which Graeme might use anxiety to his advantage. On asking him about this, Graeme recognised that anxiety did fire his creativity and helped him think and act on the spot when working in the studio. In fact, he relied and was dependent on this anxiousness and even experienced anticipatory anxiety about not getting anxious.

Understanding authenticity

Our relationship to anxiety is akin to our personal security alarm, in that anxiety holds the keys that unlock the path to our authentic self. As Sartre notes, anxiety has a paradoxical function in that it is more common to choose to ignore our anxiousness, or what he calls 'bad faith', than '[t]o act in bad faith [which] is to turn away from the authentic choosing of oneself and to act in conformity with a stereotype or role" (1943/2003: 49). Ironically, the more we attempt to evade our anxiety, the greater the inevitability that anxiety will raise its head in a less obvious and insidious form. In Graeme's case, he refused to even glimpse the vista of death but his various forms of panic attacks would leave him gasping for breath and in terror of dying.

Graeme could now make a choice to remain in his anxiousness and face his pit of despair. For Sartre, this is 'good faith'; for Heidegger (1962), it is authenticity – the capacity to stand on one's own, to carve one's own life path and not to take the easier option of following what other people say or expect. This is often confused with being genuine but, in the philosophy of existentialism, it merges the features of self-awareness, responsibility, choice, action and, ultimately, freedom. The path we choose is our path and ours alone. 'Authentic living is aware living' (van Deurzen & Adams, 2011: 92) and brings into focus our aloneness and responsibility.

Since our first meeting, I had been sitting with the feeling that Graeme was terrified, immobilised by his fear of death. This was not only about his own, inevitable demise but also the death of close loved ones. It emerged that his grandfather had died when Graeme was eight. He couldn't understand what had happened and for a long time believed his grandfather had gone on holiday and would return with his usual hug and surprise present. It was a great shock when his mother finally explained that he was never again going to walk through the front door. As a teenager, one of his school friends had died of alcohol poisoning. Graeme talked matter-of-factly about these deaths but the tears were evident as he spoke about his father's incurable cancer. It was inconceivable to Graeme that his father could be so sanguine about his prognosis and was turning to philosophy as a source of comfort, and he did his best to avoid seeing and spending time with him.

In our fifth session Graeme mentioned that he had run out of excuses for not visiting his parents, which was when I decided to broach the topic of death with him (see mortality and how it intersects with the other sections in the wheel). Although the phenomenological process describes in detail the need to stay present with the client through bracketing, description and equalisation, it is also true that, at certain times, we break this 'rule' to check or to hesitantly suggest an idea that might shift the client's perception more acutely. In the time-limited approach, as the pressure of time comes to the fore, I am aware that I will raise inherent contradictions in the client's story or proffer alternative hypotheses regarding their personal self-theories more quickly than in longer-term therapy.

For Heidegger, death is always with us, from the moment we are born. *Dasein* is a being-towards-death that is ever present and comes to the fore at various life junctures where change is thrust upon us. Endings, whether they be physical, such as the termination of a relationship, or emotional, such as shifting our worldview, evoke a 'movement-toward-death'; they connect us with our death anxiety (Spinelli, 2016: 135). In this fifth session, I deliberately decided to ask Graeme about his beliefs about death and what he found so scary. As we spoke, he realised that, when his grandfather died, he was ignorant of the concept of death. As a witness to his father's grief, he had been the bystander but had never spoken to anyone about his own emotional loss. To understand that he would never again see someone whom he loved and who loved him was both incomprehensible and frightening. Graeme was now approaching his father's impending death with a similar sense of doom.

Worldview, values, beliefs and challenging sedimentation

A feature of inauthenticity or bad faith is Merleau-Ponty's (1962) idea of sedimentation, which is when our belief and value systems get so entrenched and stuck that we are unable to see beyond what we believe is true. As clients begin to explore their underlying beliefs, it soon becomes apparent that some elements of their worldview are open and flexible, while other parts are closed and rigid. Our worldview is our perception of how we stand in the world, who we believe we are, how we understand others and how we imagine they view us, as well as our attitudes towards the larger world of our family, work, social, political and environmental situations. Indeed, by viewing the 'worldview' in the context of the whole wheel, one can gain a greater perspective of how it intersects with the existential givens and universal concerns.

Intertwined with Graeme's anxiousness around dying was the sedimented belief that his father had sold out, abandoned his dreams of becoming a pilot and the freedom of flying, and instead opted for the family life, with a steady but boring job. Graeme didn't want to repeat his father's 'mistakes' of being grounded and, at the age of 31, he appeared to be facing the same fork in the road as his father, having to make a decision to surrender his lifestyle that he so prized, marry Kate and take on the package of responsibilities that he felt was inescapable. Through some convoluted logic, Graeme believed that, if he remained carefree and unencumbered, he would live a long and happy life. This sedimented stance was a direct and subjective interpretation of how he viewed his father's decision. Indeed, on further exploration, Graeme spoke about the pressure his mother inflicted on his father and his father's evident unhappiness at having to succumb.

Graeme had taken on the stance that, if he was motivated, driven and a 'force to be reckoned with', he wouldn't lie down passively and die like his father. 'It's not going to happen to me!' was his underlying belief, laden with the value that he would be happy (and not die) if he remained free.

It is not that these beliefs or values are labelled as negative or maladaptive, but, as van Deurzen says: 'What ultimately matters in existential work is to determine what it is that really matters to the clients, not what ought to matter to them' (2002: 114). In other words, for clients to understand both the benefits and limitations of their belief system, they need to review how they came to inherit it, their reasons for adopting it and to reflect on how it may or may not be advantageous.

Each of our sedimented positions has an opposite – I am good/bad, handsome/ugly and so forth. In Graeme's case, his polarity of being carefree/submitting was based on his perception that his father had been passive and dominated by other people's wishes and commands. Graeme described himself as shy, generally scared that he wasn't matching up to other people's expectations and running away when confronted with potential conflict. As we explored this aspect, Graeme stumbled over his words, expressing his horror at realising the similarity to his father. I challenged him on this belief, pointing out that the hours he worked to support himself and his girlfriend were hardly irresponsible. Even his decision to return to therapy was made only after he had adequate funds to pay for it. He was kind and thoughtful towards others, which translated into his ability to produce music that sang to his clients' desires. In terms of freedom, what was Graeme evading?

Identifying choices and meaning

'Man is condemned to be free; because once thrown into the world, he is responsible for everything he does. It is up to you to give [life] a meaning'

(Sartre, 1943/2003). At our 10th session, Graeme texted three hours before his appointed time to cancel, due to work commitments. At our 11th session, I waited, feeling my anxiety rising at the thought that he may have decided to abort our sessions before the impending deadline. He arrived 15 minutes late, puffing and voicing profuse apologies for his tardiness. Describing his last few weeks of stress and insomnia, it seemed as if Graeme had taken a backward step. He was waking with nausea, heart palpitations and feeling scared. I, too, was noticing my body as my anxiety receded. I reminded Graeme (and myself) that we had one session remaining and we should reflect on what would be most beneficial for him.

One of the advantages of working within a time-limited frame is the quicker emergence of the crux of the client's life pressures, in a manner that indicates their overall approach to life and death. Graeme had already indicated that it was easier for him to run away than to confront anything that was uncomfortable deep down. I asked him how he was feeling and what he had been noticing since our last time together, with the added knowledge that we had only today and next week's session left. Before replying, Graeme paused, saying that it would have been easier not to come but he had remembered our first session and his promise to himself not to run, even though he felt so anxious. Staying with his anxiety, rather than trying to 'cure' it, I worked with what Graeme was experiencing in his body, asking him to describe what he was feeling.

Graeme spoke about how frightened he was. Change is perplexing in that there is both a movement towards future possibilities and simultaneously the fear of disruption to our perceived sense of safety. I coaxed him to stay with his body-sense and images arose of the isolated child who was often left out of games and social events at school. The picture Graeme painted was of a child of about seven years of age who was sad and confused and had no sense of what he could do to be liked. As the image grew, he spoke about his father and his fear of his dying. Death was so final and he didn't want to say goodbye.

Before finishing our penultimate session, I tentatively asked whether his father's choice to stop his travels, marry and have children might have been more proactive and considered than Graeme initially believed.

Final session – responsibility and freedom

Graeme seemed more solid as he arrived for his final session. He admitted that he had been fearful of saying goodbye and had come reluctantly. What brought him was his increasing awareness that it was easier for him to run rather than face his demons. He said that, at his core, he knew he wanted to face his father, to get to know him better, and not only as a paternal figure; he wanted, above all, to understand how he was coping with his illness and impending death. He had organised a fishing weekend for just the two of them and was both excited and nervous at the prospect. We talked about how it might also be important for his father to talk to his son about dying and perhaps for Graeme to ask him about how he wanted to be remembered.

Reflections

An essential component of any change is linked to a shift in perception when reflecting on past emotionally- and negatively-charged events. The phenomenologist Edmund Husserl wrote about time as 'lived experience', in that we only experience the past and, indeed, our anticipated future from our present perspective. This 'past as "the-past-as-currently-lived-and-future-directed"' (Spinelli, 2007: 43) implies that our past is now totally moveable and in stasis. We can both add and detract from our narrative of an event, constructing stories to fit our current perspective. Graeme had begun to review the same stories from his past with a different emotional understanding. He was beginning to notice that his original dislike of feeling different had paved the way for his current life choices. For instance, he had chosen an unpredictable and unconventional work environment, which left him little time for anything else. He liked this lifestyle; he felt different and special and enjoyed being noticed. The tension between this 'special' lifestyle and the lure of the conventional marriage-and-family way of life still existed but Graeme was now less torn, noting that he was only 31 and had time for both. This statement illuminated an enormous shift in his sedimented attitude. When we are able to entertain the possibility of 'both and', it immediately opens up prospects of something different.

Endings do not only feature when we are working in a time-aware approach; time and temporality are a constant within the therapeutic relationship. Each session has a beginning and an end, as well as the stretch of time between sessions. All therapy, whether brief or open-ended, is time-limited, and integrating the passage of time and the inevitability of ending into the therapeutic work helps engender a more realistic life-attitude in clients: one that is more at ease with the life/death, beginning/ending tension that is part of being human. This matches Heidegger's (1962) belief that we only become true to our self by confronting and making meaning of our ultimate finitude. This is our freedom.

Discussion with the editor

Simon: You write that your 'particular existential approach understands that the awareness of ending evokes emotional responses from both the client and therapist. Generally, anxieties will emerge sooner and more explicitly than in longer-term therapy'. Can you say more about the impact on the therapist? What is it like to work with a model that makes such an explicit connection between time and the possibility of change? Have you developed specific forms of training and supervision in response to the potentially heightened level of anxiety that practitioners may experience?

Alison: Yes, anxiety does seem to be more palpable when working with a limited number of sessions. It's not always pleasant but, if I practise what I preach, then noticing my anxiety is my personal wake-up call. This allows me to tune into my felt sense and to be curious about what might be happening for my client. I remember noticing a deep panic in my lower abdomen when Graeme didn't turn up for his 10th session. Focusing in on this, my personal fear of rejection came into my awareness. Yes, this is an old demon of mine but also one of Graeme's so my felt-sense understanding helped me to gently prod Graeme to talk more about his fear of ending and how, although it was easier for him to walk away, it might be worth his while to face his feelings of rejection.

In terms of training, yes, time and its limitations are integral to our work at the Centre for Existential Practice. We also talk and work with the existential, given that anxiety is an aspect of living that's always there, continually in the background. The limit of time is one way of bringing it into the foreground to be understood.

Simon: You note the increasing prevalence of time-limited therapy. You write: 'there are numerous modalities, ranging from psychodynamic to solution-focused approaches, that encompass a range of different solutions to working within a specified timeframe'. To what extent would it be true to say that these approaches introduce an existential given – the time limit – into the room, and so are, in some respects, 'unintentionally existential', while your own approach is distinctive and distinctively efficacious because it addresses this aspect of therapy explicitly and centre stage rather than implicitly?

Alison: I wish I could say that agencies that have a time limit to their sessions do work with the theme of time but, as far as I'm aware, in Australia this is not the case. Most practitioners will work with some kind of goal and, if that's not achieved at the close of the sessions, will attempt to garner additional sessions, refer on or talk about achievements gained as part of the closing session.

Simon: You begin with a single Wheel of Existence but explain that, eventually, many different wheels were developed and 'used for a variety of teaching programmes, including supervision, coaching and mediation'. I wonder which elements of the wheel are constant and define it as a wheel? Can you say more about, for example, how a Wheel of Existence can be used in supervision, and what is changed and what remains the same? I guess 'time' is always present at the core?

Alison: Time doesn't always have to be at the core of the wheel but it can slip neatly into one of the sections. This is the case with the Wheel of Supervision that I created in my doctorate, which has since become the frame for understanding and integrating our teaching of supervision at the Centre for Existential Practice. The beauty of the wheel concept is that it is flexible and can incorporate different givens and existential themes. My father, Freddie, had numerous folders on his computer for coaching, mediation and, before he died, some preliminary ideas on paradoxes.

Simon: How do you see your model of time-limited existential therapy developing in the future, both in terms of the development of its theoretical base and its promulgation as a mode of practice?

Alison: I would love to see the adoption and integration of time in all therapies. It's intrinsic to how we live our lives and our passage towards death; it's integral to any existential approach and an honouring of the philosophical tradition.

References

Adams M (2013). *A Concise Introduction to Existential Counselling*. London: Sage.

de Shazer S, Dolan Y with Korman H, Trepper TS, McCollom E, Berg IK (2007). *More Than Miracles: the state of the art of solution-focused brief therapy*. Binghamtom, NY: Haworth Press.

Heidegger M (1962). *Being and Time*. Oxford: Basil Blackwell.

Kierkegaard S (1846/2009). *Concluding Unscientific Postscript to the Philosophical Crumbs* (A Hannay ed & trans). Cambridge: Cambridge University Press.

Merleau-Ponty M (1962). *The Phenomenology of Perception* (C Smith trans). London: Routledge & Kegan Paul.

Rogers CR (1961). *On Becoming a Person*. London: Constable.

Sartre J-P (1943/2003). *Being and Nothingness: an essay in phenomenological ontology* (H Barnes trans). London: Routledge.

Spinelli E (2016). Experiencing change: an existential perspective. In: Schulenberg S (ed). *Clarifying and Furthering Existential Psychotherapy: theories, methods and practices*. Basel: Springer (pp131–142).

Spinelli E (2015). *Practising Existential Therapy: the relational world* (2nd ed). London: Sage.

Spinelli E (2007). *Practising Existential Therapy: the relational world*. London: Sage.

Strasser A (2016). The relational world of existential therapy and counselling. In: Noble C, Day E (eds). *Psychotherapy and Counselling: reflections on practice*. Oxford: Oxford University Press (pp100–114).

Strasser F, Strasser A (1997). *Existential Time Limited Therapy: the wheel of existence*. Chichester: John Wiley.

Taft J (1933). *The Dynamics of Therapy in a Controlled Relationship*. New York, NY: Dover.

van Deurzen E (2002). *Existential Counselling and Therapy in Practice*. London: Sage.

van Deurzen E, Adams M (2011). *Skills in Existential Counselling and Psychotherapy*. London: Sage.

16

The face of abuse: the responsibility of the psychotherapist as witness

Georgia Feliou

The beginning of wisdom is the clarification of concepts.
(Antisthenes)

I live in Athens and I work with adults. My basic training was in integrative psychotherapy. By that time, I was already attracted to the person-centred approach, as well as to the American humanistic-existential approach, through my studies but also through my individual therapy. When I first read about the British School of Existential Analysis (Cooper, 2003: 128), for my master's, I felt I was coming home. I became fascinated by it, explored it more and finally applied it in my practice.

The British School has a strong phenomenological basis. Phenomenology, however, is a very rich philosophical tradition and, although the British School seems to be more affected by the transcendental phenomenology of Edmund Husserl, the ontological phenomenology of Martin Heidegger, the existential phenomenology of Jean-Paul Sartre or the embodiment phenomenology of Maurice Merleau-Ponty (see van Manen, 2016), it leaves space, I feel, for the exploration of new frontiers, while also providing a firm ground to stand on. A number of factors, including plain curiosity, the belief that the rich phenomenological tradition has much more to offer to existential-phenomenological psychotherapy, my academic background in philosophy and my theist disposition led me to the study of phenomenologists such as Paul Ricoeur, Emmanuel Levinas and Jean-Luc Marion. Marion is a French philosopher with a major impact on phenomenology. He is considered to be an expert in Descartes and he has produced a rich body of work. In his phenomenological 'trilogy', *Reduction and Giveness* (1998), *Being Given* (2002a), and *In Excess* (2002b), he investigates the revelation of phenomena: that is, the possibility of a phenomenon to appear, what constitutes a phenomenon, and how a phenomenon relates to us.

Marionian phenomenology

In Marion's 'radical' phenomenology (see van Manen, 2016: 177–182), and in particular his study of what he calls 'saturated phenomena', I discovered a powerful tool for understanding and exploring, within the therapeutic relationship, catalytic events that have affected the clients in an 'irrevocable' manner. Marion helps us examine and explore what is happening at the receptive end of our interaction with a phenomenon – when *we* are its receiver. Briefly, according to Marionian phenomenology, saturated phenomena are the phenomena that are bigger than both our experience of them and any meaning we might try to ascribe to them; thus, they are always open to an infinite number of interpretations. In this sense, they are received as a gift – not always a welcome gift but one in the sense that it is not requested. There are four types of saturated phenomena: the event, the flesh, the idol and the icon. The Shoah (the Holocaust) is an example of an event in Marionian sense. Birth and death are also considered to be events in this sense. An example of flesh is pain: it will always exceed our intentionality and impose itself on us. An example of idol is a work of art, while an exemplar of icon is the other human being (whom, because of his/her alterity, we can never fully understand, know or control) (Marion, 1998, 2002a, 2002b).

A saturated phenomenon relates to us first. Even if the phenomenon is identifiable and clear in its nature (for instance, a deadly tsunami), the ways it relates to each person it comes in contact with and the different impacts it has on each are countless and unpredictable. The encounter, and its short- and long-term consequences, can only be interpreted or described *ad hoc* and are always understood only partially. Therefore, in cases of saturated phenomena, the subject is not the *producer* of any truth the phenomenon might reveal but the *witness* of the phenomenon – its 'worker' (Marion, 2008: 142–144). As a witness, the subject does not constitute the phenomenon; on the contrary, he is very often constituted by it. The psychotherapist (apart from being herself a saturated phenomenon for the client) is the direct witness of the client (representing here the saturated phenomenon of the icon) and the indirect witness of the events (that have been received as saturated phenomena) described by the client. Being a witness does not mean that the therapist is constantly a passive receiver; at some point, she is called to respond by taking up the responsibility of her own description of the event and presenting it to the client for critical discussion. She is also called to witness how the client has been so far constituted by the events described, knowing that any understanding she might have will always be limited, if not limiting; the same goes for the client.

Marionian phenomenology, thus, will colour the whole of this chapter, since abuse involves three saturated phenomena that are in relation to each other: the abuser (icon), the abuse (event) and the abused (icon). I have been studying the issue of abuse, and in particular psychological abuse, because I believe it is connected to the problem of violence – one of the prime indicators of the dark side of human beings. This dark side may include the Jungian 'Shadow'– whatever we deem evil or immoral and deny in ourselves and, overall, whatever might result in what we ordinarily call cruelty, monstrosity or malice. Although this side scares me, I feel compelled to face it and explore it. This side also touches a grey area that intrigues me: the area between psychology/psychotherapy and ethics.

General information on abuse

The peculiarity of psychological abuse is that it seems to have no face; there is no physical evidence pointing to it. Thus, we often fail to see it. This invisibility makes the phenomenon elusive and difficult to observe. Generally speaking:

> Psychological/emotional abuse may be defined as incidents of recurring criticism, denigration, and/or verbal aggression against a person, as well as acts to isolate and/or dominate another person. Psychological/ emotional abuse includes ridicule, stalking, destroying the property of the victim, emotional withdrawal, threats, and restrictive engulfment (i.e., socially isolating the victim…). The purpose of such behaviour is to induce fear and to punish and control the victim. (Renzetti, 2008)

It is a 'continuous violation of the victim's freedom, rights and resources' through either isolation and dominance (ie. deprivation of resources) or verbal emotional abuse (wilful inflicting of emotional pain through humiliation, for instance) (Pilafova, 2010). We may distinguish between active emotional abuse (insults, threats, devaluation) and passive emotional neglect (inability on the part of the parent to provide security, love and care due to a mental illness, for instance) (Christensen, cited in Loue, 2005: 317). Another way of seeing psychological abuse is to emphasise its relational aspect: that is, to see certain relationships as abusive as opposed to noting abusive events *in* a relationship (Loue, 2005: 315).

Psychological abuse has partly a subjective nature. Much depends on non-measurable factors such as the tone of voice, the context of the occurrences, facial expressions and insinuations. What one person considers a dynamic, intense or even loving expression of feelings, another may find abusive or suffocating (Renzetti, 2008 ; Pilafova, 2010 ; Sullivan, 2009). Intent also plays an important role.

The consequences for the victim include poor physical health (Pilafova, 2010); difficulty in regulating emotions (impaired emotion or negative emotions such as apathy, despair, hatred) (O'Hagan, 2006: 49); depression, lack of motivation, confusion, difficulty in concentrating or making decisions, low self-esteem, self-blame, loss of sense of personal value, hopelessness, emotional dependence, panic attacks, difficulty in sleeping and anxiety (O'Hagan, 2006: 48–50, 52–55; Horne, 2008). The social/relational consequences include poor social integration; poor work or school performance; lack of support network and related isolation, and inability to distinguish between a normative and an abusive relationship (Horne, 2008). On the cognitive level, they include problems with memory, with attention, with moral reasoning, with speech and perception (O'Hagan, 2006: 46–56) and learned helplessness – abused people are convinced that there is nothing they can do to escape the abuse (Escobar, 2010).

Therapists and organisations dealing with abuse (Sanderson, 2010; Sanderson, 2008; Horne, 2008; Herman, 1992) offer the following goals for treatment of abuse in general, which can also be applied in cases of psychological abuse. The most important parameter is safety: physical and emotional. Other goals include the establishment of a social support network; the empowerment of the client for the restoration of control and power over her/his life; the development of the capacity to distinguish an abusive relationship from a non-abusive one; getting away from guilt (by realising that they are not responsible for causing the abuse or stopping it); the restoration of relationship with self; reconnecting to life and to others; affect regulation (understanding and regulating overwhelming emotions); working with loss and the mourning process; finding meaning in the events, and becoming able to tolerate some degree of uncertainty.

Existential-phenomenological concerns

A cursory inquiry revealed no specific references to the existential approach and abuse. Regarding domestic abuse,[1] existential therapy is reported to emphasise the person's search for meaning and his/her responsibility for his/her own choices in life (Sanderson, 2008: 63–64). For existential psychotherapy, safety is the first priority for the person. Other issues typically explored in existential psychotherapy (such as isolation, loss, absurdity and so forth) are also explored when dealing with domestic abuse.

A discussion about an existential approach to abuse raises two important concerns that could arise from misinterpreting basic existential-phenomenological concepts and could cause a lot of harm. The first is related to phenomenological practice. The emphasis on the exploration of the subjective worldview of the client, combined with the practice of epoché, makes the therapist reluctant to categorise behaviours and even diagnose, and this is quite justifiable (see, for example, Spinelli, 2007: 68–69; van Deurzen & Adams, 2011: 125; Szazs, 1984). However, every theoretical approach must have at least one exception or it becomes a dogma. Abuse is, for me, the perfect candidate for one reason: violence.

Violence, apart from being destructive, even deadly, very often strips human beings of everything that is human about them. Aggression, while hardly absent from the animal world, does not necessarily signify violence that is deliberately malevolent and unprompted or unwarranted by the circumstances. For example, a father does not really need to grab his four-year-old baby, swing her like a hammer and bang her against the wall until she dies, just to keep her quiet. Yet it happens.

Generally speaking, by using the phenomenological method, the existential-phenomenological psychotherapist leaves room for the emergence of an innovative *description* of the world, which implies a different and possibly more liberating interpretation of it. If the therapist characterises certain behaviours or gives a diagnosis, she may steer the client towards a specific direction that could imprison her in a specific worldview. In addition, such a practice could well constitute a form of violence itself, effectively turning the client into a prospective recipient of that violence. An example of this might be the stigma associated with schizophrenia. On the other hand, we cannot be fixated on the negative connotations of words; nor can we define the whole of

---

1. Domestic abuse, domestic violence, gender-based violence and abuse in general are inter-related terms often studied together. See for example, European Agency for Fundamental Rights (2014).

a person from just one characteristic or behaviour. We communicate by using language to describe and name the world around us. Therefore, within certain contexts, calling a slap on the face or an insult a violent act does not constitute a restrictive characterisation; it is a description and a denunciation at the same time. The moral implications in such cases are grave and the psychotherapist cannot avoid them. Some cultures (for instance, Eastern European) would not easily accept psychological abuse as a form of violence (Pilafova, 2010). The issue of homophobia (related to this case study) asks us to be even more vigilant (Loue, 2005: 326–327). We should not confuse beliefs with values (as happens with cultural relativism); we must realise that violence is an issue of fundamental human rights, which are a universal value, and at some point in our lives we are called to take a stand against any violation of those rights. This point might emerge during a therapeutic session. We are obliged to respond and rise up to this challenge, otherwise we concur with the violations and even appear to approve of them.

The second concern is related to the existential concept of responsibility, which is closely connected to freedom of choice. We are faced with the givens of existence (thrown-ness), towards which we are free to choose our stance – and we are responsible for our choices. This, overbearing as it might be, is nevertheless empowering and shows us that we have some kind of control over our lives: that we are not passive victims of life but the active scripters of it.

The ability to live with the tensions related to the above-mentioned issues, the realisation of our limitations, the paradox of existence and the striving for a more authentic life are explored in psychotherapeutic practice and are believed to lead to a fuller, revitalised life.

Yet, there is a pitfall. This is not the place to explore the issue of free will, towards which existentialism has taken a positive stance. I am simply exploring the *felt sense* of people – clients who have a different story to tell. Let us explore the example of Victor Frankl. His experience during the Shoah tells us that, even in the darkest moment in human history, we have some freedom: the freedom to choose how we face the events. Yet, leaving aside other population groups, Victor Frankl's example is one in six million. Making such a rare case an example to be followed may raise very high expectations of the clients or even ourselves as therapists.

To begin with, the Shoah was not an existential given but a saturated phenomenon. To say that we *can* choose how to deal with such an event is not only an overestimation but a misunderstanding. It sets the bar too high for an average human being and makes him feel weak and quite *dis*-empowered, instead of feeling strong. Too much emphasis on personal responsibility runs the danger of encouraging blame, as it gives the impression that any inequality or, indeed, failure is a strong indication of personal incompetence (Rosanvallon, 2014: 247–252). From this angle, this misinterpretation of the existential-phenomenological approach, as I see it, could be unfair, if not damaging, especially for a victim of abuse (who is defined as a victim by the law and who *feels* like a victim).

It also completely ignores another important concept in existential theory and practice – that of relatedness (Spinelli, 2007). The relationship between the therapist and the client can unlock the *potential* of the client to get in touch with a different way of *being-in-the-world* and of *being-with-others* and thus the *potential* to face life's adversities with a different attitude. Potentiality is not equivalent to certitude and does not necessarily point to a specific course of action or, indeed, to any course of action at all. It would be as if we claimed that, because we could all potentially be saints, we can actually be saints if we choose to be virtuous. This is a denial of the reality of human existence and experience, of fortuity, of the existence of talent, and, for theists, the denial of grace.

The relationship can also hold the potential inability or unwillingness of the client to 'change'. Finally, it points to the obvious conclusion that the way we face the existential givens is not an isolated (if not solipsistic) condition but a relational process. In my view, the existential-phenomenological paradigm acknowledges that we are not only our deeds, we are also what we endure or undergo. To say that we are free to choose our attitude towards our circumstances *at all times* is to say we are not changed by the world around us: that we are fixed, unalterable and thus predetermined.

Case study

Helen was a 25-year-old woman who came to see me because she wanted to work on her relationship with her parents and on her introversion: she wanted to somehow deal with her parents' intrusiveness on her life and with the fact that she did not talk much – she was having trouble with her current girlfriend on that account. Later on, she said she was also having difficulty sleeping, that she had frequent 'panic attacks' (meaning that, at times, she would feel very stressed and would have difficulty breathing), and that she had difficulty remembering things (appointments, events and so forth). When she came to see me, she was unemployed.

Her relationship with her parents got even worse when they found out about her relationship with another woman. Her father, in particular, would swear, was very sarcastic, threatened her every day for hours when she was at home, and was very intrusive (he searched her belongings, including accessing her mobile phone and laptop). She could not hide anything and she had absolutely no privacy. Her mother agreed with the father's behaviour. She had been depressive for as long Helen could remember, following the loss of a child born before Helen, who died at the age of two. Helen's mother had always been unresponsive to Helen's emotional needs, with rare exceptions. She had developed a kind of germ phobia and would forbid Helen from choosing and touching her own clothes, obliging her to ask for them (even her underwear) every time she needed to get dressed. For a very long time, Helen felt responsible for her sister's death and wished she were dead so that her parents could be happy. Ever since she was a child, she felt she could not rely on her parents emotionally, but only practically (for food, shelter, clothing and so forth). They were both very strict (for instance, they would not let her go out and play with other children but would not explain why), they were not particularly tender, if at all, and they were ready to blame her for every incident that occurred (for instance, at school with other pupils). Her other sister, who was older than her, was subjected to the same treatment but managed to 'escape', Helen said, when she got married because she became pregnant. At school Helen had suffered from almost constant bullying by her classmates.

It took a few sessions for her to construct a coherent narrative and share all this information. It was difficult for her to talk in therapy; she would only communicate very laconically and had great difficulty connecting to her feelings and expressing them. She was unable to provide details about events. For the first three or four sessions, she would call me or send text messages outside my office hours, trying to share information and feelings. When we discussed this later on, it emerged that she had experienced her parents, and other close relationships, as being so intrusive in her life and so unresponsive to her needs and feelings that she felt that the safest place to hide was within her own self. Direct communication increased her anxiety, as she would instantly feel threatened. Being outside the therapy room gave her the space and distance she needed in order to express herself.

One day, she came to the office looking very sad and even more withdrawn than usual. She told me that she had been ill the previous week and she was shivering, with high fever (it was winter time), but her parents did not turn the heating on, saying that it was her fault she got sick; that it was due to the 'life she's leading'.

G: Excuse me, but for six sessions you're telling me all those things that your parents do and say to you and now you're telling me that they left you shivering in fever without turning the heating on? This is psychological abuse, you know. Nobody should treat another person like this.

H: Yeah... My girlfriend told me the same thing many times... She believes the same thing as you.

G: What do you think about what your girlfriend and I believe?

H: They don't treat me right, I know. But they say it's my fault. But then again, they never treated me right. What was my fault when I was a child?

Being the indirect witness of a behaviour that, to me, was clearly cruel and the direct witness of another human being who was obviously in distress, I felt obliged to name what I thought was going on, only to discover that Helen had already been 'exposed' to this viewpoint and was thinking about it. The fact that other people saw and put a name to what she was only able to feel helped her, as she said herself later, to gradually trust this felt sense. In other words, it helped her listen to herself more.

Right from the start, Helen could think clearly – or that had been my impression. She realised that what her parents were doing was irrational. She said so repeatedly. She believed she had the right to be who she wanted. This conviction was, I believe, her greatest ally.

H: Two nights ago, I was heading towards the bathroom. He [the father] followed me, shouting at me, calling me names. My mother did not show up but I could hear her from the other room saying how right he was. He was in the bathroom and I told him to go out because I really needed to use it. He ignored me and continued swearing at me. I told him again that he must go out because I had to use the bathroom. Then he started shouting at me, telling me how rude and disrespectful I was and that this was not a way to behave to my father and that all this was due to the 'new company' that I kept.

G: You mean to tell me that he would not leave the bathroom while you needed to use it and he called you disrespectful for asking him to?

H: Yes.

G: How did you feel then?

H: Well, what he did was completely irrational and I told him that. He would not listen.

G: You think his behaviour was irrational.

H: Yes, but you know... I know what he's doing is not right but I believe he only does this because he cannot understand me – but he loves me.

G: What is it that he cannot understand?

H: How I think, how I feel, who I am.

G: This is why he reacts this way, you say?

H: Yeah. I mean what he does is awful but he cares...

G: I have no doubt he cares and loves you. However, I keep thinking there must be better ways to express care and affection. I mean, there *are* other ways.

H: Yeah, I know... It felt kind of weird he would not get out of the bathroom...

G: Weird in what sense?

H: Well, it's the bathroom, you know? As we say, 'even the King is alone in there'. He doesn't respect my privacy and basically it was kind of aggressive [she looked fearful].

G: You mean you got scared?

H: ...

G: I see you're silent and I'm wondering what's going on...

H: I'm just thinking...

G: Would you like to share?

H: I'm just thinking...

Challenging the way her father expressed his love helped Helen to begin to come closer to her feelings. Slowly, she started expressing her anger and fear. She also started to explore and communicate her feelings in the sessions, instead of trying to communicate them outside the therapeutic framework. Memories of her self-loathing started coming to the surface. She said she started realising she had very low self-esteem; that she was so very afraid of rejection that she could not express herself. Slowly, she started expressing her need for acceptance, tenderness and love. She also began being more assertive towards her parents and relatives. At the same time, she made tremendous efforts to find a job – any job. She finally achieved it. It was quite an accomplishment in Greece's current, straitened socio-political circumstances. At some point she expressed her need to leave her parents' house and find a place of her own, and she did so after a while.

Towards the end of our work together, we discussed the whole issue of psychological abuse.

G: How was it for you when I told you that I believed you were psychologically abused by your parents?

H: It felt kind of heavy. Something inside me broke down.

G: What was that? In what way was it broken down?

H: It was like a heavy realisation. I could not hide from it any longer...

G: From what?

H: From that truth. I had to face it. I had to do something about it.

[...]

G: What is psychological abuse for *you*?

H: It is when you impose yourself on others against their will. You don't respect what they want, what they need; you don't respect the other as a person. You want to have it your way at any cost. Initially, I wanted to believe that my parents were only overprotective, overreacting. After they found out about my relationship and their behaviour got much worse, I was kind of forced to realise that this was not right. And that it had been going on for many years – since I was a child.

G: And now how do you feel about that?

H: I don't accept certain things. I don't let others do what they want with me... and it's OK.

Conclusion

In a relationship, we constitute the other and we are constituted by him/her through reverse intentionality.[2] This can be very damaging in cases of abuse but potentially very healing in a therapeutic relationship. By naming violent behaviour as such, the psychotherapist is exposing it and at the same time

---

2. The notion is explored by Ricoeur, Levinas and Marion. In reverse intentionality (or counter-intentionality), 'the I is constituted by the look of the other, through the icon' (Horner, 2005: 7–8). The nature of the saturated phenomenon, in particular the icon, is such that, on its encounter with us, the intentionality is reversed so that I am envisaged by the phenomenon (for instance, the other) instead of envisaging it. See also the beginning of this chapter.

acts as a moral agent: in other words, she acts responsibly – she relates as a person to a person who is being violated. She also acts responsibly towards incidents of violence. A question arises: wouldn't this suggest a directive, or even a patronising attitude on the part of the therapist? I believe not, since the therapist describes the event as *she understands it* (limited as this understanding might be) and tries to relate this felt-sense to the client, clarifying in the process that this is her own sense, *her* worldview. By so doing, she gives a living example of what it is like to engage in a relationship in an authentic and responsible way, in complete contrast to an abusive way.

When dealing with psychological abuse, or any type of abuse, apart from issues of safety, relatedness plays the most important role for an existential/phenomenological therapist. It is through this relatedness that the client will be given a chance to explore alternative ways of *being-in-the-world* and of *being-with-others* and hopefully break free from any fears or sedimentations around how a relationship with self and others is or could be. In this way the client is given a chance to realise her *potentiality* for freedom. Whether this potentiality will be actualised, and what the consequences and implications are if it is not, is the subject of another discussion.

Discussion with the editor

Simon: Reading your chapter, it was clear that psychological abuse is an important subject for you, and I got the sense that you do not feel it is accorded sufficient attention in the psychotherapy literature and perhaps in practice too. If that is the case, I wonder why you think it is so, and what you think can be done to change the situation.

Georgia: I believe that the subject is not discussed much by we existential-phenomenological therapists. I do not know why, although this whole issue that involves violence, abuse, bullying and so forth is an important subject. After all, we live in a quite violent world. I have seen a few articles on aggression, but aggression is not the same thing. What can we do to change this? Well, the first step is to talk about it. I am certain that the existential approach has a lot to offer in this field and I hope that this chapter will be used as the beginning of a fruitful dialogue and – why not? – a research project based on existential/phenomenological tools.

Simon: I found the notion of 'saturated phenomena' quite intriguing. On the one hand I can see, I think, how the four types might each be said to exceed our intentionality and impose themselves on us, but on the other hand I wondered if, in some sense, this might be said of all phenomena, with the possible exception of ourselves? And so, I wondered also what it means to think of the psychotherapist as a saturated phenomenon and, perhaps more important, what the implications of this might be for the theory and practice of therapy?

Georgia: Not all phenomena are saturated. We also have what Marion calls 'poor' (for instance, mathematical idealities) and 'common' (for instance, physical objects) phenomena. A canvas is a common phenomenon. A work of art, a painting, is a saturated phenomenon. The painting presents us with a challenge; it overwhelms us. A mere canvas does not. A painting commands our attention even for a few seconds. The other human being is a saturated phenomenon: s/he is irreducible to any of her/his traits or characteristics; s/he represents the total otherness that exceeds both our intentionality and our intuition; s/he exceeds any typology or prediction.

The psychotherapist may very well overwhelm the client, and vice versa. As saturated phenomena, both may be life-changing for each other. It is, therefore, a relationship that is potentially catalytic for both, regardless of our intention. This means that I do not know when or how I will be catalytic for the other or who, when and how will be catalytic for me. In this sense, this too is a risky relationship, with unanticipated results for both. Marion's work made me realise on a deep level that I have no control whatsoever of the relationship. This helps me be more alert and aware of the fact that neither the client nor I have any power over each other and over the relationship, and at the same time that we both have much more power than we can ever possibly imagine. It is a peculiar type of 'thrownness': it is as if we are thrown into a quantum world – a world that is known for its indeterminacy. This is quite grounding, since it leads to a deep awareness of uncertainty and undermines illusions of grandeur.

On a more theoretical level, Marion's study of saturated phenomena clearly shows that psychotherapy will never come under the category of science and that social sciences (including psychology) can never be sciences in the same way that physical sciences are. This is not the place to open up a discussion on this but, broadly speaking, physical sciences study poor and common phenomena and the social sciences study saturated phenomena. Any effort on the part of social sciences to imitate the physical sciences (in their methodology, for instance) damages both the progress and the credibility of the former, which should, in my view, turn their attention exclusively to phenomenology (as a starting point) and draw their research tools from there.

Simon: You don't explicitly return to Marion's theories in your discussion of your work with Helen. Can you say something about how they influenced your clinical practice with her, and perhaps in general?

Georgia: Marion provided me with a powerful tool to better understand my relationship with saturated phenomena, whether these are another human being or the life events described. He studies and emphasises the receptive end of our relationship to them. The emphasis is on what is happening to me and not on what I am doing. Saturated phenomena create a shock; they invade our individuality and strip from us any security and comfort. We lose ourselves to them. Marion's work helps me accept that I stand small in front of them. At last I see and admit *their power over me*; they are indeed sweeping. It's not that I am incompetent – I am deluged. This is a totally different viewpoint: I am legitimised to feel weak. I realise that I cannot be active or in control all the time and that I can surrender to circumstances. I realise that there are circumstances where the only thing I can do is surrender. Saturated phenomena may deprive us of choice; they certainly deprive us of control. This is not necessarily a bad thing because in this way they make us open up to the miracle of life. It is certainly a powerful thing, though. We need to honour this in therapy.

As existential-phenomenological psychotherapists, we have underestimated the receptive part of our interaction with the world. Helen needed the space, the time and the help to explore, understand and name what happened to her as exactly that: something that happened *to* her. As a witness of all these, I was called to accompany her in this journey and take the responsibility to explore, understand and name as well. Only after the completion of this process was there the possibility of creating space and time for discussing the next step: what now? What am I to do next? *Is there* anything I can do?

Simon: I think you identify something quite important when you reflect on the possible consequences in existential therapy of 'too much emphasis on personal responsibility'. While perhaps not precisely analogous, I have often thought that we need to take care when quoting Nietzsche's aphorism 'What does not kill me makes me stronger', since in my experience clients can be maimed by life events.

Georgia: Indeed. I remember a few years ago, I was walking the streets of Athens with a woman who was training in existential therapy. We were talking passionately about this subject, stressing how dangerous this aphorism can be when, brilliant as she is, she came up with the following paraphrase: 'What does not kill me may very well cripple me.' I could not have said it better myself.

References

Cooper M (2003). *Existential Therapies*. London: Sage.

Escobar S (2010). Cycle of violence, theory of. In: Fisher BS, Lab SP (eds). *Encyclopaedia of Victimology and Crime Prevention*. Thousand Oaks, CA: Sage Publications.

European Agency for Fundamental Rights (2014). *Violence against women: an EU-wide survey*. Vienna: European Agency for Fundamental Rights. http://fra.europa.eu/sites/default/files/fra-2014-vaw-survey-main-results-apr14_en.pdf (accessed 28 May 2018).

Herman JL (1992). *Trauma and Recovery*. New York, NY: Basic Books.

Horne S (2008). Abuse. In: Leong F. *Encyclopaedia of Counseling*. Thousand Oaks, CA: Sage Publications.

Horner R (2005). *Jean-Luc Marion: a theo-logical introduction*. Farnham: Ashgate.

Loue S (2005). Redefining the emotional and psychological abuse and maltreatment of children: legal implications. *The Journal of Legal Medicine* 26(3): 311–337.

Marion J-L (2008). *The Visible and the Revealed* (CM Gschwandtner et al, trans). New York, NY: Fordham University Press.

Marion J-L (2002a). *Being Given: toward a phenomenology of giveness* (JL Kosky trans). Stanford, CA: Stanford University Press.

Marion J-L (2002b). *In Excess: studies in saturated phenomena* (R Horner & V Berraud trans). New York, NY: Fordham University Press.

Marion J-L (1998). *Reduction and Giveness: investigations of Husserl, Heidegger, and phenomenology* (TA Carlson trans). Evanston, IL: Northwestern University Press.

O'Hagan K (2006). *Identifying Emotional and Psychological Abuse: a guide for childcare professionals*. Maidenhead: McGraw-Hill Education.

Pilafova A (2010). Psychological/emotional abuse. In: Fisher BS, Lab SP (eds). *Encyclopaedia of Victimology and Crime Prevention*. Thousand Oaks, CA: Sage Publications.

Renzetti C (2008). Psychological/emotional abuse. In: Renzetti C, Edleson J. *Encyclopaedia of Interpersonal Violence*. Thousand Oaks, CA: Sage Publications.

Rosanvallon P (2014). *La Societé des Égaux*. Athens: Polis.

Sanderson C (2010). *Introduction to Counselling Survivors of Interpersonal Trauma*. London: Jessica Kingsley.

Sanderson C (2008). *Counselling Survivors of Domestic Abuse*. London: Jessica Kingsley.

Spinelli E (2007). *Practising Existential Psychotherapy: the relational world*. London: Sage.

Sullivan L (ed) (2009). Abuse. In: *The Sage Glossary of the Social and Behavioral Sciences*. Thousand Oaks, CA: Sage Publications.

Szasz T (1984). *The Myth of Mental Illness: foundations of a theory of personal conduct* (revised ed). London: HarperCollins.

van Deurzen E, Adams M (2011). *Skills in Existential Counselling and Psychotherapy*. London: Sage.

van Manen M (2016). *Phenomenology of Practice: meaning-giving methods in phenomenological research and writing*. London: Routledge.

17

Lost for words: using existential experimentation in a GP practice

Mark Rayner and Randolph Quinault

> I see now that the path I choose through the maze makes me what I am. I am not only a thing, but also a way of being – one of many ways – and knowing the paths I have followed and the ones left to take will help me understand what I am becoming. (Keyes, 1966: 154)

Existential experimentation (EE) is an innovative therapy combining existential attitudes, a phenomenological method and recovery and humanistic principles to provide an intervention in NHS primary care to clients who present with living difficulties. It is based on research that indicates that a large proportion of positive outcomes from therapy is related to either the therapeutic relationship or to context or client factors. In short, the client and the client's lived experience and relationship with their therapist are key, not the specific techniques or model used. EE therefore focuses on both the therapeutic relationship itself and what clients themselves need to own and work on to achieve recovery. The approach is innovative in that it challenges the medical model by contextualising distress and aims to intervene early, when there is greater chance of achieving recovery.

The therapy itself takes the form of existential philosophy applied to practice. It addresses the breadth of human experience in order to focus on notions of choice, responsibility and agency. Emphasis is placed on the client being aware of their place in their difficulties. The intervention is phenomenological in that the therapist applies the three basic tenets of phenomenology:

- description rather than explanation
- bracketing all presuppositions about the client and his or her difficulties in order to see the world through their eyes and walk in their shoes, so that the therapy can maintain a focus on their lived experience rather than the therapist's knowledge or expertise
- horizontalisation, in that, as far as possible, all aspects of the client's experience are given the same attention.

The therapy is recovery based: that is, it recognises that life is a journey and encourages clients to recognise this and see their difficulties as opportunities for understanding, exploration and acceptance. Finally, in line with the notion of recovery and goal setting, the intervention follows humanistic principles in that it strives to promote the fulfilment of the person's potential.

The intervention is also readily delivered within an NHS context. The public sector demands that therapies must be manualised, so we have written what we call the structure and principles for EE (Rayner & Vitali, 2016), to comply with these requirements and for routine data collection. However, EE is an individualised therapy, recognising that everyone is different and will have their own, unique experience of common difficulties like depression.

Origins of the EE approach

EE emerged alongside the Improving Access to Psychological Therapies (IAPT) programme – the huge, government-funded initiative, brainchild of economist Professor Lord Richard Layard, to introduce a national primary care talking therapy service across England, delivering primarily CBT. At the time (from 2004 onwards), I (Mark) was working in a secondary mental health service in the NHS, where I was noticing the growing expectations on us to measure and monitor progress and outcomes of psychological therapy, especially as I was practising a type of therapy – existential – that was not included among the psychological therapies recommended by NICE (the National Institute for Clinical Excellence, as it was then called). I decided to start using outcome measures that were compatible with those routinely used in IAPT services: the General Anxiety Disorder scale (GAD-7), which measures anxiety, the Personal Health Questionnaire (PHQ-9), which measures depression, and two of the Clinical Outcome Routine Evaluation

(CORE) scales: the CORE 5-OM and the CORE Goal Attainment Form (GAF). The CORE-5 OM consists of five questions and is used in every session to monitor the client's presenting problems. The first page of the GAF is used at the start of therapy, when the client is asked to define up to four goals that they would like to achieve by its end, and again at the end, when the client is asked to rate the degree to which they have achieved their goals on a 4-point scale and to state what they found helpful or not helpful about the therapy. It is important to stress that an existentially informed therapy is not primarily concerned with the GAD-7, PHQ-9 and CORE 5-OM questions in and of themselves. Rather, it regards the asking and answering of these questions as indicative of the client's active engagement with therapy. Also, unlike the therapies offered in IAPT, while EE is guided by a written protocol and structure (Rayner & Vitali, 2016), it is not manualised, and it considers change to be about more than just change in behaviour; important change can occur in understanding too.

EASE Wellbeing CIC, which I founded, has developed and delivers the EE approach and conducts ongoing reseach, service evaluation and monitoring and measurement of outcomes. Initially, I launched a pilot EE service in a GP surgery in the borough where I worked. This was in 2006–09, when IAPT was being piloted in two test sites, in Newham and Doncaster. As IAPT began to be rolled out nationally from 2010, I further developed what I had begun, working with six to eight honorary trainee psychotherapists and counselling psychologists. This service was able to radically reduce both waiting times for treatment and rates of referrals on to secondary care.

Theoretical basis of EE

In UK primary care settings, mental health problems are commonly assessed or diagnosed (Goldberg & Huxley, 1992). The most common diagnoses of mental disorders recorded in primary care services (Ormel et al, 1994; Ansseau et al, 2004; King et al, 2008) come under the category of mood disorders (12–13% of UK cases) and anxiety disorders (8–10% of UK cases). Diagnoses of depression are predominantly (90%) co-morbid with another mental or physical disorder (Vuorilehto, Melartin & Isometsä, 2005). In other words, it is very likely that a client who presents with depression will have more than one difficulty. It may be, for example, a combination of depression and isolation because they are unable to get out of their house due to a physical disability, or depression and anxiety due to being bullied at work or at school. In addressing the breadth of human experience, EE pays attention to these other issues in order to challenge the mind-body split and to respond to dual or multiple issues that trouble a person.

EE is a short-term, integrative psychological therapy that follows the recovery approach (Shepherd, Boardman & Slade, 2008). It draws on the phenomenological approach to therapy described by Spinelli (2005, 2015), the existential-humanistic therapy of Schneider and Krug (2010), and the pragmatic approach to short-term existential therapy developed by Lantz and Walsh (2007). Its conceptualisation was also strongly influenced by Asay and Lambert (1999) and Cuijpers et al (2012), who analysed decades of psychotherapy research and demonstrated that what they called 'external factors' (now commonly known as 'context-related' or 'client-attributable' factors) are each responsible for 40% of positive therapeutic outcomes, while treatment techniques, skills or elements of the therapy relating specifically to the modality are responsible for approximately 15%. Thus, factors to do with the client or their context – factors primarily outside the counselling room – play a much greater role in the outcomes of therapy than the therapeutic techniques or modality. Moreover, earlier research by Orlinsky, Grawe and Parks (1994) found that the extent to which the client actively participates in therapy seems to be a particularly strong predictor of its effectiveness. It is for this reason that, although there is a structure and protocol for the delivery of EE, it remains individualised in that it is focused on and responsive to and seeks primarily to engage with the experience of the individual client.

Cuijpers and colleagues, in that same study (2012), also attempted to single out the contribution to client outcomes of therapist factors that are common across all psychotherapies, and were able to confirm the strong importance of the therapeutic relationship and its components. Norcross and Lambert (2011) similarly sought to identify the most consistent and important elements that seem to contribute to an effective therapeutic relationship. These were, they concluded:

- *the therapeutic alliance* – defined as 'an emergent quality of partnership and mutual collaboration between therapist and client' (Norcross & Lambert 2011: 13)

- *empathy* – the attempt to access the private, perceptual world of the other (Rogers, 1980)

- *goal consensus and co-operation* – the agreement between the therapist and client about 'the nature of the problem for which the client is seeking help, goals for treatment, and the way that the two parties will work together to achieve these goals' (Norcross & Lambert 2011: 15)

- *repairing ruptures* – the process whereby the therapist addresses episodes of tension or breakdown in the relationship with the client (Safran & Muran, 2000)
- a*dapting the relationship to the different stages of change* – ensuring the therapist–client relationship keeps pace with the client's pace of change (Norcross & Lambert 2011; Norcross, Krebs & Prochaska, 2011; Rosen, 2000).

These findings have since been updated and refined by Wampold (2015). These are all elements that have been incorporated in EE. It is thus informed by evidence from clinical practice and theoretical and conceptual models.

How is EE delivered?

The therapy begins with a screening by the GP that simply asks what difficulties the client is experiencing and how they impact on their life. If therapy is thought to be possibly appropriate, this is followed by an assessment by an EE therapist, conducted in two parts. Initially, the therapist seeks to clarify the client's presenting concerns, background, medication, previous contact with services and level of risk. The second part of the assessment is a session devoted to goal setting. We recognise that goal setting, while necessary, does not capture the breadth of the client's experience. In other words, if a person wants to sail from England to France and achieves this, they have achieved their goal, but we also consider that, in so doing, they have been exposed to other factors, such as the fresh air, sea waves, a sense of freedom and so forth. The assessor uses a repertory grid pre- and post-therapy to gather data on how the client sees themselves, significant others and aspects of their life.

The assessment is usually followed a week later by the first of six weekly therapy sessions. These begin with a phenomenological enquiry, reviewing the person's assumptions, values, beliefs and attitudes in order to explore their world views. The therapy focuses on enabling the client to become who they would like to be by working with the dynamic tensions of being in a familiar, safe place, while exploring what it may be like to reach for somewhere that may feel unfamiliar, uncertain and perhaps risky. Thus, it ceases to be about change (doing something different) but is, rather, about exploring the tension between the safety of the known but unhelpful and taking the risk to reconstruct the previously known and lost or abandoned or reach out into the unknown to find new spaces.

Towards the end of the six sessions, the work turns to the application of what has been learned to other difficulties of living. In the last session, we complete a post-therapy review to assess change in self-construct and use the CORE GAF to assess to what extent the goals listed at the beginning have been achieved and record what was and was not helpful about therapy. Finally, we conduct a three- and six-month follow-up session to determine whether the gains made in therapy have been maintained.

Case study

The clinical vignette that follows is intended to illustrate how the EE therapist moves metaphorically away from the centre of the therapeutic arena and invites the client to occupy this space. The client, who I shall call George, was a married man in his late 40s, with two children. He was referred to the EE therapist by his GP. The sessions took place at the GP's surgery, in a private room.

As previously stated, while EE is guided by a written protocol, it is not a manualised approach and does not follow a set of interventions delivered in stages throughout the six sessions. Its explicitly idiographic approach both allows the therapist to stay closer to the lived experiences of the client throughout the six weeks of treatment and offers greater freedom for creativity within the therapeutic encounter. While acknowledging the non-linear nature of the therapeutic process, it is possible to broadly divide the work with George into three interlinked phases: 1) descriptive assessment and goal setting; 2) phenomenological elucidation, and 3) experimentation in the world.

1) Descriptive assessment and goal setting

George came to his assessment session with me (Mark), tightly grasping a folder full of notes. He explained that, five years previously, he had been diagnosed with a benign brain tumour. Although non-malignant, the tumour was pressing on the communication centres of his brain, resulting in aphasia, which meant he found it difficult to express what he wanted to say. He explained that he often had difficulty remembering words – even simple words like 'table'. He felt that the memories were there but he just could not access them. His response to this 'forgetfulness' was to carry this folder of notes with him and write things down. It gave him a sense of greater security that he would not forget something he had been told.

It was immediately striking just how important words were for George. He had been top of his class academically at school and had studied English at university. He was now self-employed, running a company with his wife, where he relied heavily on his abilities to draft and present written materials. He told me, 'Words are what I do.' Over time he had grown more used to the effects of the tumour and believed he had developed ways to work around it by thinking up alternative words when he couldn't find the ones he wanted. However, his fear of forgetting had made him highly anxious about his work, which in turn had placed strains on his relationship with his wife. He never knew when he would forget a word, and he was fearful of telling people about his tumour in case it detrimentally affected his business.

George described feeling depressed – 'but not in a clinical sense'. It seemed to me to be more that he was worried about the possibility of forgetting and its impact on his work and relationship. He also expressed sadness about his perceived loss of ability. He had told his GP, 'If I were run over by a bus tomorrow, I wouldn't be as bothered as you might expect' – a statement that would usually be immediately understood as suicidal ideation. But what emerged for me in our initial meeting was a sense that his sadness and hopelessness were associated with his preoccupation with remembering information that he formerly prided himself on being easily able to recall. He said he sometimes felt as if he was living in a perpetual present, and I understood him to be saying he was engaged in a constant struggle to hold onto or regain what he had lost – that is, words.

George also spoke about his parents. His father was dead but, when alive, had focused entirely on George's mother and keeping her happy. George described his mother as high maintenance and very needy. In his words, 'Her need to have her child about her was not normal.' He said she regarded the world as there for the sole purpose of helping her – a task he took on after his father died. He went on to explain that she was good at making him feeling guilty about not giving her enough attention.

When asked what his goals for therapy were, George did not, surprisingly, say he wanted to achieve some technique for helping him regain his facility with words. Rather, he said he wanted to gain some perspective on his anxieties so that he could move beyond blaming everything on the effects of his tumour.

2) Phenomenological elucidation

First session

George arrived 20 minutes early for our first therapy session, again tightly grasping his folder of notes. I observed how he immediately attempted to establish a regimented plan for how the session would progress. Given that he and I had discussed in our initial meeting that he wanted to move beyond what he was currently experiencing, it felt important not to let him do this and instead to create a space in which he could sit in silence and experience the tension in his current position, rather than seek the means by which his anxiety could be alleviated. As the moments of silence passed, George shifted uncomfortably in his seat. Reflecting this back to him, I suggested that this wordless void reminded him of his own moments of forgetting, when he would be gripped by anxiety. He then expressed his worry that his forgetfulness made him more dependent on his wife – needier – and that, as he became needier, his wife would be forced into the same relational position to him as he occupied with his mother. Reflecting on the session thus far, I observed how important words seemed to George and his sense of identity. He responded by describing himself as a 'wordsmith', a one-trick pony whose one party trick was words.

It was clear that words were not only the currency of his business but formed the building blocks of his identity and self-esteem. Therefore, I asked George to think what it would be like for him to be without words and to stay with the anxiety that silence brings. He was not enthusiastic but, as part of the EE process, I invited him to try it out. I also asked him not to not write down afterwards what had happened in the session and to come to our next session without his folder of notes – to stay with the uncertainty and bring his forgetfulness into the room. My aim was to create a space in which we might notice the tension between holding onto his previously useful but now sedimented views, attitudes and ways of being and identifying and letting go of them. By 'sedimented' I mean a process whereby certain views, beliefs, attitudes or assumptions can, over time, become hardened and obstructive, like debris that has fallen into a stream, so as to change the natural 'flow' of a person's life. Our aim in therapy would be to create an opportunity, albeit a scary and unfamiliar opportunity, for George to look at whether those ways of coping that formerly gave him a secure sense of identity might actually be hindering him and causing some of the anxieties that he felt.

Second session

George again arrived on time for his next session and I immediately noted both the absence of his folder and his increased agitation. As if to compensate for the loss of his notes, he began the session by trying to recollect as much as he possibly could from the previous session. When he became worried that he could not remember everything, we discussed how unsafe he felt without his 'comfort blanket' of words. He explained that he felt worthless; he had habitually wielded his verbal erudition and eloquence – derived in part from his university education – like a shield. It not only made him feel strong and self-assured but also hid his vulnerabilities from others. Bereft of this shield, he felt inadequate in comparison with his peers and that he had little left to offer others.

I was intrigued by George's assessment of his self-worth and its dependency on what he could offer others. I also noted that, whenever he responded to an intervention of mine, he would preface his words with, 'I don't mean to be insulting...' or 'I don't mean to frustrate you...' George was neither insulting nor frustrating, although I did wonder if his reluctant move into an unknown space, devoid of words, might have provoked in him a sense of frustration with me. When I remarked on this, he explained that he wanted a good outcome to our sessions together so that I would be happy. I was reminded of, and reflected back to George, what he had said about his 'needy' mother; his desire to give me a good outcome seemed to me to be an expression of his sedimented need always to please others. George was taken aback by just how much his interactions with me mirrored his relationship with his mother – particularly with regard to his sense of neediness and guilt. We also noticed that he believed that, if he were able to make me happy, it would alleviate the sense of guilt that he carried with him always. This is one of the central challenges of this way of practising therapy, in that we moved our focus away from the content of his concerns to his relationship to them.

3) *Experimentation in the world*

George was again on time for our third session. I noted that not only had he again left his folder at home, but also that his scores on the self-completed CORE-5 OM, PHQ-9 and GAD-7 questionnaires were significantly improved from the previous weeks. He began by stating that he was feeling much more 'chipper' that day and began to tell me what had happened that morning. It had been his turn to get the kids to school on time. However, despite his plans, they had been late getting out of bed. Usually, this would have left him flustered and anxious that things were not proceeding according to plan. However, that morning, rather than responding as he would have normally – with a sense of urgency – he had been able to choose to stay with the uncertainty and just go with the flow. Yes, the children might be slightly late for school, but he had been able to tell himself that this was not necessarily a major problem. He described the whole experience as 'a bit of a blur', but noted that he had, nonetheless, felt happier. I thought the description of the 'blur' revealed something very important. While still being George, he had wrestled with what would previously have made him anxious, had faced the uncertainty of who George would be if he were not anxious, and was at that moment in a place where his sense of himself was transitioning from someone to someone else, becoming but not yet arrived. Hence, this sense of 'blur'.

George seemed to be experimenting with a different way of being-in-the-world by going with the flow. I pondered with him if a similar approach could be taken to his fear of forgetting: instead of fixating on trying to remember a particular word or name, he could just go with the flow. In discussing this, we used the metaphor of a jazz musician who has to play a piece of music and, in the middle of a performance, forgets the next note in the tune. Faced with this dilemma, the musician may freeze with anxiety as he desperately tries to remember what the next note is. Alternatively, he can choose to improvise up or down the scale, or indeed change the scale altogether. Put succinctly, if forgetting was a given in George's life, how would he choose to respond to situations when he forgot?

George responded positively to my analogy and explained that he was very fond of jazz music and played jazz piano in his free time. He also related an episode from his childhood when he had been playing the piano at a school concert and had forgotten the music. He had been mortified, but everyone had been very kind to him. We considered this episode in the context of his fears about how others would react to his forgetting – particularly in his professional career. It was clear that, when he had forgotten words at work, no clients had responded negatively. George acknowledged this but repeated that he felt unsafe when he forgot something: he had dropped the shield and he felt exposed and extremely nervous about having to seek help from others. We then discussed how hard it must be for him to come to sessions with me: not only was he seeking help but I was encouraging him to stay with his forgetfulness and the consequent feelings of exposure and danger.

George then described his fear that the important people in his life – particularly his wife – would reject him if his condition deteriorated any more. He described a science fiction story in which the protagonist, a man with a very low IQ, has experimental treatment that makes him a genius. Written from the perspective of the protagonist, the novel describes his experience of getting smarter, only then to face the effects of the treatment wearing off and reversion back to his original state. There was no evidence that the significant people in his life would reject George if his condition deteriorated. However, as previously described, it was clear that the fear of rejection had played a significant role in George's relationship with his mother. He described her as a 'bottomless pit of need' – an insecure narcissist who saw him as being there simply to fulfil her needs.

It seemed that being able to find words or meet the needs of others were both extremely important to him, as his identity was quite entwined with them. His fear was that, if he were not able to be 'this' George, he would be rejected by work associates or his wife, for example.

Fourth session

In the fourth session, George was again without his folder, and again his questionnaire scores were an improvement on the previous week. He began the session by talking about his weight. His friends had commented on how he had put on weight. He explained that he was reverting to the weight he had been when he was younger, but that he would prefer to stay slimmer. He then said he thought the fear of losing control lay at the heart of all his problems. I was intrigued that he had begun the session by telling me this, in light of the science fiction novel he had mentioned the previous week. It had occurred to me that perhaps George was describing himself metaphorically through the people in the novel, so I had found the book and read it – *Flowers for Algernon* by Daniel Keyes (1966).

We discussed the parallel between the character in the novel and George. George's original talent for using words had allowed him to go to a good university, which further improved this ability. But now, with the effects of the tumour, he feared he was losing his ability with language, losing control and reverting to a state where he could not rely on his original talent. George was impressed that I knew the story as he hadn't mentioned it by name the previous week because he had forgotten the title. He explained that he had re-read the novel many times in his life – particularly in recent years – and he identified very strongly with the protagonist. As we discussed his fear of reversion, I noted that there was no evidence that his tumour was malignant or that he would deteriorate to a still less able state. In this way, we were able to alight on the phenomenological expression of his concerns in his current life being tied to former aspects of his identity and it became even more clear that loss of control was the superordinate theme in all the narratives.

George had found meaning in his life through his mastery of words. But now the effects of the tumour were a given to which he had to respond. The challenge facing him was to find whether he could respond to this given positively – whether he could reorganise his life to find another way of living meaningfully – another way of being-in-the-world. We then discussed how he and his wife could respond to the given of forgetting. I suggested he could allow his wife to take on more of his responsibilities, if he could give up some of his need for control. This was a difficult move for George to consider; he worried it would put more pressure on his wife. I also suggested they could collaborate in writing lists for him that would act as aide-memoires. Thus, he would no longer be trying to 'hold onto his notes' lest he forget something; he would be embracing the unknown by acknowledging his needs for an aide-memoire. We discussed George's concern about this co-operation and his worry that he would be giving up the sense of personal control and safety that he derived from creating and carrying his personal lists with him. We also discussed his dislike that, whenever he thought about taking on a new responsibility, his first response was to create a list. He ended the session by stating, 'I'm pretty certain the solution to my problems doesn't lie in a list!'

Fifth session

At the fifth session, still folderless, George told me he felt more upbeat and motivated, but that the self-completion questionnaires hadn't really allowed him to capture this. He seemed in a positive and proactive mood and began the session by reporting back on the steps he had taken in the preceding week to try to live with the notion of not necessarily having control or giving it to something (a list) or someone else (his wife). Not only had he relied less heavily on lists, but he had also started to take back responsibility for certain tasks from his wife. He might not be able to complete these tasks as quickly or efficiently as his wife, but he could still complete them in time, to an acceptable standard, he said. He also said he had been expressing his anger more. We discussed how this was difficult for him, because of his fear that if he expressed anger, people would reject him. Again, there was no evidence to support this conclusion, and he described how everyone else in his family regularly lost their temper but forgave and forgot 10 minutes later.

He told me that he had been playing a lot more jazz piano in the last week and had listened to records that he hadn't played in a long while – particularly Miles Davis. He said, 'I've been using keys and modes that I do not normally use,' which I understood as a metaphor for his experimentation with new ways of being-in-the-world. I too am a fan of Miles Davis, and I repeated what I had read once about his style of playing. Early in his career, Miles had realised that he could not play as fast as the leading Bebop musicians Charlie Parker and Dizzy Gillespie. However, although slower, he could play deeper, and this led to the birth of a whole new movement in jazz. Bringing this back to George, I commented that, while he might not be able to work as fast as his wife, it didn't mean he couldn't produce great work at his own pace.

At the end of the session I observed that, for the first time, George had not made any mention that week of his brain tumour and its effects. He smiled and explained that thoughts about his tumour had faded into the background in the preceding week.

Sixth session

At his final session George's scores were still good, but he took out a notepad and pen and asked me to remind him of what we had talked about during the preceding weeks, while he took some notes. It seemed that his anxiety had returned, but perhaps this was a different sort of anxiety – one associated with the ending of therapy? Either way, he was back to relying on his former ways of controlling the unknown. I acknowledged his anxiety and discussed his request in the context of his expressed desire to rid himself of his dependence on lists. So, rather than listing for him what we had spent the previous weeks discussing, I used open questions to encourage him to remember what he could. As we did this, George scribbled down some notes on his pad. At the end of the session, I invited him to consider what it would feel like to tear up the notes he had just written or put them away for a few weeks and then, without checking them, see what he remembered that felt most salient for him.

As the session drew to a close, George said that he hoped to see me again some time – although not in a client-therapist relationship. Before leaving the room, he shook my hand, said I was good at what I did, and that he would recommend me to his friends. Could this be interpreted as the client wanting to please the therapist, or a recognition that he had found the process helpful? Or was it a euphemism for saying goodbye to me as his therapist, with all the possible anxieties that such a situation might invoke?

George's comments

We had already asked George to give written consent for us to write up the case as a study. We sent the case study to him and invited him to check the words we had ascribed to him to ensure we hadn't given them a different meaning. It also seemed appropriate to ask him if he would like to give us feedback about the therapy and, in his own words, describe what had happened for him. He sent us the two paragraphs below.

> I think that the most useful part of this therapy was when I was helped to the conclusion that large parts of my previous self-image were no longer appropriate or of any use to me. I was encouraged to consider how I might be able to change these and to jettison the parts where I was desperately attempting to hold on to earlier talent, failing, and

consequently feeling depression, inadequacy and guilt. It was also useful to explore the reasons why I should feel so threatened by the change in my life and to think about whether, in practice, it actually affected every element of who I was.

My experience of this process initially caused some fear as I worried that crutches I had been using, including writing lists, were going to be kicked out from under me. In practice, the process helped me consider other, more appropriate methods, such as relying more on jazz-like improvisation in work and at home. It went some way towards helping me to largely accept my own limitations but also to think about ways of getting around them.

Discussion with the editor

Simon: If I have understood correctly, the distinctive characteristic of EE is the way in which you attempt to help clients reframe their perceived difficulties into goals that describe where they wish to be. This sounds intriguing as, at least initially, it appears to depart from the generally-held view of existential therapy that the therapist avoids goal setting in favour of accompanying the client on a rigorous exploration of the personal meaning of whatever they bring into sessions. Can you say more about this key part of the EE approach?

Mark/Randolph: I (Mark) think that there is an increasing recognition that it is possible to work with goals from an existential perspective – see, for example, the recent work of Mackrill (2010) and Cooper and Law (2018). Goal setting starts with a phenomenological exploration in which the therapist attempts to attune themselves to the client's unique way of being and to make sense of their presenting problems. The therapist will explicitly ask clients to describe how they believe therapy may be of assistance to them and what form they think this help may take. The goals that emerge are highly contextualised and narrative-rich descriptions of change that the client has elaborated, which provide inspiration to the therapist for the work ahead.

Simon: You write that you complied with the IAPT requirement to use formal outcomes measures, but that EE is not manualised; it simply follows a written protocol. In some respects, it seems you have managed to successfully engage with the NHS and with NICE, while retaining the spirit of existentialism and phenomenology. As you will be aware, many existential practitioners are wary of becoming involved with the NHS and NICE – are there any lessons that might be drawn from your own experience? I also wonder what the data told you about the nature of existential therapy that would be helpful to share with other existential therapists.

Mark/Randolph: First, we view depression not as an entity but as part of lived experience that is to be unravelled and understood as a language used by many to express their relationship to themselves, others and the world. Second, we believe future generations will take a broader view of notions like depression as current thinking is moving towards this more adequate understanding of what are perceived as mental disorders. Therefore, presentation of depression as though it were a 'something' will increasingly become challenged by approaches like EE.

Simon: You write about EE as constituting a challenge to the dominance of the medical model and broadly cognitive (I guess manualisable) approaches to delivering therapy in the context of the NHS. I wonder, to what extent do you feel you have been able to influence other practitioners in this area? My sense is that, whenever we attempt to make changes, we come up against opposition from stakeholders who feel their own position is threatened. Do you have examples of how you have argued for your initiative in the face of opposition?

Mark/Randolph: The structure of EE by its very nature is operationalised, not manualised, since we recognise that one cannot simply manualise an approach because therapy sessions, while needing to adhere to a protocol to demonstrate to commissioners that it is effective and replicable, inevitably contain elements and sessions that are intertwined and overlap. Therefore, the word 'manualised' is not used as it suggests a linear approach to the work. Yes, this has been a struggle to convey to stakeholders but we have stuck to it and the results are evident and reports from clients demonstrate that they have benefited from way we work.

Simon: And, perhaps conversely, I wonder about the extent to which a cost-effective way of engaging more holistically with NHS clients might be welcomed by very many service users and service providers. I noted in a keynote address to the BPS way back in 2006 (du Plock, 2006) that the increasing marketisation of NHS healthcare and its associated reframing of power relationships (or at least the language used to describe these relationships) in terms of consumers and customers (rather than patients) and service providers (rather than experts) have the potential to demystify some aspects of healthcare. It may be that EE and the trend to democratisation of healthcare fit together very well…

Mark/Randolph: In our paper 'CORE Blimey!' (Rayner & Vitali, 2014), you will find that clinicians and clients have both engaged in and produced results that demonstrate the effectiveness of working with what are called goals, as they have achieved to a very high degree the positions wished for at the outset of their articulation of their difficulties.

Simon: You say you 'strive to maintain an individualised way of delivering these [EE] structures', but you also note that ways of working must be replicable if they are to be approved by NICE. It sounds like the provision of training in EE is going to become important in the future – can you say something about this?

Mark/Randolph: All our trainee clinicians are invited to attend initial training sessions during which they are given the opportunity to fully acquaint themselves with our model and the EE structure and protocol paper (Rayner & Vitali, 2016). However, while essential, training alone is not enough. To ensure adherence to the EE protocol, trainees are required to attend weekly group supervision with peers and senior clinicians. This provides an opportunity to reflect on their clinical work within the EE paradigm and for supervisors to monitor adherence to the spirit of the protocol.

References

Ansseau M, Dierick M, Buntinkx F, Cnockaert P, De Smedt J, Van Den Haute M, Vander Mijnsbrugge D (2004). High prevalence of mental disorders in primary care. *Journal of Affective Disorders* 78(1): 49–55.

Asay TP, Lambert MJ (1999). The empirical case for the common factors in therapy: quantitative findings. In: Hubble MA, Duncan BL, Miller SD (ed). *The Heart and Soul of Change: what works in therapy*. Washington, DC: American Psychological Association (pp23–55).

Cooper M, Law D (2018). *Working with Goals in Psychotherapy and Counselling*. Oxford: Oxford University Press.

Cuijpers P, Driessen E, Hollon SD, van Oppen P, Barth J, Andersson G (2012). The efficacy of non-directive supportive therapy for adult depression: a meta-analysis. *Clinical Psychology Review* 32(4): 280–291.

du Plock S (2006). Just what is it that makes contemporary counselling psychology so different, so appealing? *Counselling Psychology Review* 21(3): 22–32.

Goldberg DP, Huxley P (1992). *Common Mental Disorders: a bio-social model*. London: Tavistock/Routledge.

Keyes D (1966). *Flowers for Algernon*. London: Millenium.

King M, Semlyen J, See Tai S, Killaspy H, Osborn D, Popelyuk D, Nazareth I (2008). A systematic review of mental disorder, suicide, and deliberate self harm in lesbian, gay and bisexual people. *BMC Psychiatry* 8: 70.

Lantz J, Walsh J (2007). *Short-term Intervention in Clinical Practice*. Oxford: Oxford University Press.

Mackrill T (2010). Goal consensus and collaboration in psychotherapy – an existential rationale. *Journal of Humanistic Psychology* 50(1): 96–107.

Norcross JC, Krebs P, Prochaska JO (2011). Stages of change. *Journal of Clinical Psychology* 67(2):143–154.

Norcross JC, Lambert MJ (2011). Evidence-based therapy relationships. In: Norcross JC (ed). *Psychotherapy Relationships that Work: evidence-based responsiveness* (2nd ed). Oxford: Oxford University Press (pp3–23).

Orlinsky DE, Grawe K, Parks BK (1994). Process and outcome in psychotherapy: noch einmal. In: Bergin AE, Garfield SL (eds). *Handbook of Psychotherapy and Behavior Change*. Oxford: John Wiley & Sons (pp270–376).

Ormel J, VonKorff M, Ustun TB, Pini S, Korten A, Oldehinkel T (1994). Common mental disorders and disability across cultures: results from the WHO Collaborative Study on psychological problems in general health care. *JAMA* 272(22): 1741–1748.

Rayner M, Vitali D (2016). Existential Experimentation: structure and principles for a short-term psychological therapy. *Journal of Humanistic Psychology* 5(2): 194–213.

Rayner M, Vitali D (2014). CORE blimey! Existential therapy scores GOALS! *Existential Analysis: Journal of the Society for Existential Analysis* 25(2): 296–314.

Rogers CR (1980). *A Way of Being*. Boston, MA: Houghton Mifflin.

Rosen CS (2000). Is the sequencing of change processes by stage consistent across health problems? A meta-analysis. *Health Psychology* 19(6): 593–604.

Safran JD, Muran JC (2000). *Negotiating the Therapeutic Alliance: a relational treatment guide*. New York, NY: Guilford Press.

Schneider KJ, Krug OT (2010). *Existential-Humanistic Therapy*. Washington, DC: American Psychological Association.

Shepherd G, Boardman J, Slade M (2008). *Making Recovery a Reality*. London: Sainsbury Centre for Mental Health.

Spinelli E (2015). *Practising Existential Psychotherapy: the relational world* (2nd ed). London: Sage.

Spinelli E (2005). *The Interpreted World: an introduction to phenomenological psychology*. London. Sage.

Vuorilehto M, Melartin T, Isometsä E (2005). Depressive disorders in primary care: recurrent, chronic, and co-morbid. *Psychological Medicine* 35(05): 673–682.

Wampold BE (2015). How important are the common factors in psychotherapy? An update. *World Psychiatry* 14(3): 270–277.

18

An existential view on traumatic grief: the four-worlds model

Chloe Paidoussis-Mitchell

When a sudden death occurs, a seriously disruptive and psychologically difficult journey begins for the bereaved. Most of the literature on trauma and sudden loss is framed within a cognitive constructivist paradigm and this is very useful and relevant to any existential counselling approach. My contribution here is not to compete with established thinking on narrative restructuring of loss (Neimeyer, 2006, 2007) but instead to highlight how this sits very well alongside existentialism. Clinical psychology is invested in assessing risk through the lens of maladaptive responses to traumatic loss (Kauffman, 2002; Stroebe & Schut, 2007), and I appreciate that some people who experience traumatic loss do need specialist care to cope with their trauma and find trauma-recovery cognitive behaviour therapy programmes helpful.

What I believe is missing from the literature is an existentially informed clinical model for traumatic grief. This may be because, as existentialists, we do not like to frame our work in fixed modalities. However, in the past 15 years of working as a grief psychologist, I have found that an existentially informed approach to therapeutic recovery from a traumatic bereavement is absolutely relevant and appropriate – given the nature of the psychological journey, which seems entirely existential and meaning driven. In this chapter, I will set out my way of working with clients who have to learn to live with the sudden and traumatic death of a loved one.

Loss is classified as traumatic if a) it was unexpected; b) the person bereaved was not prepared for it, and c) there was nothing that could be done to prevent it from happening. These criteria are in line with the *DSM-5* (APA, 2013) diagnostic criteria for a traumatic event in the diagnosis of post-traumatic stress disorder.

I am an existentially trained counselling psychologist and have developed an expertise in trauma and grief, having conducted my doctoral research into the phenomenology of traumatic loss. This was the first study on the lived experience of traumatic bereavement to be published (Paidoussis-Mitchell, 2012). I now conduct long- and short-term therapy in private practice and have worked in NHS primary care counselling settings. This field is a passion of mine and I continue to supervise a number of doctoral research projects on grief, trauma and loss.

When working with traumatic grief, I have observed that psychological responses are unique to the individual. What helps clients recover and embrace life again is a therapeutic relationship of trust, care and compassion, where they feel witnessed, understood and validated. Although the stories I hear are harrowing, and often the emotional depths of despair and rage are intense and feel impossibly hard to bear, I have learned to develop a holding and compassionate attitude to all grief responses. There is no normal here.

In my view, responses to traumatic loss are not pathological, although of course some of the symptoms may seem so (such as feeling paralysing fear and anxiety and recurring heart palpitations and panic attacks). These are all psychological responses that express the profound shake-up involved, where normal no longer seems normal and there is a re-discovery of what it means to be (Paidoussis-Mitchell, 2012).

Sudden loss throws people violently into a state of psychological groundlessness, where they realise that there is no certainty, no safety and no fixed meaning in life; nothing is permanent and they too face death. It is deeply frightening, alienating, isolating and disorientating and the bereaved person feels confused in what it now means to live. Experiencing meaninglessness is at the heart of traumatic grief and, paradoxically, it is the way out of it. Those who have experienced traumatic bereavement attempt to create a sense of meaning out of circumstances that seem to lack it (Smith Landsman, 2002).

The four-worlds model of traumatic loss

The first step in establishing a therapeutic relationship with a traumatically bereaved client is to allow death in (Barnett, 2009). Reflecting on what happened and what it was like – phenomenologically – is not re-traumatising but, rather, validating for the client. In my experience, creating a holding, containing space for the client to narratively reveal their lived experience of their trauma and grief implicitly informs them that everything about their experience is valid and that I am prepared to face it with them.

As an existentialist, I believe that our psychological make up comprises four psychological, mental and emotional dimensions: the physical (*Umwelt*), the social (*Mitwelt*), the personal (*Eigenwelt*) and the spiritual (*Überwelt*). All of us encounter the world through these dimensions and we shape our attitude towards our experience of each dimension based on what meaning we make of our experience and what implied beliefs we hold onto about our life. It is my view that psychological wellbeing emerges when we authentically reflect on our engagement with each dimension. Key questions emerge in the therapeutic work with traumatic grief, about:

- how we find meaning
- how we relate to the unavoidable anxiety associated with sudden death
- how we respond to distressing emotions, such as rage, despair, sadness
- how we make sense of the here-and-now and what can come next
- how we allow ourselves to engage with opportunities that present themselves in making meaning out of our significant relationships and projects.

Each dimension merits some description and all of them are equally important.

The **personal dimension** is about how people relate to themselves. Do they nourish and invest in their relationship with themselves? In my experience, often clients who end up in therapy don't like themselves much and their therapeutic recovery is all about that.

The **physical dimension** is about understanding how clients relate to their environment and to the givens of their natural world. This includes their attitude to their body, to material possessions, to health and illness and to their own mortality. Through reflections on this dimension, I can start to appreciate the extent to which the client is resiliently facing death and what this means for their wellbeing and the here-and-now.

The **social dimension** is important because it is really disrupted by traumatic grief. It is the significance of the deceased and the bereaved person's attachment to them that causes grief to be painful and traumatic. So, in revealing this dimension, the client can reflect on their sense of belonging and the extent to which they feel others care about them. Work on this dimension focuses primarily on how the client navigates their experience of alienation, isolation and detachment. Storolow (2007) has illustrated very touchingly the sense of profound alienation he felt from everyone in his life after he woke up next to his dead wife. My intention with traumatic grief work is to help the client understand what loss has done to their sense of relating to others and to uncover the extent to which they themselves are contributing to extending the period of alienation.

In the **spiritual dimension** (van Deurzen, 1988), people relate to the unknown and create a philosophical, value-based outlook in order to experience meaning in life. Working in this dimension provides the framework for ongoing meaning and can be the place where healing occurs. Key questions emerge about what is meaningful to the client.

Case study

This work was conducted in my private practice and the details of my client have been changed to maintain her anonymity. She was self-referred and privately funded and keen to have counselling once a week. Suzanne was 40 years old and explained that she wanted help with how she was feeling about herself and life in general.

a) The beginning of therapy – getting to know her

Suzanne arrives on time for her first appointment, smiles a little, and walks in shyly and sits down. I introduce myself, explain the basics of our work, including confidentiality and how important it is that she feels we can create a space for her to address the issues she wants to. So our initial session focuses on us both seeing how we relate to each other. I invite her to settle in, get comfortable and tell me about herself.

Suzanne: I'm glad I came today. I was wondering whether to cancel. But then I thought I mustn't… I must do something about the situation I am in.

Chloe: I'm glad you came too. It's good to put a face to your voice. You said on the phone that you had had a lot of trauma in your life and I am wondering what you'd like to share with me today.

Suzanne: My daughter died 20 years ago. She was nearly five. She was killed in a car crash with my mum... I don't remember that much to be honest. I was like a zombie... I don't know how I got through it... Well, sort of got through it... I have an 18-year-old son too – that's complicated. I need to talk about him too. I am engaged to a great guy. We want to get married next year. But I'm a mess... really... I have terrible insomnia, I hardly ever sleep.

I am aware that, with her opening contributions, Suzanne refers to three dimensions of her existence: the physical (she can't sleep), the personal (she feels she's a mess), the social (her relationships to son and fiancé). The spiritual one is notably absent and I am thinking that this is probably fitting and the reason she is in therapy with me. It is too early at this stage to start delving into any one of these and I attempt to work phenomenologically with her so she can direct our journey.

Suzanne: I am a mess. My GP has me on 25mg of citalopram. I get panic. Terrible feelings of panic. Most days I don't actually want to leave my sofa. Especially at night.

Chloe: What's that like for you?"

Suzanne: Oh, words can't explain...There is nothing I can say to... I'm still very sad about what happened. It's been like 20 years. Most people don't imagine that I am stuck like this.

I notice that there is so much going on for me at this moment that I want to pause and pay attention to the space between us. I bracket the sense that I too would be a mess if I lost my daughter or son so tragically. I find the possibility of such a loss an unbearable thought and I feel a deep compassion for Suzanne.

Chloe: It must be devastating to have lost your little girl.

Suzanne begins to describe the devastating events and the circumstances of her losses, which are painful, distressing and deeply sad. The more she reveals, the more she seems confused by the intensity and rawness of her pain, and when I ask her what it's been like to carry on living, she describes her authentic terror.

Suzanne: I'm terrified. Just so uncertain about everything. It feels like... I am just so scared... to be.

Suzanne seems stuck existentially, living with raw uncertainty, panic, fear and inertia. I don't yet know whether her feelings of panic are about the inevitability and unpredictability of her life or about taking the leap of faith to invest in present meaningful relationships. I imagine probably both and I suspect one impacts the other.

I ask her to reflect on what she makes of our first session so far.

Suzanne: I feel like I can speak openly here. I want to come and deal with the losses I have had in my life. I am just so full of sadness. I am still there, 20 years ago. The shock was so deep.

I suggest that she has not yet had the chance to really acknowledge the impact of her trauma and propose that we start to unpack what life has been like for her.

b) The personal dimension

We start by paying attention to her actual embodied experience, digging into her personal dimension phenomenologically.

Chloe: What's it been like for you?

Suzanne: Not good really… It was horrific. I couldn't believe it. I don't know how I carried on living.

Chloe: How did you?

Suzanne: I don't actually know. It's unspeakable… I was so shocked. So, disconnected. From everything. Everyone…

Suzanne is deeply upset, tears run down her face and I feel her devastation. This is a story of horrific loss and I can't begin to imagine the trauma she's been through. I want to be with her through this but I feel upset and tearful and am comfortable showing her my own vulnerability. I take her openness towards me as a positive sign.

Suzanne: I just kept thinking I wasn't there to keep her safe. I just couldn't protect her. I am her mum. I should have kept her safe. I felt so guilty. Really, really guilty.

Suzanne continues to cry and I find myself holding the space for us, unbearably heavy with devastation though it is. I feel it is crucial that I can bear this. If she had to, I must bear it too. I want her to know I care and the only way I can seem to achieve this is to listen attentively and openly. I am sure my emotions are evident to Suzanne but there is no space to explore this yet. We are so deep in the personal dimension, the social dimension is not accessible yet.

Suzanne: I felt like my body had detached… It was like I left my body. I didn't know what I was doing. Or thinking. It was completely shocking. Nothing can prepare you for it. I had so much to deal with. I didn't think I could deal with any of it.

Suzanne shakes with devastation. Her embodied reaction is powerful and it's clear she has been living with the shattering ontological impact just beneath the surface.

Suzanne: It's so sad… I'm still totally devastated.

We work through many sessions with her expressing the impact of these tragic losses, and it feels raw. She engages with a plethora of emotions, including rage, anger, despair and lostness. It takes many sessions to bear it, to sit with the uncertainty of being, with the impact of such an awakening. I am struck by Suzanne's courage and resilience. This is no walk in the park. She is shattered and strong. The human spirit humbles me and touches me. The sessions are hard but the relationship we are building feels therapeutic.

Paramount to developing Suzanne's personal dimension is helping her highlight and attend to her relationship with herself.

Chloe: What about you? What do you make of you?

Suzanne: I don't like me. I felt frozen. I was unhinged for a long time. For years… Oh god. Yes. Yes… After they died, I did go off the rails a lot with drugs and stuff. I drank to get paralytic. I was known as the wild party girl. I'd sleep around with anybody. I'd disappear for days on end, leaving my son with a neighbour. I did go off and do lots of drugs. Reckless.

She is so upset by these reflections, she sobs and sobs. The tears are heavy with the loss of her own self and her potential for being a good mum, and she carries the guilt of having wasted the chance to make it all good with her remaining child. This is in itself devastating and requires so much courage on her part. I have to dig deep to create a psychological space between us in order to bear this rawness. I think I cope well but I find myself crying in supervision. Some of Suzanne's pain resides within me and I must take care.

Suzanne: I was such a shit mother. I really was… Horrible mother.

Chloe: You are being very hard on yourself. You were young and shattered by tragedy.

I notice that I want to protect her from any further isolation and self-battering. I hope that she can take this observation in and she seems to find it difficult because we are still in the personal dimension, where she needs to attend to healing her relationship with herself and eventually create a meaningful one. Currently she is not there.

Suzanne: Well, I have been shit. I couldn't actually help it. It makes me very sad… I really didn't want that. I do love him. So very much. But I was so lost and scared. I had no guidance. No support and everybody expected me to be fine after a couple of years but I wasn't. So, I lived as though I wasn't really in me. I was avoiding me… numbing the pain.

This is a profound observation and paves the way for her to start to step into herself and seek meaning in herself. There are sessions where she considers what it would mean if she could accept herself and acknowledge the devastation of her losses. Eventually she seems to start to relate to herself with compassion.

Suzanne: I've made a lot of mistakes but I have suffered a lot too. Unfortunately, I can't turn back the clock but I do want to sort things out now. It won't be easy but I want to try.

c) The social dimension

In making sense of who she is, Suzanne comes face to face with her social dimension and acknowledges her profound isolation and alienation during the last 20 years. This takes many sessions, as she realises she's had very little security from an early age. She'd been bullied at school, and felt she had no real friends. Her only best friend was her mum and, on losing her, she felt an intense alienation. She couldn't grasp how others had coped or made sense of the traumas.

Suzanne: They all seemed fine. I wasn't. But nobody seemed to notice. I didn't understand why I couldn't get my act together. I can see now. But back then, I was so lost, so alone. I think I might say something to them.

Chloe: What would you like to say?

Suzanne: I'd like to ask them to help me remember Kerry and my mMum. Especially with my son. We could go to the graves and put flowers. I never do that.

Suzanne is starting to consider addressing her isolation and speaking to her family members about what life has really been like for her. She feels this is important, not in their bearing witness to her life but also for these relationships to grow in the future.

Suzanne: I'd like to tell him [her father] that I felt completely alone. I was so alone. I don't resent anybody but I felt very hurt that nobody cared for me. Nobody really understood what it was like for me. I felt so alone… and now I feel so guilty.

Chloe: What do you feel guilty about?

Suanne: I feel guilty because losing my mother is harder for me than losing my daughter… It's awful isn't it?

Chloe: No.

Suzanne: Losing Mum meant I was totally alone. I had to raise my son alone. Nobody understood what I was going through. How I woke up every day… Of course, I'll always be devastated to have lost Kerry. Always. That will never go away. But losing my mum, I can't come to terms with. I'm her age now… I miss her even more and I realise now how young she was. It's so sad and really terrifying. Beyond anything… Pulling the floor from under you. Scary.

Chloe: Living with no certainty.

Suzanne: Yes. I feel like I've wasted lots of time. I was reckless and the guilt I carry is huge. I can't change the past, can I?

Chloe: No, but you can change the present. You can attend to what matters to you now.

Suzanne: Mmm… I want to make things good with my son. I really must. I don't know if he'll let me but I want to try. I did let him down. Massively… but I want to stop that now. I want to explain how much I struggled. I know what matters now. Back then, I don't think I could bear it. But all my tears have helped me see. I used to think I was weak but maybe it's been the other way round. I have been strong. I can be strong.

Her engagement with therapy is inspiring and motivating for me. I feel we are making good progress and that she is developing resilience in both her personal and social dimension.

d) The physical dimension

Suzanne's physical dimension is profoundly shaken by her proximity to death. For her, death hasn't presented an opportunity. It has been so terrifying, she has been so alone, she has had to withdraw in order to survive.

Suzanne: I couldn't possibly get close to anybody. I would be too vulnerable.

Chloe: What do you mean?

Suzanne: I'd be too frightened.

Chloe: Of?

Suzanne: Them dying… it's caused a lot of problems with my son. So many arguments. I haven't really been there for him. I call him but we don't see each other much. He's a typical teenager. He's very angry with me.

Chloe: What's it been like for you?

Although Suzanne seems to be focused on the social dimension, it is important to appreciate that these dimensions are interwoven, one impacting on the other. As the therapy progresses, it is evident that Suzanne has lived through such an embodied fear of death that she has shut down on all psychological fronts, trying to avoid the potential for more loss.

Suzanne: I have been living with such a fear.

Chloe: Fear of?

Suzanne: Life.

She describes feeling physically vulnerable every day, and says she never stops thinking about death. This panics her.

Suzanne: I'm always aware of death. When my partner goes out. When my son goes out at night. When I get in a car. When I wake up every morning. I always think about death. It's always there. It's exhausting. It's terrifying actually. It freezes me. I can't actually sleep at all… 'cause I have this feeling of blackness… total nothingness… And I try and escape it by staying awake. I watch a lot of stupid telly. I'm just so exhausted.

Chloe: You want to stop feeling like that.

Suzanne: Yes, I do. But it's so difficult. You just never know what could happen, right?

Chloe: None of us do. What's it like for you?

Suzanne: Horrible. I have stopped living. Hiding on my sofa.

Suzanne recognizes that she is stuck with paralysing fear. She feels the threat of annihilation. This has caused her to avoid intimacy and she starts to see this. I put it to her and this normalises it for her so that she can accept herself and explore future options.

Eventually Suzanne starts to recognise that, although she can't prevent another traumatic loss, she can perhaps make the most of life by searching and investing her energy into what is meaningful.

e) The spiritual dimension

At this point, we start to engage with her spiritual dimension, which is where a lot of her healing occurs. When she reflects on this dimension, she starts to appreciate that she can find meaning, that she does have some options, such as investing in her relationship with her partner and with her son.

She starts to use the sessions as a space where she can discuss her alternatives, and she practises what she could say and what she could do. One of her primary concerns is to dare to trust her partner. This is a challenge, as it relies on Suzanne letting go of her fear and trusting that she can journey in life safely. We spend a few sessions exploring what this relationship means to her, what the risk is and how she can relate to her partner in a way that is secure. She starts to develop a greater sense of ownership. This is not always easy for her, but it does lead to her feeling much more present.

Her primary concern is her relationship with her son and she manages to create a space where they can feel closer to each other. On the anniversary of the accident, she invites him to mark the day at the cemetery with her and this allows them to speak more candidly and kindly to each other. She has spoken to him and explained her distress, her sense of fear and her alienation and he has been kind and caring in response. She has apologised for the mistakes in his childhood, has felt heard and has felt that, although it hurt him, she now has the opportunity to show her devotion to him. Fundamental to her attending to this dimension is the belief that she can show him care and love and can become a good-enough mother, which is the most meaningful aspect of her life. She values this immensely and creating the opportunity for it is essential to her way forward. This gives her hope that she can rise again.

Once Suzanne has considered ways in which she can engage meaningfully in significant relationships, we reach the end of her therapy. This is something we agree together, and she engages in the ending beautifully. We spend time reflecting on this ending and how, in the therapeutic process, she was able to meet herself and listen to her body, to her heart, to her inner voice of what it's actually been like. Suzanne says she had not had the chance to do that in real life but is very thankful for the opportunity to do it with me. I am touched and humbled by her openness, courage and spirit. I feel my being able to share that with her is meaningful in its own right. In the therapeutic process, Suzanne has learned how to engage with her existential condition and with the existential promise of her ongoing life. I feel privileged to have had the chance to relate to her in this deep and vulnerable way.

Conclusion

The existential journey presented above illustrates how behaviours and symptoms that emerge in response to traumatic loss are not pathological but ontological. Suzanne could have been diagnosed with acute anxiety disorder or major depressive disorder. However, this would have missed the point of her ontological distress. Creating an inter-relational therapeutic space where she could authentically reflect on the ontological impact of her trauma allowed her the opportunity to rise again and face life with resilience. The focus on her four worlds (the four psychological dimensions) allowed her the opportunity to interpret life through her givens (meaning, anxiety, death and isolation). At the end of therapy, Suzanne could engage with and articulate the meaning life held for her, could appreciate the extensive and paralysing impact of her anxiety about death, could identify that she had carried meaninglessness with her for 20 years and could recognise that she had been living in an alienated state not only from significant others but also from herself. The four-worlds model of existential therapy allowed her to seek meaning and grow in confidence and self-esteem.

The existential approach is particularly suited to the traumatically bereaved because it is possible that difficulties with being are about authentic engagement with oneself, the world and significant others in it. In Suzanne's case, she did not want to reflect on the existential givens of her being and she turned to reckless behaviours such as drug-taking and drinking excessively to cope with an immobilising anxiety and fear of life. Her ontological struggle was immense and time was not a healer (which is the traditional view) (Horowitz, 1997). Dominant psychological paradigms centre on the reconstruction of more informed assumptive worlds (Kauffman, 2002) and the re-authoring of the story of loss in order to find meaning as a way of gaining a new appreciation of life (Murphy et al, 2003). My approach does not conflict with these ideas. The existential approach has something important to add, though – the idea that human beings are grounded in a state of inter-relatedness (Spinelli, 2007).

Suzanne's struggle with her traumatic losses highlights the existential struggle for meaning centred on finding a way to be authentically inter-relational on all of four psychological dimensions (that is, paying attention to and nurturing herself, important others in her life and her future). Achieving this is where resilience and growth occurred – not through correcting her maladaptive behaviours. Suzanne's journey demonstrates to us all that our temporal existence is full of opportunity and meaning if we permit it and confront it. I hope that this case study ignites further discussions on the nature of trauma and loss that go beyond narrative reconstructions and pathological constructs.

Discussion with editor

Simon: You explore the topic of traumatic bereavement and loss within the context of what you refer to as 'the existential counselling psychology paradigm'. I think the degree to which existential-phenomenological perspectives on therapy have found a home in counselling psychology and have been enthusiastically championed by many counselling psychologists has been quite remarkable, but the reasons for this are not always clear. Can you say what you mean when you refer to it as a specific paradigm?

Chloe: When I refer to the existential psychological paradigm, I mean that I will work therapeutically with an attitude or a stance that is informed by existential-phenomenological philosophy, which challenges the fundamental assumptions of the natural sciences framework of counselling psychology. This approach focuses on clarifying the nature, meaning and essence of psychological phenomena as they are described and experienced in an inter-subjective, inter-relational way by the client. The question of what it is like to be and what it means to be is revealed through reflective, descriptive practice. This means that in this paradigm counselling psychologists focus on revealing ontological and ontic responses through descriptive, non-prescriptive inquiry and examining the specific ways in which an individual is experiencing and navigating life. This approach denies the division between object and subject and suggests that the meaning of existence is co-constituted in our relationship with ourselves, others and the world. Our being in the world is interpreted (Spinelli, 2002) and the therapeutic alliance co-constructed between therapist and client when both parties reflect authentically on their intention to reveal the essence of the client's way of being in a descriptive, non-judgemental, open and curious exploration, free of fixed interpretations. In the existential paradigm, the ontic behaviours are understood in terms of their relationship with the client's ontological struggles. In this way, the client's world reveals itself in all of its interpreted glory.

Simon: I am intrigued by your use of what has become known as the 'four-worlds model' in working with trauma. While writers often refer to this model, few say how it can actually be used in practice. Can you expand a little on the historical development of the four existential dimensions? I believe the first three were proposed by the Swiss psychiatrist Ludwig Binswanger, and Emmy van Deurzen has propounded the fourth?

Chloe: Yes, Ludwig Binswager (1881–1966) was a Swiss psychiatrist who was influenced originally by Freud and later by Heidegger. He moved from a psychiatric understanding to an existential one (having rejected Freud's biological determinism). His focus was on revealing his patient's 'relatedness and world design' (van Deurzen & Kenward, 2005: 24). He expanded the notion of Heidegger's *Dasein* (being-in-the-world) into the three worlds of being: a) *Umwelt* – the physical dimension; b) *Mitwelt* – the social dimension, and c) *Eigenwelt* – the personal dimension. These together constitute the person's *Weltanschauung*, which is essentially how a person views their experience of being in the world. Emmy van Deurzen (1984) proposed the addition of the spiritual dimension, the *Überwelt*, based on Heidegger's later works. This includes one's attitude to a meaningful being-in-the- world. The point of the four-worlds model is to use it as a framework for understanding what the client's experience of being is and to identify where the client may have blind spots or disruptions that lead to stuckness and ontic behaviours that are catastrophic or detrimental to the client's psychological wellbeing.

Simon: In the course of reading your chapter, I think I have gained a greater insight into how bearing the four existential dimensions in mind can provide a valuable organising framework for the practitioner. What exactly is it, do you think, about the use of these dimensions that helps a client to find meaning in what at the outset seems to be very justifiable paralysis – what is so powerful about them?

Chloe: The opportunity to authentically reflect and describe the experience the client is having in each existential dimension (without pathologising or expecting explications and explanations) allows the client to nurture and invest in the relational choices s/he is presented with in life. This means that traumatically bereaved clients can emerge in their full and complicated emotional responses and be witnessed by another in such a way that they feel understood, valid and heard in the paralysing nature of their trauma. The ontic response to the ontological disturbance is revealed through the exploration of the four worlds and in this way the nature of what it means for the client to be is understood and embraced. Rather than be corrected, fixed or expected to recover, they can – through their descriptive journey – accept, trust, meet, like and look forward in themselves, in their being in life and in their meaningful relationships. The four-worlds approach allows for the therapeutic alliance, which is in my view the most important therapeutic condition, to be co-constructed by the client and the therapist and allows for existential meaning and promise to be landscaped.

Simon: You argue for an approach to trauma that focuses on its ontological impact rather than ontic responses. In a time where manualisation and evidence-based practice are increasingly promoted, I wonder what you see as the future for your non-pathologising approach to working with trauma. Do you have plans for disseminating it more widely?

Chloe: I am not sure what the future of my approach is. I feel that the mental health professions are preoccupied with the idea of recovery and systems have been developed that de-humanise suffering and despair. In my view, resilience emerges in response to suffering if people feel that their experience of being has been supported, understood and validated. Paying attention only to the ontic response that emerges in behaviours is missing the point. I am not suggesting that the ontic is ignored. Quite the opposite. I propose that the ontic is understood in light of the ontological, so that the essence of the psychological struggle or disturbance is healed. I hope to continue to share my view on this through further writing and presenting my work in workshops and conferences. The suggestion is not to exclude other approaches to trauma but rather to use the existential approach to deepen expansion of the therapeutic work and create long-lasting adaptations in people's lives. I feel that the existential approach works very well with narrative reconstructive therapies that focus on helping traumatised clients develop meaning in their life. I welcome discussions, reflections and further opportunities to share my views on trauma and hope to be able to publish a more detailed book on this in the near future.

References

APA (2013). *Diagnostic and Statistical Manual of Mental Disorders* (5th ed). Washington, DC: American Psychiatric Publishing.

Barnett L (ed) (2009). *When Death Enters the Therapeutic Space. existential perspectives in psychotherapy and counselling*. Hove: Routledge.

Horowitz M (1997). *Stress Response Syndromes* (3rd ed). Northvale, NH: Jason Aronson.

Kauffman J (2002). Safety and the assumptive world – a theory of traumatic loss. In: Kauffman J (ed). *Loss of the Assumptive World: a theory of traumatic loss*. New York, NY: Brunner-Routledge (pp205–212).

Murphy SA, Johnson LC, Wu L, Fan JJ, Lohan J (2003). Bereaved parents' outcomes 4 to 60 months after their children's deaths by accident, suicide, or homicide: a comparative study demonstrating difference. *Death Studies* 27(1): 39–61.

Neimeyer RA (2007). *Meaning Reconstruction and the Experience of Loss*. Washington, DC: American Psychological Press.

Neimeyer RA (2006). Re-storying loss: fostering growth in the posttraumatic narrative. In: Calhoun L, Tedeschi R (eds). *Handbook of Posttraumatic Growth: research and practice*. Manhaw, NJ: Lawrence Erlbaum (pp67–80).

Paidoussis-Mitchell C (2012). The phenomenology of traumatic bereavement. *The International Journal of Existential Analysis* 24(1): 48–56.

Smith Landsman I (2002). Crises of meaning in trauma and loss. In: Kauffman J (eds). *Loss of the Assumptive World: a theory of traumatic loss*. New York, NY: Brunner-Routledge (pp13–31).

Spinelli E (2007). *Practising Existential Psychotherapy: the relational world*. London: Sage.

Spinelli E (2002). *The Interpreted World: an introduction to phenomenological psychology*. London: Sage.

Stolorow R (2007). *Trauma and Human Existence: autobiographical, psychoanalytic and philosophical references*. Abingdon: Routledge.

Stroebe M, Schut H (2007). Meaning-making in the dual process model of coping with bereavement. In: Neimeyer R (eds). *Meaning Reconstruction and the Experience of Loss*. Washington, DC: American Psychological Press (pp55–76).

van Deurzen E (2002). *Existential Counselling and Psychotherapy in Practice*. London: Sage.

van Deurzen E (1988). *Existential Counselling in Practice*. London: Sage.

van Deursen E (1984). Existential therapy. In: Dryden W (ed). *Individual Therapy in Britain*. London: Harper & Row.

van Deurzen E, Kenward R (2005). *Dictionary of Existential Psychotherapy and Counselling*. London: Sage.

19

Two hats: the case study as viewed by the therapist-researcher

Prunella Gee

In this chapter, I present extracts from a case study produced for the purposes of existential-phenomenological psychology research into the impact of retirement on men and reflect on the convergences and divergences between therapy and research. The case is longitudinal, gathered at three time-points: four months before retirement and six and 15 months after retirement, making this a 19-month-long investigation.

As well as presenting data and interpretative analysis, I will comment on the tensions inherent in research carried out for a psychology PhD (which this was) by a psychotherapist (which I am). Qualitative research, generally, poses ethical issues, largely due to the interviewer/participant relationship, which, while by no means a therapeutic one, can inadvertently lead to some degree of therapeutic interaction for the participant. This is why psychotherapists need to pay particular attention to which 'hat' (therapist or researcher) they are wearing, and this can sometimes feel like treading a very fine line. There is a stark reminder of this difficulty in Kvale & Brinkmann (2009: 75):

> With an expression from a therapist-researcher [...], an experienced interviewer's knowledge of how to create rapport and get through a participant's defences may serve as a 'Trojan horse' to get inside areas of a person's life where they were not invited. The use of such indirect techniques, which are ethically legitimate with the mutual interest of

therapeutic relations, become ethically questionable when applied to research.

There is, I suggest, an added difficulty for an existential psychotherapist using a phenomenological-hermeneutical methodology – the dividing veil is all the harder to discern.

But the interviewing process is not the only one to demand caution. Interpretative phenomenological analysis (IPA), which was the methodology I used, encourages what, to a neutral therapist, might feel like extravagant interpretations that depart far from the data before returning with (hopefully) added insight. Despite the full acknowledgement that the interpretation is an aggregation of the participant's and researcher's own world-views, a therapist would probably be right to be hesitant about adopting so interpretative a role. Although the principle of horizontalisation (Spinelli, 2005), where no information is privileged over any other until there is a deep understanding of context, applies equally to both types of exploration, the underlying motivation for doing the work in the first place and what is being sought differ.

The more positive side of this cautionary coin is that the methods used in psychology research may have something to lend to psychotherapy, and perhaps, though to a lesser extent, *vice versa*.

So, I propose three areas of exploration:

1. The presentation of extracts of data and analysis from one case (out of nine) in a longitudinal cross-case study entitled 'The psychological impact of retirement on men', to demonstrate the remarkable symbiosis or 'fit' between later-life issues and the existential lens.

2. An examination of the pitfalls that arise for the researcher/therapist when considering a single case.

3. What insights each journey towards a written case may have to offer the other (therapist and researcher).

I have annotated the case study with bracketed numbers. Afterwards I will comment on each numbered section. However, I suggest that the reader ignores the numbers on initial reading, in order to receive both the case in its simplest form and the notes contextually. (I will also quote the relevant text in the notes, so only those who wish for a wider context need look back).

The case study

Roger (65) had worked for most of his career in the financial sector (investment management) and was shortly to retire voluntarily [1]. I first spoke to him four months before his retirement – he was friendly, open and deeply interested in the process of retirement and what it would mean for him. I am making a point of recording my experience of him here, because I was surprised at times how differently he appeared on paper [2]. While still in work, then, but imminently retiring, this is what he told me:

> ... it's got to the stage now, I think, but nobody's said anything, where I'm slightly to one side... in fact I'm being put a bit in the long grass [...] the people put... ringfence you... well he can't do that because he's going to be 65 next [...] I think you just get parked. You're out of the equation and that's where you are.

Roger's statement contains five powerful images: being 'slightly to one side' (a de-centring, but it's unspoken – 'nobody's said anything' – suggesting a subtle, uncomfortable ostracism); 'put in the long grass' (ageing, useless); 'ringfenced' (a pariah, untouchable); 'parked' (discarded, manhandled and de-humanised), and 'out of the equation' (excluded from the inner circle – but also an 'equation' is made up of a partnership, so the balancing act between him and work is no longer in place). Before he has even left work, sidelining, rejection and invisibility, in his mind, have already begun in force [3]. 'It's got to the stage' suggests inevitability, as if Roger knew all along it would 'come to this'. His use of the definite article before 'people' endows them with a collective identity, a certain facelessness. Above all, there is a distinct lack of agency. Despite his voluntary retirement status, Roger seems powerless.

It is important to remember that this type of research is not sociological – I am not exploring how a person may be treated by others when their retirement date is known and imminent (however interesting a study that may be); I am researching the phenomenological experience of the person retiring. It is perfectly possible that there is simply pragmatism at play when looked at from the point of view of the 'perpetrators': 'He will not be here in four months' time, so we will not give him the work.' For Roger, however, it feels personal, and I note that he uses the phrase 'He can't do that because he's going to be 65' rather than 'because he is retiring' – it is Roger himself who conflates retirement and ageing.

It is interesting to compare his feelings around his current work situation with his description of the medical tests he occasionally undergoes:

> I've got to the stage where people want to do tests on me... and so far without finding anything... you think to yourself am I an experiment bag... you know... how many pins do you want to put in just to get the answer no? Obviously, they do it because I'm showing little symptoms here and there but there's nothing happening. And you think well... come back in six months and it'll still be the same [4].

He again uses the phrase 'got to the stage', suggesting determinate expectations on his part that, provided one lives long enough, 'this is what happens'. 'People want to do tests on me,' he says (one can almost hear him whisper it behind his hand, as the 'mad scientists' eye him up and down) but in reality, these 'people' (again the sinister 'other') are his doctor, and/or those he is referred to for tests. 'Showing little symptoms here and there' could be read as 'I'm ageing', something he equates with becoming 'object', fair game for use as 'an experiment bag'. It is a potent image. An experiment bag and a human being could hardly have less in common: the former object is powerless, responseless and lifeless. It is as if retirement may herald a 'living death' [5]. Perhaps this is a long-held 'sedimented' world-view about Roger's relationship to retirement (which means ageing, which means losing agency, which means becoming 'object'). Is this why 'the people' who are still in work are perceived as holding the power. 'Sedimentation', which has been extensively explored by Spinelli (1989), following Merleau-Ponty (1945/1965), describes a fixity of viewpoint brought about by the way one has experienced, and then continues to experience, the world. The best description of 'sedimentation' I know comes from van Deurzen and Adams (2011: 57): '... it is as if the sediments of the river of life fall to the river floor and give us an increasingly solid but illusory sense of identity...' These sedimentations can just as well apply to expectations inculcated early. To children, the retired are often perceived as ancient beings who serve no purpose, and an ageing stereotype internalised in childhood, reinforced for decades, may become a self-stereotype.

Roger continues:

> ... by going to work I get a pay cheque because I've earned it, and now I'm going to have money coming in that I haven't... earned... I haven't been out gathering... hunting and gathering for it. It's just going to be the fruits of having gone to work [...] it's like oil without machines.

Again, I note the fear of passivity – hunting and gathering is bread-winning, and the bread-winner is the active mover and shaker. The recipient of 'unearned' money becomes 'object' (it is worth noting that this view was idiosyncratic – my other participants perceived their pension as most definitely 'earned'). So Roger, looking for ways to be active and 'subject', tells me he would like to join a choir:

> … but the erm… [fingers tapping] we went to a concert last week and looked at the choir… and I thought… ummm… I'm not sure about that… they said, 'Well come along and see how you feel about it.' You know that's… I'm not wanting to plunge into you know… suddenly playing bowls or snooker or you know, something I haven't done before…

The fingers tap, the ambivalence sets in, he says he does not want to 'plunge in' as if the unknown depths could be cold and dangerous, and then, without warning, he reveals three fears: bowls and snooker (certainly the former tends to be the domain of the retired) and 'something I haven't done before…' We are looking squarely at an issue of identity. Then:

> One thing about work is, even if you're not enjoying it, it keeps you mentally alert and challenged and sometimes I go to a reunion, which I do probably every year, with former colleagues in places that I've worked at in the city. I find that really, really stimulating. Because these guys are sharp and you know I… I could guarantee, if you put us all in a room again, we'd build a fantastic business and it's that sort of erm… edge that I miss, I really do erm… and it's er… I suppose it's what I miss in social life. We haven't got [tapping table] enough people in our group – you know, we can all laugh and joke and have a good time but it's not the sharp – it could be sharp wit, it could be sharp thinking – it could be erm… you know, something that just gets you going – instead of just existing.

In contrast to the pins sticking into the unresponsive experiment bag in imminent and early retirement, sharpness, while fully involved at work, is the very thing that 'gets you going' and, crucially, it is the thing that provides the difference between living and 'just existing'.

I ask how he anticipates being at home with his wife in his new capacity:

> Roger: I will want to be having… my time, in that when I go to the office [in his home] it's my time. So when I'm doing what I want to do… have to

be doing – that's my time and it's not social intercourse and 'let's have a coffee together'. It's definitely I'm doing what I'm doing and I want to be left alone to do what I'm doing [6].

Me: OK. Slightly imitating going off to work.

Roger: Yes. Yes. I can't see myself sitting around in a sitting room, feet in the air, reading a newspaper just to spend the time of day, I mean I just can't see that. You know we're not just going to sit in a room.

Is this Roger's feared image of 'just existing'? Is this the living death? When asked about his interests and plans for retirement, he says:

You know… I'm not yet ready to read things about old people […] I mean you could actually bury yourself in silver surfing and I don't want to do that. It's not that I don't want to be associated with it… it's just that… I don't need to.

At this point, it is impossible to miss the implication of the word 'bury', which hardly needs me to make an interpretation. Retirement, whatever the modern rhetoric, does, it seems, often act as a marker that brings awareness of one's own extinction into much sharper focus. But there are other interpretations. Is Roger anxious about 'burying' his familiar identity under a shuffling new one, indeed 'hiding his light under a bushel'? And might he, in clinging to his worker identity, be stifling the emergence of new (or added) identities that may in turn give rise to meaning and purpose?

I arrived for the second interview, six months after Roger had retired, ready to mark the changes – the mellowing, the joy, the dramatic revelations, the disillusion, or whatever might come to meet me. Was I surprised that I was hearing much the same rhetoric? Partly yes (because time had passed and circumstances were different) and partly no (because I had developed a keen sense that Roger's attitude was not so much situational as sedimented and based on fears of the future that had not yet had a chance to be identified and processed).

At time 2, therefore, one might be forgiven for thinking we were still engaged in our conversation of 10 months ago.

Roger: The whole retirement thing is something that seems to be thrust on people rather than you just move into it… and say now I'm ret…

people tell you you're retired, people tell you your retirement age, people tell you you're going to have a bus pass, people tell you you're going to have a senior rail card [...] it's society telling you you're past your best.

Me: Is that what it feels like?

Roger: Well that's what [little laugh]... yeah.

Me: Would there be another way of looking at it?

Roger: Such as?

Me: Er... society telling you you've earned a rest...

Roger: A big thank you [laughing]?!!! Thank you for what you've done, we'll give you this.

Me: Yeah.

Roger: Well I suppose you could [laughter].

The 'they' have another face now – it is 'society' who are the culprits – 'telling you you're past your best' and 'they tell you your retirement age'. There is a sense of returning to childhood (or fear of entering a second one) where everybody else either 'tells you' or 'speaks for you'.

At time 3 however, there is a subtle but notable difference emerging:

There's a sort of... what's the word... inability to think that one can actually make a difference any more... You think... well my opinion doesn't really matter [...] the opinion formers are all 20 years younger...

Although he is speaking now from the experience of 15 months of retirement, and the overall expression of powerlessness is similar, there is a telling change. He begins with the impersonal: 'There's a sort of... what's the word... inability to think that one can actually make a difference any more...,' and although the subject ('there's a') is neutral (ie. not 'owned', which would be represented as 'I don't seem to be able to make a difference any more'), and although he uses 'one' and 'you', both distancing techniques, there are finally the words 'inability to think', which grammatically can only refer to him. He also says 'You think' before stating that his opinion doesn't matter, instead of making a bald statement that would suggest that 'others think'. There's just the smallest hint that, if his opinions don't matter anymore, that idea may lie within. I am not suggesting that there is no sidelining, or that there are not opinion formers who do not value his input, but that the feeling is his, and therefore there is, potentially, a narrative that could be changed; the perception that this is 'how it must always be' is challengeable.

Another change that occurs at time 3 is that Roger begins, as it were, to 'speak his own subtext'. This, I believe, is evidence that he is coming to terms with retirement (or is it ageing?) and is no longer afraid to name what troubles him:

> … certainly I feel that I stopped work at a time when I could still have made a contribution.

The words can simply be translated as 'I hadn't finished, my working life was incomplete'. They also suggest that, for Roger, the ability to 'contribute' is the domain of both the younger and the working person. When I ask what retirement now means for him, he replies:

> … not going to paid employment, that's it… a working chapter now closed. I'm now on the next chapter which is 'Not working' and whatever happens, happens…

It is significant that, although retirement is 'the next chapter', the title of which might be 'A new beginning', 'Different strokes', 'Starting again' or some such positive, it is here expressed as a negative, an absence (and, I can't help observing, a compelling *double entendre*) – 'not working', making work the subject and retirement the object. At time 2, while commenting on the fact that retirement means you can travel during working hours, he offers:

> I might catch a train mid-week… to go to London or… you know… just to… catch a train… and you are travelling with people like you, so you look around and you think… hang on, I'm one of these… we're all spending time that… our time… to go places and do things… erm… and er… yes…

He describes himself among other retirees, in the throes of a slowly dawning realisation that 'you are travelling with people like you' – note the use of the third person 'you', the distancing, the caution; 'so you look around and you think…' shock-horror to the point where he cannot keep up the distancing: 'I'm one of these…' The 'these' suggests an alien species from which he recoils – and that they are using up time somewhat aimlessly, and that, because he's on the train with them and looks like them, he cannot escape the fact that he is behaving exactly as they are, 'spending time' but going... where? This could be a scene from a Bergman film, shot in black and white, impassive pale faces passing mysteriously by into the unknown. Put like that, there are echoes of ageing and closer proximity to death. So, from a reluctant identification as 'one of these', we reach the inevitable distancing:

> I see them all around me... I was sitting in a car park at the station and I saw people driving around and I thought: 'You look retired... you look old enough to be retired'... and this is the time of day when they all come out... that's when they're around and then they go home and disappear...

They 'come out' at a certain time of day and then 'go home and disappear', but now they are 'all around' him. At time 3 he has most definitely distanced himself from 'the retired' – he is enclosed in a car, peering unseen at 'the creatures' through glass, and they are 'driving around' as he studies them: 'You look retired... you look old enough to be retired.' We have a sense that they are absolutely nothing to do with him – he has projected retirement away – he is no part of 'them' (the 'they'). They are the un-dead (the living dead) – zombies driving around in their little machines, expressionless, who come out at a certain time of the day, 'just existing', soulless shells, disembodied, disconnected, ghostly beings – they make manifest the lack of stimulation he feared would be the case.

We may here remember Roger's words:

> One thing about work is, even if you're not enjoying it, it keeps you mentally alert and challenged [...] I find that really, really stimulating [...] these guys are sharp [...] it's that... edge that I miss – it could be sharp wit, it could be sharp thinking – it could be erm... you know something that just gets you going – instead of just existing.

At time 3 we see the tangible results of Roger's 19 months of processing:

> There is an awareness which is probably greater now than before that there is a limited time left... we are both fit, we both walk, we both enjoy doing anything we want to, but we don't know how long that's going to remain, so we really do want to make the most of it while we can [7].

The existential fit

Yalom's (1980) organisation of existentialism around 'the four ultimate concerns' – death, freedom, isolation, and meaninglessness – and van Deurzen-Smith's (1984) endowment of dimensions of existence – the physical, social, psychological and spiritual – as a further means of interrogating data, have proved not only indispensable but unavoidable in my retirement explorations. I have here provided only a glimpse of Roger's retirement experience, but identity questions such as 'Who am I now?', 'Who am I going to be?', 'Where do I fit?', 'How long have I got?' and 'What am I for?' become ultimate concerns when: a) a marker that points to one's own ageing and mortality is drawn; b) a provided structure is removed and one is 'condemned to be free' (Sartre, 1943/1958); c) belonging is no longer guaranteed (awareness of existential isolation), and d) the very purpose of existence is called into question. Retirement, however, can provide some of the greatest opportunities for taking existential responsibility (for authenticity); indeed, Maglio and colleagues (2005) refer to employment as a 'dyadic dilemma' that renounces freedom for security.

And what of the identity of ageing? With our Western tendency to avoid the subject of death, David Ekerdt (2010), one of the foremost and most prolific American retirement researchers and *not* an existential researcher, has noted the 'existential discomfort' that underlies many retirement research findings. Gilleard and Higgs (2007) see this, he says, as 'third-agers fending off the fourth age, resisting any identity as old or elderly', and he adds: 'Perhaps the brevity of lifetime is at the heart of it' (p78). So, it may well follow that people will not see retirement as a comfortable way to be defined, even if they enjoy the retirement lifestyle (Teuscher, 2010) – an easily overlooked distinction.

A study of retirement serves another purpose too – it shows us human life, *all* human life, without many of the props that mask the underlying realities of existence. Ekerdt even asserts that 'retirement is no longer a concern solely for the second half of life… the earliest reaches of adulthood are being colonized by frequent reminders that it takes individual effort to achieve retirement' (2004: 3). He also tells us retirement evolved because it has two main functions: the first is societal – to manage succession within social groups – and the second is to fulfil the individual's inclination to withdraw from labour and responsibility in later life, although he adds: 'It is less clear whether this is a developmental need or a response to cultural suggestion' and he reminds us that 'every cohort retires in the context of its times' (2010: 69).

The above paragraph gives some indication of the aforementioned tensions between the psychology and the psychotherapy 'hats'. Psychology is, on the whole, ultimately looking for some generalisability (it is true that very small-sample qualitative research will only be contributory to existing research when there are enough studies to suggest the results can be generalised), but psychotherapy stays with the particular. The two are not contradictory of course – Goethe (quoted in Hermans, 1988: 785) said: 'The particular eternally underlies the general: the general eternally has to comply with the particular', and it does appear that the deeper we dig into the depths of consciousness, the more alike human beings become. The data I provided above formed part of my completed PhD not simply in their own right but because they reflected those of other participants in cross-case comparison and were therefore considered, if not 'significant' in a quantitative technical sense, at least 'of significant interest'. So how can researchers and therapists remain true to their cause while both struggle to remain 'experience-close'?

Who could learn what from whom?

I will turn now to the numbers I have inserted throughout the chapter, to ask the researcher, the therapist and the researcher-who-happens-to-be-therapist, 'Who could learn what from whom?'

1. Voluntary retirement?

'Roger (65) had worked for most of his career in the financial sector (investment management) and was shortly to retire voluntarily.'

The first thing I would like to draw specific attention to is Roger's official retirement status: voluntary. And yet, listening to him, one could be forgiven for thinking he was being made redundant. I learned from all my participants how important it was not to make assumptions based on retirement status – 'voluntary' and 'agency' do not necessarily go together. Even as the process (in pre-retirement) began, Roger experienced abandonment and lack of agency. The questions that arise for a researcher are probably those such as, 'What does it feel like?', 'What is causing this?', 'How is this being processed?' A therapist is likely to begin with the same questions but want to take them further: 'Does this feeling remind the client of other events in their life?'; 'Is it familiar?' They would probably want to take time to explore family and friendship dynamics and the client's relationship with responsibility and agency. In three meetings over 19 months, such things can be touched on but there is a danger that, if the researcher/therapist is alerted to their participant's 'ways-of-being-in-the-world' they may be too quick to make assumptions; they will need to exercise caution: 1) not to probe where not invited; 2) to be aware of their own fore-understandings (Heidegger, 1962) so as not to over-identify; 3) to remember that they will not be able to follow up openings, and 4) to remain mindful that the participant is giving them a gift without asking for anything in return, and that no money has changed hands. This is neither a professional relationship nor a friendship.

These are subjects too big for this exploration, but the saliency is that the *relationship itself* between researcher and participant and between therapist and client are hugely different. Just as the therapist/researcher has difficulty stepping back from assumptions that cannot be checked out and contextualised satisfactorily, conversely, the therapist lacks the gift of the written transcript, the luxury of long contemplation over specific and revealing grammatical constructions, and the freedom to indulge in extravagant experimental interpretations, and therefore might be slower to notice what is right in front of them. Then there is the big question for therapists: how much is change being sought (or desired), how much is integration and acceptance the goal, or is one simply accompanying someone on their journey of self-exploration? The researcher is not seeking change – though I came close when I asked: 'Would there be another way of looking at it (retirement)?' This is a borderline example that is probably legitimate in this case, simply to widen the enquiry, but in a more emotional context it might open up unexpected new insights for the participant, who will have nowhere to take them. It is, of course, important to acknowledge that the encounter itself, any encounter, will bring about change for both parties.

For a researcher there is an added complication – that of whether one is a descriptive phenomenologist (after Husserl) or whether one is an interpretative phenomenologist (after Heidegger). If the former, it is perfectly possible to engage one's participant as a 'co-researcher' and take the transcribed data back to them to see if they feel accurately represented. That way an ongoing relationship can be formed, depending on the time, effort and intimacy both parties are prepared to put into the endeavour. If, however, the researcher is using interpretative phenomenological analysis, my experience is that it would be undesirable to return to the participant as they may well not recognise themselves and may take offence that you have strayed so far from their data in order to seek a deeper truth. This is a profound ethical question and cannot be explored here. However, it is one of the disadvantages an interpreter has over both a describer and a therapist, the latter being able to interpret over months or years in conjunction with their clients. The therapist/researcher has further questions to ask themselves here: should they attempt to restrict interpretation to analysis and resist interpreting while interviewing, and is such a thing even possible?

2. Advantages and disadvantages of a written transcript

'I was surprised at times how differently he appeared on paper.'

One obvious advantage of verbatim written research over a fleeting, verbal, 50-minute therapy session is that one can peruse the words, the pronoun use, the grammatical patterns, the hesitations, the slips of the tongue. Separated from their owners, these can produce an almost alchemical effect. A researcher studying transcripts in depth and at leisure will remember the participant's voice, face, body language and 'essence', and these are all essential clues to what is being experienced. However, they can be misleading – the isolated *written* words can seriously contradict the body language of the smiling, friendly, helpful person in front of one. Do therapists ever suggest they record a session and discuss the transcription with a client?

3. Collapsing time

'Before he has even left work, side-lining, rejection and invisibility, in his mind, have already begun in force.'

Yalom has reminded us that we are always going somewhere:

> The 'not yet' influences our behaviour in many formidable ways. Within one, at both conscious and unconscious levels, there is a sense of purpose, an idealized self, a series of goals for which one strives, an awareness of destiny and ultimate death. (1980: 364)

But, just as we are always going somewhere, so we also come from somewhere. Because I am able to compare on paper the different time points along the longitudinal spectrum, I am able to see that the months before retirement have coloured the retirement experience itself – an example of existential collapsing time, as Merleau-Ponty pointed out (1945/1965): 'The present still holds onto the immediate past without positing it as an object' (in other words, the past is not separate, it is part of the current experience). With my therapist 'hat' on, the collapsed past, present and future of the client will be in the room but may be easier to miss than when words have been inscribed on paper. I refer, of course, not only to the ability to read those words on the page but also to the whole process: the interview itself; listening to the recording; struggling to decipher phrases; the long, laborious but absorbing effort of transcription (best done, I believe, by researchers themselves); the musing on the results, and the creativity of the analytic interpretative process.

4. Interrogation of the literature

'I've got to the stage where people want to do tests on me...'

Interrogation of the extant literature is a necessary and central element of research. Here is an example. Teuscher (2010) looked at how the self-image of the retired differs from that of the working population, and how people's self-definition as professionals or retirees is predicted. As part of that exploration, she gave us two distinct characterisations of old age that are called upon to form a self-concept: 1) a pre-industrial one (Borscheid, 1994), in which old age was seen as an escalation of frailty and as being near to death (the 'biological' version), where only those whose mental and physical strength had diminished were viewed as old; 2) a 'socio-political concept', where the onset of old age is defined by the receipt of a pension.

The latter was corroborated in studies where people were asked to say when they thought 'being old' began. Babladelis (1978) was informed by his participants that it was around 60; Harris, Page and Begay (1988) were given 65–69, which both corresponded with workforce exit, not frailty or mental decline, thus mirroring a socio-political rather than biological definition. Teuscher also found that retirees with a more positive attitude to older age rated their status of being retired as more important as a characterisation than respondents with a more negative attitude. This throws plenty of light on Roger's standpoint and therefore experience, and it might be helpful to therapists to borrow more frequently than they do from research in order to distinguish between individual experience and cultural suggestion. For instance, Teuscher's (2010) research also finds that individuals are conscious of the value of their own social group in comparison with others. Michinov, Fouquereau and Fernandez (2008) add that identification with social groups serves to meet individual needs, including the needs for self-enhancement, affiliation and a sense of identity – but, at that point at least, Roger did not appear to wish to identify with a group called 'the retired'.

5. Using imagery

'An experiment bag and a human being could hardly have less in common: the former object is powerless, response-less and lifeless. It is as if retirement may herald a "living death".'

Imagery is a tool shared by both psychological researcher and therapist – for the therapist, the emergence of an image (such as the 'experiment bag') can be a rich source of information and much can flow from it if they care to follow up in the moment (they may also jot it down for later discussion). It is, of course, perfectly legitimate for the researcher/therapist, who is probably 'itching' to follow up, to do so but, again, they must be aware of where it may lead and what the participant may be left with. For instance, if I had asked Roger what an 'experiment bag' meant for him, it might have confronted him with his own unconscious fears and, again, left him with nowhere to process this new understanding.

I confess to not having been aware of the 'zombie' imagery until I saw it on paper. What, after interpretation, takes on a sinister, other-worldly quality might have been delivered in the most mundane way. Certainly, I did not feel it appropriate to go back to Roger after my analysis and open up talk of the un-dead. (Even in therapy, I would wait until I had built a solid trust with my client.) It was, however, useful for me to spend time exploring these data, comparing them with those from other participants who described themselves as ghosts in early retirement, and consulting informative literature. For instance, the philosopher David Chalmers (1996) has identified the 'Hollywood zombie' (reanimated, flesh-eating corpses), the 'Haitian zombie' (living people deprived of soul and free will) and 'philosophical zombies' (they look like humans, but lack consciousness). In a paper entitled 'Some kind of virus: the zombie as body and as trope', Webb and Byrnand give us the following:

> Because the idea of the zombie travels so widely, and across so many fields, it has become a very familiar character, one that participates in narratives of the body, of life and death, of good and evil; one that gestures to alterity […] species-ism, the inescapable, the immutable. Thus, it takes us to 'the other side' – alienation, death, and what is worse than death: the state of being undead. (2008: 83)

It is perhaps ironic that writers and filmmakers from HG Wells, Fritz Laing and Charlie Chaplin to Edgar Wright (*Shaun of the Dead*), have used zombification to represent the exploitation of low-wage labour and people who do dull or undesirable jobs that require only machine-like skills. In Roger's world, it is the worker who is seen as alive, and the 'role-less' retired are the zombies. We might ask ourselves how this came about.

Taking a phenomenological viewpoint on what he calls 'corporealized and disembodied minds', Fuchs (2005) speaks of the 'as' structure of the body as an effective means of expression and communication, where there is 'an implicit resonance between [others'] expressions and our own bodily and emotional reactions' (p98). In 'intersubjective perception', the body acquires the capacity to put itself virtually in the place of another body and to transpose the perceived actions into its own motor schema. In light of Fuch's potent quotation, we can recognise Roger's fascinated gaze fixed on his mirroring ghouls (becoming almost ghoul-like himself in the process). Merleau-Ponty (1945/1965) referred to this 'noninferential process of empathic perception' as a 'transfer of the corporeal schema', which he attributed to a primordial sphere of 'intercorporeality'. Here, of course, I am referring to such data as Roger's comment: 'I see them all around me [...] I saw people driving around and I thought: "You look retired... you look old enough to be retired"... and this is the time of day when they all come out... that's when they're around and then they go home and disappear...' Because there is an 'intercorporeal empathic perception' occurring for Roger, he fights heroically to attribute this unwanted 'zombie-like half-life' to the disdained other and not to himself.

6. The spatial and the temporal

'I will want to be having... my time, in that when I go to the office [in his home], it's my time.'

Roger is preparing to have boundaries in retirement (going off to his home office and guarding *his* space and *his* time – his physical and temporal world) that will denote serious business, and we are reminded that there was a 'mine-ness', an ownership of his time, provided by the workplace. This mineness can sometimes be threatened by marriage or cohabitation, and work can act as the antidote. 'Mine-ness' is a Heideggerian concept that describes the subjective awareness that it is 'me' who looks, feels and interprets – nobody else – so the object or matter of concern is partly made up of 'me'. This is why the researcher in this field needs to look at the whole person. Existential-phenomenological therapists and researchers alike will probably know their Heidegger, so this is something shared, but the researcher is *writing* about it, so keeps in mind that Heidegger's structure of *Dasein* is an aid to insight.

7. How much do both participant and client 'get there on their own?'

'There is an awareness which is probably greater now than before that there is a

limited time left… we are both fit, we both walk, we both enjoy doing anything we want to, but we don't know how long that's going to remain, so we really do want to make the most of it while we can.'

Researchers do not have to ask themselves my question above, because there is nothing sought in terms of insight, growth, acceptance or change from or for the participant. But it is clear that Roger's journey through 19 months of pre- and post-retirement, at whatever trajectory and however subtly, demonstrates all of the latter. Loosely, he experiences, refuses ownership, blames, rails, softens, acknowledges and takes responsibility (much the same journey that therapists may witness in their clients). The assumption must be that this is a result of both talking about his experience and the passage of time. Roger's central fear, that retirement will mean he is not truly living but just existing, that he will be object rather than subject and that the *'they'* will dictate from a position of power, is both the driver of other themes and the result of a sense of missing agency. Stimulation appears unattainable, partly due to his resistance to the retirement image, which is conflated with ageing and thereby 'rules out' certain social retirement activities that might have provided motivation. When he does acknowledge he is on 'the next chapter', he titles it 'Not working'.

I wonder how much time therapy supervisors spend reminding (or reassuring) therapists feeling 'stuck' with clients that they do not have to *do* anything except, having laid the existential ground, stay close, listen, reflect, ask and wait. To 'be with'/accompany a person on their exploration and notice what it is in their worldview(s) that may trip them up and make life uncomfortable, what they might come to recognise as inauthentic (whether any givens of existence are being denied), where responsibility is being avoided and where the possibility of choice goes unrecognised, is largely their task. One encouragement that Roger's researched experience may have to offer therapists is how much he wittingly or unwittingly did his own work to transcend his fears and his ambivalence, as illustrated by his time 3 statement: 'There is an awareness which is probably greater now than before that there is a limited time left […] so we really do want to make the most of it while we can.' Heidegger thought that in the midst of life we are in death and that, without this great motivator, it is impossible to live life to the full. Retirement would appear to be the provider of a golden opportunity to live, rather than to 'just exist'.

Discussion with the editor

Simon: It is often said that therapeutic practice constitutes a form of research – when we meet with clients we, effectively, become co-researchers with them of their worlds. Reading your chapter, I was interested to see the ways in which your research is both similar to and distinct from the approaches adopted by other contributors to this book. With regard to similarities, I think your approach to interrogating the literature, using imagery and paying attention to the spatial and temporal, all look like clinical 'best practice'. When I supervise, I encourage supervisees to 'play' with imagery, and practice that is not informed by research literature is, I think, questionable and even unethical. I wondered if, when you say, 'the methods used in psychology research may have something to lend to psychotherapy, and perhaps, though to a lesser extent, *vice versa*', this is what you have in mind?

Prue: I suspect you have brought to my attention something I had not thought of. I was making the assumption that researchers make more use of extant research literature than do therapists, and certainly your question has made me wonder how much I myself use literature when wearing my therapist hat – I think probably not enough, as I struggle to find time to keep notes and book appointments. On second thoughts, I think there are two levels of 'using the literature' in practice – one is the unconscious use of accumulated knowledge from prior reading and absorption of the literature; the other is the conscious seeking out of material when specific issues arise. I was suggesting that my researcher side finds the latter comes more naturally and my therapist side could probably learn from that. As for imagery, as I said in the chapter, it is so much easier to work with imagery when it is a central strand of your methodology, when it is to be found on paper and time can be spent on it after sessions. So yes, that's why I was suggesting that psychotherapy may have 'less' to lend to psychology in both these instances. I like your reflection that therapeutic practice constitutes a form of research – yes… of course. I think, because I am presenting part of what has been a long, recent and all-consuming project, I may have underplayed that aspect. Perhaps there is room for a considered piece solely looking at what psychotherapy can teach research. It would be interesting.

Simon: I found myself resonating strongly with you when you 'wonder how much time therapy supervisors spend reminding (or reassuring) therapists feeling "stuck" with clients that they do not have to *do* anything except, having laid the existential ground, stay close, listen, reflect, ask and wait. To "be with"/ accompany a person on their exploration and notice what it is in their world-view(s) that may trip them up and make life uncomfortable, what they might come to recognise as inauthentic (whether any givens of existence are being denied), where responsibility is being avoided and where the possibility of choice goes unrecognised, is largely their task.' To a very large extent, I think this sums up the role of the existential-phenomenological therapist, and in my work as a supervisor I tend to think of this as the foundation upon which clinical practice is built.

You go on to say, 'One encouragement that Roger's researched experience may have to offer therapists is how much he wittingly or unwittingly did his own work to transcend his fears and his ambivalence...' I, in my turn, wonder about this 'researched experience': do you think there was a Hawthorne effect (Wickstrom & Bendix 2000) at work here – did Roger find participating in the research therapeutic?

Prue: I'm not sure I know the answer, particularly because there was no follow-up. However, I can only imagine that, one way or another, being a research participant is profound and will produce many effects. There is also the dynamic between researcher and researched to consider. For instance, I wrote in the reflective section of my PhD: 'I am a woman interviewing men – there is, I believe, an inevitable tension here – many men are more comfortable confiding in a woman but may wish to please in a way they would not trouble to do with a man, raising potential issues around the data collected. This had obvious up-sides – they worked hard to provide full stories, they wanted to share emotions as well as facts because they picked up that this was what I "wanted". The down-side was that sometimes I had the impression they might be "over-egging the pudding". I do hope I haven't opened up a whole new subject here! For whatever reason, time or dialogue, Roger did appear, over the 19 months, to move into a more comfortable relationship with his new self, without therapy.

Simon: I spend a lot of my time facilitating experienced and fully-qualified therapists to undertake practice-based research. One of the things I tell them at the outset of their research journey is that they can expect to feel challenged and nurtured, both personally and professionally, by the process. How has the experience of undertaking this research impacted, however subtly, on your sense of yourself as a clinician or led you to change how you work with clients?

Prue: Oh, that's a good question! At the outset let me say that I have absolutely no doubt that, as a direct result of doing this PhD (and remember, it was in psychology, not psychotherapy), I have become a much better therapist. But this could be for so many reasons: 1) by establishing that the existential approach is no longer an optional extra but an underlying world view that informs everything I do, whether I am consciously thinking about it or not – I did not train as an existential therapist, but the use of IPA and its in-depth exploration of phenomenology, which resonates so completely with me, has 'settled that question'; 2) by becoming increasingly aware of the influence I (reluctantly, usually) have as a 'professional' (therapist hat) and the 'expert' (researcher hat), and, although I think I occasionally work w*ith* this awareness of influence in therapy, more often I try to resist it; 3) because my research experience has made me more conscious of people's vulnerability – my participants were innocents (in terms of therapeutic exchange), willing to share some secrets with me for nothing in return – I felt an enormous responsibility to be gentle and tactful at all times, and that has spilled over into my practice, and even when (or *especially* when) challenges are necessary, I am more aware of fragility. For myself, I feel privileged to be entrusted with the job of passing on experience (researcher) and being present as that experience is being processed (therapist) and the ongoing journey must be to avoid unwittingly abusing that privilege in either case.

References

Babladelis G (1978). Sex-role concepts and flexibility on measures of thinking, feeling, and behaving. *Psychological Reports* 42(1): 99–105.

Borscheid P (1994). Der alte mensch in der vegangenheit [The old person in the past]. In: Baltes P, Mittlestrauß J, Staudinger U (eds). *Alter und Altern: ein interdisziplinärer studientext [Age and Ageing: an interdisciplinary reading]*. Berlin: de Gruyter (pp35–61).

Chalmers DJ (1996). *The Conscious Mind: in search of a fundamental theory*. New York, NY: Oxford University Press.

Ekerdt DJ (2010). Frontiers of research on work and retirement. *Journal of Gerontology: Social Sciences* 65B(1): 69–80.

Ekerdt DJ (2004). Born to retire: the foreshortened life course. *The Gerontologist* 44(1): 3–9.

Fuchs T (2005). Corporealized and disembodied minds: a phenomenological view of the body in melancholia and schizophrenia. *Philosophy, Psychiatry, & Psychology* 12(2): 95–107.

Gilleard C, Higgs P (2007). The third age and the baby boomers. *International Journal of Ageing and Later Life* 2(2): 13–30.

Harris MB, Page P, Begay C (1988). Attitudes toward aging in a Southwestern sample: effects of ethnicity, age, and sex. *Psychological Reports* 62(3): 735–746.

Heidegger M (1962). *Being and Time* (J Macquarrie, E Robinson trans). New York, NY: Harper.

Hermans HJM (1988). On the integration of nomothetic and idiographic research methods in the study of personal meaning. *Journal of Personality* 56(4): 785–812.

Kvale S, Brinkmann S (2009). *Learning the Craft of Qualitative Research Interviewing.* Thousand Oaks, CA: Sage Publications.

Maglio AT, Butterfield LD, Borgen WA (2005). Existential considerations for contemporary career counseling. *Journal of Employment Counseling* 42(2): 75-92.

Merleau-Ponty M (1945/1965). *Phenomenology of Perception.* (C Smith trans). London: Routledge & Kegan Paul.

Michinov E, Fouquereau E, Fernandez A (2008). Retirees' social identity and satisfaction with retirement. *The International Journal of Aging & Human Development* 66(3): 175-194.

Sartre J-P (1943/1958). *Being and Nothingness.* London: Methuen & Co.

Spinelli E (2005). *The Interpreted World: an introduction to phenomenological psychology* (2nd ed). London: Sage.

Spinelli E (1989). *The Interpreted World: an introduction to phenomenological psychology.* London: Sage.

Teuscher U (2010). Change and persistence of personal identities after the transition to retirement. *The International Journal of Aging & Human Development* 70(1): 89-106.

van Deurzen E, Adams M (2011). *Skills in Existential Counselling & Psychotherapy.* London: Sage.

van Deurzen-Smith E (1984). *Existential Therapy: individual therapy in Britain.* London: Harper & Row.

Webb J, Byrnand S (2008). Some kind of virus: the zombie as body and as trope. *Body & Society* 14(2): 83-98.

Wickstrom G, Bendix T (2000). The 'Hawthorne effect' – what did the original Hawthorne studies actually show? *Scandinavian Journal of Work, Environment & Health* 26(4): 363-367.

Yalom ID (1980). *Existential Psychotherapy* (vol 1). New York, NY: Basic Books.

20

Living towards death in a technologically mediated existence

Elaine Kasket

> Death whirs continuously beneath the membrane of life.
> (Yalom, 1980: 29)

Of all sentient beings on earth, only we humans are capable of recognising and contemplating our eventual deaths. Unlike creatures that may witness and understand the death of others but not grasp that it will also be their fate, we connect the loss of loved ones to our own finitude, and our feelings of grief are intertwined with deep anxiety about our own mortality. Yalom refers to the 'primordial' quality of our fears about death (Yalom, 1980: 29), and this is not surprising, for what else in human existence is so inexorable, so certain, so inescapable? What is more difficult to imagine than the snuffing out of our life, the erasure of the physical and mental self? What is harder to accept than the fact that we cannot stop its happening? Little wonder that '*Dasein*... flee[s] in the face of it' (Heidegger, 1962: 295).

Existential philosophers have hypothesised many ways in which *Dasein* dodges awareness of its death (see Cooper & Adams, 2005). We find solace in religion, imagining an afterlife where we will be happily reunited with loved ones and live on in a different way. We reassure ourselves that we look after ourselves well, or that we are young, death is unlikely to happen for ages; we say, we don't have to worry about that yet. Reading a newspaper article that says we are more likely to be crushed by falling furniture than killed in a terrorist attack, we take comfort that our bookshelves are tethered to the wall. We strive to make our marks on the world, attaching our names to buildings, books, streets and companies, or producing children who will carry forward our genetic legacies and visit our graves. We drink or drug or otherwise numb ourselves to forget the inevitable. We hold death beyond the threshold of our awareness by staying busily distracted, planning the next holiday, binge-watching television programmes, having dinner with friends. Finally – and critically, for the purposes of this chapter – we seek out 'ultimate rescuers' that will help us escape death. Yalom (1980) listed God, parents, therapists and doctors as ultimate rescuers, but there is another, one that is increasingly involved in our experience of death: technology.

The time in which we now live is often referred to as the 'digital age' and I would argue that it is the most significant transformative event for the human race since the invention of the printing press and, before that, the emergence of language. Writing in the 1970s, Heidegger said that 'the peak of [the] abolition of every possibility of remoteness is reached by television, which will soon pervade and dominate the whole machinery of communication' (1971: 163). He was wrong about the peak having been reached, of course. Social networking sites now dominate that machinery, particularly Facebook, which, with over a billion regular users, is now the primary means of technologically mediated communication.

Cyberspace in general and social networking sites in particular have opened up new possibilities for us to be with one another in a digital world, in which there is 'a cellphone in every pocket, a computer in every backpack, and big information technology systems in back offices everywhere' (Mayer-Schönberger & Cukier, 2013: 4). Multifunctional web-connected devices allow us to capture, store, retain and access words, images and other aspects of self-representation on an unimaginably massive scale, via smartphones, tablets, laptops, watches, fitness monitors, video cameras on bicycle helmets and computers attached to eyeglasses. Descartes' duality of being has shifted to a triumvirate: *res cogitans* (being of mind), *res extensa* (being of body) and *res digitalis* (digital being) (Kim, 2001). Using technology to stay alive is hardly new, but historically those strategies were focused on the physical body: pharmaceuticals, surgery, seatbelts, air bags, bullet-proof vests, vitamins, healthy food, exercise. With the extension into digital being, we have perhaps found new ways to try to cheat death. Victor Mayer-Schönberger, a professor at the Oxford Internet Institute, argues that 'digital memory offers us a strategy of continuity and preservation to transcend our individual mortality. By using digital memory… we live on' (2011; 91).

The interface between humans, digital-age technologies and death is a strangely paradoxical one. Looking at a bus full of people immersed in their phones, one could call this a 'state of forgetfulness of being, [in which] one lives in the world of things and immerses oneself in the everyday diversions of life: … "levelled down", absorbed in "idle chatter", lost in the "they"' (Yalom, 1980: 30–31). This automatic, almost compulsive activity could be seen as Heidegger saw it, as a way of defending against death (Cooper & Adams, 2005), one version of the 'tranquillization, which forces *Dasein* away from [awareness of] its death' (Heidegger, 1962: 298) If Heidegger was correct that being ceaselessly preoccupied and active is an effective way of evading consciousness of one's mortality, then the millions of people glued to their devices would be less anxious about death than their analogue-age forebears.

On the other hand, awareness of death and mortality can be brought far nearer via all this voluminous, readily accessible data. In 2015, a terrorist attack targeted ordinary people of Paris who were going about their normal lives. Because modern technology has ensured that nearly every phone has a video camera, there was horrific and moving footage of the Bataclan theatre, of the back alley into which people attempted to make their escape and the restaurant where others were killed. Because information is now beamed instantaneously across the globe, these images rapidly became available to us at the flick of our fingertips. We saw photos of victims, followed connections to their social media profiles, witnessed the grief of their loved ones on videos, recognised ourselves in their lives – by extension, we could vividly imagine that their deaths could have been ours. We were forced to confront reminders that death can strike at any instant, and that it happens to people very much like us. The very things that can serve to fascinate and distract us – the internet and the devices through which we access it – can throw mortality in our faces.

Social networking itself, however, offers an even more striking paradox. Applications like Facebook and other social networking sites are a primary modern nexus of Heidegger's 'fascination', an immediate way to immerse ourselves in everydayness and to be distracted from whatever uncomfortable awarenesses might be lurking at the edges of our consciousness. They can be viewed as the very essence of idle chatter. On the other hand, as we post on Facebook or Twitter or anywhere else on the internet, we are building our 'digital legacies', and these are substantive phenomena. Profiles on Facebook are not just scattered detritus of one's life but can be coherent representations of being-with-others-in-the-world: complex, ever-evolving correlates of your physical existence. Facebook has explicitly positioned itself in its marketing as the site of your 'autobiography', and after you are dead, this remains as a posthumously persistent representation of who you were.

At no time does this fact become more evident than when people on your friends list die. The 'whirring of death beneath the fabric of life' (Yalom, 1980: 29) increasingly thrums throughout Facebook; because of its popularity and the fact that profiles may be retained when a person has died, it has been estimated that, by 2060, there will be more dead than live people on the site. In 2015, a feature enabling users to request profile removal on death was added to Facebook settings; if these preferences are left unstated, however, only a next of kin can successfully petition the site to remove a profile posthumously. As the statistics currently stand, if Facebook were a country, it would be the world's third largest. Actual, physical countries have designated spaces for the living and the dead; the dead and their memorials reside in pockets of land, in places one must deliberately choose to visit. Facebook is not like that. Instead, it is like a country where memorials to the dead are scattered through the streets where the living walk. What does it mean for our relationship with death now that such a phenomenon exists?

This chapter will look at these questions within the context of my therapy with a recently bereaved 21-year-old woman. It shows how profoundly this client's experience of death – and life – was affected by her socially networked existence. The themes that arose in my work with her are ones that I am increasingly encountering in the consulting room, and I suspect that this is the case for many readers. I hope to illustrate through this case that my being knowledgeable about these phenomena greatly enhanced my ability to work well with this client, and to convey that, in today's world, practitioners must be able to work with the existential implications of modern technologies. First, though, I want to mention something about how research has informed my practice.

Informing practice and theory through research

Very soon after Facebook became available to the general public in 2006, I came across the profile of a young woman who had passed away. I saw her loved ones continuing to interact with that profile – continuing to write her messages, post comments on photographs, and otherwise use her profile as a site for mourning and memorialisation. Fascinated, I formally studied this phenomenon with a qualitative study, examining mourners' experiences through interviews and looking at their online behaviours through analysis of their posts on memorialisation (Kasket, 2012). The discoveries made through this study inform my work as a psychotherapist and as a trainer who teaches bereavement counsellors about the modern landscape of death and bereavement. Death in the context of digital technologies continues to be my primary area of research and scholarship.

The experiences uncovered by my research have been significant in their existential implications. First, my participants felt that the profile of their lost loved one was the closest thing imaginable to the 'real person'. One said, '[If the profile were deleted] it would feel like I wouldn't be able to talk to her properly… it would be deleting the last bit of her that's still almost real.' My research participants talked about, on one hand, seeing the representation of their friend as incredibly durable – *forever, eternal* – and, on the other hand, being aware of its non-durability, that it could disappear into nothing by the act of a Facebook employee at the behest of a bereaved family member. 'Digital beings can either endure forever, without any change, or disappear instantly without leaving a trace. Digital beings have two contradictory possibilities simultaneously: eternal endurance and instant vanishment' (Kim, 2001: 101). This has a huge impact on the modern bereavement experience, as we will see in the case below.

Second, my young participants – all in their early 20s – naturally assumed that the deceased was in receipt of communications. They had no illusion that the flesh-and-blood person was gone and would not be posting on Facebook; in fact, this response void was a reminder of the person's physical absence. They did, however, believe that the person was somehow *there* and would read and understand. This is perhaps merely an extension of the phenomenology of existence in a digital age: as 'digital natives', all my participants had grown up with the experience that to send something into the ether is to trust that it has been received, and this felt sense continued, despite the acknowledged physical non-being of their friend. This sensation is also perhaps linked to the vividness of many online digital representations: in the profile left behind, a kind of embodiment within the digital realm remained, and the relationship with that embodied being was experienced not as an interaction with a *thing* but as an interaction with another *Dasein* that was still sentient in some way.

Like many observers of contemporary 'selfie culture' – the often-criticised tendency to frequently capture and disseminate photographs of the self – I have wondered at the compulsive collection and dissemination of personal images and minute details of people's personal lives. As a psychotherapist, however, I have also wondered whether this apparent self-centredness is actually a pre-reflective attempt to achieve a kind of immortality in the digital sphere. Is building an online self-representation a way of denying and avoiding death? Does exposure to and interaction with dead loved ones' profiles make us more authentically aware of our *own* being-towards-death, mobilising us to make the most of our existence? Does it change how we live? Or does it merely draw us into the comforting, death-denying thought that, like our dead Facebook friends, we too will continue to live on in a digital version of heaven? The following account of my therapeutic work with Tanya (a pseudonym), while it does not answer all of these questions, casts light on some of them.

A case example of death and bereavement in the digital age

While I always practise with an existential sensibility, I am a counselling psychologist rather than a pure existential-phenomenological therapist. As such, I practise pluralistically, adapting my approach to the client's presentation, needs and preferences. As the questions I pose in the above section make clear, however, the Heideggerian influence on my thinking is undeniable. In common with other existential thinkers, my attention is orientated towards 'intrinsic dimensions of Being and our place within them' (Cohn, 1997: 15): being-in-the-world, being-in-the-world-with-others, thrownness, freedom and choice, embodiment and mortality. In Tanya's case, and in the case of many other bereaved clients I have seen, the existential-phenomenological approach felt a natural fit for us both, and the private practice setting in which I work made it possible to freely choose this.

Tanya, a 21-year-old university student, came to see me in my private practice. Tanya had lost her cousin, Steven (also a pseudonym), in a car accident three months previously, and she had been devastated by grief and loss. Tanya and Steven were nearly the same age and, because of the closeness of their two families, they had grown up almost as siblings. Both were early adopters of Facebook, having had accounts since the age of 16, and both had used it avidly, frequently posting photographs and using it as their main vehicle for communication when they were not physically together. Tanya showed me her profile and Steven's profile on her phone – the record of their close relationship was clear in literally hundreds of photos and what would have amounted to thousands of printed pages of written material. They were further connected through a network of mutual friends and family, with whom each had interacted both online and in the physical world.

Up until recently, Tanya said, she had been feeling gradually better. The thing that had helped her most to date, she said, was staying connected with Steven via Facebook. At first it had been hard to look at his page – most of their friends had found out about the death via Facebook and had flooded to his page to try to find out more information and post grief-stricken, disbelieving messages. Tanya said that this had initially made the loss too raw and real. After a while, however, the contact became comforting, and she was spending perhaps a half an hour a day looking at Steven's profile, at messages and photographs of him on her own profile and at private messages between her and Steven stored in her Messenger. She incorporated this into her daily life, flicking over to his profile now and again when she was on Facebook anyway, and spending some time there. Although her aunt had given her a few physical items that had belonged to Steven, these were not as important to her as his Facebook. 'I don't feel as much of a connection to him if I look at his stuff or spend time in his room,' she said. 'I send him messages maybe every other day. I feel like that's my big connection to him. I know it sounds weird to say that I'm pretty sure he can see it, I'm not religious or anything, but it just feels like he's there and I can feel close to him as long as the profile is there.'

The reason for her presenting to therapy was that Tanya's mother, deeply concerned about Tanya's continued interaction with Steven's Facebook profile and believing that it was not 'healthy' for Tanya to be spending so much time on it, had conferred with Tanya's aunt. Tanya's aunt was also bothered by Steven's profile, but in a different way. She did not approve of the way that Steven and his friends expressed themselves and the photos they posted on his profile, and she was not comfortable with that being part of his lasting legacy. Hearing about this conversation, Tanya had become terrified that her aunt and uncle might remove the profile. 'I know I could print out all the stuff, the memories stuff,' she said, 'but it wouldn't be the same, he wouldn't be there anymore, I'd feel like I couldn't reach him.' She had become so anxious at the prospect of removal that she continually checked her phone, could not concentrate on her studies or her work and kept leaving her aunt and uncle tearful, pleading messages, which only further convinced Tanya's mother that she was morbidly preoccupied with Steven's Facebook.

Continuing bonds (Klass & Walter, 2001) is a theory of grief that challenges notions of 'moving on' after a death, instead arguing that we readjust, redefine and continue our relationships with the dead, and that this is a normal and adaptive phenomenon. Because I am knowledgeable about continuing bonds and the way they can manifest in the context of social networking, I did not fully share Tanya's mother's concerns; I also heard in Tanya's account how she was using the profile in some ways to come to terms with the reality of her loss. I was aware from my own research and scholarship that mourners may feel traumatised by profile removal – losing access to treasured photographs and communications, without choice or control, can be experienced as losing the person all over again. My first instinct, therefore, was a practical, interventionist one – that is, how could we prevent Tanya's aunt and uncle from removing Steven's Facebook page? Something felt not right, though, about continuing to pursue this avenue. To clear space for clients' individual experiences, I employ the classic phenomenological rules of epoché, description and equalisation, and I had to consciously invoke the rule of epoché here, instead of rushing in with my assumptions and imposing a course of action on Tanya. Instead, I began tuning in with my sense of unease to understand it better.

On deeper reflection, I realised that, rather than Tanya's sense of a continuing bond being intrapsychic or based on the performance of ritual or observances of a more flexible, adaptable nature, her sense of a continuing bond was *dependent* on a particular digital being – on the continued existence of the Facebook profile. The reality of Steven's finitude was only made bearable by the continuance of something that made it feel like he was 'still there', something between an avatar – a computerised, graphical representation of a person – and a kind of holographic projection. In this way, I was aware that Tanya was in some ways fleeing from the full existential reality of Steven's death, and that her need to keep him 'still there' rendered her paralysed with anxiety at the danger of profile removal.

I was transparent with Tanya about what my first thought had been. I reflected, aloud, on something that is a modern-day situational given: much of our connection takes place online, and so many – perhaps most – of our externalised memories are stored there too. 'If you had a shoebox full of notes, physical video tapes and photos of Steven, and those were your memories of him, it would be a literal crime for your aunt and uncle to creep in and steal that box of memories and burn it,' I said. 'But they have the legal right to take that Facebook page down.' Tanya had actually described Steven's Facebook profile as 'kind of like a little piece of immortality', but she and I both realised, with that spontaneous analogy, that the virtual Steven too could disappear, as Kim (2001) describes, in a moment of instant vanishment – just like the physical Steven had.

Tanya's demeanour and posture at first had been one of nervous tension – jaw clenched, muscles tight; she was suffused with anxiety at the prospect that the profile might be taken down and with fury at her aunt and uncle for threatening this. Having lost Steven in a way that she could never have anticipated or prevented, she had hoped to prevent further experiences of loss. In this moment, however, she realised that, however tightly she held on to Steven's profile, she could not necessarily prevent its disappearance. For a couple of sessions afterwards, this opened up a deeper wellspring of grief, to which I responded with deep empathy but which I did not seek to suppress or ameliorate. As our sessions continued, Tanya and I confronted the pain of inevitable, unpreventable loss, and as a therapist it was often hard for me as well to sit with the reality of this. Tanya's loss made me think of my own loved ones; it was difficult for me to not flee in the face of this awareness as well. I had to use considerable self-reflection to be able to stay with Tanya and with her increased confrontation with the reality of Steven being gone.

As the sessions continued, Tanya began considering how she could – and how she would like to – continue to carry a sense of Steven forward with her, even if the profile ceased to be. All this while it had not been removed and Tanya had continued to visit it, but she noticed that she was feeling less anxious. She was also using it slightly differently at this point. Whereas before she had focused on scrolling through photos and messages, lately she had been writing more direct messages using the private Facebook Messenger, telling Steven about her therapy and about all the feelings that she was experiencing. She read out one of the messages to me during a session: 'I know I might not always be able to talk to you this way. I know this page might not always be here. I want to feel like I can have you with me in my heart, like it doesn't matter if this is here or not. I'm scared. But I'm starting to feel like maybe I could.'

I asked Tanya what she thought it might be to 'carry him in her heart', to somehow embody Steven herself in her own life. I wondered whether, having more fully realised and accepted the finitude of existence, Tanya would be able to translate this awareness into being motivated to grasp hold of her life and make it all that it could be, to be more aware of what mattered to her. Indeed, this question and the discussion that followed seemed to shift Tanya into this frame of mind. She began talking about what she wanted her own life to be – what values she wanted to live by, what she wanted to stand for, the qualities that Steven had that she wanted to nurture in herself. I asked her about what those were. 'He was very happy,' she said. 'Very joyful. He was honest, and really kind. I want to be that. If I have children, I want them to be that. It's how I'd like to be remembered too, how I remember him.'

Interestingly, Tanya admitted towards the latter part of our work that she had actually understood her aunt's displeasure at some of Steven's posts, and she had found them distasteful as well. She described that, in Steven's digital self-representation and his bantering with his friends, his kindness and honesty were less evident; his joyfulness took the form of a rather sarcastic humour that was less gentle than that favoured by his face-to-face self. She was not even sure whether Steven himself would have liked the idea of them. 'He probably never thought about it,' she said. 'He didn't know he was going to die. They're on his "permanent record" now! Maybe he'd laugh about it. I don't know.'

As a 21-year-old digital native herself, Tanya knew that, as had been the case for her cousin, an accessible digital representation of herself would persist online after her physical death, unless she actively tried to prevent it. Steven's death and the events that followed it made Tanya more aware not only of her own mortality but of her digital legacy too. In the last part of our work she began to consider the implications of this for the life she wanted to live and the choices she would make. 'I'm a lot more thoughtful about what I post online now,' she said. 'That stuff is something that my friends and family will see long after I'm gone, and I want them to be able to do that, if they want.' Although she could no more control, predict or prevent her death than Stephen had been able to, Tanya left our work together feeling that she *did* still have the power to shape her life, and the digital reflections of that life that she is sure to leave behind.

Conclusion

Wherever the internet reaches, *Dasein* exists in a technologically permeated world, and that mode of being-in-the-world makes itself known in therapy in myriad ways, not just around bereavement and loss. Perhaps it is fitting then that this, the final case study in the book, sensitises the reader to the existential implications of these technologies – those of the present day and the infinitely more complex and fascinating technologies that are still to emerge. Engaging with the work of the modern-day scholars who have used Heideggerian philosophy to better understand being-in-the-digital-world – with texts like *On the Internet* (Dreyfus, 2009) and *The Phenomenology of Digital Being* (Kim, 2001) – has made me a more skilled psychotherapist, both inside and outside of the bereavement context. The existential practitioner who embraces and is curious about these realities is a practitioner who is all the better equipped to work in this new world, where the future, as they say, is now.

Discussion with the editor

Simon: You write about the importance of being knowledgeable about technology, and you also say that practitioners need to be able to work with the existential implications of technology. I wonder how much we need to know about this technology – by which I don't mean that we should be wilfully ignorant but that, in my experience, what is important in therapy is the meaning that clients give to phenomena. The outstanding phenomenon for me in reading your chapter is 'loss' and how your client attempts to make sense of it. And a slightly different point, perhaps, is the one often made that the technology itself seems quite neutral; the significant thing is how we use it.

Elaine: Actually, what I always emphasise is that it's *not* necessary to know about technology in detail to better understand its impact and function in the modern-day bereavement landscape. When I speak to 'digital immigrant' bereavement practitioners, one of their abiding concerns is that they must become experts about this or become adopters of these technologies themselves in order to function in practice. They're relieved when they realise that this isn't the case. On the other hand, a different kind of knowledge – the knowledge that familiar theories and philosophical concepts can be applied within this relatively unfamiliar context – is extremely useful for the digital immigrant practitioner. And, as you say, for existential practitioners the aim would be to understand the meaning of technology in an individual client's experience of bereavement. It's not a problem unless it's a problem! Technologically mediated mourning isn't problematic *per se*, but I've seen a lot of 'Luddite' practitioners assume it to be so because of their own unexamined preconceptions.

Simon: While we existential therapists (and I know you work pluralistically) talk constantly about the limitations of human existence, it strikes me that, in your research focus and in much of your clinical practice, you have chosen to put yourself in a really challenging place. I wonder what this feels like and how you sustain yourself?

Elaine: I think there are many practitioners, existential practitioners included, who might be comfortable talking about limitations of existence but who shy away from 'deathwork', including palliative care contexts and bereavement counselling. For those that choose it, I think it feels manageable because there is a strong sense of vocation and privilege. Deathwork is difficult and intense, but if it feels meaningful and worthwhile, it's sustaining, even when it's draining. In my scholarly work, I'm sustained by sheer fascination and excitement, because the contemporary interfaces of life, death and technology are incredibly intellectually challenging and complex. We're really living in extraordinary times.

Simon: Can you say a little more about Klass's concept of continuing bonds? It sounds as though this is significant for your own practice.

Elaine: Before the publication of *Continuing Bonds* (Klass, Silverman & Nickman, 1996), most bereavement counselling was still based on models of grief that assumed it was necessary to 'decathect' from the dead, to 'resolve' grief, to 'move on'. If a bereaved person hadn't 'moved on' after a certain period of time, grief might be seen as 'complicated' or 'unresolved'. *Continuing Bonds* strongly made the counter-argument that our bonds with the dead change but they don't need to end and that a continuing attachment to the dead is not necessarily pathological. This view is actually the one that most societies have always held, explicitly or implicitly, but 20th century Western psychology diverted us from that for a time, and the pendulum is swinging back the other way now. I'm actually doing a chapter on technologically mediated continuing bonds for the second edition of Klass's book, so that's exciting!

Simon: When I read 'By using digital memory... we live on' I wondered what this actually means. I remember Tim LeBon, in his 2001 text *Wise Therapy*, has a case study in which a young woman facing death enters into philosophical counselling. In the course of this, she is presented with the argument that she continues after physical death via the transmission of her genes and her memes – replicants of her ideas. But LeBon notes that this is little comfort. It 'blurs the distinction between her memes and her*self*' (p12), and it is the loss of her self, her personal extinction, which concerns her. So, I suppose what I am getting at here is that losing oneself in the everyday and 'living on' are quite distinct things. I wonder if people really do believe they 'live on' in some 'digital version of Heaven' – this feels quite fascinating in what is generally a secular age.

Elaine: This is one of my wonderings too. I'm terribly interested in the extent to which people are starting to experience digital technology and digitally stored information as extensions of their bodies and minds. The more that this is our lived experience, the more we may come to assume or feel that we will be 'living on' after our physical deaths, but that's just a hypothesis. This is an incredibly fertile area for research and scholarship, and I can hardly wait to see what evolves over the next decades.

References

Cohn H (1997). *Existential Thought and Therapeutic Practice: an introduction to existential psychotherapy*. London: Sage.

Cooper M, Adams M (2005). Death. In: van Deurzen E, Arnold-Baker C (eds). *Existential Perspectives on Human Issues: a handbook for therapeutic practice*. London: Palgrave Macmillan (pp78–85).

Dreyfus H (2009). *On the Internet* (2nd ed). New York, NY: Routledge.

Heidegger M (1971). *Poetry, Language, Thought*. New York, NY: Harper & Row.

Heidegger M (1962). *Being and Time* (J Macquarrie, E Robinson trans). New York, NY: Harper & Row.

Kasket E (2012). Continuing bonds in the age of social networking. *Bereavement Care 31*(2): 62–69.

Kim J (2001). Phenomenology of digital-being. *Human Studies 24*(1–2): 87–111.

Klass D, Walter T (2001). Processes of grieving: how bonds are continued. In: Stroebe M, Hansson R, Stroebe W, Schut H (eds). *Handbook of Bereavement Research: consequences, coping and care*. Washington, DC: American Psychological Association (pp431–448).

Klass D, Silverman PR, Nickman SL (eds) (1996). *Continuing Bonds: new understandings of grief*. Abingdon: Routledge.

LeBon T (2001). *Wise Therapy: philosophy for counsellors*. London: Sage.

Mayer-Schönberger V (2011). *Delete: the virtue of forgetting in the digital age*. Cambridge, MA: Princeton University Press.

Mayer-Schönberger V, Cukier K (2013). *Big Data: a revolution that will transform how we live, work and think*. London: John Murray.

Yalom I (1980). *Existential Psychotherapy*. New York, NY: Basic Books.

Afterword
Simon du Plock

Each of the chapters in this text has sought to address a different 'problem of living' in order to show how each existential-phenomenological therapist works with their client's experience. The contributors to the book have also attempted to take some initial steps to revitalise the concept of the case study as it may most usefully support existential therapeutic practice. In arguing for something more akin to studies of the ways in which individual therapists and clients engage with these 'problems of living', they do not necessarily eschew approaches that draw on developments in systematic case study research. They do, though, illustrate the value of coherent 'stories' that take the subjective experience of both client and therapist seriously and provide inspiration for fellow practitioners who, on reading them, are able to recognise some aspect of the narrative that speaks to them as containing some truth about what it means to struggle with human existence. Making such a connection is likely to help readers reflect on their own practice.

The contributors have also sought to show how they have each either made some innovation to theory or have applied existing theory in a creative, new way, and in the process they have attempted, as the subheading of the book indicates, to 'translate theory into practice'. Some readers, especially those familiar with systematic case studies, might have been surprised at the broadly narrative approach adopted by the majority of contributors to this book. I would argue, though, that writing in narrative form has the advantage of encouraging the reader to identify powerfully with the protagonists and care about how they will resolve the issues with which they are engaged.

Examples of how to work using an existential-phenomenological approach are relatively rare. Case vignettes crop up quite frequently throughout the literature, but comprehensive examples of clinical work are mostly limited to the publications of two or three of the most prominent figures in our field. The current text probably represents the largest number of existential case studies to be offered together in the past 20 years. I am very grateful to the authors for providing these insights into their work, and I hope those readers who are also practitioners will find much to encourage and inspire them in this book.

Contributors

Professor Simon du Plock is Head of the Faculty of Post-Qualification and Professional Doctorates at the Metanoia Institute, London, UK. He is a chartered counselling psychologist, an Associate Fellow of the BPS, a founding member of the BPS Register of Psychologists Specialising in Psychotherapy and a BPS applied psychology practice supervisor. He is also a Fellow of the Royal Society for Medicine and a UKCP-registered psychotherapist. He lectures internationally on aspects of existential therapy, and has authored over 80 books, book chapters, and papers in peer-reviewed academic journals. In 2006, he became the first Western therapist to be made an honorary member of the East European Association for Existential Therapy, in recognition of his contribution to the development of collaboration between East and West European existential psychotherapy.

Helen Acton is a UKCP-registered existential psychotherapist on the staff at Trinity College, University of Cambridge, where she works with undergraduate and graduate students, and in private practice, where she has a particular interest and background in working with LGBTQI clients. She trained at Regent's College and her work on sexual orientation has previously been published in the *Journal for Existential Analysis*.

Martin Adams is an existential psychotherapist and supervisor and a lecturer at the New School of Psychotherapy. He is the author of *A Concise Introduction to Existential Counselling* (2013) and co-author, with Emmy van Deurzen, of *Skills in Existential Counselling and Psychotherapy* (2nd ed) (2016). He has contributed to the *Wiley World Handbook for Existential Therapy* (2018) and his most recent book is *An Existential Approach to Human Development:*

Philosophical and Therapeutic Perspectives (2018). He is co-editor of the journal *Existential Analysis*. His primary interests are in the application of existential thinking to both human development and creativity, including artistic creativity. He is a sculptor.

Dr Zack Eleftheriadou is a chartered counselling psychologist, chartered scientist and a Fellow of the British Psychological Society. She qualified as an integrative psychotherapist in 1993 and is strongly influenced by existential and phenomenological theory. She is also a psychoanalytic psychotherapist and a UKCP-registered child psychotherapist. Since 1990, she has lectured and published widely in the cross-cultural field, including *Psychotherapy and Culture: weaving inner and outer worlds* (2010). She runs her own consultancy in north London, working with children and adults, and is a supervisor and an external examiner for doctoral programmes and child psychotherapy trainings.

Georgia Feliou is an existential psychotherapist certified by the European Association for Psychotherapy working with individuals and couples in private practice in Athens, Greece. Her latest work is 'Saturated phenomena and their relationship to "extreme experiences": a phenomenological comparison between mystical experiences and psychotic and depressive experiences based on Jean-Luc Marion's philosophy', published in *Existential Analysis*. Building on that work, she is jointly engaged in qualitative research on mystical and psychotic experiences. She is a member of the Hearing Voices Network – Greece.

Dr Verity J Gavin began her professional life as a social anthropologist working in the Indian subcontinent and among ethnic minorities in Britain. After directing an innovative research project at London University, she moved into a senior research post, which she left in response to restrictions imposed by the policies of Margaret Thatcher. She developed creative ways of working with severely disturbed children and adolescents while pursuing her own personal creative work and training. Her training in the early days of Regent's College with Emmy van Deurzen, Ernesto Spinelli and Hans Cohn convinced her of two themes that have guided her work ever since: the potential contribution of existential therapy to therapeutic work with children and the contribution of creative ways of working with adults in existential therapy. Verity was able to develop both these when she moved to southern France in 1990, and in 2005 she began training qualified psychotherapists, clinical psychologists and child psychiatrists over a two-year period in Brussels, Lyon and Avignon.

Contributors

Dr Prunella Gee is a BACP-registered psychotherapist working in private practice in north London and a sessional therapist for the Nightingale Hospital. She came to both psychotherapy and academia later in life, having been an actor in theatre, TV and film for over three decades. She gained her PhD in psychology from Birkbeck University under the supervision of Dr Jonathan Smith, the originator of Interpretative Phenomenological Analysis (IPA). This re-ignited a love of all things phenomenological and existential initiated at Regent's College many years earlier. She is an occasional guest lecturer at The New School of Psychotherapy and Counselling.

Dr Elaine Kasket is an HCPC-registered counselling psychologist, BACP-accredited psychotherapist and independent practitioner. Having trained in the existential modality during her MA, and having worked for many years on a counselling psychology doctoral programme with existential approaches at its heart, she now weaves existential principles and ideas into her clinical work with bereavement and a variety of other presenting issues. Her research has appeared several times in *Existential Analysis* and she authored a chapter on existential approaches in *Counselling Psychology: a textbook for study and practice* (2017). Her decade-long study of death in the digital age has culminated in *All the Ghosts in the Machine*, a non-fiction book for a general readership, due to be published in 2019.

Dr Ryan Kemp is a consultant clinical psychologist and Director of Therapies in Central & North West London (CNWL) NHS Foundation Trust. Ryan is a chartered psychologist and Associate Fellow of the British Psychological Society (BPS) and a member of the Society for Existential Analysis. Previously he was Chair of the Faculty of Addiction in the BPS and Head of Psychology in Addictions in CNWL. In addition to extensive experience with drug and alcohol addictions, Ryan has also worked with gambling and technology addictions. His first book, *Transcending Addiction*, was published in 2018.

Rimantas Kočiūnas is an existential therapist and supervisor, Professor of Psychology in Vilnius University, Lithuania, and Director of the Institute of Humanistic and Existential Psychology in Birštonas, Lithuania. He is also Secretary General of the East European Association for Existential Psychotherapy.

Darren Langdridge is Professor of Psychology and Sexuality at the Open University (UK), Honorary Professor of Psychology at Aalborg University (Denmark), and a UKCP accredited existential psychotherapist working in private practice. Darren has for many years researched and written on sexualities, critical theory and psychotherapy. He is the author/co-editor of a number of books, including *Existential Counselling and Psychotherapy* (2012), *Phenomenological Psychology: theory, research and method* (2007), *Safe, Sane and Consensual: contemporary perspectives on sadomasochism* (with MJ Barker, 2007) and *Understanding Non-monogamies* (with MJ Barker, 2012). Darren also founded the journal *Psychology & Sexuality*, which seeks to advance the boundaries of work in the psychology of sexualities.

Dr Greg Madison is an existential psychologist, psychotherapist, writer and lecturer. As well as maintaining a private practice, Greg travels frequently to teach focusing and experiential-existential therapy, and founded the London Focusing Institute for professional and public courses in embodied listening and relating. He retains his independence from institutional affiliations and is active in progressive movements. Greg has edited two texts on focusing-oriented psychotherapy and co-edited a book on existential psychotherapy. Greg was born in Canada and has special interests in the experiences of belonging and 'home'. He has written a non-academic book about leaving home called *The End of Belonging*.

Dr Chloe Paidoussis-Mitchell is a BPS chartered psychologist and HCPC registered counselling psychologist with a passion for promoting psychological health and wellbeing. She regularly blogs on grief, trauma, depression and loss and publishes work to eradicate prejudice and stigma surrounding mental health. Chloe runs a private practice and is an academic and clinical practice supervisor at The Existential Academy in London. She has published extensively on grief, loss and trauma.

Randolph Skomer Quinault is an integrative psychotherapist and a lead clinician at Ease Wellbeing. He has spent many years working in the migration field with asylum-seekers, refugees and victims of trafficking. He has also developed award-winning training on vicarious trauma.

Mark Rayner is a UKCP registered psychotherapist, Chief Executive Officer of EASE Wellbeing CIC and a psychological therapist and consultant supervisor in Barnet, Enfield and Haringey NHS Mental Health Trust. His professional focus is on delivering existential-phenomenological psychological therapy in the public sector, understanding the essential qualities in therapeutic relationships, and monitoring and measurement in existential-phenomenological psychotherapy.

Dr Christina Richards is an accredited psychotherapist with BACP and an Associate Fellow of the BPS, which she represents to NHS England's Clinical Reference Group on Gender Identity Services. She is Senior Specialist Psychology Associate at the Nottinghamshire Healthcare NHS Trust Gender Clinic and Clinical Research Fellow at West London Mental Health NHS Trust (Charing Cross) Gender Clinic. She lectures and publishes on trans, sexualities and critical mental health, both within academia and to third sector and statutory bodies, and is a co-founder of BiUK and co-author of the *Bisexuality Report (2012)*. As well as other papers, reports and book chapters, she is the co-author of the *BPS Guidelines and Literature Review for Counselling Sexual and Gender Minority Clients* (2012); *Sexuality and Gender for Mental Health Professionals: a practical guide* (2013) and co-editor of the 2015 *Palgrave Handbook of the Psychology of Sexuality and Gender*.

Dr Julie Scheiner is a chartered counselling psychologist and visiting lecturer at the New School of Psychotherapy and Counselling, London and maintains a private practice.

Sasha van Deurzen-Smith is an existential coach and academic registrar at the New School of Psychotherapy and Counselling, where she is also the course leader of the MA in existential coaching and deputy course leader for the MA in existential and humanistic pastoral care and MSc in autism and related neurodevelopmental conditions. The daughter of Emmy van Deurzen, Sasha grew up around existential philosophy and practice and was one of the first in the world to attain an MA in existential coaching. She specialises in working with creativity, self-esteem and adults with an autism spectrum disorder.

Dr Alison Strasser is the founder and Director of the Centre for Existential Practice in Sydney, Australia. She is a practising existential psychotherapist, coach and supervisor. She is also an educator with a passion for imparting how existential themes can be integrated into every therapeutic approach. Alison co-authored *Time-Limited Existential Therapy* with her father, Dr Freddie Strasser, and she is currently working on a revised edition.

Name index

A
Acton, H 5, 44–55, 334
Adams, M 5, 29–43, 240–41, 247–48, 253, 264, 319–20, 322, 332, 334
American Psychiatric Association (APA) 137, 147, 151, 283, 297
Ansseau M 267, 280
Armstrong PB 225, 231
Asay TP 268, 280
Ashworth P 58–60, 69
Aujoulat I 157, 166

B
Babladelis G 312, 318
Bakolis I 187, 198
Baltes PB 29–30, 42, 318
Barber P 159, 166
Barnes HE 9, 39–40, 42–43, 53–55, 70, 232, 248
Barnett L 13, 18, 28, 83, 283, 297
Barton J 187, 198
Bates A 184, 198
Bayne R 158, 166
Behar R 156, 165–66
Binswanger L 7, 13, 28, 59, 69, 105, 115, 188, 295
Borscheid P 312, 318
Boss M 6, 57–60, 69
Breuer J 216, 231
British Psychological Society (BPS) 138, 142, 151, 279, 335, 336–39
Bromberg PM 172, 176, 180
Buber M 183, 190, 198
Burman E 30, 43
Bury M 157, 166

C
Cannon B 39, 43, 51, 53, 55
Casementm P 106, 115
Cawley R 184, 198
Chalmers DJ 313, 318
Chang LC 161, 166
Charmaz K 157, 166
Charon R 162, 166
Chawla L 187, 198
Clark JN 151, 157, 166
Clayton J 227–28, 231
Cohn HW 4, 9, 26, 29, 43, 57, 69, 85, 101, 118, 121–22, 124, 135, 325, 332, 335
Cole CM 137, 151
Colizzi M 137, 151
Connor C 184, 198
Cooper M 118, 146, 151, 249, 263, 278, 280, 320, 322, 332
Corbin J 157, 166
Costley C 165–66
Crabtree C 44, 55
Crawford MB 30, 43
Cuijpers P 268, 280
Cushman P 201, 211

D
Deary V 162, 166
de Beauvoir S 29, 39, 140, 151, 231
Derrida J 204, 211
de Shazer S 238, 247
DeVries MW 171, 180
Dickinson T 137, 151
Domhoff GW 56, 69
Dreyfus HL 30, 43, 329, 332
Duffell P 111, 115
Dupee FW 221, 231
du Plock S v, vi, 1– 9, 55, 84–101, 154–67, 211, 213–232, 280, 333, 334

E
EAGALA, 182, 184–85, 198
Eagleton T 216, 231
Edel L 217–22, 224, 226, 231
Ekerdt DJ 308, 318
Ellis C 155, 166
Ellis H 140, 151
Escobar S 252, 263
Ettner R 143, 151
European Agency for Fundamental Rights, 253, 263

F
Feliou G 8, 249–264, 336
Fine AH 183, 187, 198
Fishman D 163, 167
Fosshage JL 58, 69
Freud S 1, 56, 69, 187, 194, 198, 216, 222, 231, 295
Fromm E 58, 69
Fuchs T 314, 318

G
Gallwey T 102, 115
Garrow S 118, 135
Gavin VJ 5, 10–28, 333, 335
Gee P 8, 299–319, 336
Gelder MG 143, 151
Gendlin ET 13, 28, 58, 69, 72, 77, 81, 83
Gijs L 143, 151

Gilleard C 308, 318
Giorgi A 59, 69
Glouberman D 107, 115
Goldberg DP 267, 280
Gonsalves C 170, 180

H

Hall C 57, 69, 232
Hannah B 183, 198
Haraldsen IR 137, 151
Harris MB 312, 318
Hawton K 146, 151
Heidegger M 28–30, 43, 57–58, 60, 70, 104, 106, 115, 135, 170–71, 180, 239, 241–42, 247, 295–96, 310, 314–15, 318, 320–22, 332
Herdt G 140, 151
Herman JL 252, 263
Hill DB 137, 151
Hillman J 231
Hirschfeld M 140, 151
Hora T 118, 135
Horne S 252, 263
Horner R 259, 263
Horowitz M 294, 297
Hoshiai M 137, 151
Hunt C 158, 167
Husserl E 60, 70, 103–4, 115, 172, 180, 245, 249, 263, 310

I

Internation Coach Federation (ICF) 102, 115

J

Jacobsen B 118–19, 121, 135
Jaenicke U 57, 70
James H 8, 157, 166, 213, 215, 217–32
Jung C 29, 56, 69–70, 183, 187, 198

K

Kant I 104, 115
Kaplan F 223, 232
Karban B 34, 43
Kasket E 9, 320–32, 336
Kasket E, 332
Kauffman J 282, 294, 297
Kemp R 7, 200–12, 336
Kersting A 138, 152
Keyes D 265, 275, 280
Khantzian EJ 201, 207, 211–12
Kim J 321, 324, 327, 329, 332
King M 162, 166, 258, 267, 281
Kissane DW 118, 136
Klass D 326, 331–32
Klontz BT 183, 198

Kočiūnas R 6, 7, 117–36, 336
Kohanov L 186, 198
Krafft-Ebing R, von 140, 153
Kvale S 299, 319

L

Laing RD 30, 33, 43, 213–15, 217–18, 230, 232, 313
Langdridge, 5, 56–70, 337
Lantz J 268, 281
Lawrence AA 138, 152
LeBon T 331–32
Leighton T 141, 152
Lev AI 138, 152
Levey M 224, 232
Loden S 56, 70
Loewenberg H 138, 152
Loue S 252, 254, 263

M

Mackrill T 278, 281
Madison G 6, 13, 18, 28, 71–83, 337
Maglio AT 308, 319
Marion J-L 8, 250, 259, 261–63
May R 85, 101, 119, 160, 167, 170–71, 176, 180
McCulloch L 184, 198
McLeod J 2, 9, 146, 151, 155, 167
McWilliam CL 161, 167
Medina M 45–46, 50–52, 55, 140, 152
Merleau-Ponty M 29–30, 39, 43, 60, 70, 242, 248–49, 302, 311, 314, 319
Mezirow J 112, 115
Michinov E 312, 319
Milton M 55, 140, 152
Mitchell SA 169, 180
Moon P 46, 48, 55
Mukaddes NM 143, 152
Mullan H 118–20, 124, 136
Murphy SA 294, 297

N

Natural England 187, 199
Neimeyer RA 282, 297–98
NHS England 143, 152, 339
Norcross JC 268–69, 281

O

O'Hagan K 252, 263
Orlinsky DE 268, 281
Ormel J 267, 281
Overholser JC 120, 136

P

Paidoussis-Mitchell C 8, 282–98, 337
Parsons M 106, 115

Paterson B 161–62, 167
Pennebaker JW 158, 167
Perkins BL 187, 199
Philips D 158, 167
Pilafova A 251, 252, 254, 263
Poole A 222, 232
Preusch P 184, 199
Proust M 213, 218, 231–32

Q

Quinault R 8, 265–81, 337

R

Raymond MJ 143, 152
Rayner M 8, 265–81, 337
Reith G 204, 212
Renzetti C 251–52, 263
Richards C 7, 137–53, 338
Ricoeur P 6, 61, 68, 70, 250, 259
Riede MR 184, 199
Rodrigues VA 46, 51, 55, 140, 152
Rogers CR 236, 248, 268, 281
Rosanvallon P 255, 263
Rosen CS 269, 281
Roszak T 188, 199
Royal College of Psychiatrists, 142, 153
Ryan R 187, 199

S

Safran JD 269, 281
Sanderson C 252–53, 263
Sartre J-P 3, 9, 29, 31, 38–39, 41–45, 51–53, 55, 60, 70, 213, 230–32, 241, 244, 248–49
Schafer R 68, 70
Scheiner J 7, 182–99, 338
Schneider KJ 268, 281
Seal LJ 142, 152–53
Seikowski K 138, 153
Shaffer HJ, 101
Shaffer JBP 214, 232
Shepherd G 268, 281
Simon L 138, 153
Smith Landsman I 283, 297
Smith S, 229, 232
Solomon RC 45, 55
Sousa D 159, 167
Spinelli E 26, 28, 84–85, 87, 89, 101, 118–19, 170–72, 181, 214–15, 248, 281, 294–95, 298, 319
Spira JL 118, 136
Stern D 169, 172, 176, 181
Storolow RD 176, 181, 285
Storr A 228, 232

Strasser, 8, 233–35, 237, 239, 241, 243, 245, 247–48, 339
Strasser A 8, 233–48
Strasser F 8, 233–35, 248
Stroebe M 282, 298, 332
Sullivan L 252, 263
Szasz T 264

T

Taft J 233, 248
Tallis R 30, 43
Tantam D 118, 136
Teuscher U 308, 312, 319
Trivedi L 183, 199

V

van der Kolk BA 173, 175, 180, 181
van der Veer 176, 181
van Deurzen E, v–vi, 7, 13, 18, 26, 28, 46, 55, 59, 70, 72, 84, 101, 105, 116, 118, 119, 136, 174, 188, 199, 241, 243, 248, 253, 264, 285, 295, 298, 302, 319, 332, 334, 335
van Deurzen-Smith E 59, 70, 116, 170, 171, 173, 181, 214, 227, 232, 308, 319
van Deurzen-Smith S 6, 102–16, 338
Vedfelt O 56, 58, 70
Ventegodt S 118, 136
Vuorilehto M 267, 281

W

Walters GD 86–87, 101
Wampold BE 269, 281
Wardle H 200, 212
Warnock M 230, 232
Webb J 313, 319
Weegmann M 207, 212
Welleck R 215, 232
White W 208, 212
World Health Organisation (WHO), 200, 212, 281
Wickstrom G 317, 319
Wilson EO 188, 199
Winnicott DW 12, 28, 214
Witemb SA 118, 136
World Professional Association for Transgender Health (WPATH) 152–53

Y

Yalom I 9, 31, 43, 118–20, 124, 136, 170, 178, 181, 190, 311, 319, 320–23, 332

Subject index

A
addiction 6, 7, 84–101, 200–212, 337
ageing 5, 301–2, 306–8, 315, 318
alienation 203, 211, 231, 285, 289, 293, 313
anxiety disorder (*see also* General Anxiety Disorder Scale (GAD-7)) 2, 293
art 26, 222, 226–29, 250, 261
authenticity 4, 32, 38, 106, 141, 227, 241, 308
autonomy 34, 214
autotherapy 223, 228

B
bad faith 41, 44–45, 49, 51, 54, 146, 223, 241–42
being-in-the-world 57, 59, 87, 121, 129, 146, 171, 210, 223–24, 236, 239, 325, 329
    way-of-, 87, 124, 217, 228, 255, 260, 274–76, 309
being-with- 7, 18, 85, 121, 127, 133, 139, 165
    others 7, 85, 121, 133, 255, 260
    others-in-the-world 322
    the-client 160
bereavement 283, 298, 324–25, 329–32, 337
    traumatic 8, 282–83, 294, 297
birth 30–32, 39, 41, 250
British School of Existential Analysis 249

C
case study research 2, 9, 155, 165, 333
chronic fatigue syndrome 155
cisgender 138, 142
cognitive analysis 6, 82
co-researcher 155, 310
couple-construct 87–89, 92, 97, 99
creativity 6, 14, 61, 68–69, 227–28, 241, 270, 336
cultural symbolic system 5, 15

D
dasein 14–16, 100, 118, 242, 295, 314, 324, 329
    avoiding death 320, 322
    movings of, 13
    -opening 13–14
    -relating 13–14
death 32, 41, 203, 211, 240, 242, 308, 313, 315, 320–32
    being-towards-, 60, 141, 242
    movement-toward, 242
digital age 321, 324–25
digital memory 321, 331
dimensions of existence 59, 67, 105, 113, 308
doing-to 161, 165
dreamworld 58, 67

E
eigenwelt 59, 105, 188–89, 284, 295
embodied phenomenological attitude 5, 21
engulfment 215, 217, 251
existential
    anxiety 21, 23, 31, 132, 213, 230
    coaching 6, 102–3, 113–15, 339
    givens 3, 124, 140, 180, 235, 242, 255, 293–94
    -phenomenological therapy 72, 155, 159
existential philosophy 7, 45, 52, 115, 120, 144, 177–78, 213, 234, 265
experience, bodily 6, 75, 82

F
facticity 5, 40–41, 44–46, 51, 53–54
focusing 72, 83, 338
four dimensions of human existence 7, 13, 18, 21, 24, 27, 59, 67, 105, 113, 171
four ultimate concerns 308
four-worlds model of traumatic bereavement and loss 8, 188, 282–83, 295–96

G
gender dysphoria 7, 142–43, 145–47, 151–52
gender identity 7, 138, 144, 146, 151–53
General Anxiety Disorder scale (GAD-7) 266, 273
goal setting 266, 269–70, 278
grief 282–98, 326, 328, 331
group dynamics 117, 126
guilt 4, 126, 252, 273

H
here-and-now 81, 100, 126, 130–31, 173, 284
here-is-a-new-person 85, 160
homophobia 254
horizontalisation 113, 173, 266, 300
human development 5, 29–30, 32, 38–39, 42, 319

I
I-am experience 160
imagination 61, 68, 104–5, 221

implosion 215, 217
Improving Access to Psychological Therapies
    (IAPT) 266–67, 278
individuality 32, 262
Interpretative Phenomenological Analysis
    (IPA) 337
intuition 104–5
isolation 107, 170, 178–80, 251–53, 285,
    289–90, 293, 308
    existential, 308

L

Law of Existential Consequence 33, 41
lifeworld 59–60, 62, 65, 67, 69, 202, 208
    fractions 60, 67
literature 6, 213, 215–17, 229–32
lived experience 45–46, 52, 148, 154, 174, 245,
    265–66
lived time 5, 32
loss 48, 51, 170, 179, 242, 252–53, 282–83,
    285, 293–94, 297–98, 329–30

M

Major Depressive Disorder (MDD) 293
manualised therapy 266, 279
Marionian phenomenology 250–51
maturity 32, 127
    stages of, 120
meaninglessness 171, 178, 283, 293, 308
metaphor 68, 106–7, 274, 276
    therapy 187
mitwelt 6, 23, 59, 105, 188–89, 284, 295
moment-by-moment
    experience 71
    phenomenological awareness 72
    relationship 75, 81
mortality 30, 80, 189, 239, 242, 284, 308,
    320–22, 325, 329
myalgic encephalomyelitis 155

N

narrative identity 61, 66–68
natality 30
National Health Service (NHS) 142, 144, 150,
    158, 265–66, 278–79
National Institute for Health and Care
    (formerly Clinical) Excellence
    (NICE) 197, 266, 278, 280
neuroscience 30, 180
neurosis 216, 229
NHS primary care 8, 265, 283
non-verbal communication 15

O

ontic concerns 57, 59, 62, 67
ontological
    insecurity 8, 213–18, 220, 222–24, 226–28,
        230, 232
    security 213, 217, 225
original project 5, 31, 33, 38, 40, 53

P

paradoxes 32, 39, 121, 247
paraphrenia 222
participant observation 5, 13
past 4, 33, 40, 81–82, 172–73, 176–77, 235,
    245, 311
Personal Health Questionnaire (PHQ-9) 266, 273
petrification 215, 217
phenomenological
    attitude 5–6, 14, 21, 113, 129
    enquiry 145–46, 159, 269
    method 18, 57–58, 69, 104, 155, 164, 253,
        265
philosophical consultancy 114
physicality 7, 32, 138
play 12, 15–16, 19–22, 59, 61, 67–69, 316
pre-reflective choice 53–54
problems of living 114, 333
psychoanalysis 1, 26, 39, 169, 177, 209
psychoeducation 114
psychological abuse 8, 251–52, 254, 257,
    259–60, 263
psychological 'dis-ease' 3
psychology research 299–300, 316
psychosis 143, 226, 229–30

R

refugee 7, 168–72, 174, 176, 178–80
relationality, paradox of 32
relational space 5, 14, 21
research, case study 2, 9, 155, 165, 333
retirement 160, 299–315
ritual 16, 215, 327

S

schizoid process 8, 213, 227
sedimentation 242, 260
self
    -medication 6, 201
    -structure 87
sexual orientation 5, 44–46, 49, 51–55, 335
situated
    client as, 3
    dasien, 100
    freedom 41, 51

social networking 321–22, 326, 332
stage theories 5, 29, 42

T

therapeutic alliance 3, 68, 87, 100, 173, 195, 268, 281, 295–96
therapeutic relationship 3, 7, 63, 169, 177, 185, 194, 197, 245, 250, 259, 265, 268, 283
therapy world 5, 10, 13–14, 25
'they' 305, 307, 315
three movings of *dasein* 13–15
thrownness 31, 33, 261, 325
trans people 137
traumatic bereavement (*See* bereavement, traumatic)
twelve-step traditions 208

U

überwelt 24, 59, 105, 188–89, 284, 296
umwelt 20, 59, 105, 188–89, 284, 295
uncertainty 78, 129–30, 238, 240
ungroundedness 30

V

violence 66, 251, 253–54, 260, 263

W

Wheel of Existence 234–35, 247
wisdom 32, 249